Afro-Cuban Diasporas
in the Atlantic World

Rochester Studies in
African History and the Diaspora

Toyin Falola, Senior Editor
The Frances Higginbotham Nalle Centennial Professor in History
University of Texas at Austin

(ISSN: 1092–5228)

A complete list of titles in the Rochester Studies in African History and the Diaspora, in order of publication, may be found at the end of this book.

Afro-Cuban Diasporas
in the Atlantic World

Solimar Otero

UNIVERSITY OF ROCHESTER PRESS

Copyright © 2010 by Solimar Otero

All Rights Reserved. Except as permitted under current legislation, no part of this work may be photocopied, stored in a retrieval system, published, performed in public, adapted, broadcast, transmitted, recorded, or reproduced in any form or by any means, without the prior permission of the copyright owner.

First published 2010
Reprinted in paperback 2013

University of Rochester Press
668 Mt. Hope Avenue, Rochester, NY 14620, USA
www.urpress.com
and Boydell & Brewer Limited
PO Box 9, Woodbridge, Suffolk IP12 3DF, UK
www.boydellandbrewer.com

ISSN: 1092-5228
Hardcover ISBN: 978-1-58046-326-3
Paperback ISBN 978-1-58046-473-4

Library of Congress Cataloging-in-Publication Data
Otero, Solimar.
  Afro-Cuban diasporas in the Atlantic world / Solimar Otero.
      p. cm. — (Rochester studies in African history and the diaspora, ISSN 1092-5228 ; v 45)
  Includes bibliographical references and index.
ISBN 978-1-58046-326-3 (hardcover : alk. paper) 1. Yoruba (African people)—Cuba—History—19th century. 2. Yoruba (African people)—Cuba—Ethnic identity. 3. Yoruba (African people)—Cuba—Migrations—History—19th century. 4. Cubans—Nigeria—Lagos—History—19th century. 5. Return migration—Nigeria—Lagos—History—19th century. 6. Nigeria—Emigration and immigration—History—19th century. 7. Cuba—Emigration and immigration—History—19th century. 8. African diaspora. I. Title.
  F1789.Y6O84 2010
  305.896'33307291—dc22

2010004861

A catalogue record for this title is available from the British Library.

This publication is printed on acid-free paper.
Printed in the United States of America

This book is dedicated to the memory of
my grandmother, Lila Melchor García.

Contents

	List of Illustrations	viii
	Acknowledgments	ix
	Introduction	1
1	Grassroots Africans: Havana's "Lagosians"	23
2	Returning to Lagos: Making the *Oja* Home	51
3	"Second Diasporas": Reception in the Bight of Benin	74
4	Situating Lagosian, Caribbean, and Latin American Diasporas	88
5	Creating Afrocubanos: Public Cultures in a Circum-Atlantic Perspective	111
	Conclusion: Flow, Community, and Diaspora	140
	Appendix: Case Studies of Returnees to Lagos from Havana, Cuba	157
	Notes	163
	Bibliography	199
	Index	241

Illustrations

Figures

1	The Cuban Lodge, Campos Square, Lagos	91
2	Grave of Mrs. Anastasia Gooding, Ikoyi Cemetery, Lagos	96
3	Grave of Hilario Campos and Johana Cicelia Munis, Ikoyi Cemetery, Lagos	97
4	Mrs. Ola Vincent, granddaughter of Hilario Campos, at the grave of her aunt and grandfather, Ikoyi Cemetery, Lagos	98

Maps

1	The Atlantic World showing Havana and Lagos	xi

Illustrations on author's website: http://www.lsu.edu/faculty/solimar/

    Community center for the "Popo Aguda"

    Omoba Prince T. Olusí

    Child devotee of Olokun, Eyo masquerade, Lagos

    Chief Lola Bamgboshe Martins, *olowo* of the Songo Egungun

    The Bamgboshe Martins House, Lagos

    Bamgboshe Egungun shrine, Lagos

    Hilario Campos, Afrocubano repatriate to Lagos

    The Cuban Lodge, Campos Square, Lagos

    Mrs. Catherine Aderemi Gooding-King

    Grave of Mrs. Anastasia Gooding, Ikoyi Cemetery, Lagos

    Grave of Hilario Campos and Johana Cicelia Munis, Ikoyi Cemetery, Lagos

    Mrs. Ola Vincent, granddaughter of Hilario Campos, at the grave of her aunt and grandfather, Ikoyi Cemetery, Lagos

Acknowledgments

There are so many people to thank for their help in the development of this project. First and foremost, I need to thank members of the Campos family, Mrs. Ola Vincent and Mrs. Aderemi Gooding-King of Lagos, for their generosity in sharing their memories of their grandfather Hilario Campos with me. In Lagos, I was indebted to the wisdom of *agbalagba*, of elders like Chief Lola Bamgboshe Martins and Prince T. Olusí, who both shared their knowledge of the Aguda and the city over many conversations. Also indispensible to me was the guidance of Dr. Ajikobi of the University of Lagos, who introduced me to the Olokun House, whose members provided much assistance and were generous with their time. I must thank as well the Oshe family, which housed me during both of my field sojourns in Eko.

In the United States, many people were responsible for making this work possible. I want to thank Dr. Yiwola Awoyale of the University of Pennsylvania's Language Data Consortium for his patient work with me on Yoruba and Lucumí. Prince Yekinni Atanda of Oshogbo also assisted me with connections and with visits to Oshogbo and Lagos during my fieldwork. The insights he provided into *esin ibile*, or traditional Yoruba religion, while I was visiting his home in Philadelphia, were invaluable to me. I am grateful to Sandra Barnes, Roger Abrahams, J. Lorand Matory, and Dan Ben-Amos for their support in the initial stages of this project, which began at the University of Pennsylvania in 1999. Along the way, colleagues like Katherine Henninger, Pallavi Rastogi, Carolyn Ware, and Gale Sutherland of Louisiana State University read earlier versions of chapters of the book and provided valuable insights. Their adroit comments were essential to the refining of important aspects of the text. I would especially like to thank Myriam Chancy for her support and valuable advice in formulating the text in an innovative manner that reflected my view of the Atlantic world. My dear friends and fellow folklorists Frank de Caro and Rosan Jordon were also instrumental in giving me much-needed advice on completing the project. I would like to especially thank Toyin Falola for his reading and support of the manuscript.

I am thankful to my family in Cuba, especially for their support of my work and of my visits throughout the years I have spent on this project. My mother María Melchor, my father Raymond Otero, and my brother Rai Otero were crucial in their moral support of this long and complicated project. My aunt and uncle, Blanca and Robert Alvarez, were also involved in supporting this work with love and affection. My husband, Eric Mayer, tirelessly stood by my side as I revised and edited the volume.

I am indebted to the West African Research Association and the Fulbright Program for supporting this project and facilitating my fieldwork in Lagos. I also need to thank Guillermo Ferreyra, Robin Roberts, and Margaret Parker of the College of Arts and Sciences at Louisiana State University for their support of this project and its completion.

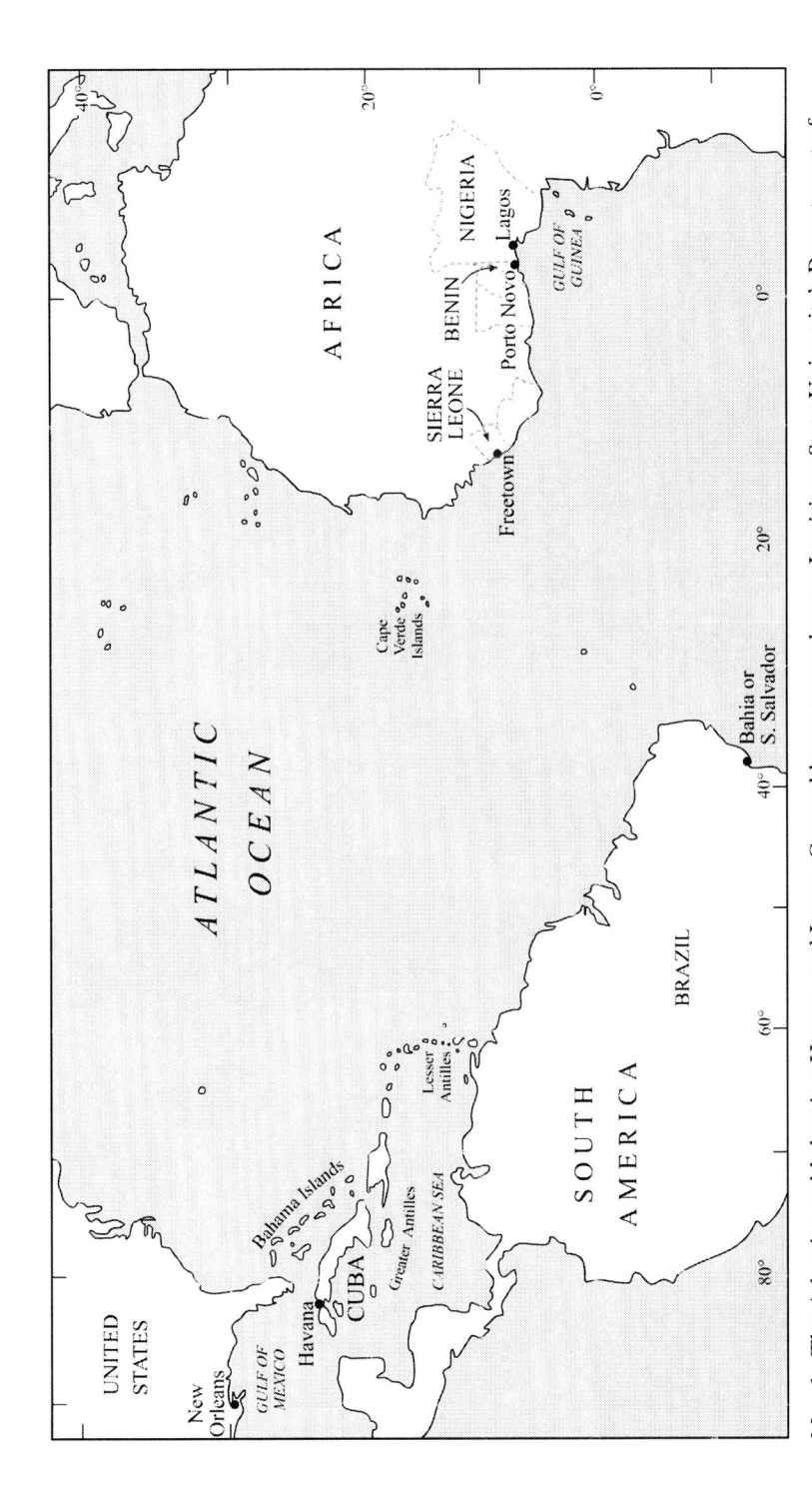

Map 1. The Atlantic world showing Havana and Lagos. Created by cartographers at Louisiana State University's Department of Geography and Anthropology.

Introduction

"Aiye ni oja, orun ni ile."
The world is a marketplace; heaven is home.

—Traditional Yoruba proverb

For the Yoruba, the phrase *orunile* captures the notion of home that one carries with oneself from birth.[1] The idea is that we leave heaven, our home, to embark on a journey into the world, a marketplace. The marketplace referred to here is a West African marketplace where almost any kind of transaction may occur. It is a public space full of possibilities, danger, and wonder. In the Yoruba *oja*, the key component is the negotiation of the value of something through verbal barter. It is a sphere of performance where there are winners and losers. Individuals are encouraged to use forceful rhetoric, mastering the art of persuasion and profiting from it. Following this metaphor, then, the world is a place where we try our luck, hone our potential as individuals, and eventually leave at the end of the day. What we take back home with us from the marketplace is the dilemma we are all faced with in our human existence. Along these lines, then, the moment we are born illustrates our dispersal into the diaspora of the world. I usually write about how this ontological position creates a uniquely African and Caribbean mode of understanding the human being's place in the world in the genres of memoir and novels based on Yoruba mythological narratives.[2] Here, I would like to offer a story of a similar kind of journey of dispersal and return that spans generations and the Atlantic region.

The present volume grows out of exploring the contours of the above dilemma in relation to the Afrolatino Atlantic world. I am particularly interested in the Afro-Cuban diaspora that has existed between Lagos, Nigeria, and Havana, Cuba, from the nineteenth century into our current era. Africans who also identified with living in Cuba or Brazil, or Afrolatinos, as they are called here, moved across the Atlantic, looking for home, between the Americas and Africa in successive waves. Their economic savvy and cultural resiliency left lasting legacies in the diasporic communities they helped to create in the Caribbean and West Africa. Moving along this well-worn path, Afrolatinos made their mark in Southampton, Freetown, Ouidah, and Lagos—places deeply touched by the cross-migration of Africans from the Americas.[3] These communities have always been ambulatory, transnational, and ethnically diverse. Subsequently they were influenced by and also contributed to the formation of the Cuban and Nigerian sense of nationhood in pervasive ways.

Emancipated slaves of Yoruba descent moved back and forth between Havana, Cuba, and Lagos, Nigeria, in the nineteenth century. In Cuba, they were Havana's "Lagosians"; in Lagos, they became part of a heterogeneous Afrolatino group known as the Aguda. The Aguda include a population of repatriated Cubans who, along with Brazilian repatriates, established their own community in Lagos, Nigeria. The communities that grew out of these Afrolatino migrations were deeply committed to hard work, education, and economic advancement in their new homes, on many shores, and against great odds. These values held true for those in Havana living as emancipated slaves, and later for members of the Aguda arriving in Lagos as repatriated Africans. The material presented in this volume illustrates just a few of the ways in which these communities have made a lasting impression in Africa and the Americas. One adhesive element not to be forgotten is the lasting and shared element of different forms of *orisha* worship active among these fluid communities at the present time and throughout history.[4]

This volume is the work of a folklorist interested in how history, memory, and culture operate in the social imagination over time. Folklore as a discipline combines literary, ethnographic, historical, linguistic, and other methodologies in order to look at subjects that are otherwise missed by utilizing solely one approach. Henry Glassie, Roger Abrahams, Richard Bauman, Charles Briggs, Alan Dundes, Dan Ben-Amos, Sabina Magliocco, and Regina Bendix are just a few of the folklorists who have grappled with the difficulties of being part of a discipline and turning to subjects of study that are often misunderstood or overlooked in the academy.[5] One major area that folklorists study, in a wide range of genres, is the poetics of everyday life. I use my interdisciplinary research organically, to get closer to those poetics through a plurality of approaches. In this volume, I move from an analysis of the lives and context of Lagosians living in Cuba in the nineteenth century to my own ethnography carried out in Nigeria, and then into the emerging public sphere and civic culture reflected in nineteenth-century Cuban letters by and about Afro-Cubans. To give an analogy, the field of Yoruba studies in general mirrors that of the folklorist in marking out spaces of recognition for important cultural work done by community artists and leaders.[6] Both folklorists and Yoruba scholars employ innovative interdisciplinary tools and rigorous methodologies that help move academic discourses into spaces in the lived world where critical work is being done. This book is written in this spirit of collaboration, which challenges the terms of engagement as to whose narrative or history is important to study, how, and why.[7]

It is daunting to contemplate the multiple manifestations of Yoruba-inspired communities and cultures emerging in the nineteenth century between Africa and the Americas. In an attempt to learn something new about the variety of these "Yoruba" legacies, I want to revise the terms of engagement traditionally found in African American and Africanist approaches to the study of the African diaspora. In this volume, the focus is turned away from the view that Africa and the United States are the only viable starting points for the exploration of the African diaspora. Afro-Atlantic communities and the diasporic worlds they made are highlighted here, especially those ambulant populations stemming from Cuba, along with the creolizing discourses these may or may not contain. I take the term "creolization" in the manner suggested by Roger Abrahams in his essay "Questions of Criolian Contagion."[8] Here, Abrahams suggests that "creolization" is a term misunderstood by most cultural theorists because of their propensity to look for "purity" of origins in the attempt to explain cultural admixture. Like Abrahams, I am influenced by the linguistic use of the term "creolization" because of its ability to describe the process of ubiquitous admixture. This process in the Atlantic world occurred and occurs in a context of cyclical, dynamic, real, and imagined cultural encounters.

My perspective breaks with that of others who have studied the African diaspora in the Herskovitsian sense in that it refutes certain key aspects—especially the idea of "retention" of African cultural traits that are later mixed with European traits—of the idea of creolization as understood traditionally among anthropologists and sociologists.[9] These ideas have changed in African studies over the last few decades, and I take Andrew Apter's lead here in rethinking the idea of syncretism along with creolization.[10] Thus, I locate certain processes of cultural carrying and admixture as *both* African and Caribbean ways of constructing community. One of the main points addressed in this volume is that what we consider to be a particularly innovative Caribbean or American way of creating new cultures is actually also very African. This book means to emphasize Afro-Atlantic, in a cyclical sense of the word, ways of knowing and constructing society.

These diasporic sensibilities become the major elements that formulate the nature of creolized cultures in terms of their portability and pliability. The experiences of movement and flow in the African diaspora, indeed, in diaspora in general as a phenomenon, are not superficial. They are fundamental to the production of culture and community, especially in the contexts of Havana, Lagos, and Yorubaland in the nineteenth century. In other words, the idea that this kind of study is in contradistinction to the unidirectional view of the study of the African diaspora is precisely the point. With this in mind, I purposely use the term "Afrolatino" from time to time because it refers to communities that identify with being both African and

4 *Introduction*

Latin American, and with a range of places called "home" located in the way these two geographic spaces are reimagined.

Diasporic communities in Afro-Atlantic societies creatively used notions of home and history. For the Yoruba, broadly defined, the united aforementioned tropes of heaven and home have found fertile routes for legitimizing new ethnic, cultural, and religious associations. The organizational tools used by communities engaged in revitalizing Yoruba religion and identity in Cuba helped to create this national identity.[11] We can say that a similar, marked presence was felt in Lagos when Afrolatinos began repatriating to that island in the nineteenth century.[12] A transnational legacy was acutely felt, in terms of both quotidian history and folk narrative, as Afrolatinos such as members of the Aguda nurtured the perception of creolized alliances and disbursed allegiances. Fortunately for the returnees, the accessibility and elasticity of New World identity formation fitted nicely into the Lagosian framework for incorporating new communities. In the Lagosian context, spaces for the incorporation of new communities were always reserved, since newcomers could easily be legitimized as belonging through the pliant extension of genealogies, alliances, and connections found in place in the city's social structure. For the Aguda, a larger context for circum-Atlantic cultural exchanges was understood to be well under way, in the Bight of Benin as a whole, from the eighteenth century on.[13]

Organization of the Volume

This volume is organized to emphasize the fluid nature of the formation of Afrolatino identity. Again, "Afrolatino" is used here to describe certain kinds of identifiable constructions of transnationalism, culture, society, and religion across the African diaspora in specific contexts. Our entry point for discussing the Aguda circum-Atlantic communities begins with the actual movement of Havana Lagosians, like Martin Marino, back to West Africa in the nineteenth century. Here we see how Afro-Cubans asserted their desire to capture "home" between Africa and Cuba on fluid and self-identified terms.

The construction of these very categories, "Cuban" and "African," represents multiple and distinct nationalistic dilemmas that are at the heart of a nineteenth-century impetus toward self-definition for African and Atlantic communities.[14] In the Cuban context, by the close of the nineteenth century, Afro-Cubans were both lauded as national heroes and despised as Blacks on the island. These deep discrepancies in approaches toward Black Cubans certainly aided the unrest that plagued Cuba up to Castro's revolution of 1959, and some say up to the current era.[15] The focus in this volume, then, is to reveal how some "Yoruba" found "home" in multiple places along the Atlantic, but especially in conjunction with Cuba, where even today Cuban quotidian life reveals the depth of this connection and shared association through religious practice. Traditionally thought of as a one-way street, the Cuban-Yoruba diaspora, in the manifestation of the Aguda, allows for a consideration of this identity from a different vantage point. As members of the Aguda, self-identified descendants of Afro-Cubans living in Lagos have been imagining Cuba as a distant, almost romantic, homeland. This social process forces us to recognize the pervasive nature of nostalgia, memory, and the role of the imagination in creating community in transnational populations. The relationship of memory to the imagination is a fundamental component of how we understand, receive, and acknowledge the experiences of communities like the Aguda in different registers.[16]

The second half of this volume deals with ethnographic fieldwork carried out among the Aguda in Nigeria. I will say more about my ethnographic positioning below, but I will note here that I worked with the Campos family in Lagos in a manner similar to that of Ruth Behar in her work on Jewish diasporas, presented in *An Island Called Home: Returning to Jewish Cuba*, in terms of discovering personal spaces of remembering, imagination, and memory through fieldwork. Immediately, local narratives and family histories started to flower and unfold in response to my questions. Like members of the Jewish diaspora from Cuba in the United States, Afrolatinos brought their new, creolized, and Latin American cultural practices to Africa with them. As influential repatriates, the Afrolatino Aguda who returned to the Bight of Benin during the nineteenth century literally re-created, especially through architectural aesthetics, some of the spaces that they inhabited in Lagos, Sierra Leone, and Ouidah.[17] Through architecture, religion, language, and quotidian life, the Aguda redeposited some of their own legacies of Afro-Atlantic diasporic culture into West Africa.

Finally, this volume pieces together the innovative notions of diaspora that the narratives of the Aguda seem to suggest. Yet, it is clear that the depth and the breadth of the actual experiences of this community cannot be contained in any one volume. Chapter 5 necessarily returns to the Cuban dilemma of identifying the African as part of Cuban national culture as a model for understanding the legacies of a transnational creolization that is densely layered and cyclical in light of the evidence I am providing here. The conclusion to this volume pieces together my consideration of the main theoretical discussions of the Afro-Atlantic diaspora in light of the new perspectives that the history of the Aguda urges upon us. I also hope, however, that the explanation of my perspective on diaspora and colonialism in the Afro-Atlantic world is helpful in contextualizing the Aguda in terms of the important ideas and research that have preceded this study. This is especially true because the materials I reveal here are only pieces of a complex transnational narrative that includes clues to yet "undisclosed" transmigrations across the Atlantic. In many ways, scholars are just beginning to understand what many have known for years: culture is a process and history is reconstructive. This volume forces us to think about possibilities and people's own social agency over the definition of their identity and the telling of their history.

The countries of the Atlantic world have been the forced and voluntary stopping places for many West Africans. Thus, the ways in which Cuba and Nigeria have been transformed continue in the lives of Africans and Latin Americans living in many places around the world, including the United States. More research still needs to be conducted that gears itself toward understanding the resiliency of diasporic communities globally, as many communities are being displaced through war, disease, and globalization. As people with limited options, emancipated slaves who returned to Africa revealed that out of despair can come agency; out of dispersal, unity. I urge others to ask the impossible questions, to seek more information about the ways dislocated people view and empower themselves in the social and imaginative practice of journeying "home."

Ethnographic Memory and Atlantic Diasporas

The family histories of the communities I worked with as an ethnographer in Lagos suggested that their forefathers and mothers recycled and imported "African" diasporic sensibilities, like the continuation of a portable religious culture, that helped them change their national identity while settled in Cuba.[18] Upon their return, the Afro-Cuban Aguda continued to make themselves felt as prominent and unique contributors to civil society especially in Lagos, Nigeria.[19] This last aspect revealed itself in the interviews given by Mrs. Aderemi Gooding-King and Mrs. Ola Vincent, the granddaughters of Hilario Campos, the founder of the Cuban Lodge in Lagos. As a folklorist and ethnographer, my challenge was to speak to the sisters about their Cuban roots without forcing any connections that they themselves did not see. In other words, I needed to get them to talk about how they felt about being Afro-Cuban without suggesting that they must identify with this label and the history it implies.

What occurred when I sat down to speak with Mrs. Ola Vincent and Mrs. Aderemi Gooding-King was a process of recovery that mirrored my own search for Cuba. In previous fieldwork done in Cuba on the Yoruba-based religion of Santería, I was struck by the complex layers of association between Cuban spiritual entities and Yoruba identity in religious performances and rituals.[20] The density of the interplay led me to believe something fundamental occurred in the nineteenth century in Cuba that shaped the ways in which Yoruba-Cubans described in this book would be received and, in the case of the Aguda in Lagos, would present themselves to the world. In my work with Mrs. Ola Vincent and Mrs. Gooding-King, this view was elaborated upon, as the Campos family built their reputation in Lagos as Aguda from Cuba who were distinct and respected because of their unique contributions to Lagosian society. These contributions were recognized as Cuban, as Campos built a lodge in the middle of the Aguda neighborhood indicating this unique origin. As I sat at the Cuban Lodge, speaking with Mrs. Gooding-King, I realized that our conversations were a collaboration in recovering Cuba.

By recovering Cuba I mean retrieving what the idea of Cuba means to a descendant of a Cuban diaspora. While I was looking for a unique counter-working of a Yoruba diaspora in the Atlantic world in the Aguda, I also found a straightforward Cuban diaspora. Cuban diasporas are embedded in discourses of longing, nostalgia, and the reconstruction of home through the performance of culture and ritual.[21] Attempts to recover a lost Cuban past can be found in a range of global and temporal examples, especially in literature and film.[22] In my ethnographic fieldwork with the Campos family, I also found these recognizable traces of a Cuban diaspora in the form of narrative family history. Together, through ethnographic interviews, my collaborators and I were able to locate how they imagined Cuba in their family past. We were also able to speak reflexively to each other about that process in thinking about our own mixed identities within that diasporic formation. Talking about the mixture of Catholicism and *orisha* worship found in both Cuba and Lagos solidified the ways in which we understood how Yoruba diasporas from both Cuba and Brazil not only came full circle but also created a new kind of Atlantic identity in the Aguda.

Along these lines, I also spoke to Lagosian community leader and royal family member Prince T. Olusí of the Isaleko section of the city. Our conversations centered on Lagosian royal history as represented through traditional narratives found in the Ifa divination corpus. Olusí was intensely interested in this project and generously provided his insight on how the Aguda were and are perceived in Lagosian civil society. He also explained his perspectives on the responsibilities of authority from a traditional Yoruba framework. As an ethnographer and a folklorist, I was keenly interested in Olusí's own role as a community leader who served a range of constituencies successfully. He became a true collaborator in terms of helping me understand how mythological understandings of the past, like those found in the *odu* of the *Ifa* divination corpus, are deeply connected to the moment. These connections, I learned through Olusí, represent potentialities for weaving together disparate elements in a larger design. The pattern that emerged represented a deeply cyclical set of experiences in the Atlantic world that held over time. The perpetuation of these interrelated Atlantic understandings are actively renewed by the global popularity of *orisha* worship and the importance Cuba and Nigeria hold for ritual training today.[23]

Resituating Afrolatino Identities in the Americas and Africa

I want to propose a different framework for looking at movement in the Afro-Atlantic diaspora. Rather than looking at this movement from a unidirectional perspective, the present volume emphasizes how Afro-Atlantic communities moved back and forth, between and within "home" and new settlements. In both conceptual and lived ways, people who were engaged in the process of Afro-Atlantic diasporic movement poured back and forth across boundaries against incredible odds and with great agency. The Yoruba in Cuba and the Yoruba-Cubans in Nigeria addressed in this volume form just one example of this kind of transmigration between historically related communities. The impetus for transmigration is here rooted in a nostalgic longing that is reexperienced in the relocations of communities away from their place of origin.

Within the context of slavery, individuals moving around in the Afro-Atlantic world traveled with a cultural frame of reference that included social strategies for the creation of new identities.[24] Those in flux were constantly reinventing their sense of identity, history, and place, out of necessity. The invention of the idea of home was an important part of this process of identification in diasporic communities. The idea of home acted as a conceptual buoy that placed its own reference in the pliable realm of cultural production. People moving in Afro-Atlantic diasporas had to reinvent home in repeated and repeatable ways. This meant that Afro-Atlantic communities that emerged in places like Cuba had to carry old cultural ways and create new ones through their travels. The concept and the practice of diaspora in this context, then, informs Afro-Atlantic communities' production of the world from their own perspective, influencing deeply, often on a grassroots level, national and transnational identities.

West Africans who created these kinds of Afro-diasporic communities were well versed in how transnationality and nationality are interdependent in nature. Transnationality and nationality, as a form of transculturalism, informed the clusters of cultural products that situated meaning in African cultures from very early on.[25] In this manner, the history of the Caribbean and West Africa grew together through what would now be described as "globalization," "transnationalism," or the "creolization" of cultures and peoples.[26] These kinds of cultural strategies are not new; they represent recurring ways of making identity and place, through time. By reexamining the intense cultural negotiations that took place in the African diaspora, we can begin to think about the creation of "African" ways of being that permeated public culture and folklore in much of the Caribbean and Latin America.[27]

Approaches to the Study of the African Diaspora in the Americas

However, similar certain experiences of dispersal may seem to be, structurally, historical contexts shape the situations and reactions of relocated groups. The study of the African diaspora in the Americas is unique in that it provides a range of challenges to the supposed one-way movement of diasporas and their cultural creations. Multiple approaches often reflect the nature of the society from which such studies emerge. Consequently, societies that identify with being creolized, like those found in Cuba, the Caribbean, and Latin America, reflect an approach to the study of the African diaspora that emphasizes cultural admixture. In North America, a more bifurcated racial analysis has usually come to the fore as sociological and historical studies have tried to unravel the deep divide that still locates whole populations, sloppily, in a phenotypic typology. The largest source of misunderstanding between these different schools of analysis is that the latter mistakes the transculturation of creolized societies for the assimilation of bifurcated societies. The truth lies in between. Creolized Latin American societies are much more racist than the official rhetoric allows. And North American society contains much more cultural fluidity and admixture than is usually attributed to its culture. Consequently, the study of the African diaspora should include multiple diasporas, migrations, and a plethora of approaches that mirror the density of their cultural contexts.

Repeatedly, Afro-Atlantic culture has been characterized by the search for "authentic" African cultural markers, though these seem elusive. One example comes from the field of folklore around the mid-twentieth century, involving a major debate, on the "African-ness" of African American folktales in North America, between folklorist Richard Dorson and anthropologist William Bascom.[28] For Dorson, African American folktales were distinctly "American" or even "European" in nature. For Bascom, the tales found especially in Cuba and Brazil but also in the United States represented direct correlates of tales found in West Africa, especially among the Yoruba. The crucial question that this debate about "authenticity" raised was: when and where does a distinguishable "African" culture begin and end for Afro-Atlantic communities? In the context of the Afro-Atlantic world, the debate between Dorson and Bascom represented the anxiety that the labels "African" and "European" identities evoked, especially because of the history of slavery in North America.

At the heart of the above-mentioned question is another one about the African nature of African American cultures in North America.[29] Official categorizations of what constituted African cultural traits are critiqued for the ways in which these categorizations fetishized and froze specific aspects of culture like religion and music.[30] Consequently, the already variant and mixed aspects of West African cultures were located in artificially pure and static notions of what constituted the "African," and these were also frozen in time. Though we have moved closer to looking at African cultures in the Americas as reflecting an influential set of processes rather than identifiable products, the analytical lens through which we identify these processes is still located within the same discourse of distance from the very cultural discourses of cultural production that we are trying to understand. With this in mind, I propose that turning toward folk etymology within the Afro-Atlantic world will help us to develop comparative discourses that will let us understand different kinds of sources: epistemological ones. The clue to understanding the ongoing interrelationship between African and Afro-Atlantic communities lies in listening to the meta-analysis provided by the producers of culture, about their culture, in these communities.[31]

For Afro-Atlantic communities like those of the Yoruba-Cubans and the Aguda, the construction of new societies and cultures was based on transactions and interchanges on a multitude of levels. These transactions developed an idiom with which to bargain that included actors. For most aspects of the Afro-Atlantic world, slavery was a central institution in setting the boundaries for cultural and social negotiations. However, even within these social parameters, Africans in the Americas also created their own terms of creolization and nationalism.[32] In this context, then, the Aguda's story of transmigration acts as a testament to an amazing amount of agency that operated with resilience and creativity around the baffling social context of slavery. The story of the Aguda, almost unknown until the present volume, provides us with clues suggesting that there may be many more narratives of agency, encounter, and reinvention to be uncovered in this particular transatlantic context.

With the idea in mind of exploring the ways in which colonial identities may have been fluid, it is interesting to consider Rolena Adorno's look at primary source material from the Spanish Americas from the sixteenth and seventeenth centuries. Adorno presents a colonial history that explores the initial idea of admixture in the New World, in the Americas. In this view, Europeans, Native Americans, and Africans were constantly adapting to each other, socially, in the new context of the Americas. Adorno finds that there were many layers of resituating social identities in this colonial context.[33] Further, looking at these negotiations in the past shows that cultural merging and cultural transference do not necessarily end in cultural homogenization.[34] Micro-narratives and mini-exchanges between the above groups created the groundwork for the building of official institutions. Ultimately, even for the colonial context of the Americas as a whole, contact and incorporation between individuals, even if they were perceived in hindsight to be different or socially disparate, did result in significant connections between those participating in the creation of new societies.

Thus, it is important to consider the notion of creolization here. If people were admixing so early on, creolization must have been a perpetuating force in the Americas. African and indigenous social organizations and cultures did not disappear in the construction of colonial empires in the Americas.[35] Afro-Atlantic communities especially displayed a cultural propensity for innovation that allowed them to perpetuate their folklore in a manner that also influenced the building of postcolonial societies. The ability to perpetuate and manipulate cultural identity about home in a fluid manner became an important and powerful strategy for the construction of the nation in the Caribbean, but especially in Cuba. In fact, many Africans became Afrolatinos because of the way they influenced the new societies forming in the colonial Americas—and in Africa as well.[36] The Aguda in Lagos, Nigeria, are an example of such a group.

Roger Abrahams observes how Caribbean notions of creolization transgress North American boundaries of culture and race.[37] Thus, the belief in the idea of "purity," rather than what he calls "creolized contagion," keeps North American understandings of African diasporic ethnicity and culture bifurcated. However, Latin American and Caribbean nationalisms and identities are based on applauding, on the surface at least, the end product of creolization. The "local" community, or *el pueblo* in Latin American and Spanish-speaking Caribbean contexts, not unproblematically sings a tune of happy miscegenation as representative of the nation, the home-grown or *lo criollo*. This approach has been critiqued by scholars who see this kind of nationalism, especially in Cuba, as a sort of political charade or blackface presentation.[38] However, this critique often tends to ignore the deep semiotic power that the performance of African culture holds in Cuban society.[39] In regard to Afro-Atlantic diasporas, in the colonial context we see that Africans were present in multiple ways, whether through creolization or in a type of culture of resistance, as found in maroon communities like *palenques* or *quilombos*, for example.

Creativity and innovation on the part of Africans in the Americas have been portrayed as part of the construction of their new *criollo* identities.[40] Very few ethnologists in Cuba relied upon a comparative ethnographic study of similar traditions found in Africa to justify their findings. The end result has been localized studies that illustrate in great detail the manifestation of particular African cultural traits in one place in time. Due to this, the processes underlying the regeneration and invention of African ways of being have not really been conceptualized. Though they were aware of the African antecedents of the materials they were working with, Cuban ethnologists like Lachateñere and Barnet, for example, could not locate the "syncretized" nature of religions like Santería and Palo Mayombe within the cultural sensibilities of West African religious culture.[41] Yet, it is clear that the tendency toward admixture and incorporation already existed in religious cultures in Africa.

In this way, the Caribbean is seen as the primary locus for the process of cultural admixture that we identify with Afro-Caribbean cultures.[42] Yet, if we focus solely on the Caribbean as the site for Afro-Atlantic creolization, we ignore vast aspects of the processes of cultural creolization that were created in Africa and transplanted to the Caribbean. That is to say, the incorporative strategy of cultural assemblage usually associated with Afro-Cuban *criollismo* is distinctly African in origin. Here again I am focusing on the process, not the products, of cultural amalgamation, and this switches the emphasis toward understanding which cultural epistemologies are at work in Caribbean creolization. I am arguing that traditional African ways of knowing are central in how Caribbean communities adapt and create culture. As social agents in this process, many itinerant Africans founded social, political, and cultural organizations that were transnational and culturally varied.[43] In the end, a combination of social strategies was assembled in order to create a "certain way," or the *de cierta manera* way, of blending culture that Benítez Rojo alludes to for the Caribbean.[44] However, a dominant force in the perpetual creation of that pliant and recognizable Caribbean *criollo* culture is the African cultural philosophy of creolized incorporation.

African languages, religions, and aesthetics are found in the quotidian culture of Cuba and its diasporas. Cuban folklorist Fernando Ortiz suggested early on that a variety of West African, and especially Yoruba, epistemologies of culture building are present in nineteenth- and twentieth-century Cuba.[45] In his detailed ethnomusicological study of African music in Cuba, *La africanía de la música folklórica de Cuba*, Ortiz undertakes a comparative analysis of the music, poetry, and instruments of Cuban and West African folk music.[46] His conclusions are similar to those of Abrahams (above), in that he sees no room for purity in describing the culture that is practiced in the everyday context of folklife:

> No puede hablarse de "música absoluta" sino por absurdo convencionalismo.... No hay música "pura."
>
> [One cannot speak of "absolute music" except with an absurd [sense of] conventionalism.... There is no "pure" music.][47]

For Ortiz, there is no such thing as "pure" music. Ortiz's work emphasizes the idea of process, especially that of transculturation, in the making of Cuban, especially Afro-Cuban, culture.[48] When looking for connections between Cuban and Yoruba music and performance, for example, we cannot locate a "pure" form of any one ritual act or song, because these are living and changing performances that only can be located as "authentic" through an artificial construction involving the freezing of cultural forms.

It is more illuminating to consider how these expressions are used and reinvented, and how they actively borrow pieces from past and new expressions. This tells us more about cultural legacies borrowed from Africa, especially from the Yoruba in Cuba, because these cultural performances are always amalgamated and shifting.[49] Thus, I am suggesting that we focus on the similarity of process rather than forms, that we compare strategies of creolization throughout the Atlantic world.

This helps us to see that both Yoruba and Cuban cultural and religious performances were collaborative on their own terms when these cultures continued to engage each other both in Cuba and Lagos in the nineteenth century. These collaborations also included the semiotics of material culture and folk cultural expressions, as in altar-building traditions.[50] Within Afro-Atlantic diasporas, this kind of collaborative use of aesthetics between cultural performances, which established an interplay between the idea of Cuba and the idea of Africa, created a conveyor belt that helped Afrolatinos to imagine themselves in multiple ways, as well as to imagine belonging to more than one place. In the case being considered here, both Cuba and Africa acted as sites for creatively imagining a fluid identity that expressed itself through cultural performances. For the Aguda in Lagos and the Yoruba in Havana, this continuum operated within a motion found both in a social imaginary and in actual migration and settlement. The suggestion here is that a deeper tradition of creolization coming from the Yoruba themselves can be recognized in Cuban cultural aesthetics and also serves as a referent for these two communities. This occurred in a manner that was not static; neither was the performance of Yoruba cultural identity in Cuba essentialized into an object of purity of cultural forms. We can say that Afro-Atlantic diasporas here used cultural practices, and cultural change, as part of a historical continuum.

When we look at the context of the Cuban/Yoruba/Aguda diaspora, we see the ethnic and social heterogeneity of the Europeans, Africans, and Native Americans present in the worlds they encountered. The Yoruba presence here is felt in different stages in the Americas, because the idea is that this particular ethnicity is elastic both in Africa and in its own diaspora.[51] It also takes on a different character through time. From the mid-nineteenth century on, a later wave of "Yoruba" cultural impact was strongly felt in Latin America and the Caribbean. The Ogun Ajakaiye, or the great civil wars of the Yoruba on the African continent, accounted for a growing number of prisoners of war being sold into slavery during this era.[52] Before this period, the majority of slaves came from the Congo region, primarily being moved into the Southern United States and Brazil.[53] Yet, the way we understand the idea of Yoruba identity, as an imaginative site for creating home and community, is dependent on its portability and capacity for layering new elements of culture in ways that feel traditional.

A large part of the contextual framework that surrounded communities like the Aguda was that the Spanish, Portuguese, and British empires all played different and shifting roles in the American colonies over time. The three empires had conflicting ideas about the slavery of Africans, the forced incorporation of indigenous peoples into their colonies, and the importation of Asian labor into plantation building in the Americas. Connected to and layered within that shifting context between the empires were the different emergent African communities in the Americas that moved around between these systems. These communities had to continually re-create a sense of history and place that allowed for the ethnic incorporation of a variety of African but also Asian, indigenous, and native-born peoples.[54] This process of ethnic mixing in the colonial worlds in the Americas became a model for the building of postcolonial identities in the region.

Yet ethnic mixing also shaped the way diasporic communities, like the Aguda of Lagos, reintegrated themselves into the already heterogeneous Yoruba society. Individuals traveling through the Afro-Atlantic world understood how to work within cross-cultural and transnational contexts that allowed them to view ethnicity and nationality with elasticity. By the time returnees like Hilario Campos established their homes in Lagos in the nineteenth century, they were well versed in how to make multiethnic families, and communities by extension, work. For example, the Cuban Aguda of Lagos intermarried with immigrants from Sierra Leone, or Saros. This showed their willingness to use the mode of diaspora as a form of identification, rather than as an indicator of a pure national or ethnic origin. Thus, the quality of movement became a quality by which a community could be defined, and by which a community could also define itself.

Though different empires approached slavery differently, slavery did not exist in isolated places in the Americas. It seems obvious, but slavery was a momentous, transnational phenomenon that required the movement of a diversity of people back and forth across the Atlantic. A huge variety of people circulated through the geographic channels used for slavery, for a variety of reasons. Slavery did, for the most part, dictate the social, political, and economic reality of these routes. Yet, other quotidian legacies and movements also came about in that context. The Aguda who moved to Lagos from Cuba used the routes established by the slave trade to make it safely back home to Africa. The Aguda repatriation, then, asks us to rethink how conglomerates of communities, like the returning Yoruba-Cubans, may negotiate different kinds of agency within restricted and specifically located geographic contexts.

In this volume I am interested in suggesting that the Aguda displayed social agency in the way they experienced their lives, in how they enacted the daily performance of living, in their folklife.[55] Their decisions, whether to repatriate or to stay in Cuba, were real and complicated. One way to begin to imagine their voices is through examining what has been reported about their quotidian lives, but especially in terms of Afro-Cuban religious culture. Traditional Yoruba and Afro-Cuban religious cultures see ritual as affecting the realms of social agency and power. This is especially the case for African and African diasporic public rituals that are performed in order to dislocate, in some fashion, official discourses.[56] These domains of agency work at different frequencies from the kinds of social power experienced in the political public sphere as understood statically.[57] In the Caribbean and in Yorubaland, the realm of the unseen is a powerful social tool, albeit a secret one, that engenders the ability to use certain kinds of power. So the ways that we understand the public sphere should take into account how far beliefs in the agency of other frequencies are present for groups like the Aguda. Also, we must recognize that belief in the use of sorcery for political gain is very real, though rarely openly talked about, in African, Caribbean, and Afro-American contexts.[58]

Imagine a context, then, that includes a variety of interested individuals: traders, emancipated slaves, slaves, laborers, war heroes, prisoners of war, pirates, religious leaders, and other personalities coming from Africa, Asia, the Americas, and Europe.[59] This is the context for the Aguda moving back to Africa from Cuba. The world that existed was truly heterogeneous, with well-traveled individuals from diverse backgrounds crossing back and forth across the Atlantic. And this world was just as complicated and diverse for at least three centuries. Power relationships and hegemonic forces did play a role in who got to go where and when. Yet, as in our world today, different kinds of societies existed side by side, sometimes in conflict, contact, and negotiation with each other. Due to this complexity, communities like the Aguda were able to move and reassemble themselves in different contexts. Their vitality as a community through this transmigration had much to do with their ability to reimagine themselves in reference to their different experiences of diaspora.

Religion and Africans in the Americas

Folk Catholicism played a key role, as a compatible set of traditions and beliefs, for setting the framework for a new religious merging with African practices. In all of the interactions of people and culture described here, "folk" means the lived praxis rather than the official pedagogy of Catholicism among local communities in the Afro-Atlantic world. One example of how this quotidian combining worked in Cuba is the ritual association between La Caridad del Cobre, the virgin patron of Cuba, and the *orisha* Ochún of the Oshogbo area of Nigeria.[60] The ways in which La Caridad del Cobre and Ochún interacted and interact for believers are complex in terms of decisive realms of influence and conflation. This kind of Catholicism, like the folk Catholicism found in Europe, was informed with belief in the supernatural, miracles, saints as deities, and the efficacy and agency of believers to affect the world around them. In the Caribbean and Latin America, folk Catholicism was intimately tied to these magical beliefs but also to performing nationalism in the public adherence to specific local saints and virgins, like La Caridad del Cobre in Cuba or La Virgen de Guadalupe for Mexico.[61] There are many more examples in Cuba, Mexico, and Brazil of this process of the merging of indigenous and African deities with Iberian Catholicism in new, local ways that one can consider to be a religious aspect of *criolloismo* or *mestizaje*. It was on the level of the grassroots, everyday, lived practice of folk belief based on similar supernatural grounds that Yoruba traditional religion and Catholicism became incorporated into a larger, unique range of practices that one can now identify as Cuban folk religion.[62] Catholicism played a role in how the Aguda from Cuba identified themselves within Lagosian society. Connections between the traditional Yoruba religion and Catholicism remain constant for the Aguda because of the fuel that the admixture found in Cuban folk religion provided for founding community leaders in making these connections.

Shared folk practices in Lagos included the adoration of saints and deities, the observation of carnival and festival, and a belief in magico-religious phenomena on sacrificial and ritual grounds.[63] Historically, similar incorporative processes had already occurred in Africa, with outside beliefs being incorporated into traditional religion; these beliefs included other ethnic rituals, Islam, and, in the Congo, Portuguese folk Catholicism.[64] This added a context of past familiarity with the merging of diverse African and European religious cultures for those entering the African diaspora with these experiences.[65]

In Cuba, groups of ethnic Yoruba and Congo, as well as other African ethnicities, patronized the Catholic fraternal orders of *cabildos*. The idea of being part of a secret society made sense religiously for the African-born *bozales* and the Cuban-born *criollos* involved in African religions in Cuba.[66] This was so because the structure of religious sects, *awo*, in traditional Yoruba religion was one of secrecy based on a spiritual lineage that operated like a family. The structure of an *awo*, like a *cabildo*, was based on hierarchical association that included initiation and oath taking. Also, *cabildos*, as established in Andalusia and in Havana, were complicated, mixed entities that served various religious and civic functions in organizing the public sphere.[67] In the context of fifteenth- and sixteenth-century Spain, Judaism, Islam, and Christianity were enmeshed in many ways, especially in Seville. In Seville, *cabildos* were especially abundant in the era, and their role dealt with negotiating socioreligious affairs in the public sphere on the continent.[68] In turn, we see that Afro-Cuban *cabildos* developed out of a context in which both traditional African fraternal associations and Spanish civic brotherhoods influenced the new Cuban version of religious and social affiliation.

In Afro-Cuban *cabildos*, members made their devotions to Catholic saints and to *criollo* and African ancestors, as well as to other combinations of beings that affected their spiritual worlds. Ties among *cabildo* members were economically fostered and respected.[69] The heterogeneity of African home cultures was also expressed through associations within and between Cuba's *cabildos*.[70] These organizations helped new *emancipados*, free people of color, slaves, and laborers of African heritage re-create a complex set of associations, especially through religious and cultural performances, that always referred back to a kind of home. Besides reinventing mutual aid organizations based on a rather cosmopolitan understanding of community formation, individuals who participated in the *cabildos* also fostered new local identities that nurtured nationalism in Africa. Within these contexts in the Americas, Afrolatinos used nuanced ideas about the multiplicity of national identities and created new *naciones*, or new ethnic groups. Inside Cuba these were aligned with a *cabildo*'s choice of affiliation, or combination of affiliations, to pasts that indicated specific kinds of origins in Africa.[71] This "African" reassociation enriched the variety of linguistic, musical, religious, and political aesthetics that dominated the creation of Afro-Cuban civil society.

Scholars, families, and local communities speak about the movement of people and religion back to Africa from the Americas, especially from Cuba to Lagos.[72] In a dialogue about cultural legacy and origins, discussions about the cross-migration of Afrolatino, meaning both Afro-Cuban and Afro-Brazilian, religious cultures to Africa and back again begin to circulate.[73] The question of legacy creates confusion when looking at Candomblé, Santería, and *esin ibile*, or traditional Yoruba religion. All of these traditions are closely related ritually: in the practice of initiation, in the performance style of dance and drumming, and in the consistent understanding of a shared mythological corpus of divine beings. Thus, in thinking about how Cubans of Yoruba descent understood their Afro-Atlantic religious practices when they came back to a Protestant and Muslim Lagos, we can begin to understand the uniqueness of their own vision as a diasporic community through this lens. One way in which they continued to practice Afro-Atlantic religion was to remain Catholic in this context. This raises questions as to whether this Atlantic strategy of extending traditional Yoruba religion was brought back over to Africa. The Cuban narratives presented in the ethnographic section of this volume directly address the possibility of this kind of religious transmigration across the Atlantic.

Cultural assemblage, as a folk methodology of community formation, is usually based on a set of aesthetics, and it helps foster the ownership of distinction and difference.[74] This ability to connect allows groups like the

Aguda to emerge as coming from but also arriving anew to Lagos. Narratives of connectivity are often based on religious epistemologies set deeply within traditional Yoruba religion. These narratives, as in the traditional mythologies found in the *odu*, the *itan*, and the *pataki* of Cuba, are themselves embedded with cross-references to themselves. The stories themselves transmigrate genre and offer up for any one deity a multitude of identities and locations of existence. The word *itan* refers to a narrative that is also understood as a kind of history. As models, the founding oral texts in traditional Yoruba and Afro-Cuban religion emphasize mobility, change, and adaptation. These religious narratives use the idea of assemblage as a way of both carrying and then later unpacking the identities of the deities that are believed to be part of the experience of moving around. In referring to themselves as Lagosians in Havana or Aguda in Lagos, Yoruba who had lived in Cuba identified with their traditional religious culture by using the traditional notion of cultural assemblage, *asa*, with regard to folk Catholicism and their new Afrolatino identities. Their religious worldview gave them narrative guidelines to follow in reinventing themselves perpetually as an itinerant community.

The Yoruba in Cuba used traditional ways of inventing culture that focused on the folk methodology of assemblage that is being described here. Again, one can look at the religious music of *orisha* worship in Cuba in order to find out more about how the process works. Ortiz, in his "Orígenes de la poesía y el canto entre los negros africanos" (The Origins of Poetry and Song among Africans): points out Yoruba folk strategies that exemplify the way an embedded semiotics is applied in religious contexts in order to provide a folk metacommentary on the performance process.[75] By layering appellations for deities in orature and song, a process that Ortiz has recognized as *kasha* among the Yoruba, the performers are creating avenues for the manifestation of multiple expressions of the divine. This religious and performative technique is also acknowledged in the performer's own metacommentary on *kasha*. *Kasha* provides a kind of reflexive cultural commentary that is traditional in religious performances in Africa. In Cuba, it is also brought out in religious performances. Here is an example Ortiz gives us of *kasha* in a liturgical song for the *orisha* Yemayá.[76] As Ortiz writes,

> The same [kind of religious complexity] occurs among Afro-Cubans, in whose religion(s) the gods receive diverse names, in the manner of "avocations" taken from existing episodes from their mythology or simply expressions of their excellence. *So much so that they have been fonts of incessant confusion, at least for ethnographers, that still have not been cleared up. The black gods not only have diverse names in their own religion, but also with quick syncretism they incorporate the names of gods from other African religions and Christian saints, and even others invented in Cuba.* . . . This ritualistic polynomality, or recitation of the diverse names of each of the gods, and also many of them [*orisha*, gods] in the same invocation, is so characteristic that in the Yoruba language there

exists a special name that signifies this occurrence in ritual: *kasha*, which is used in religious songs in Afro-Cuban *Santería*. In this manner, one of the songs to the goddess Yemayá says:

Emi odé, omó odé
omó odé, emi odé
Káchú, ma má iyá, gbe le yó[77]

As Ortiz notes above, many different Afro-Cuban religious cultures deal with divine manifestations as negotiations of multiplicity and wholeness. Indeed, the Spanish translation from the Lucumí that Ortiz provides follows the lyrical format of Cuban popular rumba music and verse.[78] Ortiz also notes that special names and words are unintelligible, intentionally, to outsiders and even priests.[79] Using consistently subverted and shifting signifiers, we see that in Santería, religious musical performers, priests, and practitioners invert the notion of sacredness. It is also understood that not all of the varied manifestations of one *orisha* can ever fully be embodied in a space or within the body of a priest(ess). Thus, the understanding of the multiple names and manifestations of immense deities, like Yemayá, is accurately expressed by an embedded semiotic process.

Processes like *kasha*, the layering of names in invocation, and the commentary provided on that layering process, simulate the way in which itinerant Yoruba communities perform their identity and affiliation through time. The deities provide role models for the formation of community and history through ritual performance. This performativity of different stages of the lives of *orisha* in quotation (through naming) operates within a flexible metadiscursive structure. The quotation of traditional appellations, along with new words in new languages, such as Spanish or Kikongo, fits with traditional Yoruba praise-naming traditions, such as *oriki*, in Africa.[80] The past becomes manifest in the present through the ritual calling of the deity, of his or her names, and that past is layered, amalgamated, and open to new meanings. This created a space for the Yoruba in Cuba to understand themselves as a part of Africa, through their traditional religion of *esin ibile*, and, as a part of Cuba, through their new religion of Santería as well.

Understanding the power of discourse in performance is important when dealing with the Yoruba in the Atlantic world. *Kasha*, like *pipe* (calling the deities down by listing their titles of honor orally), manifests itself in the power of the act of utterance, of *ofo*.[81] This kind of religious performance was brought to Cuba by the Yoruba, who taught their way of worship to others. The Yoruba word for folklore, *atenedenu*—literally, "mouth to mouth"—signals the importance of the act of transmission in setting the parameters of making "folklore" for the Yoruba.[82] Orature, speaking well, as in convincingly and with skill, is valued in daily speech, as in religious performances.[83] Yoruba groups like the Lucumí and the Aguda were especially invested in creating new kinds of "Yoruba" ethnic cultures through religious performances that layered origins in a kind of work known as "ethnogenesis." According to J. D. Y. Peel, in Nigeria, *Kasha, pipe,* and *mojuba* are shared rituals that use the act of naming as a creative commemoration that relies on skilled speakers and listeners.[84] These traditions of naming the past in performance mirror the Afro-Atlantic diaspora in the present, in that they are also symbiotically re-created through a reflexive exegesis.

Transnationality and Globalization in Latin and North American Contexts

At the base of the construction of Latin American cultures was the encounter of different diasporic peoples. Africans and Asians came as slaves and laborers, Europeans of many backgrounds converged on the "new" continents for a number of reasons, and the indigenous populations struggled to survive these encroachments upon their homes. Jorge Klor de Alva proposes to access the specifics of the cultural negotiations of these groups by conducting careful readings of texts provided by Spanish and Portuguese expansionists.[85] When these texts are augmented by readings in African American (in a broad sense) autobiography, we can begin to reconstruct the complex and heterogeneous milieu of the culture of engagement in the Americas.[86]

Rolena Adorno also calls for a close reading of texts and situations arising from Spanish colonial America in the late sixteenth century and the seventeenth century.[87] Adorno's approach is similar to Klor de Alva's in demanding a more responsible and specific usage of the terms "colonial" and "postcolonial" for different historical contexts. One of the key features of this argument, also found in Angel Rama's *La ciudad letrada* (The Lettered City), is that we should not apply contemporary understandings of metropole and periphery, or our perception of the limits of those terms from our current vantage point, to previous manifestations of the scale of societies in colonial situations.[88] The main thrust of his work is to explore how different stages of literary discourses in the colony grew to create independent, postcolonial, and creolized nations.

In this vein of reimagining the building of the Atlantic world and Latin America, Alejandro de la Fuente recently used a careful reading of Havana in the sixteenth century, concluding that this port city was imbued with an international sense of importance because of its unique transitional positioning as a site for exchange.[89] J. R. Thornton and Linda M. Heywood also carefully excavate notions of slavery, Atlantic Creole identities, and port cities in the context of British, Dutch, and Central African exchanges in this circum-Atlantic trajectory for the sixteenth and seventeenth centuries.[90] These works demonstrate how Africans from a range of ethnicities were important actors in Atlantic history from early on in the colonial period. Their significance includes their lasting influence on the shape of the Atlantic cultures and economies that connected together Africa, Europe, the Americas, and the Caribbean. The specific example of this influence that developed in the nineteenth century in the form of the exchanges between the Aguda and the Havana Lagosians reiterates the importance of looking for historical narratives originating from creolized and subaltern spaces that may be obscured by a top-heavy historiography.

The production of culture in Cuba during the colonial period was fraught with heterogeneous views and internal contestations. What we would now call varied transnational and diasporic communities produced global discourses in Cuba: some were elite, others were resistant, and some had mixed allegiances as far as the Spanish crown was concerned. One important point to think about in this historical context is the fact that elite and folk histories were not necessarily separated in terms of spheres for the creation of histories. For example, Yoruba oral history can be seen as both elite and folk history in both the Nigerian and the Cuban contexts, depending on one's vantage point.[91] More specifically, in Nigeria, Yoruba traditional history certainly belonged to an elite class, while the same stories in Cuba became the stories of slaves, and thus became labeled as folk history. Though contexts such as these may change the reading of the history, in terms of whether it is folk or elite, the principal characters and the narrative voice in either Yoruba or Cuban contexts call for the community to use its own history as a form of reassociation with prestige. In the Nigerian context, Samuel Crowther and Samuel Johnson also wrote "official" histories, based on their transnational experiences, that helped to foster a Yoruba version of pan-Africanism from the mid-nineteenth century to the early twentieth century.[92]

Diasporic communities in the Americas between the sixteenth and nineteenth centuries, whether they were European, African, or newly "American," participated in transnational and global discourses that reveal processes more commonly associated with contemporary cultural production. That is, these cultural conversations were established by demographic encounters that took place in historically dense zones of interaction like Havana and Lagos. In this volume I will explore how the Aguda traversed and re-created this particular area of the African diaspora in ways that reveal shifting notions of home. I will then uncover some of the narratives provided by modern-day Aguda that emphasize their feelings about the importance for their grandfather, Hilario Campos, the founder of the Cuban Lodge in Lagos, of being both Cuban and Yoruba. Though Campos was born in Cuba, he felt so strongly about his African roots that he took his two sisters back to Lagos with him in the late nineteenth century. Yet, in Lagos, Campos began to feel a sense of nostalgia for Cuba, which brings this family's narrative full circle. I will talk about the deep connection with Cuba that is still spoken about by

Campos's descendants in modern-day Lagos. Their stories reveal a deep and interesting propensity for diasporic association with a homeland that resides primarily within a family's memories. Their longing for Cuba resembles that of many first- and second-generation Cuban Americans, whose idea of Cuba belongs more to the realms of fantasy and family legend than to actual experiences on the island.[93]

Though the site for nostalgic longing changed from Africa to Cuba in later generations of the Aguda, the process of diasporic remembering in this community remains similar. The longing for a home that one cannot readily encounter inspires feelings of pride and nostalgia. I found that the Aguda in Lagos did the work of association in their attempts to retrieve their heritage through an inherited social imaginary. I believe that this kind of imaginative reconstruction and recovery is well entrenched in the language of loss and discovery. Families and communities that are separated by distance, time, and lack of physical contact are especially prone to developing this kind of framework for remembering, and for developing new communities based on their memories.[94]

I aim to provide the reader with an opportunity to consider the important role that the layered language of diaspora—as hope, longing, and memory—plays in shaping our contemporary understandings of folk history. Indeed, the relationship of the imagination to memory and the practice of reconstructing history is embedded in how we understand ourselves in relation to a past.[95] And the transnational nature of an "Atlantic" imaginary is also at play in how the past is remembered, understood, re-created, performed, and put into narrative in a range of contexts.[96] In this book, the narratives about the past provided by the Aguda and the contexts that their ancestors traversed speak to an important aspect of Afro-Cuban and Yoruba connections that has been little explored: that of Africa "remembering" Cuba. We will find that the seeds sown in this diaspora begin in the mind, in the imaginative reconstruction of home that belongs to a time and place that is perceived with historical intangibility, that is irretrievable in its loss, and that is bittersweet in its remembering. The effects of these reconstructions are very real, as they continue to produce viable and unique Atlantic cultures rooted in this past.

1

Grassroots Africans

Havana's "Lagosians"

Dolores Real

It was June 7, 1854, and Dolores Real was forty years old. She had lived for thirty years, most of her life, in the city of Havana, Cuba. She was now heading back to her city of birth in Africa: Lagos, Nigeria. When she was just a small girl, Spanish slavers took her to Cuba aboard what she remembered as a large vessel. She and the others were dropped off at the town of Cardenas. From there, they were taken to the slave barracks in the island's capital, Havana, where she stayed for one month, awaiting her fate.

Dolores was then sold to a free Yoruba woman and a fellow Lagosian, Carmen Real. Carmen named her Dolores (her original Yoruba name is unknown) and took her in as a laborer. Carmen, a laundress, employed Dolores in the trade and taught her the necessary skills. Carmen also had eight or nine other female slaves working for her at the time. Six years later, Dolores was sold to Father Leon, for whom she worked as a domestic. It took seven years for her to save up the 450 pesos she needed to buy her freedom from the clergyman. On her own, Dolores returned to the trade she had learned from Carmen, and worked as a laundress, earning about fifteen pesos a month. She worked her way home, literally, saving what she could from these modest earnings until she was able to pay the 140 pesos it cost her for passage back to Lagos.

At the time when she gave her testimony to British officials, Dolores was certain that her mother and three brothers would be waiting and preparing for her return on the other side. Over the years, she had diligently stayed in contact with them, by word of mouth, through messages delivered by arriving slaves and emancipated repatriates moving in and out of Cuba and Lagos. For the four months prior to her departure, she was especially active in communicating messages via this Havana–Lagos grapevine. The short biography reported here was recorded by officers of the British Anti-Slavery Squadron as she embarked on her voyage back to Africa.[1] This and other narratives of the life histories of Havana Lagosians provide some new and specific observations on the multidimensional nature of the Atlantic world for Africans moving across the ocean during the nineteenth century.

The African Diaspora and the British Antislavery Movement

The Evangelical Movement of the late eighteenth century, which fostered the development of organizations like the Church Missionary Society, led British and European writers to examine slavery and its role in the Americas. During the 1760s–1780s in England, a keen interest was shown by Quaker leaders, like doctor John Fothergill, who was inspired by the antislavery publications of Anthony Benezet, in commenting upon and changing public opinion about the nature of the development of contemporary empires and economic markets in light of slavery and its immorality.[2] On a broader scale, emerging collections and treatises on world history displayed a preoccupation with the idea of philanthropic religious interest in the conditions of the transatlantic slave trade.[3] A European constituency of abolitionists began to exhibit a fervor for developing antislavery societies across the Atlantic world.[4]

The antislavery leaders Granville Sharp, James Ramsay, and Thomas Clarkson provide examples of staunch early British opposition to the Atlantic slave system. According to Christopher Leslie Brown's *Moral Capital*, a historical narrative providing a simple picture of an inevitable movement toward philanthropy does not tell the entire story of British abolitionism.[5] Though they were labeled philanthropic, the worldview of these leaders was one in which the existing social and cultural hierarchies that fostered slavery more accurately represented their positions vis-à-vis the Other, especially Africans. Such philanthropists usually attempted to "civilize" through the imposition of religious, educational, and social institutions. However, the notion of Africa, and of Africans and other nonwhites, for that matter, suggested by this European context of ideas existed on a conceptual plane that could not recognize, address, or account for some of the on-the-ground strategies and networks that Africans were already creating to battle and subvert slavery. The abolitionist movement, as Brown suggests, exhibited a rare shift from the cultural paradigm dominating the Atlantic world, one in which the economics and culture of the plantation relied heavily on slavery. This shift originated as an offshoot of the Quakers in particular.[6] Thus, the partnerships fostered by British philanthropists and emancipated slaves were created out of two distinct worldviews that perhaps met haphazardly, and mainly, in the realm of praxis.

On a larger scale, the argument presented by eighteenth-century British abolitionists was not one of pure human interest but one that, rather, was involved in a power struggle over the position and importance of diverse European institutions with regard to the lives of native, Creole, and slave populations in the Americas.[7] This larger scramble for power over the lives of Others thus represented embedded and emerging struggles for political power within Britain.[8] Motivating these interconnected discussions about slavery and the role of abolitionism in the Atlantic world was the overarching British concern over contemporary international threats to the empire, especially in regard to the roles of the coempires of Spain and Portugal.

It was no accident that active abolitionists of the late eighteenth and early nineteenth centuries, like James Stephens and Zachary Macaulay, spent years of their ministry in the West Indies.[9] Experiences in the Americas, as well as in Africa proper, provided links and established networks for British abolitionists that created "native" constituencies and converts. In this manner, Africans and individuals of African descent were led to support ministries that seemed to improve their situation and condition. However, these allegiances were often contested cultural and political sites where religious practices were reshaped to resemble the traditional practices of the populations in the process of conversion.[10]

The Church Missionary Society (CMS) was founded in 1799 by abolitionists William Wilberforce, Henry Venn, and Thornton. This influential missionary organization played an active role in establishing Christianity in West Africa, but especially among the Yoruba in Lagos. It also provided an infrastructure for creating an educational system all over Africa, but again, most visibly in "Yoruba" strongholds like Lagos. Through its monopoly on educational institutions, the CMS served as a major instrument of religious and cultural instruction, from an "English" perspective—with some African reworking—in West Africa. Coupland put the motives of the British abolitionists' acculturation campaigns succinctly:

> It must not be supposed that either Wilberforce or any of his collaborators were interested only in that one aspect [abolition] of the humanitarian movement. . . . It is not enough, they felt, to stop injuring the Africans: an attempt should be made to help them, to give them the best instead of the worst of what European civilization had to offer.[11]

Coupland went on to name the three "C's"—elements that the CMS was eager to promote: Christianity, commerce, and colonization.[12] Thus, missionary organizations like the CMS were seeking paternalistic routes toward guiding their foreign congregations. Other British abolitionist interest groups interested in "civilizing" Africans on African soil developed a growing interest in repatriation as a strategy with a multitude of ends, especially the movement of transatlantic Blacks to the newly formed settlement of Sierra Leone.[13] Though there might have been a legitimate interest in abolishing slavery in the late eighteenth century, the eventual goal of some groups and individuals in the abolitionist movement included "civilizing" the African or Indian Other.[14] Though it is not a new observation, we can make a correlation between the paternalistic allegiances described above and those found in nineteenth-century Cuba, in the patronage of *belles artes* by the powerful

Domingo del Monte, whose patronage of Afro-Cuban writers and abolition was perhaps spurred by a similar civilizing undercurrent.[15]

Repatriation to Africa of postslavery African populations was one means offered by abolitionists like Granville Sharp of locating sites for new ministries and societies.[16] It was key that Sierra Leone was a favored locale for missionaries training and organizing Africans from the Atlantic diaspora to engage in further missionary work, on the continent and abroad. A settlement in Africa provided a space for African Americans, Africans, and Europeans that allowed for a negotiation of identity, religion, and politics in a site reinvented as an African home. Africans moving around in the Atlantic world used Sierra Leone as a focal point for creating networks to provide grassroots information about the conditions of postemancipation labor in the Caribbean.[17] From early on, Africans in the Americas also created significant emancipated communities in the Spanish circum-Caribbean.[18] These enclaves of freed people were connected on a transatlantic scale in terms of movement and range of citizens. It is obvious that both vernacular and official information circulating between remaining Spanish and British slave societies about these communities created a shared consciousness about resistance and freedom among Africans and their descendants in the Atlantic world.

The transnational nature of British abolitionism, when coupled with African diasporic participation in fighting for freedom from slavery, allowed for the development of a Black Atlantic consciousness that had a dissonance in its roots. For some British abolitionists in the late eighteenth century, Africa provided opportunities for the advancement of British trade and colonial expansion to make up for losses in the Americas, rather than a purely altruistic alternative to the slave trade. One example given by Brown concerns the case of the colony of Sierra Leone, in connection with which Joséph "Flycatcher" Banks, and others like Malachy Postlethwayt, tried to "sell" abolition to the English public and political leaders as profitable, as advantageous to England if the goal of profiting directly from African soil and labor was pursued.[19] Sierra Leone was initially established in 1787 by the British and by Black loyalists who had fled from the American Revolution as a place of asylum for Africans in America fleeing reenslavement. Sierra Leone played a crucial role for both the British and Africans in the diaspora as a working example of different interests coming together in favor of abolitionism.

Afro-Atlantic abolitionism was also moving in transnational ways toward African repatriation in the late eighteenth century.[20] The formation of a creolized Black consciousness was under way, in the creation of a discourse about different kinds of freedom and routes toward that freedom. People of African descent worked in a kind of transatlantic alliance for freedom, often crossing ethnic, linguistic, religious, and continental lines in a process that saw some significant cross-migrations in the nineteenth century that were identified as "African" in multiple ways.[21] In many ways, early British and Afro-Atlantic approaches to slavery and self-determination, which offered repatriation to Africa as solution, illustrated a reordering in the Atlantic transnational imagination that was occurring at that period and continued into the nineteenth century. Havana's Lagosians and the Cuban Aguda in Lagos were good examples of populations who navigated the waters of slavery, emancipation, and repatriation that developed out of the transnational conceptualization of the Atlantic order in the eighteenth century. During the nineteenth century, romantic notions of repatriation to Lagos and of the idea of Yorubaland held by Sierra Leone's Creoles mirrored those of the Aguda. The reordering of the Atlantic world that occurred in the establishment of abolitionist, albeit colonial, enclaves in Africa in the late eighteenth century by the British and by diasporic Africans from North America created the conditions for the Saros and the Aguda to come to Lagos looking for their ancestral roots and for self-determination a hundred years later.[22] Movements like those to and from Sierra Leone and other places in Africa to the Caribbean and back were also known in Bahamian and Trinidadian contexts.[23]

A moment in this reordering of the Atlantic world that shook up Afro-Atlantic, American, and European abolitionists alike occurred in 1772 when James Somerset was brought to England from Virginia by his owner Charles Stewart. Somerset ran away, was recaptured, and then shipped to Jamaica for resale. Somerset brought the issue of his status to the West Indian courts. The judge in this case, Judge Mansfield, was eager to settle the case in favor of Somerset. Mansfield clearly urged Stewart to set Somerset free of his own accord. And, on June 22, 1772, Mansfield dismissed Stewart's claim, ruling in favor of Somerset's freedom.[24] The Somerset case ignited British, American, and African diasporic abolitionism in the Atlantic world.

Brown provides examples of the resulting momentum. These included the growing movement of Black petitioners in Massachusetts in 1773, which directly confronted the colonial legislature in a spirit of abolitionism and anticolonialism.[25] Ex-slave Olaudah Equiano, who had gained an official position with the British government in 1786, in which he was managing provisions for Sierra Leone, used this position to criticize the mismanagement of the colony, and was dismissed.[26] Writers of African descent in this era of the creation of new Atlantic diasporas, like Wheatley and Sancho, were not merely tokens, but represented a varied contribution to the antislavery discourse that intersected with European and American discourses of abolition in a shared public sphere.[27] Thus, Equiano and these other emerging Black figures represented some of the ways in which Africans acculturated to European modes of discourse pushed themselves into the public sphere and created a space for their voices in the civil discourse about slavery, and about colonialism, in the late eighteenth century. These instances foreshadow, in several ways, the legal avenues, albeit limited, that were used by many in a varied set of struggles for freedom in the Atlantic world.

This search for agency by Africans in the Atlantic diaspora also included small acts of freedom and the use of alternate discourses and routes that circumvented the models and systems that transatlantic slavery had set up, or indeed used these models and systems in order to "get back" to Africa in terms of their actual return, as well as in terms of the creation of aesthetics and vernacular cultures in the Americas.[28] The latter, the creation of quotidian cultures that connected people to Africa and to a transnational Atlantic Blackness, opened up the possibility of conversing across the Atlantic with Africa in a manner that created a space in which Africans could imagine themselves in relation to the Americas as well.[29]

Places like Lagos and Havana contained these aesthetic cross-migrations as potential spaces of home. This was especially true in terms of the Afro-Christian retransformation of place and identity that both the Yoruba Cubans and the Aguda performed in Cuba and Lagos. The new *cabildos* and Catholic churches became infused with a portable historical performance containing transcultural negotiations of ritual and identity. Indeed these *cabildos* incorporated *criollo* and "authentic" notions of a range of being African in Cuba—often simultaneously mixing and clarifying ethnic origins.[30] "Africa" became a portable origin that also allowed for new beginnings away from slavery in repatriation experiences and in cultural performances. However, individuals and communities differed in terms of their ethnicity, their origins, and the experiences they acquired in their transatlantic migrations. And this meant that they brought with them their own culturally informed senses of how to build their new societies, especially in terms of future shape and content. One can imagine that even as early as the late eighteenth century, organizations like the Sierra Leone Company, made up of British abolitionist missionaries, were challenged to find that the voices of repatriated Africans included a multitude of perspectives with differing ideas on how to proceed in terms of identity, religion, language, culture, education and so on. The diverse parties of repatriates, who came to the bargaining table with different goals, means, and assumptions in mind in terms of types of spaces of home in "Africa," came together through the performance of an Afro-Christian cultural identity in both Sierra Leone and Lagos.[31]

Indeed, by 1820, the Mixed Commission Courts, operating in Havana, Cuba, and Freetown, Sierra Leone, had established a method for the repatriation of *emancipados* to Africa from Cuba.[32] Due to publications like the *Anti-Slavery Reporter*, established in 1823 and edited by Zachary Macaulay, information circulated among abolitionists about the cross-diasporic networks that focused on reuniting slaves of African descent with the continent and with their families.[33] The publication also served to sway British public opinion toward the abolition of slavery. However, many of those who were emancipated at sea became cheap labor for the plantations in the Caribbean—including Trinidad, the Bahamas, and Cuba.[34] Individuals emancipated at sea would eventually contend with the Mixed Commission Courts as a way to determine their status in the new societies in which they found themselves. In places like Havana, the courts dealt with a plethora of individuals who came from different parts of Africa, but also from other parts of the Caribbean. The courts themselves, according to Rosanne Adderley, provided such detailed records in Havana in the registers of different ethnic origins of freed individuals that we can only infer that certain cultural mores and affiliations were imported directly into the emerging "Afro-Cuban" public sphere.[35]

The Mixed Commission Courts in Africa and the Caribbean

The British Anti-Slavery Squadron began cruising the coast of West Africa in hope of implementing the Slave Trade Act of 1807. This was an agreement between Spain, France, and Britain outlawing future traffic in people from Africa to the Americas. About one-sixth of the British navy was dedicated to the effort, which not only affected Cuba and the Spanish Caribbean, but also deeply touched the populations of the British Caribbean in places like the Bahamas and Trinidad well into the nineteenth century in terms of redistributing emancipated Africans in a circum-Atlantic manner.[36] It was during the squadron's encounters with ships flying other nations' flags that we find slaves being taken to Havana from Lagos, as *emancipados*, or emancipated slaves, who, ironically, had to work to pay for their freedom.[37] In Havana, the newly arrived Africans would work and wait as their status was negotiated by the multinational Mixed Commission Courts.[38] However, such negotiations often proved unsatisfactory for all parties involved, especially for the Africans waiting in slave barracks in Havana, because of the differences in policy between countries in regard to slavery and the status of individuals emancipated at sea. This was especially true with regard to Spanish officials, who were unwilling to administer *emancipados* who had been liberated at sea by the British but placed in Cuba's slave society. The result was that in 1833 the British took over the task of monitoring *emancipados* in Havana.[39]

The Mixed Commission Courts tried to negotiate the elaborate transnational policies concerning *emancipados* and their legal status in the multiple sites of the Atlantic diaspora. It was understood that the transnational nature of the legal and personal status of individuals from Africa was an *Atlantic* concern, though perhaps it was not referred to as such at the time. International organizations, like the Mixed Commission Courts, anticipated the fluid and fluctuating nature of understandings of the region that indicated an understanding of the complex global identities emerging from these contexts. It was the treaty of 1817 between Spain and Britain that had set up the Mixed Commission Courts in Sierra Leone and Havana, Cuba, in anticipation of growing discussions about the status of the *emancipados*.[40] According to Martinez-Fernandez, however, these Mixed Commission Courts began operating in an official capacity in 1820.[41]

The picture was complicated, and the need for the Mixed Commission Courts was reaffirmed, by the activities of the slave traders and the nations that supported their activities. Ships wanting to avoid inspection by the British squadron often flew other nations' flags and were stocked with falsified documentation. There was also illegal slave trading, originating from intercolonial trade between Atlantic ports, which had been established in Cuba as early as the late sixteenth century.[42] Illegal slave traders had the support of parties and nations that provided them with the means to hide their true intentions from the squadron in a variety of ways. Of course, parties to treaties with Britain, like Spain and Portugal, which continued to profit from the trade, denied any involvement when it was necessary, while aiding the slave trade when it was convenient to do so. The United States aided the illegal slave trade to Cuba, and around the middle to the late 1830s, U.S. officials were actively involved in international fraud. The involvement of the United States could be characterized in the following way:

> After the Treaties of 1833 and 1835 they [illegal slavers] shifted to the Portuguese, and after the British Act of 1839 to the only flag which continued to afford immunity from the search [of the ships], the Stars and Stripes. . . . And to make themselves more secure the smugglers provided themselves, in the case the flag were questioned, with fraudulent American papers. Thus American ships were bought by Spaniards and used for the Cuban Trade under the pretense of being still American. It became an open, a notorious scandal.[43]

As scandalous as this seemed at the time, nevertheless there was a less than vigorous effort on the part of Spanish judges in the Mixed Commission Courts in Havana to rectify the status of slaves brought in by falsified, illegal means and documentation. Indeed, the numbers of persons with undetermined status increased significantly between 1810 and 1846, when it was reported that some 116,800 individuals were intercepted on slaving ships at sea.[44] For Africans living in Havana at the time, this meant that they usually waited for the courts' decisions as *emancipados*, in a state between free and slave, while working and living on their own in Havana's ethnic neighborhoods. Those wishing to make the trip back to Africa, especially to Lagos, would often have to wait years for the financial, legal, and political opportunity to embark on their journey. Since they had had to wait so long, many had acquired spouses and children in Cuba, and brought these along with them. These returnees were individuals who had developed an "Afrocubano" identity alongside their African identity over the years, and they would carry both of these identities back to Africa with them.[45] This dual frame of reference became a factor in the lives of the repatriates who settled in Lagos.

For Spanish court officials and British judges, their differing agendas and the high level of conflict of interest made the speedy rectification of the status of illegally held slaves a political impossibility.[46] The unclear status of Havana's large and growing African and Black *criollo* labor force was a source of strain for all of the players involved. The British had their supervisorial role at stake, the Spanish their colonial and economic control over the island, and the *emancipados* their livelihood and social legitimacy. Such was the level of concern that, in 1835, treaties between the Spanish, British, and Portuguese began addressing the issues of *emancipados* directly.[47]

In Cuba, a particular point of controversy was the role that the British monitoring of slavery played in fostering rebellions and revolts on the island. One well-known example was the controversy surrounding British antislavery commissioner David Turnbull.[48] It was believed by Spanish officials in Cuba that Turnbull had played a pivotal role in creating opposition to the government among slaves and sympathetic white *criollos*.[49] There is some debate as to whether Turnbull was directly associated with what was perceived, in the minds of Spanish officials, as the slave and abolitionist conspiracy of La Escalera in 1844.[50] Robert Paquette's seminal study of La Escalera, *Sugar Is Made with Blood*, looks closely at the debate among both Cuban and North American historians on whether there was actually a conspiracy in Cuba at the time.[51] Some argue that La Escalera was more a matter of Spanish colonial repression than an organized and transnational effort to resist colonialism and chattel slavery. Paquette's study includes a significant reconsideration of Domingo del Monte's writings, and concludes that the will to action and resistance certainly existed in an international context during the era of La Escalera among a range of social actors on the island.[52] More to the point, however, is the problem of accurately reconstructing motives, actions, and events in the aftermath of repressive government actions that included the use of torture to force confessions. How much does the story of a conspiracy owe to government paranoia, and how much to real, organized resistance?

At the core of the internationalization of sentiments in favor of abolition and resistance is the notion of a "transnational imaginary" that can be applied to Black Atlantic identities in terms of the way they were culturally reconstructed for the purpose of fighting slavery and colonialism.[53] These "imaginaries of freedom" certainly have roots in the Haitian revolution, but they also have a common meeting place in the transnational imagination in Cuba. The Aponte conspiracy of 1812 is an interesting point of remembering resistance in Cuba as connected to a transnational thirst for Black freedom in the region and fueled by transatlantic alliances—especially located in Haiti.[54] José Antonio Aponte, a former militia commander in Havana, was part of the leadership of a major Yoruba *cabildo* and a local leader among Afro-Cubans. It is important to note that other African ethnic groups also established *cabildos*, with differing degrees of acceptance of Cuban-born, *criollo* Afro-Cubans in Havana, which were also investigated closely at various times by the island's colonial government.[55]

The threat that the Aponte conspiracy represented, like La Escalera thirty years later, was both transnational and local, underground and rampant—it created a space where the contradictions of the actors and motivations of the era could be portrayed in the social imagination. This imagination worked and works in triggering instances where colonial repression and Black resistance were and are projected upon these Atlantic scares and conspiracies. Perhaps no single agreed-upon narrative will ever emerge, but we will always find that the multiple disclosures of conspiracies by colonial officials and by historians perpetually paint a world that is complicated in its fluidity, in its ability to destabilize purely bifurcated notions of racial alliance through unlikely allegiances. The inclusion of different ethnic registers, like Aponte's Yoruba affiliation, in the whole schema of this particular transnational imaginary, creates the suggestion of a pan-African connectivity that is elusive but sought after for a myriad of purposes.[56] The Cuban elites and the Spanish reacted to later revolts like the La Escalera by tightening laws and security precautions around slaves, *emancipados*, and mixed populations through the use of the Mixed Commission Court.[57] From 1844 on, in the period often referred to as the Black Scare, Spanish officials used whatever political leverage they gained from the revolt to restrict the abolitionist interpretation, from within the Mixed Commission Courts, of laws affecting the legal status of African workers, *emancipados*, and slaves.

This was especially the case in regards to the Mixed Commission Courts that grew out of the strained negotiations taking place between Britain and Spain on the island of Cuba from the mid nineteenth century on.[58] In *Fighting Slavery in the Caribbean*, Martinez-Fernandez documents the life of one British judge living in Havana while serving on the Mixed Commission Court for the Suppression of Slavery, a special session of the court. George C. Backhouse and his wife Grace Catherine moved to Cuba in 1852, a period that saw a wide transnational movement of people, especially in terms of both free and slave laborers, to and from the port of Havana.[59] Considering this challenging context in terms of factors affecting the conditions of Spanish rule, it was no surprise that Backhouse experienced an acute reticence on the part of his Iberian counterparts serving on the court.

Indeed, in both Spanish and North American governments, proslavery politicians voiced concerns over the British involvement in abolitionist activities in Cuba. For example, there was a filibustering campaign in the United States between 1848 and 1851, sponsored by southern senators, for

Cuban statehood.[60] The main impetus for U.S. politicians' interest in Cuba was the search for a ready supply of slaves to the American South. Also, some American politicians felt the need to curb British power in Latin America, a region that was increasingly viewed, through the lens of the Monroe Doctrine, as under the purview of the United States. Thus, Britain's international abolitionist activities in Cuba directly threatened both Spanish and North American claims to influence and empire-building in the region. The British abolitionist movement began asserting an international campaign following the Slave Trade Act of 1807 that blossomed into attempts to administer emancipated Africans, especially in the Spanish Caribbean through the first deliberations of the Mixed Commission Court in Havana in 1820.[61] The importance of the establishment of this court is that it introduced liberated Africans of consistent ethnic identities into a slave society. Like Havana's Lagosians, who are being explored here, those introduced to Cuba via emancipation at sea came with set ideas about their cultural identity in Africa, and they formed a range of ethnic Black associations in Cuba and Havana that came to reveal this reality. Thus, the transnationality of British abolitionism created the opportunity for Afro-Atlantic individuals to help create new social groups in both the Caribbean and Africa.[62]

The existence of a large, cosmopolitan, ethnically mixed slave and free urban population in Havana made this major Atlantic port a fertile site for negotiating the relationships between colonial centers and local creolized communities.[63] All players engaged in the push and pull of the era by creating diverse political allegiances that protected their vested interests. The most pervasive, yet unofficial, community developments were the growing Black, white, and mixed *criollo* grassroots associations that were positioned toward a dissenting (read *away* from Spain) Cuban nationalism. Though some scholars believe that the idea of Cuban nationalism as inclusive of Afro-Cuban citizenship is merely a myth, the reality is that Afro-Cuban and other Afro-Atlantic communities created new Africanized notions of citizenship in postemancipation Caribbean societies in the nineteenth century.[64] Some clues as to how such associations developed organically can be found in the case studies reviewed below. Examples of how the Havana Lagosians converged, in official and unofficial associations, to establish a significant presence in Havana illustrate early strategies of community development, some of which were later adopted by other emerging Cuban populations during the island's subsequent revolutionary wars.

There was also hostility toward British abolitionism and the Mixed Commission Courts in other parts of the African diaspora. For example, by 1845 Brazil had ceased taking part in any of the Mixed Commission Courts. Brazilian slaveholders were particularly hostile to "Lord Aberdeen's Act," an international legal attempt to undermine Brazilian slaving via the jurisdiction of the British admiralty on the high seas.[65] Cuban policy, for its part, followed the Spanish mandate tacitly to work with antislavery forces, given Spain's albeit reluctant compliance with British abolitionist treaties. Though the courts in Havana repatriated Africans freed on the high seas, the pattern was to establish a lengthy, inconsistent, and expensive process for the *emancipado* class of workers.

Slave, Free, and Indentured Labor in Nineteenth-Century Cuba

It is helpful to think about Cuba in the nineteenth century in terms of slaves, free people of color, and indentured workers as part of a larger transatlantic context. This perspective views Cuba not only as integrated economically through plantation culture and colonial expansion but also as being part of the social and cultural landscape that created potentially new ways for Africans, Afro-Cuban *criollos*, Afro-Atlantic creoles, and people of color to work together toward a civic society that would include them. In her comparative study of the construction of postslavery societies in nineteenth-century Louisiana and Cuba, *Degrees of Freedom*, Rebecca Scott depicts the context of these changing sites from the perspective of slave and free economies for people of color. This impressive study details two slave societies that do not fit a bifurcated model of race and freedom, yet Scott still focuses on seeing how a "reality of dichotomies" existed for these cosmopolitan sites.[66] Dealing mainly with the plantation of Santa Rosalia in the Santa Clara region of Cuba, she illustrates how slaves and workers of color used different stages of freedom in order to shape their own lives and future.[67] Their lives involved a testy alliance with white *criollos* in the fight for Cuban independence from Spain and later for greater representation in Cuba's new government despite U.S. interventionist policies.[68] Scott ultimately looks for a "vernacular sense of the deeper meaning of freedom" in the record.[69] Using Louisiana and Cuba as models for that freedom, Scott points toward a transatlantic imaginary of Black solidarity rooted in a racial flexibility, multiple ethnic identifications, and transnational affiliations that was found throughout the Afro-Atlantic world in the nineteenth century.[70]

In the census of 1861, a total of 232,493 individuals were counted as free people of color on the island.[71] Of this number, some 37,768 free people of color were listed as living in Havana.[72] They resided in the urban environs of Havana, especially within *barrios* and enclaves of people of similar African, Asian, or mixed ancestry.[73] Even as early as in the sixteenth century, female urban slaves known as *ganadoras* became wealthy as tavern owners, laundresses, and cooks that served the bustling port city.[74] These considerations suggest that almost from its inception, Havana's urban workforce comprised people of African or mixed ancestry. Most *emancipados* and free people of color in the nineteenth century worked day-to-day, though unsure of their exact legal and social status in Cuban colonial society, as was true of other Africans "freed" at sea by the British antislavery forces.[75] Casanovas and Paquette provide data on the occupations of both men and women free people of color in nineteenth-century Havana.[76] Their tables, for 1861 and 1847, respectively, and the life histories found in the appendix to this volume suggest that during this era male Afro-Cuban workers were increasingly represented in such skilled occupations as cigar rollers, blacksmiths, and carpenters. Further, the women worked as seamstresses, confectioners, and midwives. When corroborating this information about labor with the life histories presented below (and in the appendix), and with the narratives about the specific kinds of skills Afro-Cubans brought back to Africa with them, we see an emerging pattern. Africans and their children acquired specific skills like smithy and carpentry in Havana that they then emphasized as a cultural legacy in places like Lagos where they resettled.

It was also during this period in the mid-nineteenth century that the importation of Chinese slave labor, via the Philippines, picked up in Havana.[77] Like their African counterparts brought by the Anti-Slavery Squadron, Chinese laborers also lived with the uncertainty of their official status: were they free citizens, indentured servants, or slaves?[78] Many Asian laborers shared the slave barracks, masters, and tasks with newly arrived Africans, or *bozales*, in Cuba.[79] The issues concerning the status of nonwhite workers from Asia were also left up to the Mixed Commission Courts, thus layering tension and confusion onto the courts, the slave barracks, and the streets of Havana.

However, as the case studies below show, most of these urban workers were acutely aware of their cultural and ethnic affiliation and history vis-à-vis Africa.[80] One community that utilized the Mixed Commission Courts as a means for repatriation to its ancestral home was the Lagosian community living in Havana. Their social strategies included an international cohesiveness, within African information networks, that executed a successful counterdiasporic movement back to Lagos. In Lagos, and in London, lists of repatriates from Brazil and Cuba were compiled and distributed via the Mixed Commission Courts at these locations.[81]

El Síndico Protector de Esclavos: Cuba's Advocacy for Slaves

Another international political body that dealt with the burgeoning African labor force in Havana was the Síndico Protector de Esclavos (Syndicate for the Protection of Slaves). The syndicate was a magistrate elected by a *cabildo*, a quasi-official fraternal organization, and the magistrate's role resembled that of a judge. Unlike the Mixed Commission Court, the syndicate speedily enforced the right to liberty and repayment on behalf of slaves, indentured workers, and *emancipados*. The post held a two-year term, with a possibility of a third year of reappointment. In Havana, the syndicate's main function was to arbitrate between the complaints of slaves, *emancipados*, and newly arrived Africans and colonial law.

Though not officially part of the court, the syndicate shared physical and political space with the court in certain instances. For example, the syndicate sometimes carried out his functions in special hearings called binational antislavery courts. In these courts, which were not the same as Mixed Commission Courts, British and Spanish functionaries presided over the fate of recent arrivals from Africa. At times, the judges ruled in favor of repatriation to Africa, via either London or Sierra Leone to Lagos. For Lagosians living in Havana, we find that several utilized the syndicate's role of advocacy to advance their goals of repatriation back to Africa.[82]

In most cases, the syndicates acted as primary counsel for Africans in the Havana courts of the mid-nineteenth century. Their responsibility was to make known, and make the legal case for, the concerns and complaints of Africans in Cuba. Also, it was the syndicate who held the authority to recommend and enforce acts of repatriation to Africa for *emancipados*. In the case studies presented below, we find that some Lagosians, like railroad worker Lorenzo Clarke, successfully sought the powers of advocacy given to the syndicate. Clarke gained his freedom, economic compensation for unpaid labor, as well as a legal avenue to return to Africa.[83]

Moving between Cuba and Africa: Afro-Cubans Creating Options

One of the most noted cases of repatriation back to Africa to be heard by the Mixed Commission Court was that of John Baptiste Dosalu, or Nicolas Lucumí as he was known in Havana. An Egba Yoruba, Dosalu found himself enslaved and sent to Cuba as a prisoner of war after having fought in Abeokuta in 1855.[84] He sought release from slavery by writing to the CMS, as well as to his family back home in Lagos, through the Mixed Commission Court in Havana.[85] It was actually Samuel Crowther, perhaps the most influential member of the CMS working in West Africa, who sent the money for Dosalu's passage back to Lagos. With Crowther's and G. C. Backhouse's help, on July 10, 1856, Dosalu left the port of Havana for Lagos, where he later settled into the emerging Afrolatino Aguda community.

Dosalu's case was unique in that it showed a collaborative effort between two distinct political organizations across the Atlantic: Havana's Mixed Commission Court and Lagos's Church Missionary Society.[86] Even more remarkable was that this alliance proved efficacious during an era in the history of Cuba notorious for an active slave trade. This partnership connected these two urban centers across the African diaspora in an official capacity. Significantly, two of the most influential international organizations dealing with Africans in the nineteenth century worked together to repatriate an individual. Instances such as Dosalu's illustrate the importance of looking for "forgotten" or unusual histories to provide models for understanding, and retracking, the phenomenon of the creation of communities like the Aguda.

The *Bergantín San Antonio*: Lagosians Return Home from Havana

Afro-Cubans of especially Yoruba descent returned to Africa by their own efforts and accumulated income. They worked as free laborers, or appealed to the s*ociedades de color* (associations of people of color), as well as utilized the limited legal and official avenues open to them at the time to gain liberty and repatriation. In this historical context, more than a few Afro-Cubans owned slaves or *emancipados*. Often, this particular social and economic relationship was employed strategically to liberate spouses and family members. In other instances, wealthier Afro-Cubans and brotherhoods chose to buy someone's labor and later offered them their freedom because of ethnic affiliation or racial solidarity.[87]

These legacies are important for us to consider as we revisit the making of the Atlantic world and the nature of an epoch under constant historical reconstruction. The drive and savvy that young Afro-Cubans, especially Lagosians, in Havana had for earning enough to repatriate is a testament to the resiliency of this community. For example, it was reported that a group of urban, working-class Lagosians living in Havana had "chartered a Spanish vessel directly from Havana to Lagos, entirely at their own cost."[88] They not only possessed the funds to make the trip; they also had obtained the legal permission from the Spanish colonial government for this repatriation.[89] It also must be noted that this particular voyage to Africa was not part of the colonial Spanish regime's forced deportations, especially in terms of the introduction of the general Slave Regulations of 1844 that were one result of the reactionary political climate in the wake of the La Escalera conspiracy.[90] Mainly, the passengers of this voyage were established merchants who also brought their *criollo* children and spouses with them back to Africa.

The repatriates who left Havana for Lagos in 1844 aboard the *bergantín San Antonio* were Afro-Cubans who had saved up for their passage back to Africa. These individuals worked as bakers, tobacconists, vendors, slaves, and seamstresses; some even won the lottery to reconnect with their families. Others owned stores, married other Afro-Cubans, and would later send their children back and forth between the two port cities for schooling.

This particular return voyage occurred in 1844, earlier than is usually estimated for such repatriations. This earlier inception of return trips indicates that the migration of the Aguda consisted of various waves of movement back to Lagos from Havana throughout the nineteenth century.[91] The repatriations were also fueled by and coincided with international Yoruba pan-African social and political movements of the era that also included Bahia, Brazil, as a site.[92] The later, ca. 1880s–1890s, repatriations to Africa were influenced by renewed antislaving efforts on the part of the British. This resurgence of a former abolitionist policy ignited the return to Lagos not only of Afro-Cuban Yoruba but also of Sierra Leoneans, or Saros as they came to be known.[93]

The idea of circum-Atlantic travel between Africa and Cuba, in lived and imagined ways, formed important contexts that linked Havana and Lagos as "contiguous" urban environments. The work of the social imagination here can be exemplified by the same kind of community creativity that allowed the symbolic importation of African deities and ancestors especially in the practices of public ritual and carnival.[94] On a social and material level, for this transatlantic community, the two cities fostered linked familial networks and shared economic resources that made each city an extension of the other. The particular nature of living in dense urban and heterogeneous centers, where identity was formulated and incorporated on multiple levels, created avenues for the performance of a shifting Afro-Cuban/Yoruba affiliation on both islands. This was especially true for the Yoruba who lived "in between" Havana and Lagos, and who felt links with these communities on several levels. Due to these links, this diaspora experienced a living passageway between Africa and Cuba that, significantly, they negotiated on their own terms after the harrowing experiences of slavery, as the case studies that follow will illustrate. The concept of home, then, begins to have an innovative aspect here where portable realms of possibilities, zones of affiliation and identity, could be maneuvered not only in memory, which is vital as well, but also in lived experiences. The reality of these movements rested, however, on great sacrifice and determination on the part of individuals and families who made up this unique transatlantic group.

Havana's Lagosians: Returning Home as Afrocubanos

Lagosians living in Havana between 1830 and 1850 usually worked as urban slaves. They saved up their earnings for their freedom, then later worked to pay for their repatriation to Africa. This process was long, taking anywhere from twenty to thirty years.[95] In the interim, these Lagosians became part of a community that also called Cuba home, as they worked to build and maintain Havana's economy in the mid to late nineteenth century. Repatriates participated in Havana's urban economy in a myriad of ways, on a variety of levels—as entrepreneurs, owners of shops and of slaves, and as slaves and workers as well. By the time many were ready to repatriate to

Lagos, individuals and their Cuban-born families and mates identified in a range of ways: as *omo-eko* (children of Lagos),[96] Yoruba, Cuban, and Black *criollos*. Therefore, Havana's Lagosians created new kinds of layered identities for themselves in becoming Afrocubanos.[97] They were creolized, and they helped to creolize what would become Cuban national culture. Their success in creating these vital links between Lagos and Havana was due to their ability to navigate and recognize diasporic ways of creating opportunities and bonds across geographic boundaries. These diasporic sensibilities were skills that they brought with them to Cuba from Africa, and these were developed from the importance of Yoruba concepts of building culture that rely on social exchange, metaphor, and movement, such as the idea of *iranjo*, the journey.[98]

Yoruba cultural thinking has been, and is, rooted in religious and political understandings that emphasize the negotiation of dispersal and reaccommodation of people, goods, and ideas. Let us take an example from folk narrative still very much present in Yoruba sensibilities of cultural origins.[99] In the discourse of the ancient Yoruba mytho-political corpus, Oduduwa, the ancestral Father of the Yoruba, sent his sixteen sons out from Ile-Ife toward different regions to found the kingdoms of the Yoruba, fostering a unique kind of diasporic sensibility to the creation of culture and history.[100] In later chapters of this volume, traditional chief Prince Olusí from Isaleko, Lagos, refers to this and other traditional myths that create the foundation for contemporary understandings of transnational social and political allegiances. Use of folklore and mythology in contemporary praxis symbolizes the ways that people maintain their historical sensibilities by interpreting tradition in flexible, portable, and consistent ways. As Karin Barber and others have noted, Yoruba methods of generating tradition rely heavily upon these uses of exegesis, interpretation, and discursive strategies rooted in social performances.[101]

The narratives of the Havana Lagosians presented in this chapter illustrate how, in practice, these processes of cultural thinking can become quotidian methods for the formation of new cultural enclaves. Their strategies were both internal and external: the communities left significant public markers that transformed the landscapes of Havana and Lagos.[102] These Afrocubanos changed the face of these two urban centers by injecting a set of values that emphasized a Yoruba sense of economic enterprise, cultural flexibility, and intense community pride. What emerges from the tales of Havana Lagosians is a multicentered cultural history, one that also addresses flows of people overseas who contributed to various Afro-Atlantic understandings and historical interpretations. The narratives indicate that slaves, *emancipados*, and urban laborers of self-proclaimed Lagosian origin utilized all of these aspects of their collective identity in Havana in navigating the diasporic waters of a transnational cultural identity.[103]

The Case Studies

Lagosians living in Havana during this era reformulated in grassroots and nuanced ways the contours of the African-Atlantic diaspora. By grassroots, I mean that these communities used unofficial and official cultural sensibilities in order to reconstruct and shape their social selves. Their experiences indicate a transatlantic zone of cultural agency that thrived in the face of the international institution of slavery. The following declarations originally appeared in the *Anti-Slavery Reporter* in 1854, describing how twenty-three Cuban *emancipados*—eleven men, eight women, and four children—returned "home" to Lagos via London.[104] The first leg of their journey commenced on June 7, 1854, on board the *Avon*, a vessel owned by the Correo de Vapor de las Indias Occidentales, sailing from Havana to Southampton.[105] By July 1, the passengers were on their way to Lagos aboard the *Candare*, a ship operated by the African Navigation Company.

Upon their arrival in Southampton, the returnees were greeted by Sir Joséph Clark. It had been a difficult trip for the repatriates, and most were tired, hungry, and thirsty. Mr. and Mrs. Da Silva provided the travelers accommodations at the "Hotel for the families Da Silva," located in Queen's Terrace. The Da Silvas, of Brazilian-Yoruba origin, had resided several years in Havana, where Mr. Da Silva had worked as a civil engineer for railroad construction on the island. He recognized one of the *emancipados* as a former employee for the railroad.

The returnees expressed the desire to go to Lagos as a final destination, instead of Sierra Leone or Liberia, other important ports of repatriation serviced by the British navy. They were also understandably concerned about the possibility of being forced back into slavery by interceding ships.[106] Significantly, most of the passengers had been baptized as Catholics during their time in Cuba. Yet, most of the couples on board were bound together by custom rather than by a church wedding. Also, many of the passengers could neither read nor write, but they expressed a great desire to acquire these skills as soon as possible. This provides another indication of the repatriate community's enterprising spirit, especially as members faced the new challenge of re-creating their lives upon return to Lagos.

The life histories presented here are based on the passengers' declarations that were taken upon their boarding the *Avon* and the *Candare*. I have interlaced my own observations and analysis within the stories to highlight significant patterns, divergences, and characteristics of this rarely studied community. Also, the focus on different individuals, given one at a time, provides important, intimate portraits that flesh out the complex societal picture of these self-identified Africans who lived a good part of their lives in nineteenth-century Havana. The individual names of repatriates who lived in Havana are given below with a short narrative that provides some of the contexts for their experiences and journeys. In the interest of recovering these important "vernacular histories," I have included many details for the eight case studies from my folkloristic research. The remaining case studies, are listed in the appendix. Though only a sample of the many histories of Africans returning to Lagos from Cuba, these rich vignettes indicate a well-developed trajectory of movement and flow between these cities during the era.

My main focus here is to suggest one way to imagine the lives and contexts of Havana's Lagosians in the nineteenth century in light of the complexity and social agency that their experiences bring to the discussion of transatlantic slavery in general, and Afro-Atlantic diasporas in particular. The kinds of social strategies that the Lagosian Yoruba, and other Africans as well, displayed in Havana were continuations of ways of building community, prestige, and wealth found on the continent. And the new skills and alliances that they incorporated into these strategies from life in Havana created a rich, layered understanding of what they had to contribute to Africa as transatlantic returnees.

The life histories below highlight the first part of the two-part story we are exploring in this book, representing the very folks who went back to Lagos to begin establishing the Aguda community that now identifies with Afrolatino and Yoruba ancestry simultaneously. As in the case of Dolores Real that began in this chapter, we will see that it is the social processes of diasporic affiliation and dual-nation building that Havana's Lagosians and the Aguda are working together to bring about in the Atlantic world in this moment in the nineteenth century. Here we get a sense of the contours of the Havana side of these lived historical experiences that helped to shape what Africa means in Cuba and what Cuba means in Africa for these interrelated communities.

Lorenzo Clarke

Lorenzo Clarke was between thirty-five and thirty-eight years old when he headed for Lagos from Havana. He had lived in Havana for twenty-two years, the latter half of that time while General Tacón was the governor of the island. Lorenzo was born in Lagos but was sold into slavery as a prisoner of war during what could be described as a Yoruba interethnic conflict. He was brought to Havana from Lagos on the slaving vessel *El Negrito*, along with 560 others, the majority of whom were women captives.[107]

About two weeks before reaching Cuba *El Negrito* was intercepted by a British naval vessel. There was a struggle at sea and the two ships exchanged fire. The British vessel overpowered the slave ship, and the slaver's captain and crew were taken into British custody. The two ships, along with the unfortunate prisoners, were taken to Havana, Cuba, to await further instructions. The slaves were immediately placed in the government slave barracks, located in Alameda near El Morro. There they waited for twenty-two days until they were divided into two lots: one group was conducted to the Consulate of Cerro, and the other to the Consulate of Lucillo. These two sites were camps for runaway slaves and for Chinese indentured laborers in Cuba at the time.

Lorenzo ended up in the Consulate of Cerro, and after putting his name down for an application for manumission, he was sent to labor on public works projects for the local government. He was told that, as a condition of his labor, he had to wait no fewer than ten years before he could obtain the right to claim the status of an *emancipado*. Thus, Lorenzo had no choice but to work as a laborer for the colonial government of Havana. His status at this time resembled that of many urban Blacks in Havana, most of whom lived in between a state of slavery and freedom as laborers for either individuals or the colonial regime.

Lorenzo later found employment with the railroad on the Havana–Güines Line, where he worked steadily for twelve years. It was during this time that Lorenzo acquired his surname from the American who served as the auxiliary engineer for the line, and for whom he worked as a personal servant. Eventually, Lorenzo was able to accumulate a small savings from this work and his other various jobs. He decided to play the lottery and won a prize of 300 pesos. He entrusted the money to his employer, Clarke, for safekeeping. Clarke in turn kept Lorenzo's money for himself, returning to the United States with it in his pocket. Lorenzo posted a complaint to Don Antonio Escovedo, the secretary of the railroad company, who advised Lorenzo to take the matter to the general captain of the railroad company. Lorenzo made his claim, and the company obtained the services of the syndicate (the aforementioned *el síndico*), who then forced the American, Mr. Clarke, to return the money to his former servant.[108]

After this incident, the syndicate informed Lorenzo that he was now free to claim his status as an *emancipado*, and he received his manumission papers. After this, Lorenzo began to work on his own accord in construction. He began making good money and decided to settle down. He married María Rosalia García, also a native of Lagos (see her story in the appendix). They had three children—two boys, José and Roue, and one girl, Isabel. Even though he had started a new life in Havana, he expressed a deep wish to return to Lagos permanently.

Lorenzo applied to the British consulate for permission to go back to Africa. He took his wife and children with him to Lagos, aboard the *Candare*, for which he paid a passage of 425 pesos, total. In the end, he had prepared the way for his return through word of mouth, from information given to him by other Lagosians who had recently arrived in Havana as slaves under similar conditions to his own arrival and stay. Through these interactions, he obtained pertinent information about his relatives in Africa and prepared to make Lagos his new home.

Miguel Marino

Miguel Marino was born in Lagos and was around sixty years old when he started his journey back to his native town from Cuba. In his personal testimony to ship officials, he expressed his long-time and close familiarity with the rest of the passengers returning to Lagos. This indicated that Miguel was active in maintaining ties with other Lagosians for the twenty-four years that he had lived in Havana. Miguel's observations also illustrated that, by the time he was ready and able to return to Africa, a grassroots Lagosian diaspora was being formed in urban Havana between 1825 and 1860. (Other case studies also point to a close-knit network of kin and community, in Havana and in Lagos.) Miguel's role as an elder in the community especially highlights the importance of cohesive group formation, because these ties made on land and at sea created fertile ground for later displays of leadership among the Aguda in interactions in Lagos and in the wider Afro-Atlantic world.

Miguel came to Cuba aboard a Spanish vessel along with three hundred other slaves. He noted that British vessels were chasing the ship along the route. Once in Havana, the slaves were taken to the slave barracks in Castillo Principe. Miguel was sold to Don Juan de la Cruz, a baker, who later sold him to another baker, by the name of Don Miguel Marino. Miguel stayed with the baker until the latter's death eight years later. However, Miguel was again sold to another baker, Don Pancho Aguiar, with whom he stayed for about a year and a half.

By this time, Miguel had saved up enough money from his employment as a baker that he married a native-born Afro-Cuban woman, a *criolla*, and started a family with her. For reasons unstated in the record, this union dissolved and Miguel later remarried another African-born woman named Margarita Cabrera. He played some of his earnings in the lottery and won a prize of 1,000 pesos. He bought his and Cabrera's freedom for 500 and 300 pesos, respectively, with the prize money. Their freedom papers were expensive for the era, a cost indicative of the high level of skill that Miguel and Cabrera had obtained as contract laborers. He went on to work as a stevedore until he decided to go back to Lagos. With the fruits of this labor Miguel bought their passage for 200 pesos and took Cabrera and his daughter, Matea, with him back to Africa.

Margarita Cabrera

Margarita Cabrera, Miguel Marino's wife, was a Carabalí, an ethnic group from the interior of West Africa. In Cuba, many kinds of Africans, such as Carabalí and Congo, lived side by side with Yoruba in urban Havana. Margarita was taken from her village when she was twenty-three or twenty-four years old. She was sixty by the time she boarded the ship back to Africa with her husband and Matea, Marino's child by his first marriage. This kind of interethnic marriage between Africans in Cuba was common. In fact, it was from such unions that the construction of Afrocubano *criollo*, or native-born, identities in Cuba emerged, in both individual and communal ways.

She remembered little of her original trip to Cuba, only that the vessel was packed with other slaves. The slaves disembarked at La Punta, Havana, where Margarita was sold to a merchant named Cabrera. With Cabrera, she worked in his estates, cultivating sugarcane and coffee. Thus, her mode of work differed distinctly from that of the Yoruba/Lagosian slaves in urban Havana investigated in these case studies, in that she was doing hard labor outside of the urban center of Havana.[109] However, she stayed with Cabrera fifteen years until she was sold to Don Scipiano Aguiar, for whom she worked as a laundress for nine years.

Margarita was then bought by Manuela Muños, a Carabalí woman like herself. Muños was also a laundress who had emancipated herself with the fruits of her labor. After one and a half years of work, she agreed to sell Margarita to her husband Miguel, for 300 pesos. Thus, we see that Margarita found her freedom by being sold twice, as a slave to two other Afro-Cubans. In a sense, this was a very common legal and social strategy employed to liberate Africans among members of their own Afro-Cuban community, albeit from different initial ethnic origins.

Gabriel Crusati

Gabriel Crusati was not sure of his exact age upon boarding the vessel back to Lagos, but he guessed he was around forty years old. He had lived in Havana for twelve years after being enslaved in Lagos, his home at the time. He was brought to Cuba by a Spanish slaver with two hundred other people, the majority of whom, according to Gabriel, were women. When they arrived in Cuba, they were taken through a coastal forest, then to the slave barracks. Gabriel was sold to Don Luis Droseo, a businessman, and he did hard labor for Droseo for seven months.[110] Another businessman, Joaquin Lupicio, bought Gabriel and employed him in the mines, though Lupicio (of Brazilian origin) was a distant relative. This coincidence illustrates how the Brazilian-Cuban-Lagosian diaspora had multiple fronts, some very deep historically, and laden with geographic diversity.

In this case, Havana was one site where wealthy Afro-Brazilians, some from Lagos originally, held significant business positions on the island. Thus, it was not strange that Gabriel was employed by a Yoruba-Brazilian relative, especially since this relative practiced trade in this well-established transatlantic manner.[111] Mining, especially gold and metals, was a lucrative business for Bahians from Brazil and Lagosians from Nigeria, since the mid-1500s.[112] Wealthy Africans, especially West Africans of means, were almost always included as part of this economic interest group.[113] One should recall the Da Silvas, the owners of the Hotel for the Families of Da Silva. The Da Silvas in Cuba were Brazilian-Yoruba who lived in Havana for several years, where Mr. Da Silva worked as a civil engineer on the railroad before setting up their Southampton inn.

Gabriel, nevertheless, worked for his relative, Lupicio, for six years. He saved his money and bought his freedom for the stipulated 500 pesos. His wife, Luisa Mazorra, accompanied him at the time of the deposition. The two passengers paid 100 pesos for their passage to Lagos.

Lucas Marino

Lucas Marino, the brother of passenger Miguel Marino, was forty-five years old when he returned to Lagos, his hometown. He lived thirty-one years in Havana, where he eventually landed after an antislaving British vessel intercepted the Spanish ship that was carrying Lucas and other slaves. Upon arriving in Cuba, the British let the passengers off at Casa Blanca, and though they were not technically slaves, Lucas and the others were taken to the government slave barracks. Lucas was forced to stay in the barracks for three months before his labor was rented out to Don Manuel Marino. He worked as a water vendor, for which he was paid three pesos weekly. Lucas Marino was rented out often and saved up his earnings quickly.

After eight years, while working on the streets of Havana, Lucas was reunited by chance with his brother Miguel. Lucas described the emotional scene that ensued: the brothers embraced, cried, and rejoiced. It was remarkable that these two Lagosians found each other on the streets of Havana in such dramatic fashion. This event also indicated that there was a significant amount of freedom of movement for urban slaves, whose substantial enclaves made up Havana's local labor community.[114]

Lucas worked under Don Marino until the latter died. His work contract was passed on to Don Marino's son, who sold Lucas his walking papers for 400 pesos. Lucas married a free-born Afro-Cuban *criolla*, he had five children, and he made Havana his home until deciding to return to Africa. Lucas decided that he would go to Lagos first, make enough money for his family to join him from Cuba, and then later send for his wife and children. Lucas was certain that his brothers and sisters in Lagos were going to help him financially, making his livelihood and plans to reunite his Cuban family, in Lagos, possible.

Lucas was an *emancipado*, like others noted here, due to his arrival on a British antislaving vessel. He should not have had to pay the 400 pesos he did for his contract. These sums applied to slaves, and he was under no legal obligation to pay for his freedom, which should not have been in question. However, Lucas's case illustrates a common problem that existed in mid-nineteenth-century Havana regarding *emancipados* from abroad. Namely, their status was somewhere between slave and free, and many Spanish colonial officials, opposed to the British imposition of antislavery laws in Cuba, took advantage of this ambiguity.

Telesforo Saavedra

Born in Lagos, Telesforo Saavedra was forty-eight years old at the time of his journey. He lived twenty-nine years as an *emancipado* and later as a free person of color in Havana. He was originally brought to Cuba, along with three hundred other individuals, on a Spanish slaving vessel. Around four days before reaching the port of Havana, the ship was intercepted by a British vessel. The ship, its crew, and the passengers were taken to Havana. As was usually the case with those brought to Cuba by British interceptors, the Africans were taken to the government slave barracks and sold as *emancipados*.

Telesforo and the others waited fifteen days, after which time his labor was rented out by a government council to a confectioner of chocolates and delicacies named Saavedra. He worked under the confectioner for ten years. However, Telesforo informed officials that he was beaten and treated poorly by this employer. After serving his ten years with Don Saavedra, Telesforo moved on to a Monsieur Greffe, also a confectioner, who paid the government directly for renting out his labor. He worked for twelve years under Greffe until he had earned enough money to buy his papers. However, officials were not content to give him his documents until he paid the police a bribe for the final forms. By the time Telesforo was heading back to Lagos, he had been living as a free person of color in Havana, working as a confectioner, for seven years. He paid a total sum of 100 pesos for his passage to Africa.

Manuel Vidau

Manuel Vidau, who was forty-two years old at the time of his repatriation to Africa, was brought as a prisoner of war from Lagos to Havana in 1834. The

Spanish vessel he arrived on carried three hundred other slaves, the majority of whom were women, according to Manuel. He was sold to a merchant and tobacco roller, Don Manuel Vidau, with whom he worked for eleven years. He learned the trade of tobacco rolling proficiently, rolling an average of four hundred cigars a day. However, Don Vidau was a cruel master, humiliating and physically punishing Manuel if he did not meet a high daily quota. Eventually, Don Vidau sold his slaves and went to Spain to live off the fortune he had made in Cuba. Manuel was then sold to Don Pedro Carrera, a sugar and coffee trader. Carrera also sold his slaves, retired in Spain, and Manuel was transferred to Carrera's son, who stayed on in Havana.

By this time, Manuel began working as an *emancipado*. Rolling tobacco, he earned 6 to 7 pesos a week, of which he paid 4.5 pesos a week toward his freedom. Like many others in case studies of repatriation to Lagos from Havana, Manuel pooled his funds and played the lottery. In Manuel's case, a community of Havana Lagosians, thirty-nine individuals, assembled their resources and played for a big win, for which they equally divided and shared a prize sum of 1,600 pesos. Again, these kinds of social strategies illustrate economic savvy on the part of this particular African community in Cuba.

Manuel went on to buy his liberty for 589 pesos, a sum that illustrates that he had to gather resources from his personal savings to augment the prize money. By the time he began his journey back to Africa, he had been free for eight years, during which time he lived and worked in Havana as a tobacco roller. The fruits of this labor were enough to support his wife and adopted son, as well as pay for their passage to London, which cost a sum of 225 pesos. Manuel declared that his life in Havana was good, but he wished to return to Lagos to be with the family he had left behind. The fact that he served as a social leader of Havana's Lagosian community was demonstrated by the respectful title given to him by the others heading home on board with him on the ship: *el capitán*.

María Luisa Picard

María Luisa Picard, Manuel Vidau's wife, was also a native Lagosian returning home. At thirty-two years old, she told of how, some twenty-one years before, she was brought as a slave to Havana on a Spanish ship. She was sold from the barracks to Don José María Picard, a slave runner, for whose family she served as both a driver and a cook. After four years, she was sold to a nobleman, Don Pedro Maximo Valdes, for whom she labored as a serving maid. After two years, she was given *coartada* status, which meant she could begin paying toward her liberty. However, she was required to offer Valdes the sum of 240 pesos to begin the process. She continued to work for the Valdes family for a total of eight years. By the time of her repatriation she had been free for seven years. She had only recently taken up with Manuel at the time of her declaration. A final interesting aspect of María Luisa and Manuel's story occurred in relation to their adopted son, Manuel Aye. "Manuelito" Aye, about four years old at the time of their declaration, was left as an orphan after his parents died of cholera when he was only four months old. Manuel took in Manuelito because he was his uncle and wanted to raise the boy as his own.

Interpreting the Havana-Lagos Diaspora: A Concentric Perspective

We see that many Lagosians living in Havana in the mid to late nineteenth century had firm family and community ties that served as social and economic resources for residing in an urban setting. Many of these individuals, like our last case study described above, that of María Luisa Picard, worked and lived in Havana for an average of twenty years before returning to Lagos. This pattern indicates that this particular community acquired skills and characteristics in Cuba that made them Afrocubanos in every sense of the word. Once in Lagos, they combined their diasporic identity with that of the local communities surrounding them to form a population that was ethnically diverse and culturally complex. They brought their Afro-Cuban culture with them, and they thought of themselves and were received by the Yoruba in Lagos as Cuban-Yoruba in many ways. The kinds of experiences found in the above narratives of Havana Lagosians indicate that Africans in the Americas created viable and efficacious cultural, social, and economic networks on their own terms.

They also changed the societies they lived in, helping to creolize and create new ethnic groups in Cuba. And, as Afrocubanos, this group helped to create a unique public culture in Lagos. Living in Cuba, especially in Havana, had made an impression on them and their children; at least two generations had arrived in Lagos, as described in the narratives above. By balancing the social poles of individual recognition and communal cooperation, these Yoruba-Cubans were able to gain access to information and goods that facilitated their journeys back to Africa. These strategies were based on cultural sensibilities and epistemologies that go far beyond derivative models of resistance. Their lives did more than disrupt and circumvent hegemonic social systems and slavery. Afro-Cubans of Lagosian and other ethnic African descent in nineteenth-century Havana created prosperous communities in transnational, transatlantic contexts.

Africans who were destined to make Havana their new home utilized the opportunities for employment and personal liberty available to them within the urban neighborhoods, or barrios, of nineteenth-century Havana.[115] The above case studies clearly present individuals in Havana who aptly navigated through social, economic, and legal networks in order to reach their personal and collective goals. These goals included a range of priorities, but repeatedly the repatriates demonstrated a deep longing for their home city of Lagos. So, many chose repatriation as their way to reconnect with those left behind in their native land.

Another way this group made contact with home in Africa was by establishing information networks in Havana. Those who decided to stay in Cuba would pass information back to Lagos through repatriates like the passengers who went back on the *Avon* and *Candare*. Information would often get back to the Lagosian community in Havana through *bozales*, recently arrived slaves to Cuba. Passengers clearly indicated that they expected to find family members waiting for them in Lagos, as news was brought to them through the *bozales'* network. The documentation for the *Avon* and the *Candare* noted that this means for passing information across the Atlantic was indeed somewhat effective, if not common:

> These people [*bozales*], before being enslaved, had conversations with free blacks who had returned to Lagos from Havana some time ago. These circumstances were not uncommon. Slaves from Havana frequently come to know about their families through information provided by recently arrived *bozales* [slaves]. Freed slaves are always returning constantly to their country of origin. Several years back, a great number of them chartered a Spanish vessel, en route to Havana to Lagos, entirely at their own cost. Through them, many slaves were able to send news back to their friends [in Lagos].[116]

As Yoruba-Cubans, this community extended their sense of belonging despite the obstacles of slavery, distance, and changes in social realities and language. As when the two Marino brothers met on the streets of nineteenth-century Havana, communities in the diaspora found surprising ways to construct networks within sites of relocation by sticking together when possible. Strategies like buying other slaves related to one's ethnic group helped to reconnect ties within these groups. The actual environs of the barrios of Havana during this time period allowed urban slaves and free people of color close and fairly unsupervised interaction that created conduits for communication. The repatriates discussed above helped to develop a grassroots, transatlantic information pathway from this environment that supplied vital connections to those across the ocean. As we see with Saavedra and Clarke above, these connections included ties to the Brazilian-Yoruba community in a context that encompassed both Cuba and London and that would come together in the Aguda community in Lagos. Lagosians in Havana, as elsewhere in the Atlantic, kept tabs on their families and businesses in Africa, and likewise those in Lagos stayed in contact with Cuba.[117] Boundaries were renegotiated by enslaved and free Africans in ways that historically and culturally transformed the important urban centers of the Atlantic world in the nineteenth century and, as we will see in the following chapters, into the twentieth century and beyond.

In some of the case studies above, we see that the *criollo* children of Havana Lagosians were taken back to Lagos with their parents. Some were clearly acculturated to life in Cuba, spoke Spanish and little Yoruba, and were taking a voyage to someplace new with their parents. One such voyager was Hilario Campos, who left Cuba with his two sisters in search of the homeland in Lagos that his family in Cuba pined for. The subject of much of the second half of this book, Campos and his descendants in Lagos represent how Afro-Cuban and Yoruba diasporas overlapped each other in terms not only of movement but also of individual experiences of resettlement, return, and an imagined past.

Afro-Cubans living in Havana indeed struggled with the reality of urban slavery. However, the passengers discussed above demonstrated a resilient sense of identity and history as Africans and as Afrocubanos. Processes of social reinvention, specifically through labor, were a reality for Havana's emancipated Black population. This community turned the transatlantic slave route into a tool of social organization and international communication. They aptly challenged and transformed the international geographic, social, and cultural institutions that forced them into slavery. The very pathways that led them away from Africa were retraced, innovatively and tenaciously, as routes home for some, and as new beginnings for others. In the following chapter, we will explore the context of those new beginnings at "home" by looking at Lagos in the nineteenth century from historical, public, and folkloristic perspectives.

2

Returning to Lagos

Making the *Oja* Home

The idea of the *oja*, or the Yoruba marketplace, as home is suggested in the proverb quoted at the beginning of the introduction to this book: "Aiye ni oja, orun ni ile" (The world is a marketplace; heaven is home). Yoruba proverbs present a truncated form of meta-analysis that provides a cultural critique about both the subject matter at hand and the use of language to reflect that message.[1] They are reflexive in their deep play about the genre. The notion of the bustling, busy *oja* expressed in the proverb certainly applies to the place at which returning Africans and Afrocubanos arrived on their journey home. In that place, the Lagos of the late nineteenth century, we encounter a stage set for high royal drama, war, and trade in what was then, and still is, the largest metropolitan center in West Africa. The events that took place in this era created narratives that became easily incorporated into traditional "Yoruba" metanarratives that helped to resituate history, place, and ethnic identity in a flexible manner.[2] British colonial officers also reemphasized in their writings the narratives about Yoruba political culture in Lagos that spoke of kingdoms, villains, and heroes.[3] Lagos played an important role in imagining a site for the "quintessential" transatlantic marketplace. Storytellers, mythmakers, and community leaders merged in the environment that the Havana Lagosians encountered when they returned home.

Overview: Lagos as a Transatlantic Site

Geographically, Lagos was situated in an area made up of various small islands in a series of lagoons that serve as means of traveling from rivers in the Nigerian interior to the Atlantic Ocean.[4] The proximity of the Bight of Benin, as well as the accessibility by water of the important ethnic enclaves and markets of the Bini, Ijebu, Egba, and Awori, enhanced the islands' attractiveness for trade. From the early settlements of fishermen to the current commercial metropolis, Lagos and its neighboring islets offered a meeting place where Africans and outsiders forged alliances, fought wars, exchanged culture, and created new communities. Brazilians of Yoruba ethnicity returned to this area to influence the establishment of political and economic institutions.[5] Receptivity to newcomers became well established over time, as newcomers like the Aguda found their place in the area, especially in the influential (slave) trade zones of Ouidah and Lagos from the late eighteenth century onward.[6] The region became one of the most influential centers of economic activity, political struggle, and social change for the transatlantic world.

To go back in time, Lagos in the late fifteenth century began to develop its own sense of gravity as an important site for economic activity. Accounts suggest that Benin traders and warriors frequented Ido Island, especially. Ido was one of the region's most accessible ports via the waterways from the interior. There, an informal market was established for the exchange of a range of goods, both internal and foreign.[7] The area became a place where enterprising interlocutors established integrated marketplaces that stretched out from the Yoruba hinterland. This marketplace worked in ways that moved goods, people, and ideas in multiple directions.

Fishermen and traders, the former of Awori ethnicity and the latter of mixed Bini (from Benin) and Yoruba ancestry, met around the Ido port of Oloto during this era for trade and commerce.[8] The settlement of Aromire was the first recognized enclave conquered by the Bini in this region.[9] The Benin Kingdom, one of the largest empires to the north and east of the Yoruba kingdoms, wanted to take advantage of the burgeoning trade that attracted wealth and people to the area. The Bini were eager to establish a lasting presence in the region, extending the potential for tribute and partnership southward. Trade "ambassadors" sent by Benin (these roles would often be filled by Brazilians and Portuguese in later years) involved themselves in the early development of Lagosian trade and royal politics, especially when it came to determining trade policy.[10] The Bini, through both force and diplomacy, inserted themselves into the social fabric of the developing Lagosian political and economic structure. Some local Yoruba cooperated with Bini royalty, especially through tribute and alliance, because of the increase in economic and social status, as well as the military protection, that the Benin Kingdom could provide.

However, the Bini were not alone in their eagerness to profit from the region's accessibility for trade. A diverse range of ethnic Yoruba, including the Ijebu, moved in and out of the Lagos region from very early on. Traditional patterns of commerce developed before Benin's initial conquest. Adept and itinerant *iyaloja*, Yoruba market women, were already playing a crucial role in moving items back and forth from the Yoruba hinterland to the Lagos region when the Bini arrived. The power and influence of the *iyaloja*, aided by the emphasis on trade in the region, helped to foster the rise of rich and powerful women, like Madam Tinubu, who are an important part of Lagosian historical memory.[11]

By the seventeenth century, migrations from the rest of Yorubaland converged on the region because of trade. Communities were established by migrants like the Awori, Ijebu, Egba, and Ondo, as well as other groups from the interior. These settlements were ethnically marked, often settling in waves of dispersal and relocation. This early kind of settlement pattern helped set the stage for making Lagos the diverse, cosmopolitan place it is today. Lagos contained ethnic enclaves from its inception, and these created the foundational material and social texture of the town. For example, Ikorodu became an early place of convergence for Ijebu and Awori Yoruba traders. Descendants of these two groups later became known as Ikos, as this enclave developed its own flavor and identity.[12] Migrant groups settling in Lagos established trade partnerships with each other, with other ethnic groups, and eventually with merchants outside Africa.[13] This is important to note in comparison to the ways that Afro-Cubans of Lagosian descent were adept at business and lived an urban lifestyle while living in Havana. Their background, both in Africa and in Cuba, allowed their resettlement in Africa to take a positive turn, with the establishment of a prosperous community with transatlantic ties.

Schedules of interaction between traders followed patterns of exchange set by the movement of goods and people. Egbado and Awori Yoruba, for example, set a pattern of meeting every nine days at Ido Whorf.[14] International trade, with the Portuguese, for example, also created patterns of cultural and material exchange. The incorporation of outsiders into preexisting patterns of exchange became the rule as the convergence of people and goods in the region escalated by the late fifteenth century.[15] The place of the Aguda in the region was established later upon this pattern of incorporation and exchange. Discursive and social strategies mirrored each other in expressing the acceptance of newness into tradition through mythology and folklife. Here, folklore, in the form of narrated memory, local legend, and oral history, carefully tracked and incorporated the Bight of Benin's history into broader diasporic Yoruba and Bini metanarratives.[16]

Yoruba traditional history, or *itan*, on the Lagos region follows the discursive strategies of other Yoruba traditions of narration.[17] The reasons given for the relocation of different ethnic Yoruba communities vary: civil war, the search for economic gain, conflict at home. In the discursive realm, narratives resituate these relocations within a unifying network of a mythos-history that also has set stylistic and aesthetic components.[18] This discursive strategy interlaces Yoruba diasporic peoples and their varied homelands by reformulating spiritual and historical genealogies to include new members.[19] The new communities, like the Aguda in Lagos, become domesticated in an incorporative framework that allows new constituencies to enter a preexisting social context. Sacred genealogies for the Yoruba work toward the incorporation of people into various local communities, embracing a wide range of dispersed people into their kin groups.

This may include other Yoruba coming from elsewhere in Nigeria, or transatlantic "Yoruba"—who may have achieved that ethnic status through their spiritual affiliation with Yoruba traditional religion. The point is that the inclusion of a range of people in Yoruba communities involves the allocation of prestige. A community made up of a variety of individuals from different places provides for a kind of nationalism that relies on the expansion of the community on a translocal level.[20] The prestige factor may encourage competing claims to cosmopolitanism, where a high value is placed on the ability to create workable congregations out of many different constituencies. Lagos became an important economic and cultural center because of its inclusion of outsiders like the Aguda, the Saros, and others. The catch is that outsiders must be willing to adapt to the rules that govern the incorporative networks described here. That is, one must learn one's role in the schema of a particular social framework and perform that identity in order to be let in. The Aguda were able to perform their own brand of Yoruba identity because their Cuban identity was already becoming imbued with markers of Yoruba-ness. An example here is the Cuban nationalistic belief in ritual practices like Ifa divination, which are central to performing Cuban cultural identity.[21]

Versions of Lagosian history have accumulated in a context where narratives shift. The retelling of the past, especially through oral tradition and personal experience narratives, often serves present interests in seeking power through historical legitimacy. The kinds of power at stake in the performance of a historical narrative include economic, political, and spiritual facets of power.[22] Establishing the legitimacy of power, then, depends on creating viable links to the past that place one in an appropriate historical location in relation to present (especially oral) renderings of history.[23] The metadiscursive assemblages found in most Yoruba practices of history are performative in a manner that extends from any given moment into the past in terms of signaling past performances as citations, or "quotations," indicating a valid textual and historical connection.[24]

In Lagos, the rewards for skillfully forming links to the past set the scene for political and economic ascendancy from the city's inception. For example, Patrick Dele Cole discusses how these negotiations of history affected the *oba*-ship, or the history of kingmaking in Lagos.[25] Cole remarks especially on the power struggles between the Bini and Yoruba royalty in the region, and how this led to the development of at least two competing modes of traditional government.[26] Assertive involvement in the region's politics on the part of the Portuguese, Brazilians, and British, especially, created a venue for restructured claims to the Lagosian throne.[27] For example, the drama of Lagosian royal politics reached a significant level in the era following the 1851 British bombardment of the city.[28]

Rights to royal rule have historically been traced back to at least one prominent culture hero. The Oduduwa founding myth that ties the heterogeneous

Yoruba together is still used to determine and expand legitimacy with regard to traditional *oba*-ship. The diasporic dispersal out of Ile Ife of the sixteen sons of Oduduwa established the original kingdoms of the Yoruba.[29] Traditional legitimacy to rule over large communities rests on establishing a genealogical relationship to Oduduwa through one of the original sixteen diasporic kings. Lagos has an interesting and dense royal history because there were two avenues, through the Yoruba and the Bini, by which the founders of the region connected themselves to Oduduwa. Creative genealogy has always shaped understandings of who is residing in Lagos. In other words, leaders have gained access to different kinds of power by placing populations within different historical and social groups, thus linking communities in kinship lines that emphasize *their* heritage as legitimate cultural centers. Traditionally, the Bini have a Yoruba-based kingship and system of Ifa divination inherited from a long history of exchange with Ile Ife.[30] The other avenue of connection to Oduduwa is the mythos-narrative of Ogunfunmire, the "founder" of Lagos, who was related to Oduduwa. Both kinds of narratives created the means to establish genealogical lineage and the legitimacy of power in Lagos.[31]

The narrative of Ogunfunmire emphasizes his ties to Ile Ife and his relationship to the royal family there.[32] The Lagosian royal title of *olofin awogunjoye* is said to come from this founding figure.[33] According to traditional storytelling, Ogunfunmire was a great hunter who decided to settle in the Isheri area of Lagos. His power as a hunter was of supernatural origin, and he gained notoriety through the successful use of powerful charms, or *agbo*. He is said to have had many children while settling Lagos. He also lived for an extraordinary length of time, further evidence of his magical prowess. As with other Yoruba narratives, in Africa and the circum-Atlantic world, Ogunfunmire's remembered political and spiritual powers are significant attributes of culture heroes. The narrative also provides a broad structural basis for adding on and linking into Ogunfumire's genealogy. It allows especially for a road toward legitimate kingship in Lagos that emphasizes Ogunfunmire's connection to Oduduwa.

Ogunfunmire grew older, and he relied more heavily on his magical charms for hunting, turning himself into a snake to catch his prey. One day, tired of being controlled by their father, his children destroyed the transformative medicine while he was hunting in the form of a snake. Local legend relates that the sorcerer, lacking the means to transform himself back into a human being, was left to wander the lagoons of Lagos as a serpent for eternity.[34] Ogunfunmire's first son, Aromire, gave the land at Isheri to the Bini, who built there the traditional Lagosian royal compound called the Iga Igandanran, the Red Pepper Farm. This is still the site of the king's palace in Lagos.[35] The sons of the *olofin*, the royal leader of this Yoruba-Bini clan, took on the royal titles of the *idejo*, or land-owning chiefs, distinguished by the white caps that they wore.[36] There are reported to have been anywhere from ten to thirty-two originating *idejo* chiefs. This difference in range is due to traditional Yoruba numerical patterns.[37] Prince T. Olusí, of Lagos's Isaleko area, related to me in an interview how the various ethnic Yoruba organized themselves as the *idejo* chiefs in the new town after Ogunfunmire expired. He explained:

> So, at the inception of Lagos, there was the history of the *olofin*, who to some extent can be described as the leader, or the king of the early settlers. And, they settled at Iga [Igandanran], Iga on the island, on the other side from where we are now. And, these idejo chiefs sprang from the leadership, the crop of the leaders of various smaller communities that came to the island.
>
> For example, you have the *ijo ara*,[38] now called the *ijora*. They have their own leader.... You also have those who come from Ikoyi. Ikoyi in the hinterland of Yorubaland. They now, they also have their own leader called *onikoyi*.
>
> ... Now, it has to be explained that these leaders ... have connections with *kings* in the Yorubaland [emphasis in original]. So, when the people now come together, [at] once they recognize that someone is a prince *back home* in their kingdom [emphasis in original]. So among the Ikoyis, one candidate became the leader, became the first to [come to] Eko.[39]

As Olusí indicates above, incoming groups from the region and beyond organized themselves effectively and quickly became incorporated into the sociopolitical structure of Lagos. In carrying with them a diasporic sensibility for rearranging alliances and histories, ethnic Yoruba and repatriates like Afro-Cubans in Lagos set up social organizations that emphasized leadership and representation in the area. Indeed, the region of the Bight of Benin, as a whole, shared a set of political and economic networks in which diverse governments, economies, and communities were interlaced over time. The ways in which these communities from abroad and within affected the formation of Lagos present a layered history that comes about in a chorus of simultaneous narratives in the region and its diaspora.[40]

Mythology, Legend, and Narratives Representing the Past

After the mytho-historical era of Ogunfunmire, described above, came the era of conquest of Lagos by the Benin Kingdom. The Bini played a major role in forming royal relationships in the region.[41] The interplay of the powerful Bini, the Ijebu Yoruba, and the Portuguese created a complicated set of alliances that laid the basis for Lagosian royal politics.[42] In the nineteenth century, another web of influences came into play in Lagos: the ties created between the Egba Yoruba and the British. Missionaries played a significant role here, especially through the CMS.[43]

In many instances, the mythological narratives of Lagos, such as that of Ogunfunmire, illustrate chronologies and perspectives that are different from those provided in Western-trained historians' accounts of the Lagosian past.[44] However, the mythological narratives are remembered by the communities who "own" and tell these stories as part of their understanding of the region's history. These narratives reflect a social imaginary that allows for cohesion and understanding about accepted mythological contexts that reflect a shared historical trajectory. The construction of the verbal text gives important clues to ways in which the past is resituated in popular memory.[45] The traditional mythological narrative also allows for a space wherein people who are not necessarily acting in official capacities affect and recast local history. For folklorists interested in quotidian perspectives toward the past, notoriety and infamy are valid points of entry for recognizing contributions to the formation of community, memory, and history.[46] Often the stories deal with quotidian details and grassroots dramas contributing to a "history" that becomes memorable in its accented use of local flavor.

According to these narratives, relations between the administration at the Benin royal court and the local Lagosian rulers were tenuous. Access to trade was the main issue in most of these tales. The tension between the Benin court and the local rulers was is especially marked in terms of the way in which local elites invested in ruling from Ido reacted to Benin's intervention in local Lagosian public culture. For example, in one narrative, Aseru, a *balogun*, or warlord, from the Benin court, conquered part of Ido island.[47] Aseru died in Ido after administering the area for a short while. A Yoruba chief, Asipa, a contemporary of Aseru, was married to an important Bini woman. Asipa, who was familiar with Bini social customs, decided diplomatically to ship Aseru's body back to Benin's royal court for burial.[48] Asipa was rewarded generously for following the correct social protocol. The Benin court bestowed upon Asipa three honorary attributes of royal status: the *gbedu* drum, a special sword, and the title of *olorogun*. With these attributes, Asipa's descendants still hold an honorary title as the symbolic kings of Lagos. Not insignificantly, these titles are legitimized primarily through their association with the powerful Benin court.[49] Also important to note from this narrative is that it provides a folk explanation for the symbolic markers of royal kingship.

Oral tradition also illustrates how local and Benin styles of government are understood to be intertwined by the local community. Traditionally, legitimization of the power to rule has been established by using oral histories and narratives as political precedents.[50] Lagosian folklore also emphasizes repeatedly the early importance of wealth among Lagosian elites. The ability to rule in Lagosian contexts relies on careful diplomacy and administration of local and foreign elements, especially with regard to trade. Popular and successful Lagosian *obas* and chiefs consistently demonstrate a penchant for pooling disparate material resources, whether through trade or military support, from neighbors and visitors.[51]

Lagosian local rulers, and *obas* especially, needed to negotiate with a range of different diasporic and trade communities. This was especially important as the land in Lagos was "officially" distributed among different populations residing in the area. Traditionally, as we see in the folk narratives regarding Ogunfunmire's progeny, the *idejo* or "white cap chiefs" are considered to be the initial land administrators for the area.[52] It is not unusual for folk narrative to document the ways in which land was distributed and influence spread through the Lagosian rulers. The "traditional" aspect being discussed here is incorporative, however, of outside influences in terms of coalition building and trade in Lagos. Individual rulers who succeeded in generating status and power in the area did so by embracing outside elements and taking these elements into their own fields of influence. These community leaders were the most successful at ruling a diverse, heterogeneous, and competitive populace because of the range of options they could put into play in terms of combining the strengths of their constituencies.

Diasporic Encounters: Slaves, Returnees, and the Americas

The circum-Atlantic diasporas of the Yoruba Afro-Cubans and the Aguda had originally been dispersed by way of the Bight of Benin. The transnational cultures and societies were created out of encounters between the Bight of Benin and Cuba.[53] The creation of Afrocubanos, from an African perspective, was fraught with war, slavery, wealth, and colonialism.[54] Narrative, oral history, legend, and myth became ways of situating these grand social forces that touched smaller, albeit still transnational, communities in very real ways. Playing a role in the formation not only of Lagos but of the Bight of Benin in general were the Afrolatino Yoruba, the Aguda, who began returning from Brazil to Lagos's neighbor, Ouidah, as early as 1721.[55] The numbers of returnees to the area in general, as manumitted slaves and businessmen, continued to grow during the following centuries.[56]

Transatlantic interactions between groups intensified during the eighteenth century. Encounters between the Portuguese and West Africans occurred during the reign of Oba Akinsemoyin, between 1760 and 1775.[57] Both oral history and official sources record that the monarch invited the Portuguese, whose company included some "Brazilian slave traders," to the Yoruba kingdom.[58] Akinsemoyin may have made these contacts with the Portuguese and Brazilians earlier, during his exile in Apa, while his predecessor, Oba Gabaro, reigned in Lagos.[59] The trade that was established as a result of these contacts included the exchange of guns, ammunition, salt, tobacco, alcohol, palm oil, cloth, and slaves. This was an early example of movement across the Atlantic with a distinct Benin-Lagos-Bahia route in play.

One interesting character among Akinsemoyin's new business partners was Joao de Oliviera.[60] Oliviera was a former slave, taken to Brazil, who later returned to West Africa, became wealthy, and acted as a mediator for the opening of the slave trade in Porto Novo and Lagos.[61] Apparently, some of the early Afrolatino returnees from Brazil to the Bight of Benin, especially to Ouidah and Lagos, were keen on establishing their wealth and possessed an ambivalent set of ethics concerning the slave trade and its role in their own lives. Other powerful Portuguese and Brazilian families who were important in Benin, and subsequently in Lagos, included the Da Souzas, as well as the Martinez and Martins families.[62] Members of these influential "corporate" families included Cuban and Brazilian former slaves who had found a space in this African-based intradiasporic identity.[63] A split in terms of attitudes toward slavery and emancipation was reflected in nineteenth-century struggles over power is the Lagosian royal courts.

Indeed, the Aguda and the Saros entered into this tense climate as returnees who saw and lived the experiences of slavery, emancipation, and repatriation. As Mann and Law indicate in their works on Lagos and Ouidah, respectively, these populations inhabited a complicated climate where a unilateral attitude toward abolitionism (at least one that could be recognized by Anglo-Europeans as such) did not exist due to the local social context with regard to power and legacy.[64] However, Cuban returnees to Lagos made a concerted effort, as we saw in the life histories of former slaves in the last chapter, to use the very system of slavery itself as a means of "acquiring" spouses and neighbors whom they would free later. A similar strategy also was practiced in Lagos, whereby slaves could "own" other slaves, sometimes known as *éru*, eventually leading to the freedom of these individuals.[65] The slavery-to-emancipation experience existed on multiple levels in Lagosian society in the nineteenth century.[66] In terms of the Cuban Aguda's experience of slavery, theirs was a legacy of a long emancipation in a trans-Atlantic context. In Cuba, they worked as *emancipados* for decades before returning to Africa. One can imagine how the similarities between the two places in terms of degrees of freedom created a sense of a pan-African consciousness for those who resettled in a colonized Lagos. This "new" consciousness and a developing frustration with British colonialism fueled a transnational "Yoruba" nationalism that included Aguda from Cuba and Brazil, as well as Saros, as its main proponents.[67]

In another earlier instance, contact with the Portuguese and the Afrolatinos spurred significant cultural innovations on the part of Lagosians and neighbors alike.[68] Mediterranean, Atlantic, and Afrolatino influences arriving in the Bight of Benin affected the area's architecture, religion, art, language, political systems, and trade.[69] According to some local lore, the

Lagosian palace, the Iga Igandanran, was built with Portuguese and Bini materials during the eighteenth century.[70] Historical sources show that cultural and material exchange included noted trade expeditions to and from Bahia, Badagry, and Lagos.[71] The royal court of Oba Oshinlokun, in alliance with the Ijebu Yoruba, was especially open to political and cultural ties with Brazilian and Portuguese slave traders.[72] On the other hand, Oshinlokun's short-lived successor, Oba Adele, had different alliances in place, as he supported the British antislavery stance from the beginning of the nineteenth century on.[73] By 1820–21, Oshinlokun supplanted Adele, while the latter stayed for twelve to fourteen years in Badagry, where he connected with the Egba Yoruba, who also had ties with the British via the CMS's missionary work.[74]

Returnees from Brazil, Cuba, and Sierra Leone played a crucial role in forming the very societies they were returning to in this period and later on. Truly diasporic individuals who traded and moved between the Atlantic shores, especially to and from Brazil and Cuba, were creating new African societies in both regions. Communities and individuals that were interested in cultural and social enterprise were immediately attracted to the economic opportunities the Bight of Benin had to offer. The issue of the slave trade came to dominate politics in the Bight of Benin by the early nineteenth century. Across the Atlantic, the dependence on slaves to work plantations in the Americas displaced and relocated a huge number of Africans. Slavery indeed changed and shaped the nature of societies and cultures in the Bight of Benin, and especially Lagos, in important ways.[75]

Returnees from the diaspora played a myriad of roles in the region. Cubans and Brazilians interacted with each other and merged into a loose, flexible Afrolatino group, sometimes before even reaching Lagos.[76] The Saros, or Sierra Leoneans, were another diasporic contingent that placed itself in the Lagosian and larger political landscape. Slave traders from Brazilian backgrounds, like Ojo Martins and Domingo Martinez, made their presence felt in Lagos and the surrounding area by the mid-nineteenth century.[77] The interests of diasporic communities moving in and out of the region differed and fluctuated with the political climate.[78] In this situation, diasporic communities from the Americas shifted easily into the local political custom of coalition building across religious, cultural, and ethnic differences. This cosmopolitan approach to negotiating business, culture, and politics was well formed *even before* these individuals left the shores of the Bight of Benin.[79] Thus, the social legacy of West African culture formed a blueprint for the success and resilience of diasporic communities, even in the face of slavery.

Along with "diasporic sensibilities" came innovation and the borrowing of technologies and education.[80] The Aguda successfully utilized the colonial Latin American training and technologies they gathered in the diaspora and brought these back with them to Lagos.[81] The political and economic leadership in Lagos was made up of diasporic elements from all over the Bight of Benin, Europe, and the Atlantic world.[82] These varied contingents were versed in diplomacy and often transformed social and cultural difference to their own advantage.[83] This transformation worked for local and diasporic elites because they were able to shift paradigms in order to engage in a variety of discourses that fostered negotiation.

As in the understanding of metaphor of the Yoruba *oja* or marketplace, these negotiations were centered on performative ways of reassembling and remembering social actors and history. That is, the way alliances and enemies were made in the moment of performance contributed to the way this history has been understood and passed on. For these reasons, narrative traditions emphasizing mythological and legendary characteristics contained stylistic attributes that captivated audiences listening to narratives of the past. Further, these dramatic attributes contributed to the successful outcome for those who were understood to be the victors of these histories—in both the performative moment and the remembered history.[84] These formal characteristics, in the way of favored aesthetics, situate the ways in which the past is understood and revealed for both local and visiting communities within the region as a whole.[85]

These discursive strategies reveal how performance creates the experience of history through a range of narrative genres. In my fieldwork, investigating the Aguda presence in Lagos with Prince Olusí and with the granddaughters of Hilario Campos, I found two different examples of narrating the Aguda into the history of Lagos. In the first case, we see how the Aguda can be incorporated into the general fabric of Lagosian society as welcomed outsider ancestors. In the second case, the granddaughters were locating their family's past in the Cuban diaspora as it related to their own lives as Lagosians. In both instances, to be explored in detail later on, we see that the performances of their narratives of belonging to a common past share the stylistic elements of speaking with traditional authority about instances of social innovation and exploration on the part of Lagosian ancestors.

Alliance and Flexibility in Lagosian Cultural Scapes

Chief Lola Bamgboshe Martins, himself an Aguda, writes about the Lagosian legend, Mabinouri Dawodu, who was characterized by his panache in religious and social negotiation.[86] According to "Mabinouri Dawodu: The Merchant of Olowobowo," this patriarch of a wealthy dynasty started out as an emancipated slave in 1815. Very much like the *emancipados* in Cuba, Dawodu's father, a "Tapa" Muslim from Nupe, was brought to Lagos as a slave and was sold into the transatlantic slave trade. The father later returned to Iggo,

Lagos, under the auspices of the British naval antislavery campaign, which was growing in size along the Lagosian coast. As with the Afro-Cuban *emancipados* in urban Havana discussed in chapter 1, Dawodu's status changed when he found a patron—Chief Ogunmade on Eko Island. Dawodu worked for Ogunmade as a fisherman and farmer for over five years. Like fellow Lagosian Lucas Marino in Cuba, Dawodu decided to stay on at his patron's compound, the Isale Eko. Dawodu, like Marino, made a substantial amount of money from the commerce and trade he engaged in while under his patron's roof.

It is significant that Lagosian Yoruba from disparate places, like Marino and Dawodu, established trade and families in new environments. To obtain knowledge, power, and material gain, the Yoruba in these emerging Afro-Atlantic contexts relied on access to mobility and opportunities for making money. Many successful and knowledgeable individuals were those, like Marino and Dawodu, who combined traditional ways and innovation by "working" the patron system. Not all individuals were as successful as these two *emancipados*, but there is no evidence to suggest that their lives were extremely unusual.[87] Such individuals became successful through their capacity for navigating official and grassroots channels that provided access to social and economic mobility and status.

Diasporic sensibilities, which included flexible attitudes toward different kinds of identity, assisted in guiding the success of *emancipados*, Aguda, and Saros, traveling to and from circum-Atlantic shores.[88] For example, Dawodu's flexible attitude toward his religious identity shaped the way in which this former slave rose to high economic and social status.[89] During his life, Dawodu devoted himself to Islam, Ifa divination, and finally Christianity. He adjusted his religious devotional practice within a larger holistic framework that emphasized the stages of his life, his family's influence, and social prestige and consequence. This flexible attitude toward religious identity does not illustrate a lack of dedication. Rather, the flexibility within African approaches to religious life shows the unity of social and spiritual identity with its layered practices. With these cultural approaches in mind, we can see that Dawodu' s legacy was linked to the economic, religious, and material culture of the diasporic Aguda in Lagos. He, like other Aguda and former slaves, creatively turned shifting cultural and religious affiliation into assets.

The physical landscape of Lagos shows how the diasporic sensibilities of Yoruba religious and ethnic groups were incorporated into the city. The site of Ogunmade's compound (now the well-known CTS building) became a central meeting place for Ifa priests, or *babalawo*, CMS members, and Saro politicians like Herbert Macaulay.[90] At his death in 1874, Dawodu left seven heirs, in a legacy that closely links different religions, nationalities, and architectural styles. Dawodu explored being a Muslim as a slave and being an Ifa priest during his rise to wealth and status, and he finally converted to Christianity by the late 1860s. His son Fagbemi was also a *babalawo* in his youth and later converted to Christianity. Fagbemi was even baptized by the famous Samuel Crowther in 1868. His conversion indicated not only a shift in religious affiliation but also a rise in prestige and status in Lagosian social circles. However, a *babalawo*'s "conversion" to Christianity does not necessarily mean his abandonment of Ifa practice, since Ifa accepts all religions. This is especially so if Ifa is the core religious affiliation.[91] In any case, by the end of the nineteenth century, the Ogunmade compound exemplified a typical Lagosian site of the elite: it demonstrated a history that was cosmopolitan, international, and religiously heterogeneous.[92]

The architecture of Lagos may be our most dramatic reminder of the contributions made to the city by the Aguda and Saro immigrant populations. However, immigrants to Lagos also included several waves of ethnic Yoruba from regions like Egbaland, Ijebuland, Ondo, and Oyo. These diverse ethnic groups brought their ways to Lagos as well. The diasporic sensibilities, then, of both immigrants from abroad and migrants from the interior included aesthetics and social strategies that built personal dynasties and communities in new contexts. The family legacies that grew out of the Ogunmade compound represented this varied way of making the idea of "home" as both a place left behind and a place of new beginning. For making the marketplace home, or home the marketplace, was very much the task ahead for repatriates, ex-slaves, exiles, and immigrants in general. Lagos as a city benefited from negotiations between the ideal and the practical, as the communities that formed were full of both practical market savvy and high levels of civic pride and responsibility.

Among diasporic Yoruba in both Africa and the Americas, their aesthetics mimic religious accommodations and negotiations between different groups. The ties that hold the merging of traditional religion, Christianity, and Islam together were well in place in the African diaspora, especially in Cuba, an originating space of home for the Aguda. Dawodu's rich religious life illustrated the rule rather than the exception in terms of the interrelation of religion and social responsibility for many Yoruba.[93] Persons of high social status were expected to convert, change, and merge beliefs for the sake of communal, especially familial, harmony. An important individual's civic duty, like that of an *oba* or king, for instance, requires a spiritual component whereby he or she ideally ameliorates divisions in belief, by personal example, in the name of tolerance.[94] Supposedly "separate" religious traditions, like the traditional Yoruba *esin ibile* and Islam, have had long historical legacies of coexistence in Nigeria, especially among the Aguda and Saros of the late nineteenth and early twentieth centuries.[95] In making Lagos home, Afrolatino and ethnic Yoruba immigrants continued to bring their own experiences of negotiating cultural diversity to the table.

Royal Sagas, Lagosian Legacies

Despite the image of tolerance and decorum presented above, Lagosian royal sagas in the nineteenth century were characterized by intense competition. At issue was the political and economic control of Lagos as it became more vital and influential in world trade.[96] The Bini and Lagosian locals struggled with each other in implementing trade and trade policy for the area.[97] A series of expulsions, revolts, and manipulations plagued the reigns of Obas Oshinlokun, Oluwole, Akitoye, and Dosumu. The major figure that ignited most of the controversy and strife was Kosoko, an individual who was absolutely certain he was the legitimate *oba* of Lagos at the time.[98]

Ethnic Yoruba, the Ijebu and the Egba in particular, have exhibited a long-standing interest in and competition over trade and religion in the region.[99] Adding to an already volatile climate were the outside influences of the British, the Portuguese, the Aguda, and the Saros as these groups converged upon nineteenth-century Lagos. Local struggles quickly became international affairs in an area where such a wide range of nationalities and interests existed. The idea of diasporic negotiation referred to above also necessarily included strategies for conflict resolution that shaped how disputes were or were not settled in the city.

Before the English bombarded the city of Lagos in December 1851, things were already getting complicated between Kosoko and Akitoye. Both men claimed the Yoruba royal throne in Lagos.[100] Kosoko's exile among his allies the Bini and Ijebu in Epe was prompted by Akitoye's collaboration with the British to end slave trading in the region, supposedly in support of the palm oil, or *epo pupa*, trade.[101] This shift in trade policy went badly for Kosoko and his allies, for a large portion of their wealth and influence was established through trade, especially in slaves, with the Portuguese.[102]

Both men were backed by their European allies. Kosoko attacked Lagos with an army of 1,500 men in August 1851.[103] British Consul Campbell, acting on Akitoye's behalf in Lagos, pleaded for help from the British Royal Navy. Subsequently, when Akitoye died in September 1853, his son Dosumu took the throne with British promises of support. However, Kosoko gained favor with the population of Lagos after Akitoye signed a treaty ceding Lagos to the queen of England on January 1, 1852.[104] The political crisis deepened when the *idejo* chiefs protested against the treaty on grounds of traditional law.[105] The *idejo* chiefs argued the illegality of the treaty on the grounds that the *oba* of Lagos had no authority to cede, to the British, land that he did not traditionally own. The argument went that the land, administered traditionally by the *idejo* chiefs, was distributed by them among influential families from the region's inception as a site for settlement, and not distributed by an *oba* or king.[106]

Kosoko and Dosumu continued their intense struggle for the throne by manipulating their coalitions and ties to Yoruba from outside the Lagos region. The use of *baba isale* relationships multiplied the number and scope of the Yoruba who became invested in these nineteenth-century struggles.[107] *Baba isale* (literally, "father" or the representative of the home) relationships were expressed in social networks through which important families in several towns established cultural and material exchanges in return for political support and economic gain. These relationships were especially important in providing a framework in which distinct Yoruba ethnicities formulated a sense of community that traveled through geographic and cultural boundaries.[108] *Baba isale* relationships are crucial to understanding how Yoruba transcultural sensibilities developed over time. Diasporic Yoruba within Nigeria sent out representatives from their towns to metropolitan centers like Lagos. Below, my ethnographic collaborator, Prince Olusí, alludes to these kinds of connections in terms of how neighborhoods were formed in Lagos. This mode of social organization represents a way in which the Yoruba created cultural and political networks within their own diasporas. For Lagos, these relationships played important roles in the political sagas of the nineteenth century.

In Cuba, during the same era, we see that a kind of *baba isale* network was established by Havana Lagosians. The formation of economic and social support groups among Lagosians in Havana enabled the incorporation of new arrivals from the continent in a way that helped the Havana Lagosians to stand out as a constituency among the other Yoruba and Africans in Havana. This suggests that there may have been a transatlantic continuation of the *baba isale* concept, albeit changed and creolized within the Caribbean context with all of the cultural and social influences this implies. It is interesting to think that upon their arrival in and integration into Lagos, the Aguda brought a cyclical understanding of these relationships reflecting a thoroughly Atlantic perspective.

Lagosian "Yoruba," with their wide range of ethnicities and identities, became more united under British rule. Not wanting to become unpopular like his father, Dosumu turned against British rule. He made alliances with the Ijebu Yoruba, the French, and others in order to augment his constituency and resources.[109] The Ijebu Yoruba were a vital ethnic component in Lagos because they controlled much of the movement of trade to and from the interior of the country. Since trade played an instrumental role in incorporating other ethnic Yoruba in the politics of Lagos, Dosumu was quick to make friends with the Ijebu. Also recognizing the Ijebu's key role in controlling trade from the interior, the British interfered militarily with Ijebu trade routes in 1892.[110] The British closed off crucial trade routes from the interior to Lagos, routes that were traditionally controlled by the Ijebu. By the time the British resolved their conflict with the Ijebu, the seeds of disaffection with British rule were already taking root among prominent Yoruba and other elites in Lagos.

It is within this environment of strife, turmoil, and the reassociation of communities that the Havana Lagosians entered the scene. During this era of flux, the Cuban Aguda emerged as a subgroup of returnees who reestablished themselves by building a community in the Campos Square area of Victoria Island. Centered around the Cuban Lodge, built by Hilario Campos, the Cuban returnees converged with Brazilian and Saro repatriates through marriage and social interaction. The basis for restructuring heterogeneous communities, however, already existed in traditional understandings of Yoruba community formation. Thus, the politics of association came together in this context in a manner that displayed the rich contours of diasporic resettlement, understood in native, local ways but also in transnational ways, that fell into place in nineteenth-century Lagos.

Idejo Chiefs: Working Affiliations, Building Consensus

One way to make sense of this particular branch of Lagosian royal history is to speak to contemporary bearers of this history. Yoruba responsible for interpreting and accessing the community's history tell these narratives with rich nuance and a complexity that accompanies emic, or insider, meta-analysis. During my sojourn in Lagos, Nigeria, in 2001, I was fortunate enough to speak to the son of an *oba*, the knowledgeable Prince T. Olusí of Isaleko, in the heart of Lagos. Olusí's role as a traditional and contemporary leader allows him to evaluate the stormy history of nineteenth-century Lagos in light of ethnicity, power, and religion. As a Yoruba and a Muslim, an authority in his neighborhood, and a role model of the larger metropolitan Lagosian area, Olusí bridges the spaces that generate diversity in Lagos. His insights extend into the ways in which diasporic communities revisit boundaries and difference as sites of encounter and coalition building.

Olusí's perspective on the traditional *idejo* chiefs is particularly telling.[111] His understanding of Lagosian political history illustrates official, traditional understandings of the above sagas and narratives in the Yoruba context. In the end, Olusí's rendering of politics and history gives clues to how similarities in cultural processes may have developed among the Yoruba over time. One case in point that came up in our conversations is the Yoruba penchant for building religious networks, through *orisha* worship, in transnational ways, in both the nineteenth and twentieth centuries.[112] Olusí's generosity in speaking to me about these matters was based on an official responsibility to represent Yoruba traditional history to outsiders as a member of the royal family of Lagos. But Olusí was also aware of my own interest in looking for Yoruba sources for religious culture building in

Cuba, and there was much we could discuss about the role of *orisha* worship in both societies.

The *idejo* chiefs, according to Olusí, all represent a different region of Yorubaland. Many of the ethnic groups represented by local chiefs have organized their narratives of origin according to the symbolic cultural number of sixteen or thirty-two founding members. The value placed on these numerical formulas relies on the importance of the Ifa divination corpus for generating local histories through the divination verses of the *odu*.[113] Below, Olusí describes the role of the *idejo* in creating traditional civil society in Lagos. Note how he emphasizes the diasporic, moving nature of the positioning of the *idejo* chiefs within the Lagosian political structure. As he explains,

> What is *idejo*? It is the description of a class, because traditional chiefs ... are sometimes called "landowners." But I choose to call them—land administrators, or landlords. ... For example, you have the *ijo ara*.[114] ... You also have Oduwa, ... who came from Ibadan; [he is] the head of that one. So, [this] class of chiefs [the *idejo*], some people put them at sixteen, some would even put them at thirty-two.[115]

The prince's explanation of the *idejo* in Lagos illustrates several crucial aspects of Lagosian, maybe even Yoruba, attitudes toward political and social organization and power that were also carried to Cuba. Note that Olusí prefers the term "land administrator" instead of landowner in describing the *idejo* chief's role. Rather, he privileges the idea of negotiation, the idea of the *idejo* chiefs as a reasonable social body that worked along with the *oba* of Lagos. Along with this flexible approach to land management, Olusí reveals the diasporic nature of the *idejo*. The *idejo* chiefs came from other places in Yorubaland whose people identified a particular *idejo* chief, or emissary, as representing their interests within the Lagos region. Thus, coalition building and the movement of valuable individuals created the social milieu of Lagosian politics among the Yoruba. Certain ethnic groups used these emissaries to further their interests as immigrants to Lagos, as well as to collect and convey the issues important to their constituencies back home.

Olusí's descriptive and exacting model allows us to speak about the affiliations and networks created by communities in the Bight of Benin especially among interior political groups. He describes how different ethnicities from Yorubaland came together in *idejo* relationships in Lagos. The social strategies used for creating these associations highlighted the necessity for reinventing historical relationships. The new understandings of how people from different parts of Yorubaland were connected in Lagos, reflected a flexible approach to culture building through alliances. This approach toward affiliation has ramifications for how we understand the Yoruba influence on Cuban culture and civic life—especially in nineteenth-century Havana.

Building Coalitions: Yoruba Diasporas Organize

As we saw in the previous section, the Yoruba penchant for organizing in civil associations was an important factor in creating a traditional structure for society in nineteenth-century Lagos. This tendency toward organizing consensus was also seen in a range of sectors in the traditional Yoruba public sphere. Below, Olusí provides an analysis that adds depth and detail to the workings and layers of association found in Yoruba society. That is, it shows there is a level of intricacy and flexibility that truly serves as a model for creating constituencies. Olusí's examples of Yoruba alliance building are so telling that I quote him at length here:

> So that you find all these ethnic groups from Yorubaland . . . uniting, still forming together under one umbrella, or the other to mix. Now, having said that, then you still have some *other* organizations, *both* traditional and social—that now bring the people together, irrespective of ethnic origin. For example, now you have the Oshogbo cult. The Oshogbo cult, now, is open to *any* person willing to be a member. . . . So that you [are] now free to join, whether you are Ijebu, whether you are Egba, whether you are Ijesha. . . . It's a cultural, *cultural* umbrella.
> Then, you also have the religious group. Like say the Ifa group now.
> All the *babalawo* would come together to celebrate the Odun Ifa.[116] They . . . sometimes do it in their respective houses. But they also come *together* to do it. . . . That they now have . . . the Ifa Conclave or Society, where you have Ifa chiefs. You have the *araba*, who is the . . . head. You have the *araba*. You have eh, *awishe*; you have all these titles that are peculiar to the Ifa society. They have different grades. But, you see, it, that [the Ifa organization] also is open to *all* worshippers of Ifa, whether Ijebu, whether, whether Ilorin, whether, whether Egun, whether Ijesha. They will be promoted according to their regulation. So that also is another society.
> . . . You also have trade groups. For example, those who sell gari now, *gari naa*. Who come together, have one leader. So, so you have the trade groups. You also have those who sell plants, who come together, those who sell cloth, who come together, you know, who have various trade groups, you know. So that you have all these various platforms. You have religious groups, that bring them together irrespective of ethnic [origins]. You have trade groups, that bring them together irrespective of country. Then you also have communal groups, what you [call] *area*, area groups.[117]

As we can see, Yoruba diasporic sensibilities allow for coalition building on multiple fronts. Whether it is the *iyaloja*, the market women of Nigeria, or *babalawo*, Ifa divination priests, Yoruba communities recognize the power of building associations across regional and personal distances.[118] This includes taking into account the diversity found in a community's age sets, occupations, genders, wealth, and levels of skill and education in various fields of knowledge. Repeatedly, as Olusí described above for *babalawo* and their coalitions, as well as trade groups, civil associations are able to form out of many different reference points.

It is clear, then, that in the past as well, diverse Lagosian communities devised a sophisticated means by which to negotiate affiliation. As Barry Hallen brings out in *The Good, the Bad, and the Beautiful*, Yoruba epistemology and values are contingent upon an almost radical notion of objectivity, fairness, and firsthand experience.[119] The assessment of the value placed on certain types of knowledge, in terms of reliability and sources, is especially relevant to Olusí's observations. People decide where they belong according to a critical process of negotiation. This negotiation over the value of certain associations dominated the cultural marketplace in Lagos in the nineteenth century.

The correlation between the organization of knowledge and the organization of people became clear as Lagosians and connected communities in the Bight of Benin used vernacular discursive models to situate themselves and others.[120] In Olusí's description, there is an emphasis on how each group imagines its platform in light of the rest of Lagosian civil society. This search for appropriate associations also understands the value of the level of prestige acquired in building coalitions.[121] In the turbulent context of nineteenth-century Lagos, communities reordered coalitions so that groups could be augmented, and could also intersect on various social planes in the ways Olusí describes above. The connection created between the Aguda and the Saros as newcomers but also repatriates in the city's social life is an example of this kind of flexible grouping. As Hallen suggests about Yoruba philosophy, and Barber suggests about Yoruba religion, different ethnic Yoruba came together discursively in their many diasporas for the sake of coalition building.[122] These skills in merging cultural perspectives and social platforms were certainly brought to the African diaspora. Here, communities and nations of African descent built community and coalition across ethnic diversity and divergent social histories, especially in Cuba, through civil associations.[123]

For example, Africa-inspired organizations, like the *cabildos* in Cuba, fostered in-house economic and religious support for the pan-nationalism and cultural legitimacy of the Yoruba and other Africans in the nineteenth century.[124] In a larger sense, the Cuban *cabildos* represented the ways in which Africans in the diaspora negotiated the particularities of African creolized ethnicity, while still emulating a pan-African consciousness within their respective societies in the nineteenth century.[125] It is significant that these Black organizations also fostered transnational and localized nationalisms that simultaneously emphasized notions of Cuban-ness and African-ness.

The role of traditional religious organizations in diasporic contexts, like the Yoruba Ogboni society in nineteenth-century Cuba, served as complicated inspirations to innovation. Clearly, when faced with the social reality of slavery and second-class status in Cuba, Yoruba associations like the Afro-Cuban Ogboni society developed new applications of their social roles based on perceived traditional frameworks that were renegotiated within the context of new and emerging participation by Afrocubano *criollos* who shifted notions of African authenticity.[126] This positioning was part of a platform, very much like the platforms described by Olusí above, that reorganized the Yoruba in Cuba who shared an interest in continuing traditional civil organizations in a new environment. Being, for example, part of an Ogboni association in nineteenth-century Cuba also told people where you came from, what religion you were associated with, and the level of power and prestige you were carrying with you from Africa. However, in colonial Cuba this level of civic organization was seen as a threat by the European and white *criollo* population from an early period in the colony's history.[127]

Due to this fear of Black associations, the island's elite saw the nineteenth-century Aponte Conspiracy as originating out of Afrocubano organizations like the *cabildos* and the Ogboni.[128] "African religious leaders" were thought to be the primary organizers for "revolt against white plantation owners," though recently this perspective has been critiqued as overemphasizing the role of African "religion" in inspiring these revolts.[129] However, for Afro-Cubans, the associations remained embedded with African religious identification in terms of their sociocultural significance.[130] Religious performances that recontextualized Yoruba royal traditions in Cuban social settings emphasized a larger set of Atlantic associations that connected spiritual and political power symbolically.[131] In a related manner, an Atlanticist perspective is offered by Childs's study of the Aponte incident where he locates the rebellion within the framework of the Haitian revolution and mounting international pressure against slavery.[132]

Even in the twentieth century, postrevolutionary Cuban cultural consciousness placed its historical roots in the revolutionary acts of Afro-Cubans, especially those relating to the Ten Years' War that began in 1868.[133] Ferrer and Ayorinde speak to how this consciousness acts as a trope that reifies Afro-Cuban religion and Blackness in a selective process that can also erase the reality of racism in Cuban society.[134] This kind of reinterpretation/performance of "African" modes of resistance to slavery and colonialism allowed for a rhetoric of Cuban nationalism that both included and excluded Afrocubanos, with their new creolized identities being perceived as both domesticated and dangerous in a range of ways.[135] Afro-Cuban religion, music, and art were foregrounded as the main contributions that Africans brought to Cuban national culture. However, it is clear from the experiences of Afro-Cuban groups like Lagosians in Havana, for example, that Africans brought much along the lines of social organization, economic savvy, and diasporic community-building strategies to Cuban society and culture.

Heterogeneity in the Neighborhoods of Lagos

Lagosian and other ethnic Yoruba living in Havana from 1830 to 1890 acquired a wide range of skills and professions that they took back with them upon their repatriation to Africa. Like their Brazilian counterparts, the Nago Yoruba, who were mostly from Bahia, Cuban-Lagosians returned to Lagos carrying with them a range of professional and cultural adaptations they had developed in the Americas.[136] The Brazilian-Yoruba focused on becoming architects, traders, and engineers, and brought these skills back to the Bight of Benin. These returnees contributed to the aesthetic and economic texture of the whole region.[137] The ethnic Yoruba in Havana, conversely, became "bakers, butchers, tailors, mechanics, and the like."[138] Lagosians in Cuba formed a large part of the skilled labor force in Havana, having skills that proved lucrative enough to establish businesses, and eventually material and social networks connected to Lagos.[139]

In 1880, statistics on Lagos recorded 3,221 Aguda and 1,535 Saros living in a city with a total population of 37,458.[140] The Aguda differed from the Saros in that most of the former were Catholic, as opposed to Protestant, or specifically Anglican. The religious affiliation of the Aguda with Catholicism demonstrated certain Afro-Cuban and Afro-Brazilian legacies that they brought back to Africa.[141] Cole suggests that the Aguda were perceived to have been on friendlier terms with the indigenous Yoruba population and its culture than were the "Victorian" Saros.[142] This affinity resulted from the Aguda's identification with traditional cultural practices.

By the early twentieth century, Lagos was divided into four quarters: that of the British in Portuguese town, the Popo Maro of the Saros, the Popo Aguda of the Aguda, and on the outskirts the indigenous population.[143] These sections of the city still extended outward from the Marina, with the Aguda creating their own neighborhoods around the Holy Cross Catholic Cathedral and Campos Square. Both the cathedral and square were constructed by the Aguda, who were gifted architects and city planners.[144]

The Aguda used their transnational identities to influence the ways in which they obtained status and power in the incorporative Lagosian social schema.[145] It was within these bids for social power, explicit or implicit, that communities and individuals negotiated their collective and singular roles within this new social context. When we think of *cabildos* and *sociedades de color* in nineteenth-century Havana, we find that Afro-Cubans, especially self-identified Lucumí, negotiated and performed their social and political status through religious coalitions.[146] These performative skills were brought back to Africa and then reinterpreted in ways that augmented the cultural capital displayed by and given to the Aguda.

Situating Returnees from Abroad in Lagos

Prince Olusí made the following observations regarding returnees to Lagos:

> Those who came back from Cuba and Brazil came from a society where you have been trained not to waste resources, even labored to make your money. So they have been taught not to be wasteful. So, now they find [in Lagos upon arrival ca. 1860–90] a class of people who would be the Saros.[147] ... Saros who would want to kill three fowls, whereas the Brazilian Aguda would content himself with just one.[148]

Here Olusí points to two vital aspects that are under consideration in our exploration of diasporic community building. The first is the element of historical and social context that the Aguda population carried with it. The Cuban Aguda in Lagos carried with them the kind of work ethic that allowed them to rise in social and economic status in Cuba. They brought these attitudes back to Lagos, where they mingled with other diasporic groups, like the Saros, and the local ethnic Yoruba populations. Yet the search for social mobility became part of an Atlantic cycle, with the Cuban Aguda seeking a "Lagosian" way of community building a generation earlier in Cuba.

As Olusí suggests above, there may have been a popular perception of differences in attitude toward the allocation and use of resources between Saros and Aguda in the public arena. Olusí's observations emphasize that the Saros were interested in displaying their wealth. On the other hand, Olusí sees the Aguda as being perceived as "thrifty" in terms of economic resources. These contrasts situated by Olusí suggest that there are multiple vernacular discourses resituating the perception of the cultural and social properties of newcomers among certain sectors of the Lagosian local population.

We know that these repatriate communities that arrived in Lagos had different histories. Along with their unique backgrounds, the returnees also brought to Lagos distinct sets of social adaptations from their different diasporas. Whether in Cuba, Brazil, or Sierra Leone, their encounters with different societies and communities abroad shaped the texture of how these repatriate communities were perceived by other Lagosians. The differences in the way that Saros and Aguda were perceived to employ these adaptations informed the way they have been represented in Lagos and other places in the Bight of Benin where they resettled.[149] The Afrolatino Aguda, then, were characterized by their sensible use of economic resources.

What were the skills that Yoruba Cubans brought to Lagos? Fortunately, some clues about these skills have surfaced from the work of Cuban historian Pérez de la Riva, and also through the annals of the *Anti-Slavery Reporter* as discussed in chapter 1.[150] These sources and the interviews I conducted with Mrs. Ola Vincent and Mrs. Aderemi Gooding-King, granddaughters of

Hilario Campos, the founder of the Cuban Lodge in Lagos, give glimpses of the kinds of professions Lagosians developed in Cuba as *emancipados*.

In their movement from Cuba to Lagos, Cuban-Lagosians established the kinds of adaptations, social networks, and identities that allowed them to be upwardly mobile in terms of finances, trade, and status. In Cuba and Nigeria, then, Afrolatinos of Yoruba-Cuban stock made their mark by relying on a sense of community that valued a work ethic that fits particularly well with the itinerant rigors of diasporic life. The significance of these community values can be seen in two ways: (a) that there were some cultural sensibilities, shared by these dispersed yet connected and interactive communities, that were also based on a shared past; and (b) that there were some epistemological negotiations that people were reinventing in innovative, yet shared, ways. These two ways of explaining the connections between these groups do not rule each other out. On the contrary, their coexistence represents an extension of the kinds of cultural preparations that diasporic people often carry with them as a means of creating routes not only to survivability but also to social and economic mobility. We see that these portable values and behaviors situated Afrolatinos in both the Caribbean and Africa in positions that were flexible enough to allow them to demonstrate their mastery of the skills of negotiation and community making across the Atlantic in profound ways. Chapter 3 explicates the ways in which the members of the Cuban-Lagosian Campos family understand their history and their contribution to Lagosian cultural and civic life.

3

"Second Diasporas"

Reception in the Bight of Benin

In recent years, a deeper awareness has emerged of the sustained historical relationships across Afro-Atlantic worlds, and of the fact that the diasporas involved may be rethought in many ways.[1] Necessarily, African and American societies, spaces, and relations are now being understood as extensions of each other. These understandings include refreshing ways of seeing how communities extending from the Bight of Benin to the Caribbean and the Americas are contiguous and integrated in their histories, thus forcing us to rethink our notions of discrete regions. Along with the reconsideration of region in exploring these transnational flows is the movement of religious culture as a means to identity for Yoruba nationalities through different Atlantic contexts and societies.[2] The research offered here on the Cuban connection of the Aguda of Lagos reveals the extent of these diverse historical and cultural copenetrations, and how these flows influenced their reception in Lagos.

Movement of slaves from Africa to Brazil began early on through Portuguese colonial routes. In one study, Verger suggests that trade between Bahía in particular and Africa expanded from 1770 until 1851, and that these voyages included the selling of slaves for gold, tobacco, and sugarcane.[3] In pointing out groups of free Africans moving back and forth across the Atlantic in the early nineteenth century, Bay and Law draw our attention to prominent individual travelers, including ambassadors from African royal courts to Brazil and Cuba on voyages launched from Dahomey, Porto Novo, and Ouidah.[4] Slave trading was one activity that brought these individuals to different shores.[5] However, these routes for the negotiation of slavery also became routes for repatriation. And, importantly, free Africans, especially the Aguda, traveled across the Atlantic from the Bight of Benin to Cuba and Brazil because of the bicoastal nature of their families, businesses, and roles as traditional religious functionaries.[6] These various traditions of travel often came full circle in Lagos, a port city that was a major shipping port for the Aguda repatriates, and also for royal emissaries and other important personages.[7] In Lagos, and in the other ports mentioned above, the Brazilian slave trader was an important, and ambivalent, political player. I say ambivalent because in some instances it was the very descendants of slaves, like the powerful lineage known for the "title" of the Chachas (also known as Xa-Xas) of the Da Souza family in Ouidah, that played this role.[8] Law provides a particularly apt characterization of this group:

> Some of the Brazilian merchants involved in the slave-trade from West Africa in the nineteenth century were likewise ex-slaves: the most eminent example being Joaquim d'Almeida. . . . In Ouidah . . . an example is Sabino Vierya, originally a slave from Nupe in northern Nigeria who returned from Brazil to West Africa as a trader but fell into poverty and became a client of de Souza, who gave him land in Sogbaji, adjoining the de Souza domain in [the] Brazil quarter.[9]

Law suggests that the repatriation of slaves to West Africa from Brazil was motivated particularly by a slave revolt in Bahia in 1835.[10] In this instance, as in Cuba and other places in the Americas, repatriation was carried out as an enforced act of deportation on the part of colonial governments in the Atlantic, fueled by what was known as "Black Scares."[11] It is in the context of these forced migrations, as Pérez de la Riva suggests for Afro-Cuban repatriates returning on the bergantín *San Antonio* discussed in chapter 1, that some groups decided to go to Africa, funding the voyages with their own savings.[12] In other words, some communities negotiated the anti-African political climate in a manner that facilitated their voyages back to Africa.

Afrolatino communities also instigated repatriation to Africa. Ex-slaves returned to the Bight of Benin in successive waves during the nineteenth century for a variety of reasons. In some instances, powerful individuals engaged in the very commerce that had previously enslaved them in the Americas. These new elites negotiated important social roles for themselves in their resettled communities in Africa. Others, like the Aguda of Lagos, and earlier of Benin, returned to Africa for cultural, familial, and economic reasons. In some cases, individuals from both groups of Aguda moved back and forth, to and from Africa. Whatever the choices made by these returnees, it was specific historical contexts that fostered their different, and at times contradictory, understandings of loyalty, country, and home. In this larger context of returning to Africa, it is significant that the Cuban-Yoruba members of the Aguda identify themselves as descendants of returnees in contemporary Lagos, Nigeria, because this shows their dual frame of reference in terms of representing a truly "Atlantic" perspective.

Catholic religious practices brought back from Latin America united people of disparate national identities together under the Aguda identity. However, the kind of Catholicism that was carried back was an Africanized folk Catholicism that existed as a form of public culture in both Cuba and Brazil in the nineteenth century. These kinds of religious practices included a heavy emphasis on Yoruba cultural identification as a form of legitimation for the construction of a recognizable community in terms of ethnicity. Subsequently, the Aguda in Lagos carried back with them a sense of Yoruba-ness that was fueled by the combination of religious practices from Catholic and *orisha* traditions that are found in Candomblé and Santería.[13] These traditions created a sense of nationalism and community for the Yoruba in Latin America, and fueled the process of creating a longed-for homeland in Nigeria. The sense of Yoruba belonging that was fostered in the Caribbean and Latin America allowed the Aguda to understand their place in the world while they were in the diaspora and also when they came back home to Africa. The idea of the journey, or the *iranjo*, for the Yoruba is a central metaphor for the accumulation of knowledge and meaning, especially in the diaspora.[14] The diasporic sensibilities of Havana Lagosians and the Aguda were formulated by the experience of a journey of shared routes and Atlantic contexts. These groups also maintained a deep level of connectivity to *orisha* religious practice and cultural thinking in terms of the meaning of the journey and of home.

My conversations with Aguda elder Mrs. Aderemi Gooding-King revealed that Aguda followers of Africanized forms of Catholicism and of *orisha* worship located themselves within a subtle ritual context. This subtlety illustrates a form of code switching among the Aguda that also takes place among Afro-Cubans, with regard to Catholic and traditional African religiosity. Perhaps the combination of African Catholicism with traditional Yoruba religious culture among the Aguda in Lagos comes directly from Cuban and Brazilian ways of worship that reflected the strong nationalistic connections felt between followers of *orisha* worship in Cuba and Brazil with Yorubaland in the late nineteenth and early twentieth centuries.[15] Whatever may be the contours of such cultural carrying across the diaspora with regard to religion, no doubt an array of confluences and innovative codification of deities, rituals, and religious folk history existed for Aguda communities.

In the mid-nineteenth century, the Aguda population multiplied in the Lagos area. Along with the Aguda came repatriates from Sierra Leone, known as the Saros. The Saros have been depicted as an elite group of immigrants who emulated Victorian culture.[16] Abner Cohen's work on the Creoles of Sierra Leone shows how this group's "elite" culture was imported into Lagos via the Saros. And, more significantly here, the production of "elite" culture generated by Creoles from Sierra Leone, some of whom settled in Lagos as Saros, is grounded in multiple African reinterpretations of European cultural tropes.[17] So, in much the same way that the Aguda reinterpreted their Christian and *orisha* religious cultures in terms of their own readings of cultural identity, the Creoles of Sierra Leone reinterpreted the "Victorian" aspect of their identity in terms of their own creolized epistemological ground that spoke neither to pure African nor to pure European sensibilities. It is also interesting that the Creoles of Sierra Leone claimed

Yoruba cultural roots that allowed them to reproduce religious and social secret societies based on perceived Yoruba antecedents.[18] This process of culture building based on a Yoruba ancestry echoed what was going on in the late nineteenth century in Cuba, where "Yoruba" *cabildos* sought to reconstruct a religious and nationalist discourse centered on the construction of Lucumí identity.[19]

Several of the groups of Africans who were repatriated to Sierra Leone in the nineteenth century came from Portuguese slaving ships intercepted by the British Anti-Slavery Squadron.[20] Some Yoruba repatriates, like Samuel Ajayi Crowther and Samuel Johnson, worked in Sierra Leone under the auspices of religious organizations like the CMS before moving on to Lagos.[21] It is clear that some Creoles settling in Lagos as Saros understood their move to the city as a sort of "homecoming." Their movement between Sierra Leone and Lagos added another zone of repatriation and community formation in the Atlantic world that could also be interpreted as a "cyclical" phenomenon.

The Saros were instrumental in developing schools, churches, and a Standard Yoruba version of the Bible in Nigeria.[22] Alliances were forged across religious boundaries—for example between *babalawo* and prominent individuals, such as Crowther, in the Christian ministry—creating a form of pan-"Yoruba" national consciousness.[23] Herbert Macaulay was an influential Saro who challenged British colonial policies in Nigeria. The issue on which Macaulay was most active in voicing his opinion centered around land distribution and the management of native lands by the English.[24] Macaulay's journalism exhibited a sophisticated nationalism that fostered a "new Yoruba consciousness."[25] Though he was thought of as a Christian role model, Macaulay significantly befriended *babalawo* and was himself a trained *onisegun*, or traditional Yoruba herbalist.[26] We have seen that such fluidity in religious affiliation is an important tool for garnering prestige and power in the diverse climate of Lagosian society. Through his savvy choices of affiliation, Macaulay successfully negotiated a range of religious identities that augmented his status and influence among his contemporaries in an array of social circles that included elites in both European and African associations.

It is this kind of fluid frame of reference that allowed Saro and Aguda immigrants settling in Lagos in the nineteenth century to claim a transnational pan-"Yoruba" set of identities. These reconstructions were necessary as part of these immigrant communities' ways of belonging to Lagos. The idea of "belonging" to Lagos also included the idea of "place" in the narrated histories of Havana's and Bahia's Afrolatinos. The process of rebuilding, of relayering connections across the Atlantic diaspora, to and from Lagos, still exists in contemporary contexts as the Aguda seek to unravel and display their Afro-Atlantic roots.[27]

Legacies of Home: Caribbean and Latin American Communities in the Bight of Benin

Africans moving back and forth across the Atlantic created "home" in a wide range of ways. From as early as the late eighteenth century, Africans who had made their homes in the Americas returned to the Bight of Benin to reestablish themselves. For example, in Ouidah, powerful Brazilian families like the Da Souzas played a significant role in furthering trade, including the slave trade, between Bahia and this part of the African coast.[28] Similar diasporic communities, of Brazilian and Cuban Yoruba, the Aguda, returned throughout the nineteenth century to make Lagos their home. Their experiences abroad, as slaves and laborers in the Americas, introduced new ways of being African in terms of religious identity, ethnicity, and occupational skills.[29]

To speak of a monolithic Yoruba culture in the nineteenth century makes little sense.[30] What is understood as "Yoruba" has always been an amalgamation of many ethnic groups, from distinct towns throughout the southwestern part of modern Nigeria and Benin, which communicated with each other in a mutually intelligible language.[31] Until the late nineteenth century, the term "Yoruba" referred specifically to citizens of the Oyo kingdom.[32] With the aid of diasporic groups returning from Cuba and Brazil, plus missionaries and other repatriates from Sierra Leone, transnational Yoruba-speaking communities began to see themselves as belonging to a distinct, unified nationality.[33] Ethnic identities, noted in the dialectical distinctions and geographic diversity among Yoruba-speaking communities, brought a certain heterogeneity to this emerging nationalism. The various ethnicities, including those of the diasporic groups, produced the interrelated, yet distinct, "Yoruba" cultures now found in various parts of the world.[34] This kind of cultural reworking can be seen as a "diasporic sensibility."

Whether as Lucumí in Cuba, Nago in Brazil, or Aguda in Lagos, the ethnicities that make up the Yoruba are no strangers to relocation and cultural and economic reinvention. Traditional *orisha* worship acted as a strong, incorporative civil religion that allowed for political participation and organization on a variety of social levels and on multiethnic terms.[35] Even the deities themselves represent different areas of Yorubaland or are borrowed from neighboring places. For example, Sòngó/Chango is associated specifically with the Oyo kingdom in both Africa and Cuba.[36] Historically, people coming from this part of the Bight of Benin into the American diaspora, like the Fon/Edo and the Yoruba, brought with them strategic ways of creating alliances with other Africans and immigrant communities in the Americas.[37] These incorporative sensibilities even brought in groups from other geographic areas. In Cuba, for example, religious practices from the Congo region have been interlaced with Yoruba *orisha* practice.[38] Though this mixing is not without aspects of contention, as the reiteration of boundaries between Ocha and Palo is a constant theme among practitioners, these two sets of traditions are seen as markers of a shared Afrocubano religious culture.[39]

The religious resilience of *orisha* worship deeply influenced Christian and other African belief systems in the Caribbean and Latin America.[40] The Afro-Atlantic religious traditions of Santería, Candomblé, Shango, Umbanda, Palo, and Vodoun, were shaped by *orisha* worship from Yorubaland in deep historical and structural ways. In similar fashion, Africans returning to Yorubaland from the diaspora brought back with them to Africa a Caribbean and Latin American sense for religious and cultural creolization. When Afrolatinos came back to Lagos in the nineteenth century, the accumulative community-building strategies exemplified in Afro-Caribbean religions, especially the emphasis on incorporation and admixture, came full circle.

Invitation from Olokun: Ifa Sends for the Aguda

In Lagos, community leaders talk about culture, tradition, and the past from a range of perspectives. For example, Aguda chief Lola Bamgboshe Martins emphasized the Brazilian contribution to the city in the form of the Boa and Egungun masquerades.[41] Professor Ajikobi of the University of Lagos described in his conversations with me and in his piece "African Folklore: Its Importance in Our Development" the importance of the performance of traditional cultural forms by Nigerians of all ethnic groups in creating a valid national culture.[42] Mrs. Aderemi Gooding-King, the granddaughter of Hilario Campos, the founder of the Cuban Lodge in Campos Square, spoke to me of Cubans in Lagos. She focused on the community's interaction with and marriage into Brazilian and ethnic Yoruba communities.[43] These examples illustrate that individual cultures and traditions are a part of thinking about the Lagosian past. Cultural markers that signaled their own unique contributions helped Martins, Ajikobi, and Gooding-King to locate their past within a context of continuity with cultural performances in the present. Sometimes this continuity was presented to me in narrative form. At other times, images and memories served as the conceptual links to the community's history.

Prince Olusí of the Isaleko neighborhood, often thought of as the heart of the largest marketplace on the island, presented me with Lagosian oral history from the perspective of a royal leader. Olusí negotiated the particular and the grand in a fashion that showed how diasporic models of community building behaved in Lagos over time. What Agudas and Saros found upon their return was that they were reintegrated into Lagosian society despite their marked differences. Assisting in this process, Olusí related, were the ways in which Lagosians saw their city as fitting into the

80 *"Second Diasporas"*

larger world community. He presented oral histories that showed how the outside world was melded with Lagosian daily life (through its royalty, entrepreneurs, slaves, missionaries, and so on) in an ongoing fashion. He spoke of a traditional tale taken from the Ifa Odu, the Ifa divination verses, specific to this region of Lagos, Isaleko. This narrative comes from a divinatory corpus that bridges many gaps: the relationship between the far and the near, the supernatural and the practical, the strange and the familiar.

"Korin Itan ni Ebo Olokun": The Story of the Sacrifice to the Sea

Olusí is an *omoba*, the son of a king and the recognized prince of the Popo Saro quarter in the heart of Lagos. As such, he is expected to be an expert on Lagosian traditional history. His role as an important *oloye*, a title-holding member of one of the royal families of Lagos, gives him the opportunity and responsibility of remembering and resituating Yoruba histories in diverse contexts. Such histories are considered to be *jinle* discourses, discourses that are deeply entrenched in layers of traditional meaning. Events in such narratives are layered with a code of emergent significance that depends on the level of knowledge brought to the story on the part of listeners. Yoruba popular history about Lagos emphasizes a diverse and enterprising population and the city's role as a cosmopolitan, international center of trade for all of Africa. Olusí relates Lagosians' willingness to draw in outsiders for business and trade. This is the common perception, especially about the Aguda of old. Olusí's tale is rooted in the ways in which royalty and *orisha* worship interacted with each other and with the outside world. In the following *korin Ifa*, Ifa divination song, Lagosians were called by the gods to seek outside influences from other cultures and peoples for the sake of diversifying the city.

The narrative quoted below was recorded during an interview session at Olusí's palace. We met frequently for conversation, often accompanied by Olusí's adopted nephew, Professor Ajikobi from the African Language and Literature Department at the University of Lagos. The palace is found at the very center of one of the busiest markets in Lagos, and thus activity and frequent visitors peppered my visits. One afternoon, after speaking about the origins of the term "Aguda," Olusí recalled an *itan*, an Ifa divination tale, about the initial group of immigrants to Lagos. In the following verses, an "Ifa-centered" interpretation of the theme emerges.[44]

> Prince Olusí: And, the Portuguese at that time made friends with the *oba* [king of Lagos]. They'd give him presents, fur, felt, tobacco, things like that. So that is the initial contact which developed, trade followed, and everything. So, at that time, the Portuguese were described as *aguda*. So they—and there is a song which I will sing—

Solimar Otero: OK, very good.
Prince Olusí:—which, in Yoruba, which will describe what I have referred to. It's an historical song. It says:

[*singing*]

Mo pí ta'tàn fùn e.	I am going to tell you a history.
Itan lóó itan kìí Akinsemoyin	It is a history about Akinsemoyin,
Bábà koo tere.	Who is the father of Oko Ekotere.
Mo pí ta'tàn fùn e,	I am going to tell you a history.
Itan lóó itan kìí Akinsemoyin,	It is a history about Akinsemoyin,
Bábà ko Ekotere.	Who is the father of Ekotere.
Won dífa, dífa ó láàni n'Iga,	They consulted Ifa, they consulted at the Iga, the palace
Olokun Eko dífa mu.	It is the Olokun of Eko that is consulted.
Won dífa, dífa ó láàni n'Iga,	They consulted Ifa, they consulted at the Iga palace
Olokun Eko dífa mu.	It is the Olokun of Eko that is consulted.
N'won taá aso fùnfùn sèé títùn.	They tied a white cloth to a post.
Won wa toto osun mefa	They came along six months
taá awo bo'ton,	after the priests performed the sacrifice.
Won wa toto osun mefa	They came along six months
taá awo bo'ton,	after the priests performed the sacrifice.
Awon agbu Aguda won jo ló ké dele	They, the Aguda, were who came following after
won jo páa se a aso fùnfùn.	the white cloth.
Ebo tíí aru sokun ni eelo bádù	It is the sacrifice that is performed at the time that
Aguda wa si Eko awa.	brought the Aguda to our Eko.
Olafí dé ó eru taa'ka sólòwóò.	Slaves now compete with their masters for wealth,
Olafí dé ó eru taa'ka sólòwóò.	Slaves now compete with their masters for wealth,
Olafí dé ó eru taa'ka sólòwóò.	Slaves now compete with their masters for wealth.[45]

Olusí's explication, which followed the performance of this *itan*, challenges the notions of hegemony and colonialism as postulated by a binary

"Western" versus "non-Western" perspective. Olusí's rendition presented the Portuguese as the first set of Aguda, who were invited to come to Lagos through a sacrifice to the deity of the ocean, Olokun. This historical recollection of how Europeans and Africans encountered each other in Lagos emphasizes the pivotal role of the Lagosian ruling elite and their connection to traditional religion. Olusí's performance of the tale for me was done in his "official" capacity as a member of the Lagosian royal family. This historical song recalled the diversity of situations, players, and contexts inherent in the happenings that make up oral history.[46] In the following excerpt from Olusí's explication, we see his own interpretation of the significance of the historical narrative:

> And so, when they come here. You see, I think it is in the fourteenth century, I think, fourteenth, fifteenth century, the late fourteenth, early 1500s, yeah.[47] There is a very old song, it tells the history of the connection. . . . it tells the history of the connection. And the history that we have, King Akinsemoyin, who is very prominent in Lagos history. . . . You know, when he is the king of Lagos he is involved in the slave trade. And he is asked by one of the priests that he should make *ebo*.[48] They said that he should make *ebo*, a sacrifice to the ocean, the goddess of the ocean, Olokun.[49] So that goodness and good fortune can come to the town of Lagos that is unknown at that point in time. And the *oba* asked what are the ingredients for the *ebo*. He had to get all types of foodstuffs. . . . So they were also made as an *ebo* at the foot of the ocean. The vegetables, the oranges, they take . . . they'll throw the thing at the ocean. And this is done. And after some time, the Portuguese were at that time, in the fourteenth century,[50] sailing around the world, and, they noticed the fruits floating, on the ocean . . . and they said, "A town must be around here." And they followed the fruits to, saw a settlement, met some people. They told them, that the *oba* is at the Isaleko,[51] and they were eventually taken to the *oba*, and then contacted the Western world, there it first started. So, so that is the first contact with the Portuguese. And, the Portuguese at that time made friends with the *oba*. They'd give him presents, fur, felt, tobacco, things like that. So . . . trade followed, and everything. So, at that time, the Portuguese were described as Aguda.[52]

The singing of the *odu* and its exegesis by Olusí illustrates several key components already alluded to about African oral panegyrics.[53] Situations and explanations tied to community history shift with changing contexts. African and Afro-Atlantic diasporic communities construct, accept, and communicate oral histories that are organically useful in tying one to the past through traditional reinvention. Olusí's tale provides us with a beautiful example of this kind of resituating of oral history in the moment of performance. He highlighted in both the song and the explication of the song the uniquely self-confident and openly incorporative nature of Yoruba cultural practices.

In contemporary Cuba, as in contemporary Lagos, Olokun represents a deity of the ocean, either male or female. Olokun is also "received" in a ritual carried out by initiates of a sacred compound, or *ile*, for the purpose of "opening the roads," or *abriendo los caminos*. This is precisely the kind of function Olusí speaks of here in terms of what the *ebo* does for the town of Lagos as a whole. In Cuba, as is also believed in the ritual houses of the Ile Olokun in Lagos I worked with, we see that *ebo* for Olokun can bring good fortune and bring various opportunities for individuals. In "receiving" Olokun in Cuba, one receives ritual implements, as in the case of receiving one's *elegua* or *los guerreros*, which one cares for and creates as a religio-psychic universe, or *cuadro espiritual*. In a sense, a personal Olokun behaves like an *elegua*, in terms of navigating roads and bringing along opportunities, cleaning out negative influences, albeit on water instead of land.

In Olusí's narrative, it is not surprising that Yoruba traditional religion was the source and catalyst urging the Lagosian community to seek out new cultural and social connections. Within the perspective of the *odu* sung above, the Yoruba remained in control of the epistemology that explains the "colonial" encounter here. They held supernatural control over the relationship to the initial Aguda-Portuguese encounter and understood these power dynamics within a their own cultural center. The story turns traditional linear narratives of colonialism on their head by claiming that it was the Yoruba traditional leaders who created the opportunity for contact and trade with their ritual practices. Efficacy and power are attributed to traditional sources that can be located within the culture.

Perhaps the last lines of the song are the most haunting and resonate best with the history of the Aguda's Atlantic departure and return:

Olafí dé ó eru taa'ka sólòwóò.

[Slaves now compete with their masters for wealth.]

Olusí explained the last line of the *korin Ifa* as illustrating the promise of Lagos for turning ill fortune into a prosperous fate. He equated the slaves and servants to adventurous people who knew how to change their circumstances. He reiterated that Lagos was a safe haven for those looking for something better and that this quality has continued to attract to the city an international community of people interested in commerce. He also expressly added that the Aguda represented a renewal of prosperity for Lagos, especially in terms of turning a life of slavery into one of material success and social prestige.

Ironically, Olusí also indicated that many associated the former slaves, the Aguda, with the slave-trading Portuguese because of the perception of a shared Catholic heritage. In a related conversation and short article presented to me, bicoastal chief Bamgboshe Martins talked about the former slave Mabinouri

Dawodu, the Merchant of Ologbowo, who became a local legend for epitomizing this "Lagosian" notion of upward mobility.[54] Dawodu was remarkable in his ability to code-switch between religious faiths, embodying a fervor for *Ifa*, Christianity, and Islam at different periods in his life. Both Olusí's and Bamgboshe Martins's depictions of former slaves presented images of individuals who crossed the Atlantic back to Africa with life skills that made them particularly apt at navigating the cosmopolitanism and complexity of Lagosian social contexts. In these narratives, the city of Lagos and the Aguda become tropes for reinventing and recasting the colonial past and slavery in a manner that highlights African agency. More to the point, however, is the way in which these two tropes in particular, Lagos the place and the Aguda community, act as reminders to a larger counternarrative about power distribution in the Atlantic world.

Similar discursive strategies were used by the Yoruba in Cuba in the nineteenth century in trying to situate their role in that society as Afro-Cubans.[55] As we saw among Havana's Lagosians, and later among the Cuban Aguda in Lagos, the frame of reference of a personal narrative history becomes a significant point for locating creolized and subaltern discourses that reveal the complications of the Atlantic world in terms of the density and multiplicity of experiences and social actors. Received as a "second wave" of the Aguda, the Havana Lagosians arrived back in Lagos bringing their strategies of religious and civil association from Cuba home with them. Both facets of this diaspora, in Havana and in Lagos, used the Catholic Church as a form of civil association for organizing their communities. In Cuba, the association with the Catholic Church took the form of *cabildos* dedicated to a Catholic saint and an African cultural group, or *nación*.[56] In Lagos, the Aguda from both Cuba and Brazil, organized themselves under the umbrella of the Catholic cathedral found in Campos Square, which they designed and built themselves.[57] Thus, religious association, as understood through Catholicism and *orisha* worship by diasporic Yoruba, was a pivotal way in which the members of this transatlantic community transformed themselves. By associating through religion, they were able to create a framework for developing cultural and material resources that helped them make a place for themselves in their new homes. Yet their religious associations and civic groups also reminded them that they came from the multiple and converging homelands of Yorubaland and Cuba.

Mixing Yoruba and Afrolatino Cultures in Lagos

> They do. Like Bo[a], they call it Bo[a].[58] They do it.
> ... The Bo[a], yeah.... They do it in the, in the night.
> That *Boa*, sometimes, in the, with the sun-up, with the mother of the Yoruba, [the] *Italosha*[59]—I know that.
>
> —Mrs. Aderemi Gooding-King[60]

The deeply remembered connection to *orisha* worship in Bahia and Lagos is especially exemplified in the nineteenth-century travels of the Bamgboshe family.[61] This legacy illustrates the way in which the members of the Aguda community reestablished their "Yoruba-ness" by asserting their diasporic identity.[62] This is a process signaling a diasporic continuation of the assertion of Yoruba identity that also has been the instrument for asserting *cubanidad* and Brazilian-ness. For example, the Songo Egungun, or ancestor masquerade that is performed and displayed at Lagos is of Brazilian, Candomblé origins.[63] The *ile*, or house of worship of the masquerade, was established and is maintained by the Bamgboshe family, which was associated with the great temple houses, or *teirreros*, of Brazilian Candomblé in the late nineteenth century.[64] The existence of the *ile* at the Lagos site reveals a poignant cross-diasporic transplantation of this Afro-Atlantic religion. That we find Candomblé in Lagos may be the result of shared experiences of life in different places, bonded to community and identity through religious praxis in intimate spheres.

Whether they are Muslims, *orisha* worshippers, or Christians, people in Nigeria have respected certain official aspects of Yoruba traditional religion. Due the centrality of Ifa divination to Yoruba kingship and traditional medicine, many of the most prominent and important individuals in Lagosian society are trained as *babalawo* (Ifa priests). These respected individuals have played crucial roles throughout Yoruba history, on the continent and in the Yoruba diasporas across the Atlantic.[65] Hilario Campos was identified as a *babalawo* by his granddaughter Mrs. Gooding-King (see chapter 4). This bolstered his credibility and his ability to unite diverse and dispersed Yoruba under the roof of the Cuban Lodge. As a father on multiple levels, but especially on this religious level, he was the perfect moderator of this fluidity. That he spoke little Yoruba and acquired his Ifa training and love for his Lagosian homeland in Cuba is also an apt example of the kind of cross-referencing being explored here. The associations created in Cuba and carried out in Lagos are located within the ongoing cultural work of creating nostalgia, diaspora, and homeland for itinerant Yoruba populations in a transatlantic context. It is also unsurprising, then, that Campos's granddaughters adopt a similar association toward their other, distant homeland, Cuba, in trying to recapture their own historical past and resituate themselves in the Lagosian social landscape. These associations work off each other and point to a larger cycle of reassociation and community formation that has its roots in traditional Yoruba understandings of place and dispersal. The diasporic sensibilities they adopted helped transatlantic Yoruba communities to simultaneously manage various philosophical and religious systems. As Prince Olusí noted about the way religion is lived in a Yoruba family:

> One thing that is significant is that despite all these incursions, some people helped to get it [*orisha* worship] in. You have, over the ages, maintained the

thing. You had some people who have to tally to the religion of their fathers. Who have those who were, you know, were in the two. Who happen to be Christians, they would participate in the religion of their fathers. You know, either their village or their family, who would [say], "Let's go to church." So, you have it in those of us who are Muslims also. There are the people who participate in the Islamic religion, that pray five times a day, fasting and do it, and when it is time for the *egun*, they join in the *egun*, they join at the *ebo*, they *join* the Ifa traditions.

Also, the priests continue to condemn these things, but it has been part of our lives. And it is these [who practice] what I call "the double dealing," and those who stay faithfully with the *orisha* tradition, *that* has kept [traditional] religion to be around to this day. . . . You see, the concept of the Yoruba fathers place[s] the *oba* as, as the head of the community. Apart from being the head of the community, he is also the spiritual symbol of that community. It is their belief that all religion is under his control. That whatever *ocha*[66]—that you worship it for the whole of the community. And you are supposed to [do so] under the *oba*. You are supposed to be accountable to him. Relations, at times, someone who has been worshipping a particular deity moves from one community to another, he reports to the *oba* of the new community. So we repeat, he is an authority, he will not have his festival until he reports to the *oba* and the *oba* sanctions it. And the *oba* himself sees himself as the spiritual head of the community. He will send presents. . . . And during that festival they will pray for the community, they will also pray for the king, they will pray for *everybody*.[67]

As with the Campos family members' recognition of their Cuban patriarch as also being responsible for legitimizing their presence in Lagos as a Yoruba family, the statement by Olusí quoted above reveals a similar process in connection with the religious culture that underlies most Yoruba customs and understandings of the family, home, the individual, and community. Olusí draws on several pivotal components of Yoruba religion and civic society. Even before the arrival of the Aguda in Lagos, traditional *orisha* worship served to hold the community together under the *oba*. The diversity of religious culture found among different ethnic Yoruba related to their needs as distinct historical communities. In this manner, traditional Yoruba religion, as a civic religion, as Jacob Olupona suggests, helps maintain the diversity of communities of faith that fall under the Yoruba ethnic umbrella due to its epistemological framework based on pliability and flexibility.[68] It also, as Olusí adroitly notes, shapes differences into a larger whole.

We find in the account given above that the *oba* behaves as an example of *religious tolerance* and stability. His power traditionally rests on the ability of diverse groups being able to coexist in his territory. Thus, royal ritual work among the Yoruba emphasizes the incorporation of diversity and the achievement of unity, which helps the *oba* to ritually and socially legitimate his power over the range of communities involved. It is easy to see that Hilario Campos, as a Catholic, a Cuban-trained *babalawo*, and a founder of a whole neighborhood in Lagos, himself embodied the kind of religious tolerance and cultural flexibility of an *oba* as described by Olusí. In reality, he could not have adopted any other kind of outlook and still been successful in fulfilling his leadership role in this densely complicated cultural and social context.

As mentioned above, Olupona suggests that "community-ship" is a concept well adapted to Yoruba traditional religion in Oshogbo, Osun State.[69] Originally used to describe quotidian Indian communities by Gerald Lawson, "community-ship" as a concept allows for affiliation within particular yet highly heterogeneous populations. Within Yoruba religious communities, Olupona's adaptation of this concept is especially apt. In Oshogbo, as well as in many cosmopolitan centers of Yoruba extraction, traditional religion acts as an adhesive for a diverse range of communities. As Olusí does, Olupona places the *oba* at the center of this idea of civil religion. The *oba* becomes a magnetic force that keeps an array of Yoruba communities cohesive, celebrating the unique contribution of each to the social mandala.

The imagery of the mandala works well here as a metaphor for the intersection of Yoruba religious culture and civil society, because of the symbol's elegant complexity. Indeed, the beauty of the Yoruba technique for weaving a wide range of social fabrics together acts very much like the visual bricolage of the mandala, which relies on both precision and an overarching continuity. As any piece of a mandala acts as a new and viable center, the frame of reference of Yoruba traditional history converges and merges in a similar fashion. To be more specific, in our above example about the interconnectedness of traditional religion and royalty, we see that the discursive models that make the *oba* an epicenter of social action also allow for renderings that may shift the focal point of activity.

At the heart of competently possessing one's social place in this world is the ability to shift and reframe narratives and performances of social power through persuasive polemics—as history, song, divination, and so forth—to create new centers. These new spaces provide platforms for encounter and expression. Thus, among the Aguda in Lagos, especially, the practice of "Yoruba" traditional religion has been an exercise in mitigating the range of transatlantic platforms and perspectives as adherents have encountered each other and new contexts. The Campos family is no exception here, and its members' resilient claim to the multifaceted worlds that created their unique identity indeed resonates as characterizing a rich, living branch of the Yoruba and Cuban diasporas found worldwide. In chapter 4, we explore this legacy and the influence of religion and Cuban Aguda identity on the Lagosian landscape and civil society.[70]

4

Situating Lagosian, Caribbean, and Latin American Diasporas

> The Brazilians began to arrive in Lagos and in Ouidah at the end of the eighteenth century.... They maintained, on the Guinea Coast, Brazilian traditions: patriarchal organization of the family, architecture of homes, devotion to the cult of Senhor do Bonfin, celebrations, dances, and until recently, the Portuguese language. Were the Cubans able to make their mark with the Brazilians?
>
> —Pérez de la Riva, *Documentos para la historia de las gentes sin historia*, 30

> But they [did] come when my mother [was] alive. They [did] come from [the Cuban] embassy. And, when they walked into here—they were here, in the compound . . . at the lodge, that time my mother [was] alive. That summer they were here, she had seen them—and my mother [was] so happy. So happy that she, she wept! I remember. Ah-ha . . . that's life.
>
> —Mrs. Aderemi Gooding-King, granddaughter of Aguda Hilario Campos

Pérez de la Riva answers his own question about the Cuban presence in Lagos, Nigeria, in the negative, citing a lack of "evidence of Cuban culture" in Lagos.[1] However, as seen in the work of Cuban historian Rodolfo Sarracino and from my own interviews with Aguda of Cuban heritage there *is* evidence of Cuban contributions to the culture of the Aguda in Lagos.[2] Indeed, the very name of Campos Square, where the Cuban Lodge is located, shows that an entire area in Lagos is named after a Cuban repatriate.[3] Though Brazilian cultural aspects tend to dominate some visible forms of Aguda social performance (like the Boa masquerade held in Lagos every year), the emergence of the Aguda community as a whole represents a unique synthesis of many social and cultural diasporic groups. For example, among the immigrant groups themselves, intermixing occurred between Saro and Aguda repatriates, through marriage and business alliances, at various points of entry into this part of the Afro-Atlantic diaspora.

Yet dissecting the Aguda's cultural mélange into different, "always" separable parts is an artificial exercise. The community works because of its ability to create new combinations and alliances based on commonalities and differences. As we will see below, community leaders like Chief Bamgboshe Martins and Mrs. Ola Vincent share a sense of history, place, and experience in Lagos, although the former is of Brazilian and the latter of Cuban extraction within the Aguda community.

The main difference between Cuban and Brazilian Aguda, from Pérez de la Riva's perspective, is the socioeconomic status of Brazilian Aguda. Although he does speak to the cultural legacies Brazilians brought with them to Lagos in the opening quote above, he tends to focus on the status and prestige displayed by their visible success.[4] These conclusions are not strange, because up until the present study, scholars have tended to focus mainly on the Brazilian side of the Aguda population. Historians and cultural critics argue that the Brazilian returnees were people of money, with a long history of transnational interaction and trade between Lagos and Bahia.[5] The Brazilian side of the Lagosian–Latin American diaspora managed adroitly the admixture of wealth, prestige, high-status religious culture (for example, becoming *babalawo*), and skilled craftsmanship (becoming masons, architects), on both the Lagosian and Bahian sides of the Atlantic. The movement of this kind of cultural capital shaped in its process the places for the stopping posts of this diaspora, such as the hotel, Casa Da Silva on Queen's Terrace owned by Anthony Da Silva in Southampton, England, which housed Havana Lagosians Lorenzo Clarke and Martin Marino on their way back to Lagos.[6]

Pérez de la Riva still characterizes the repatriates as Afrolatinos. Both Cubans and Brazilians of Yoruba origin returned to Africa with a history of socialization and acculturation from their Latin American homes. Pérez de la Riva dates the beginning of the return in the late eighteenth century rather than the nineteenth century, which agrees with the findings of recent research about populations in the Bight of Benin.[7] The dates for the return of Cubans reflected in Pérez de la Riva's work and my own, 1830 to the 1860s, pose questions about the length of time and depth of contact between Afrocubano communities and the Bight of Benin.[8] Mainly, the social settings for these transatlantic voyages existed in diasporic contexts: Havana, Bahia, and Lagos. These milieus represented centers that shaped the ways that Afrolatinos came into their own in their new homes.

The lives of the Aguda break in midsentence in a long historical conversation between diasporas. The agency and innovation of *emancipados* and slaves in Havana in the nineteenth century created communities that moved through the cracks of the diasporic routes created by transatlantic slavery. Their alternate histories resituate the idea of the Atlantic world in profound ways. Social forces like slavery and colonialism impacted the lives of people and limited the choices open to them in creating their worlds and their communities.[9] Yet another look at how these choices were employed by the Havana Lagosians and the Aguda shows that people always had ways of re-creating their communities and also of expressing and recapturing their community histories. These folk and grassroots understandings of people's pasts usually highlight the ways in which these communities resisted, reformed, and resituated the terms of their own existence against what seemed impossible odds.

In this particular context, grassroots exchanges of communication had a conduit in individuals and communities that were instrumental in developing a sense of pan-Yoruba national identity and cultural innovation in Cuba, Brazil, and Nigeria. The alliances between these individuals and communities represented a form of agency and cross-dialogue in the African diaspora based on alternative discourses of identity. For example, the creolization and cross-fertilization of what were recognized to be Yoruba religious language and ritual contexts within an American context allowed for new modes of being "Yoruba." The religious cultures of both Santería and Candomblé allowed for conversations that included Native American, Asian, and other African ethnic groups, like those from the Congo, into a "Yoruba" worldview. This worldview was already expansive in Africa, but it also grew in different and particular ways of expression according to changing contexts in Latin America, as it did in Africa. What was unique, perhaps, about the Latin American versions of "Yoruba-ness" was their special connection to the national cultures of Cuba and Brazil, in which they represented "authentic" African folk and folklore.[10] These discourses of identity were not necessarily attached to tropes of resistance to or compliance with European hegemony in people's reimagination of their Yoruba identities. Rather, the cultural work of Latin American Yoruba identity formation highlighted the multifaceted nature of the communities' worldviews. Diasporic sensibilities were used in discourses that helped communities to reorient and reinvent themselves by using memory and a remembered shared past. It is important to investigate how these Afrolatino communities imagine and perform their shared past, as Africans and as Afrolatinos, since these populations have a profound effect on the way Africa, the Caribbean, and Latin America are currently located in the global imagination.

Memory, History, and the Imagination

This chapter deals with the ways in which the members of the Campos family remember their shared history and the role that the idea of Cuba plays in creating their identity in relation to other Yoruba in Lagos. Throughout my work, I have used the idea of the imagination, understood as a kind of social and individual work, in different registers—as transnational, transatlantic,

Figure 1. The Cuban Lodge, Campos Square, Lagos, 1999, photograph by author

national, local, and global.[11] At the root of the relationship between history and memory is the role of the imagination in the range of ways in which we recollect the past. Scholars dealing with history and the philosophy of history have grappled with the problem of memory, time, and narration.[12] But perhaps it is Paul Ricoeur who gets to the fundamental aspects of this dilemma in terms of the way in which history, memory, and the imagination are temporally conceptualized in Occidental philosophy.[13]

Ricoeur locates the source of distrust of memory in both Plato and Aristotle, and this distrust is at the heart of the Western historian's struggle in working with the past in the present. The rhetorical issue is the presence of the absent, and the present representation of an absent thing, which is the problematic of memory because it is located, in Plato, according to Ricoeur, in the imagination.[14] For Aristotle, again following Ricoeur's interpretation, the representation of a thing formerly perceived has as its problem the issue of the image within the act of remembering, and this is partly the historian's dilemma with regard to memory and the past. This dilemma with regard to the imagination for the historian is apparent on the microlevel of "reading" the archive, and on the macrolevel of narrating that history through writing that requires on some level the use of the imagination. Imagination is a cognitive tool that is necessary for recollecting and re-creating the past, because in the end, writing the past is based on rhetorical reimagining. The moment or event has to be reconstructed because it belongs to the past. As Ricoeur puts it, "Historiography itself, let us already say, will not succeed in setting aside the continually derided and continually reasserted conviction that the final referent of memory remains the past, whatever the pastness of the past may signify."[15] Yet both the image of the past and the act of recollection of the past are held to be suspect in Western philosophical thought. In thinking about the remembered history of the Aguda, represented by the Campos family's experiences presented below, we have a combination of registers, scales, notions of memory, the past, and history that represent Occidental, Yoruba, and Caribbean dilemmas of "pastness."[16]

Ricoeur finds that for Plato memories are ordered in an aesthetic that includes misremembering and fantasy.[17] It is important for us to consider this here, in thinking about communities like the Aguda as engaging in tropic kinds of remembrance. As Johannes Fabian has explored in a range of ways, this kind of remembering can be done with a certain amount of play and satire in the process of creating history from the "ground up."[18] Thus, there is an acknowledgment on the part of Afro-creolized communities like the Aguda that their tropic register may contradict official paradigms of history. What is important for these communities, then, are the kinds of memory that form a viable context for sustaining the community through the work of the social imagination in "remembering" the past (or present). This necessarily includes certain kinds of forgetting or misimprinting of the images of memory that

Plato found central to the act of remembering the past.[19] Thus, the memories of the Aguda that we will discuss below illustrate a kind of communal work that incorporates, denies, and resituates understood notions of the past in terms of transatlantic identity and the transatlantic diaspora. This forces us to ask questions such as whose past, whose history, whose memory, whose notion of time are being used to understand the relationship between remembering and the past. My work with the Aguda and with Afro-Cuban religious culture forces me to say that a combination of registers and scales is at work when communities reconstruct their past.

This brief consideration of some of the core dilemmas with regard to the relationship of memory to the imagination and its implications for the reconstruction of history shows us only one set of ways in which to consider the rebuilding of the past. Indeed, the notion of the past can be constructed in multiple ways even within the Occidental discourse.[20] Tied to the way in which the imagination can render any reproduction is the notion of aesthetics and how these aesthetics order the meaning of such renderings. These renderings can be "read" in multiple ways that are also governed by aesthetics. The question of whose aesthetics mirrors the question of whose past.

This is especially so for the intersecting aesthetic planes of the artist who creates an art object and for the audience when the artist and the audience come from different epistemological and cultural frameworks. Art historian Rowland Abiodun is concerned with precisely this dilemma in looking at Yoruba notions of aesthetics and a "quotidian" art criticism that develops from these aesthetics.[21] The historical reconstruction of the meaning of certain ritual art objects, like the sacred rattle, the *iroke*, found in Ifa divination, by academic art historians clashes with or ignores the important work of cultural deconstruction carried out by ritual leaders like *babalawo* in analyzing and using the art.[22] Abiodun critiques the academic art historian's arrogance in assuming that his/her "universalizing" epistemologies and aesthetics are neutral in order to control the "disciplinary discourse" and the meaning that is exported to the world about art objects like the *iroke*.[23] However, aesthetics that merge, clash, or coexist in tension are often played out within the material culture itself, creating pieces that come from a "hybrid" worldview.[24]

Narratives, like material culture, have a life that circulates outside the intention and perspectives of their producers.[25] In the realms of popular culture and "traditional culture" from African perspectives, we see overlap, invention, and play that are both self-conscious and unintended as work on popular theater and public ritual discusses.[26] The narratives about family memories that the Cuban Aguda related to me during my ethnographic fieldwork display this kind of complicated discourse. Their recollections reflect a field of reference that allows them to perform within an aesthetic of identity-play that encompasses Cuban-ness and Yoruba-ness in shifting ways. On a larger scale, the interplay between Occidental, African, and Caribbean aesthetics in their reflections and memories mirrors the struggle over the "meaning" of the cultural history of the Aguda for the outside world. The work of the folklorist here is to use these narrative performances to insert a quotidian historical framework into the larger meaning of the history of the Aguda that necessarily explores an understanding of the community's significance on its own terms.[27]

This search for significance is especially so in terms of the artistry and play of oral literature, or orature, that people use in telling their own historical narratives in Africa.[28] The very languages used to express the narratives found within a community are themselves used and constructed in a self-reflexive manner that is subject to critique by the community at large. That is, the person speaking about important subjects, like community history, is expected to speak well and within an aesthetic code that gives respect and authority to those who do so.[29] What we see in the case of my Aguda collaborators in reconstructing their family history with performances of their narrative of memory is a "competence" that demonstrates their authority in the community as a whole.[30] In other words, their ability to speak well and adeptly carries the weight of their own personal pride and prestige and that of the community.

The Cuban Aguda in Lagos

The only major historical work about the Campos family and the Cuban Lodge in Lagos was written by Cuban historian Rodolfo Sarracino.[31] Sarracino's work brings to light the various migrations back to Africa from Afro-Cubans of Yoruba ancestry that occurred as a *voluntary* process after 1844.[32] That is, Sarracino agrees with Pérez de la Riva's assertion about the repatriates to Lagos not being part of the forced expulsions that occurred in Cuba after La Escalera.[33] Where Sarracino moves away from Pérez de la Riva is in his findings of Cubans "leaving their cultural mark on the west [African] coast."[34] Sarracino dedicates one chapter of *Los que volvieron a Africa* to the Campos family in Lagos and Mantanzas, documenting their bicoastal nature through their letters and photographs. His work laid the preliminary foundations for my fieldwork conducted in Lagos among the descendants of Hilario Campos.

My fieldwork with Campos's granddaughters, Mrs. Catherine Aderemi Gooding-King and Mrs. Ola Vincent, revealed the imaginative and tropic aspects of diasporic remembering and history making that were not considered by Sarracino. I believe that my focus on folkloristics and transatlantic legacies yielded unique kinds of questions and answers that dealt primarily with the intersection between memory and oral history. The four major areas my consultants emphasized were the following: (1) the remembering of cultural markers, like Spanish-language retention in childhood at the Cuban Lodge; (2) the erection of tombstones commemorating the Cuban ancestry of the Campos family at Ikoyi Cemetery; (3) the extent of cultural admixture among other kinds of repatriates with the Campos family and with the Aguda in Lagos; and (4) evidence of creolized *orisha* traditions and folk Catholicism among Aguda returnees.

The fieldwork with Mrs. Gooding-King was conducted in Lagos, Nigeria, at the Cuban Lodge, 40 Ogunlami Street, Campos Square, in 1999 and again in 2001.[35] My conversations with Mrs. Ola Vincent took place in her home on Victoria Island in Lagos in 2001. My role in speaking to the sisters was that of a young researcher, also of Cuban background, who wanted to learn about their family in particular. They were generous in answering my questions and in leading me toward areas of importance that would otherwise have been difficult for an outsider to perceive. For example, they both stressed to me the importance of commemorating the Cuban heritage of their grandfather in the form of a tombstone, a memorial piece of public culture, which the family went to some expense to create shortly before my second visit to Lagos. I will discuss this in more detail later. But the point I want to make here is that as a folklorist engaged in re-creating aspects of their family oral history, I saw the sisters as collaborators in many respects and deferred to their authority over how to impart their narratives of home and community.[36] This created a situation in which I was shifting modes of perspective and analysis, as most ethnographers engaged in some kind of reflexive fieldwork try to do.[37] I believe that where we all met, in thinking about Cuba as an idea, a distant emblem that informed all three of our identities but was unattainable in many ways, was a place of intersection mirroring a transnational imaginary about the island that can be found across time and diaspora.[38] Below is the outline of the remembered family history of Hilario Campos obtained from my interviews.

According to Vincent, Hilario Campos's father was born in Lagos and was taken to Cuba as a slave. Roman Hilario Campos was born in Matanzas, Cuba, in 1878 and died in Lagos on December 14, 1941. While in Cuba, six children were born to the family. Two of the Campos sisters, Serafina Akitoyi and Johanna Cicelia Munis, who were born in Cuba, also returned to Lagos. They both stayed at or near the Cuban Lodge during the childhood of the Gooding sisters. Mrs. Anastasia Gooding, the mother of Mrs. Gooding-King and Mrs. Vincent, was born in Lagos on October 5, 1907, and died on April 19, 1994, at eighty-seven years of age. Mrs. Vincent and Mrs. Gooding-King remember growing up in the Cuban Lodge among Spanish-speaking family members. The language spoken at home gave them a sense of cultural distinctness that they speak about with pride and nostalgia.

From my interviews with Mrs. Ola Vincent, it appears that Hilario Campos returned to Lagos via London, like many of the other returnees from Cuba.

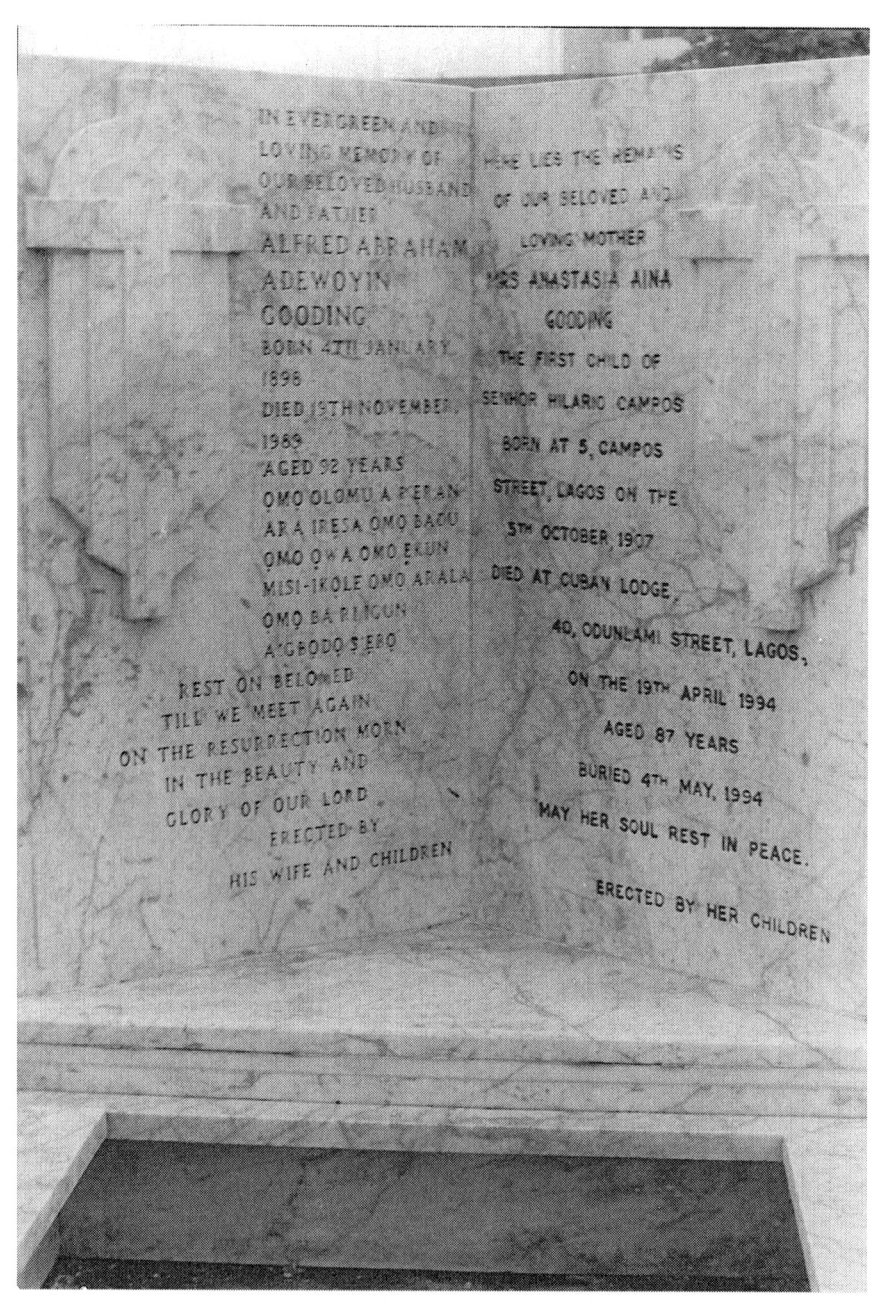

Figure 2. Grave of Mrs. Anastasia Gooding, Ikoyi Cemetery, Lagos

Figure 3. Grave of Hilario Campos and Johana Cicelia Munis, Ikoyi Cemetery, Lagos

Figure 4. Mrs. Ola Vincent, granddaughter of Hilario Campos, at the grave of her aunt and grandfather, Ikoyi Cemetery, Lagos

Recalling the Casa Da Silva in Southampton mentioned earlier, we see that there was an organized set of routes that families utilized to return to Africa. These routes are remembered as significant details of the Campos family history as other friends and family members met and stayed in London during their travels.[39] Thus, London seems to have been an important point of convergence for returnees. The most significant aspect to keep in mind here, however, was the multifaceted nature of the travels home. In the retelling of their grandfather's journey, the sisters reaffirmed for me that in remembering a diasporic legacy all the stops along the road are important.[40]

Cuban Cultural Markers among the Aguda

One of the most striking aspects missing from both Sarracino's and Pérez de la Riva's considerations of the Cuban Aguda in Lagos is the notion of cyclical cultural flows, especially in terms of religious identity, in their unique Atlantic context.[41] Neither historian really delves into the ways in which Cuban Aguda negotiated their multiple and shifting identities, as families and as a subgroup within a larger heterogeneous community of Lagos, by using creolized "Yoruba" sensibilities from abroad. That is, the cultural tools that both the Brazilian and the Cuban Aguda shared in Lagos reflect a larger set of transatlantic symbols that communicate power and prestige across borders. These symbols of prestige often call upon the important imagery of traditional religion that still legitimates political power among the Yoruba today.[42]

Consequently, many of my conversations with Mrs. Aderemi Gooding-King and Mrs. Ola Vincent revolved especially around their perception of their Cuban ancestry. The best answers came as a result of focusing on how they remembered their difference from, and similarity to, other "Yoruba" living around them in Lagos. Not unsurprisingly, the admixture already found among Lagosian ethnic Yoruba, in terms of their origin elsewhere in "Yorubaland," created a template for understanding their own place among mixed migrant populations.

One Yoruba concept that may be useful is the notion of *gbe asa*, carrying culture from one place to another. This is a notion that can apply to people keeping their customs after movement to Lagos both from the Nigerian hinterland and from across the Atlantic. Customs may be acquired, changed, and readjusted in the Lagosian milieu. However, the recognition of certain attributes as "belonging" to a particular culture is a significant way in which communities reassemble what is understood as a shifting paradigm. One of the main "markers" that allowed the sisters to speak about this kind of cultural and social differentiation was the Spanish language use surrounding them during their childhood. The following interview excerpts, first from

Mrs. Aderemi Gooding-King and then from Mrs. Ola Vincent, provide good examples of this process:

> Solimar Otero: Did they, did they speak Spanish?
> Aderemi Gooding-King: Oh yes they did! . . . Yes, with my mom. When they speak in the Yoruba language, they only know a little, little [Yoruba]. . . . [Hilario Campos spoke Spanish] Together with the sister, with his sister.

> Mrs. Ola Vincent: But, when we were small, we don't know that we belong to any foreign country, we know of Lagos. . . . So it was when we are, you know, growing gradually, that then we know that our great-grandfather is from Cuba, from Brazil, from Sierra Leone, from this, from that. . . . You know, my own grandfather, Hilario Campos. His sister, Mrs. Akitoyi, Serafina. So, they used to speak in Spanish. . . . But we don't know much about this. And, since we are young we don't know that it's going to be of good or benefit to us. . . .

> Solimar Otero: And, would they know what they are saying? Did, did your mother know Spanish?
> Mrs. Ola Vincent: Little.
> Solimar Otero: She would *hear* it though.
> Lola Bamgboshe Martins: Of course, she could *hear* it.[43]

There are several observations to be made from the sisters' and Bamgboshe Martins's responses above. One thing that is clear is that Hilario Campos spoke Spanish in the presence of Mrs. Ola Vincent and Mrs. Gooding-King to their mother, but mainly to their great-aunts, Serafina and Cicelia. All three of the elders of the Campos family were born in Cuba and came to Lagos in the late nineteenth century. After establishing the Cuban Lodge, Hilario and his sisters used the lodge as a family home and a workshop. The use of Spanish within the lodge was an important familial activity that made an impression on the sisters. Though neither one of them retained a knowledge of Spanish, they certainly were aware of the fact that it belonged to them in unique ways that made their family distinct from others. They knew there was something different, "foreign" Mrs. Ola Vincent called it, about their background. And they knew that something was operating all around them, creating a backdrop to their childhood. That these two sisters have held on to the notion of a Cuban Aguda ancestry (we see this in the pride shown in the erection of the gravestones at Ikoyi Cemetery) well into their sixties and seventies shows that though they did not acquire Spanish, they did not forget it as a significant marker of their own family's difference and identity.

Mrs. Ola Vincent's comments also specifically indicate that this difference included an admixture in her memory. When she says, "So it was when we are, you know, growing gradually, that then we know that our great-grandfather is from Cuba, from Brazil, from Sierra Leone, from this, from that," we see that she remembers an international diasporic admixture that provided the household context of her childhood. Her acceptance of the confluence of cultures and languages in the Campos homestead reveals the family's tolerance of others. It is also important to keep in mind that though this particular family was unique in its Cuban-ness, such a diversity of ethnicity, language, and religion in Lagosian households was not unusual. Rather, the Aguda added their own brand of admixture to a larger urban pool of conglomerate communities. These can especially be seen in the Popo, or neighborhood enclaves that roughly marked the location of ethnic, occupational, and class-related settlements of diverse groups in metropolitan Lagos. In reimagining Mrs. Ola Vincent's childhood at the Cuban Lodge as part of this larger, densely heterogeneous context, we perhaps come closer to understanding how cultural differentiation thrived through the change and admixture found in the application of "diasporic sensibilities" by this transatlantic Afro-Cuban/Yoruba family.

Another very interesting identity marker that the Campos example illustrates is the sense of African, specifically Lagosian, identity also developed by the family while in Cuba. Though born in Cuba, Hilario, Serafina, and Cicelia were brought to Cuba because the family obviously felt a strong connection to their Yoruba background, like Havana's Lagosians, and thus repatriated to Lagos. We see that this occurred in a second-generation context, with the experience of the homeland being relegated to the remembered culture of the childhood home. This process occurred in the cross-diasporic context of both Havana and Lagos for the Campos family.

Hilario Campos was a young man with limited Yoruba language skills when he settled in Lagos. He must have acquired a strong association with his African identity in Cuba that fueled his desire to come back home. We must also remember that Hilario's father was taken to Cuba as a slave, and that perhaps this explains the depth of the association with Yoruba culture, and home as Africa, that persisted within the family. Of particular interest here are Mrs. Vincent's comments about what she remembers her grandfather saying about his African ancestry:

> Solimar Otero: Do you think that Hilario Campos and your great-grandfather felt the sense of being Lagosian [while in Cuba]?
> Mrs. Ola Vincent: Lagosian, yes, yes. Yes. . . . [It's] *not that I think so! They said it!*—and what we are trying to do now is to find out [more information about the family] from Cuba, you know. And I don't know how we can do that. [emphasis added][44]

Here we find that Mrs. Vincent recalls a very strong sense of association with Yoruba culture, and with Lagos in particular, on the part of her grandfather, Hilario Campos. Of interest also is the way Mrs. Vincent associates the nostalgia her grandfather may have felt for Lagos while in Cuba with her own family's search for its Cuban connections. We see a parallel situation, in that neither Hilario Campos nor Mrs. Ola Vincent were actually born in the homelands with which they seek to reconnect. It is in the milieu of family history, personal folk narratives, and borrowed memory that desires for connecting across diasporas emerge and are nurtured. In the historical context of the Atlantic world in the nineteenth century, this sense of a bicoastal family history fueled the very real search for reconnections, the building of new associations, and the commemoration of the past for both the Aguda and the Afrolatinos across the Atlantic.[45] In looking at the pride and detail that went into the erection of the newer gravestones for the Campos family (see below), we see the family's need to mark their distinct history as Aguda and their unique past in the context of the larger Lagosian public sphere. Here, distinctness works to relocate the space and place of the Campos family within larger social networks. The markers serve as a sort of shared community property.

In exploring the transatlantic ramifications of this kind of social imagination, and the type of work such remembering makes possible, one would have to imagine a similar sense of difference and cultural amalgamation provided the larger social backdrop of Cuba's African communities that emerged in the nineteenth century. Again, in recalling the cacophony of African ethnicities, even distinct Yoruba communities, that existed in Cuba, we see that a similar heterogeneous sense of admixture must have created the context for the formation of distinct subgroups on the island. As already mentioned, these emerging Afrocubano identities were marked by the establishment of Black associations and *cabildos* in Cuba, and particularly in Havana. Similarly, there was the thrust toward nation building in reassembling a diverse set of communities in the name of a loosely unified Cuban and Yoruba identity. Multiple nationalisms were carried by the same groups (such as the Campos family), since these associations were incorporative and fluid in nature. The shift in frames of reference—for example, the shift to being Cuban in Lagos from being Lagosian in Cuba—reveals one way in which this diasporic community managed the wide range of identities it laid claim to.

Such processes operate over time, as in the Campos family's nostalgia and imagining of distant homelands being carried across generations. This kind of longing is a particular sort of recuperation of memory that is not necessarily owned by any one individual but by a community as a whole. It would be difficult to pinpoint one set of origins of such romantic associations with place and memory. However, we can locate the pattern of association that was redeveloped across the different temporal and geographic sites of this branch of the Aguda diaspora. In my second set of interviews with Mrs. Gooding-King, at the Cuban Lodge in 2001, despite her advanced age, she expressed a desire to "return home" to Cuba—a place that obviously operated in her imagination as a historical beacon of sorts. In the following excerpt from my interviews, she indicates her desire to go to Cuba after receiving a visit from a delegation from the Cuban Embassy:

> Mrs. Gooding-King: They [the Cuban delegation] come here to visit me. Telling me how everybody over there [in Cuba] wants to see me. Bringing [a] present to me. Telling me that I should come back *home* in time. To come and enjoy the land over there. . . . Yes, back home. Over there with my children.[46]

In following up with Mrs. Gooding-King about the meaning of these comments it was clear that she was making connections to a past that she had come to own as hers. The real familial ties, the memories of growing up different in Lagos in the Cuban Lodge, and the reassertion of these ties to Cuba by visits from a Cuban delegation and researchers like myself are all factors that contributed to her vision of Cuba as a sort of primordial home. In diasporic communities like that of the Aguda in Lagos, different modalities of the notion of home often operate in confluence with each other. The fact that Mrs. Gooding-King layered her notions of home, in terms of both temporality and place, reaffirms the tenacity of this process. It is ironic, yet fitting, that Mrs. Gooding-King indicated her desire for a reunion with the descendants of the Campos family in Cuba while sitting in the living room of the Cuban Lodge, located in Campos Square, in Lagos, Nigeria. In an extension of many kinds of cultural congruencies, Mrs. Gooding-King's wishes provided yet another instance in which remembering and dreaming work together to bring two ends of a diaspora together conceptually. Though this process of association relies heavily on the social imagination, there are also concrete markers of commemoration of the cultural heritage of the Cuban Aguda. In the next section we look at the gravestones placed by the Campos family in Ikoyi Cemetery, which constituted a kind of public historical record that contextualized and solidified the conceptual processes described above for the family, and for other Lagosian Aguda as well.[47]

Cuban Aguda Public History: Ikoyi Cemetery

One major component of the Campos family's remembered history that was emphasized to me was the burial sites of relatives in Ikoyi Cemetery. Hilario Campos, J. Cicelia Munis, and Anastasia Gooding are all buried here. Campos and Munis share a gravesite, and the history of their journey from Cuba to Lagos is inscribed on the tombstones.[48] The grave of Mrs. Anastasia Gooding, the mother of Mrs. Ola Vincent and Mrs. Aderemi Gooding-King, also bears a long and telling marker commemorating her life history in relation to the extended family. In visiting the site with Mrs. Vincent, she recalled the family's effort to make their history public in this manner. Upon taking a photo, I remember Mrs. Vincent's proud pose next to the marker of her grandfather and great-aunt. Her demeanor clearly indicated the deep sense of connection she feels with this part of her family's history. The graves' open, lengthy display of the Cuban background of the relatives buried there reveal that the Campos family sees its Aguda heritage as an important part, not only of the family's past but of Lagosian public history as a whole.

Another significant aspect of the graves is their location. Ikoyi is a part of Lagos where people of relatively high status live. The location of the graves in this area indicates a high-status association for the Aguda in the Lagosian social world. The use of Holy Cross Cathedral for the funeral services of these relatives also indicates a high level of social status for the family. The cathedral is located on Campos Square and its congregation consists of people in relatively good social and economic positions.[49] Though Mrs. Gooding-King and Mrs. Vincent are both Anglicans—due to the religious affiliation of their father, a Saro—they openly displayed pride in their family's association with the Catholic cathedral and its congregation. Indeed, Mrs. Anastasia Gooding remained a Catholic all her life, even after marrying a Saro. Cultural and religious mixing was a frequent component of the high-status repatriate families that helped to build "modern" Lagos, both literally and socially.[50] We will now look at how cultural mixing between the repatriate Aguda, both of Cuban and Brazilian origin, and the Sierra Leonean Saros figured in the Campos family. Social status and prestige are highly important markers of identity formation for all of these interrelated communities.

Cultural Mixing between the Aguda and the Saros

Intermarriage between Brazilian and Cuban Aguda was commonplace in Lagos. Adding to this admixture of repatriate families is the incorporation of Saro returnees into families like the Campos family. The mother of Mrs. Vincent and Mrs. Gooding-King married a Saro, Mr. Gooding, after being raised in the Cuban Lodge. His own family compound was at Itabalogun[51]—in the Saro area of Lagos.

The intermixing of Sierra Leonean and repatriate Cuban culture created a unique atmosphere at the Cuban Lodge. Besides being a living space, the lodge served as an artisans' workshop, run by Hilario Campos's son-in-law, Mr. Gooding. The workshop attracted a range of people as buyers and operated in different genres—such as *ese*, Yoruba traditional sculpture, and batik cloth. This kind of activity made the lodge a high-profile meeting space where the Campos family felt compelled to set an example and shine. Mrs. Gooding-King remembers the approach of her family toward the more public aspects of her home at the Cuban Lodge:

And, they [her mother and grandfather] are careful of how they dress. Particularly, they were very clean. They didn't stop, [they were] really very hardworking people. . . . The building was used for living here. . . . And we have a little shop, [a] workshop. He [Mrs. Gooding-King's father] applied himself in art. Second, [in] batik. In African sculpture, *ese*. My father sold to *oyinbo*, mostly, batik.[52]

Mrs. Gooding-King echoes the sentiments earlier expressed by Olusí with regard to the way the Aguda were perceived. They both emphasize a kind of work ethic that seemed to characterize the community. The international flavor of the Cuban Lodge provided an appropriate stage for the group's representation of itself to outsiders. Along with other kinds of Yoruba artists and visitors, art aficionados interested in traditional Yoruba artwork, particularly the European *oyinbo*, came into contact with the Campos family here in their home. One could imagine the environment of Mrs. Gooding-King's and Mrs. Vincent's childhood as filled with an array of languages and cultures. It is also important to note that at the Campos's workshop, it was repatriate Saros and Aguda who were representing Yoruba culture through traditional art genres in a context of diasporic production. Other workshops and vernacular spaces of art and architectural production were commonly associated with Aguda of both Cuban and Brazilian extraction.[53]

One question that remains is how the process of cultural mixing between Brazilian and Cuban Aguda occurred in Lagos. What would be the most appropriate way to grasp the multifaceted and geographically dispersed spaces of this copenetration? Previous literature on the subject suggests that the process must have occurred on various diasporic fronts—in Southampton, Havana, and Lagos.[54] Looking at the Campos family as a prominent example of this process within the context of the larger Lagosian Aguda community, we find that over the years the Brazilian and Cuban subsections of repatriates have indeed merged in multiple ways. Selective association by both parties has allowed for the emergence of an identifiable, collective Aguda community that embodies them both. The display of cultural customs and public performances are the sites of cultural production that most obviously articulate this emergence. Of particular note are the Boa, Christmas, and Easter masquerades performed by the Aguda community as a whole. As Mrs. Gooding-King indicates, "Masquerades, yes . . . well, they would celebrate here, at Christmas time and Easter time . . . dressing [up in] the different types. And dancing—from Cuba, and Brazil, yeah—yes, samba. There are many. They are in a group."[55]

Gooding-King's statements that "There are many" and that "They are in a group" illustrate the points made above about the complementary processes of differentiation and emergence in Aguda public performances in Lagos. The focus on dress, dance, and the different kinds of performances offered at the masquerades shows that these acts are culturally dense with ethnic coding. The redistribution of difference here is particularly managed by familial lineages.

For example, the family of Mr. Lola Bamgboshe Martins represents one of the oldest lineages of the Brazilian Aguda (not to mention the Nago Yoruba in Bahia, Brazil), responsible for conducting Aguda masquerades in Lagos.[56] It was clear that the position of Lola Martins as a "torch bearer" of diasporic traditions, on both sides of the Atlantic, was recognized as an important leadership role for *both* Cuban and Brazilian Aguda. He held the important traditional titles of Baba Egungun and Ajolojo Egungun of Lagos, indicating that he was the patriarch of the Egungun masquerades of Lagos. Indeed, Gooding-King remarked enthusiastically to me that Lola Martins was "her brother"—a term of endearment that indicated both respect and a deeply felt connection to the Bamgboshe family. Her role, as a Campos, paralleled that of Mr. Bamgboshe Martins, in that they both represented the living descendants of two of the most important poles of the Cuban and Brazilian historical legacy of the Aguda in Lagos. The Cuban and Brazilian Aguda have socially bolstered each other in ways that have recognized and respected the cultural diversity and unique contributions of their different diasporic origins in Latin America. One major adhesive readily apparent in this process was the respect for Yoruba traditional religion displayed in Cuba and Brazil in the late nineteenth century and used as a means to create different kinds of national communities in these diasporas. In the section below, we discuss the Latin American traditions of Candomblé and Santería as major means by which the Brazilian and Cuban Aguda have recognized in each other a mutual understanding of a unique kind of Yoruba and also Afrolatino identity.

Religion among the Aguda and Other Lagosians

> My grandfather [Hilario Campos] is in Ifa; they worshipped Ifa. . . . For Ifa, an Ifa priest. He did worship Ifa—He wore the, the white cloth.[57]
>
> —Mrs. Aderemi Gooding-King,
> personal interview, August 7, 1999, Lagos

As discussed above in regard to the Campos and Bamgboshe families, being "transatlantic" was an important part of their diasporic identity as Aguda living in Lagos. For Cuban and Brazilian Yoruba, their pan-diasporic identity increased and deepened their adeptness at boundary play. Religious culture is one realm of daily existence where this kind of play flourishes.

Orisha traditions, in both Brazil and Cuba, are cultural milieus in which Yoruba-ness is repeatedly enunciated.[58] As already mentioned, Bamgboshe Martins asserted to me that Brazilian-ness, and Candomblé practices especially, operated as another means to express Yoruba cultural ties in both Brazil and Nigeria.[59] The semiotic language of *orisha* worship works as an idiom for Afrolatino, especially Cuban and Brazilian, nationality and identity in both contemporary and historical contexts that characterize the fluctuating worlds of these diasporic populations.[60]

The quotidian element of *orisha* observance, as a public culture and a civil religion, has found its way back to Lagos in Brazilian and Cuban forms. Afrolatino communities left traces of their observances of *orisha* traditions in Cuba, Brazil, and Nigeria in the form of *orisha* and Catholic devotion, civic art, and personal histories. One interesting example comes from an 1859 report by the Protestant missionaries of the CMS, in which Henry Townsend remarked upon the affinities in terms of liturgical models between the Catholicism exhibited by Afrolatino returnees and *orisha* worship.[61] Townsend even goes so far as to ask: "Who could be surprised that white [Catholic] slave-traders at Lagos should consult Ifa before sending their ships to sea?"[62] Small examples of this sort reflect the CMS's distaste for both the slave trade and Catholicism. Regardless of what CMS missionaries thought, however, the Aguda communities carried their diasporic religious sensibilities, which included vernacular Afrolatino religions that married *orisha* worship with Catholicism, with them as they returned to Africa.[63] Indeed, between 1859 and 1863, the population of Brazilian and Cuban Catholics in Lagos rose significantly, almost doubling the numbers in Catholic congregations around the city.[64]

The increase has several explanations. The first is that 1859 is the year the Sociétiés des Missions Africaines (SMA), founded in Lyons, France, attempted to bring Catholicism to West Africa via Sierra Leone.[65] The SMA's efforts were later aided by the returning Aguda in Lagos, and by 1863 the Aguda had established a connection with Father Francisco Borghero, a Roman Catholic priest, and created a parish in Lagos that was specifically recognized by Rome.[66] This parish later became the foundation of a Lagosian archdiocese. However, the numerical increase of Catholics was also proportionally related to the ongoing settlement of Catholic Brazilian and Cuban repatriates to the Popo Aguda area in particular.[67] Another significant factor that later added visibility to the growing number of new Catholics in the city was the building and design of the Holy Cross proto-cathedral on Campos Square in 1879–83 by Lazaro Borges da Silva and Francisco Nobre, two Aguda architects.[68] Ultimately, it is important that we see the Aguda's connection to the religious traditions they brought back with them, which included Catholicism, Islam, and *orisha* worship, as setting the necessary foundation for the establishment of official cultural institutions in Lagos.[69]

My conversations with Mrs. Aderemi Gooding-King affirmed similar sentiments of flexibility in relation to religious and ethnic identity. Participation in forms of religious culture coded as Yoruba, Brazilian, and Cuban was and is all a part of being Aguda in Lagos. Strategies of differentiation and affiliation allowed for an Aguda version of identity that is both unique and consistent with other flexible West African tropes of identification. Yet, even within this flexible discourse, there are instances of contradiction, ambiguity, and convergence between Catholic and *orisha* traditions. This kind of layered discourse about religion is particularly Caribbean and Brazilian in its mode of code switching. Compare, for example, the statements made below about the Campos family's religious affiliation by Mrs. Gooding-King and Mrs. Vincent:

> Mrs. Ola Vincent: Yes, Hilario Campos was a Catholic. [At] Holy Cross, Holy Cross, yes, Lagos, the Catholic Mission.
> Solimar Otero: The cathedral, right? And was your mother still a Catholic?
> Mrs. Ola Vincent: Anyways, she was married to my father. My father is a Protestant. . . . But my mother never goes to the Anglican Church. . . . She said, "I am a Catholic, and I am not going to leave my church." . . . So, "But you children, you have to go with your father"'—[but]—she died a Catholic!
> Aderemi Gooding-King: They do it. Really they do worship on the island. Even the—the *orishas*—at this, at this Catholic church—all the saints here, they have meaning. . . . Oooo!! But they won't tell you. Unless the Cubans and the Brazilians they tell you all the signs. . . . ah-ha, about the [*orisha*], they won't say it, they won't. . . . The same thing with their preacher. Wherever they have their preacher it won't last. He is doing it, but he won't show it . . . openly. . . . They just don't—they just stand there by the Bible. Just bring the Bible into everything—bring it out into everything! Oh God! Those people! They don't have pride, *because my parents are from Cuba—they kept it up, that's how they know it.* And all these things they forbid their children, oh—they're not doing their job, it gets lost! . . . They're taking [traditions] away from their children. They begin losing respect for this land, and it's all lies. [emphasis added]
> Mrs. Aderemi Gooding-King: They *do* believe in the *orishas*. They do believe. Very well. Even all the saints in the Catholic church [are related to the orishas].[70]

These three excerpts were taken from my ethnographic interviews with Mrs. Ola Vincent, and Mrs. Aderemi Gooding-King. Both sisters claimed to be of the Anglican Protestant persuasion, but they were also very interested in *orisha* worship in Nigeria, and especially in Cuba. What emerges from the sisters' statements is a similarity in dilemmas about religious identity in Cuba and in Nigeria that allow for a level of code switching and concealment about faith in traditional Yoruba religion. (However, code switching occurs in many

Afro-Atlantic religious cultures besides Yoruba-derived traditions.[71]) Though highly respected members of traditional worship groups, like *babalawo*, do not hide their allegiance to the *orisha*, other community members sometimes do. Or better stated, they selectively choose the audiences and contexts where they reveal such beliefs and practices.

Also, both Mrs. Vincent and Mrs. Gooding-King associated Catholic religion with their family, and Mrs. Gooding-King especially saw a connection between the Catholic saints and the *orisha*. She indicated to me that the saints all "had meaning" associated with orisha worship. It is also interesting here that Hilario Campos was identified as solely Catholic by Vincent, but that Gooding-King identified her grandfather as both a Catholic and an Ifa priest, a *babalawo*. This kind of comfort with code switching between Catholicism and *orisha* traditions may only be found in the creolized traditions of Santería and Candomblé, in which this merging provides a way of enunciating sustained multiple identities. Culturally incorporative perspectives like those found in transatlantic *orisha* traditions rearticulate themselves here in a manner that comes full circle—as in the case of the Campos family. The religious cultures found in Lagos, Bahia, and Havana shared the diasporic sensibilities of transatlantic *orisha* worship in terms of establishing complicated and fluid alliances across disparate social terrains.

For example, like many practitioners of Santería in Cuba and Candomblé in Brazil, some Aguda preferred to keep their religious affiliation to certain *orisha* private. This legacy of caution toward one's religion is another legacy brought over from the diaspora, as many Afro-Cubans and Afro-Brazilians were forced to worship in private or accept Catholicism outwardly. In a sense, Gooding-King's critique of this behavior becomes a push to organize traditional Yoruba religion in such a way as to make it public, known, and revisable. It is clear that for Mrs. Gooding-King, there was no problem with being a Christian and then offering a passionate critique of the Western Christians' colonizing of Yoruba traditional religion. Not surprisingly, her comments regarding the lack of respect for traditional Yoruba religion relate to a kind of Yoruba nationalism that has its historical roots in the Afrolatino diaspora. This kind of shift in religious allegiance can occur due to the overall recognition of Yoruba traditional religion as a sort of organizing civil religion.[72]

However, in paradigms of secret and open praxis, a restricted lens always appears in the expression of religious culture in terms of who performs their faith openly in public. By looking at places where binaries have merged, that is, at "syncretized" religious practices, we come closer to understanding the *lived* realities of Aguda religious associations and legacies. It is here, at the moment of dual recognition, that the religious world can open up and show how vernacular religions like Santería, Candomblé and traditional *orisha* worship have become a basis for the existence of a "Yoruba" group identity on three continents.

Considering the diverse nature of ethnic groups that make up the Yoruba, one can see how the Aguda have come to represent another unique group of Yoruba who were incidentally from the Caribbean and Latin American diaspora. Like other ethnic Yoruba, like Ijebu or Egba Yoruba living in Lagos, for instance, the Aguda arrived in the city with their own unique history of dispersal and resettlement from multiple "Yoruba" diasporas. This diverse and layered diasporic type of community formation is completely consistent with recognized tropes of how "Yoruba-ness" is constructed as an ethnic identity and later reidentified within broader social contexts.[73]

The paradigm of home/diaspora has a nostalgic aspect that utilizes the language of travel, loss, and gain. It is interesting that both the Aguda and the Havana Lagosians identified with a nostalgia for home in a manner that allowed them to make their mark in their new homes by being identified with the distinctness of "being" from somewhere else.[74] These communities became important parts of defining the cosmopolitan nature of Havana and Lagos. In a way, these two cities are sites of the imagination that serve each other well as destinations, in that they reaffirm what they promise to do for one another. These promises, and also memories, operated within the social imagination through the allegories and religious performances discussed above.

For the Lucumí in Cuba, the Nago in Brazil, and the Aguda in Nigeria and Benin, public forms of display, like the Boa masquerade, were recreated to celebrate the negotiation of a range of particular localities, identities, and origins that acknowledged influences from specific home and diasporic sources.[75] These were all mixed *de cierta manera*, in a certain creolized manner that contains familiar hybrids as models, as sources of inspiration, for future play and invention.[76] For the Aguda under investigation here, their Cuban heritage provided creolized forms of culture that served as models of performance that could be carried to Lagos. For example, Hilario Campos's participation in Santería, as a *babalawo* trained in Cuba performing this identity among the Aguda of Lagos, created a space for recognizing a familiar, yet unique, way of understanding a Yoruba from Cuba.

Since Yoruba culture so deeply influenced Cuban national identity, this kind of performance behaved as a mirror of sorts, in which the Cubans and the Yoruba in nineteenth-century Lagos found a piece of themselves reflected due to this shared mythological and religious cultural context.[77] In chapter 5, we return to Cuba and the creation of an Afro-Cuban identity in the island's public sphere in the nineteenth and twentieth centuries. We will find that the transatlantic memory that informed the embrace of Cuba by the Aguda has another manifestation in the way that Cubans imagined themselves as Africans.

5

Creating Afrocubanos

Public Cultures in a Circum-Atlantic Perspective

El rayo surca, sangriento,
El lóbrego nubarrón:
Echa el barco, ciento a ciento,
Los negros por el portón.

El viento, fiero, quebraba
Los almácigos copudos;
Andaba la hilera, andaba,
De los esclavos desnudos.

El temporal sacudía
Los barracones henchidos:
Una madre con su cría
Pasaba, dando alaridos.

Rojo, como en el desierto,
Salió el sol al horizonte:
Y alumbraró un esclavo muerto,
Colgado a un seibo del monte.

Un niño lo vio: tembló
De pasión por los que gimen:
¡Y, al pie del muerto, juró
And, at the dead man's feet,

Blood-red lightning cleaves
The murky overcast:
A ship disgorges, by the hundreds,
Blacks through the hatches.

The raging winds laid low
The copious mastic trees;
And rows of naked slaves
Walked onward, onward.

The tempest shook
The swollen barracks;
A mother with her babe
Passed by, screaming.

Red as a desert sun,
The sun rose on the horizon:
And shone upon a dead slave,
Hanging on a mountain ceiba.

A small boy witnessed it:
He trembled for the groaning men;

vowed
To cleanse that crime with his life!

—José Martí, "Versos Sencillos XXX"

In this poem, Cuban poet José Martí depicts the arrival of African slaves in Cuba in a tragic manner.[1] His characterization surrounds the violence done to Africans with metaphors of nature's ferocity. The little boy in the last stanza foreshadows and represents the Cuban nation yet to be born out of this sordid past. The two tropes, of violence and nature, provide an entry point for a discussion of the development of the use of the idea of the African citizen in constructing national identity in Cuba. This idea of the emerging Afro-Cuban citizen was reformulated through re-remembering race and nation in view of the nineteenth-century wars for independence, especially the Ten Years' War and Cuba's 1895 war of independence.[2] Although it is important to consider these events in the historical construction of the idea of Afro-Cuban national identity, this chapter focuses primarily on how the literary public culture on the island provided an imaginative context for the language of history, nation, and memory. This is especially so because the rhetoric that recreates history through the study of war also informs how these very tropes are being reassembled for a range of purposes.

Here, my concern is with the Atlantic context that is remembered by Cuban and North American scholars for the Yoruba arriving in Cuba in the nineteenth century.[3] It is important to consider how we try to arrive at imaginative and social contexts for the Atlantic world that groups like the Aguda traversed in that century. We shall explore how Africans were imagined, and also how they imagined themselves to be sources of a new Cuban identity. In doing so, we get closer to understanding the tenacious cultural association that Cuban identity held for some Aguda in Lagos. It is important to consider the development in the Spanish colony and later in independent Cuba of a public culture that voiced African-ness as a form of citizenship when we explore the arrival and lives of Lagosians working as emancipated slaves and free people of color in Havana in the nineteenth century.

The Yoruba proverb that began this book, "Aiye ni oja, orun ni ile" (The world is a marketplace: heaven is home), provides apt imagery that juxtaposes the ways in which individuals and communities may relate to different situational identities. In the construction of Afro-Cuban communities in Cuba, competing notions of home were mitigated through narratives of belonging to the island. If we recontextualize the proverb in an Atlantic perspective, we see that the idea of home, as Africa instead of heaven, is a model used for the building of a new nation based on the notion of a shared place of origin. The world of the marketplace, in an Atlantic reframing, represents various stopping points in the African diaspora. These locations were sites for an amalgamation of histories and traditions that created new societies and cultures. The negotiation needed for creating these new "homes" apart from the places left behind represented a challenge for Africans, Europeans, Asians, and Native Americans thrust together by European expansionism.

Traditional folk wisdom, as displayed in the proverb quoted above, brought to these shores by Africans, became an important and forceful source for understanding and shaping new societies in the Americas. Folk belief and folk practices provided many of the social models for restructuring politics, religion, and rebellion in the places where Africans settled. For example, the image of the Afrocubano community as a multireligious entity into which traditional African cultures merged and as a site for the creation of new identities unique to the island is primarily a legacy of traditional African religious tolerance and flexibility.[4]

In looking at the formation of a Cuban public culture through writing the Afrocubano into the emerging nation, we see that it was not only the figure of the Afrocubano as citizen that was utilized for these means. There were also instances of the performance of Afro-Cuban ways of knowing, negotiating, and creating culture, especially religious culture, that were incorporated into the civil culture of Cuban society. Diasporic Africans in Cuba, especially Lagosians from Yorubaland, came from regions historically dense with cultural interaction, market activity, and linguistic variation. Folk wisdom in the form of religious practices, narrative, and vernacular speech allowed innovative epistemologies of cultural melding, from Africa, to flow into Cuban public culture. The nuanced coding of mixed religious culture, in terms of both traditional African and folk Catholic practices on the island, allowed select audiences to participate on different levels in grassroots performance in the public sphere. Examples of this kind of imagining of shared Cuban public space often centered around the performance of religious feasts and festivals for saints and gods like La Virgen de Regla, also known as Yemayá, among others.[5]

Approaches to Affiliation and Identity

How far did the involvement of Afro-Cubans go in Cuba's nineteenth-century struggle for independence? What risks did members of Afro-Cuban fraternal societies, like the *cabildos* (some of whom were often on good terms with the Spanish colonial government), take during the rise of Cuban nationalism? These were some of the same kinds of questions that Black and white *criollo* writers and activists were grappling with in mid-nineteenth-century Cuba. Both groups of *criollos* faced the challenges of not being "authentic" enough in terms of ideas of allegiances to Africa or Spain and origins in those places.[6] Yet it was the shared liminal space of being a Cuban-born *criollo*, with a whole range of hegemonic clashes contained in tension within that broad identification, that allowed for a limited amount of shared participation in the construction of the imagined community of Cubans fighting for independence in the nineteenth century. As the movement for Cuban independence, led by José Martí, the *mambistas* of the Ten Years' War, and Afro-Cuban figures like Maceo and Morúa Delgado, grew, Afrocubanos negotiated their role in a new, burgeoning, and contested Cuban civil society. The range of attitudes among Afrocubano communities mirrored the diversity of individuals involved with the formation, affiliation, and influence of *sociedades de color*, or societies of people of color.[7] Since the range of interests in Cuban independence varied along class, racial, and cultural lines in diverse ways, the answers to the questions listed at the beginning of this section are multiple on many fronts.

Some people are critical of the reality of racial incorporation into the public discourse of civil society in Cuba in both the nineteenth and twentieth centuries.[8] Studies like Aline Helg's *Our Rightful Share: The Afro-Cuban Struggle for Equality, 1886–1912* point, in part, to a bifurcated racial system that used a "myth" of Cuban racial equality in order to disenfranchise the emerging Afrocubano population after the wars of independence in the late nineteenth century. Helg also argues that this dualistic racial system was not a product of the influence of the United States on the island, but was solidified with the North American presence. The study also shows how an Afro-Cuban public sphere became dedicated to the development of Black consciousness through periodicals like *El Nuevo Criollo* and *Previsión* in the early twentieth century.[9] With this in mind, we must also remember that North American influence in the late nineteenth and early twentieth centuries in Cuba encompassed the spread of African American ideas about race, freedom, and citizenship to the island, though with often limited results, these interchanges between African Americans and Afro-Cubans highlighted a dissonance in ideas about race, culture, and nation among groups trying to work together.[10]

This is not to say that common ground for creating a transnational racial consciousness was missing. Rather, the problem is that these struggles took place within the slippery discourse of race found in a Cuban society that reified an idea of cultural creolization through the valorization of African culture in many respects, while denying racial equality in terms of social discourse and political power.[11] The issue at hand is the elision of race with culture in analyzing the ways that Africans and Blacks occupy different social categories in reaffirming national identities in Cuba.[12] These two categories refer to different kinds of cultural capital that were and are manipulated in different contexts in order to describe the elusive notion of (Afro-) Cuban identity.[13] Many of the complexities related to race in nineteenth-century and early twentieth-century Cuban society come from precisely this dilemma. How do we think about historicizing an emerging creolized nation that includes Africans without silencing the very language that can be used to signal the existence of racial inequality? Do we impose our own contemporary perspectives about race and culture by focusing on only certain formulations of these categories?

In other words, how do we recontextualize our understandings of the categories of race and culture in order to understand Cuban racial and cultural constructs from the nineteenth century on?

An example may come from taking in a comparative perspective that examines racial inequality in both Cuba and North America. In *Degrees of Freedom: Louisiana and Cuba after Slavery*, Rebecca Scott demonstrates that Black American struggles for freedom in Louisiana created bonds between Afro-Cuban activists and their Gulf Coast neighbors in the nineteenth century.[14] And, within Cuba, African and *criollo* Afrocubanos created associations that were densely layered in terms of notions of ethnic affiliation and authenticity and registered social power in terms of African-ness.[15] Looking at these intersecting, yet unique, struggles for equality, Scott grapples with notions of blackness, citizenship, and freedom in two distinct societies that share an Afro-Atlantic context. The "simultaneous" construction of two public spheres of color, through periodicals like the *Crusader* in Louisiana, and *La Igualdad* in Cuba, for example, illustrate how actors in this time period themselves struggled with redefining the contours of race, culture, and nation.[16]

Afro-Cubans and African Americans shared the experience and memory of an Afro-Atlantic past, with an eye to a consciousness based on the transatlantic circulation of information, lived experiences, and travel. Scott speaks of Antonio Maceo's 1884 visit to New Orleans, a high-profile example of a sojourner who epitomized for both African Americans and Afro-Cubans the struggle for freedom by Afro-Atlantic communities.[17] The larger legacies here are the shared emphases on knowing the world through movement, the portability of the message of liberation from slavery, and continuing attempts to make connections. These very diasporic sensibilities are what ties the actors in Scott's study to this present study of the Aguda and Havana's Lagosians. Both works suggest broader networks of exchange that represent another tier of involvement in this very same Atlantic context. Afro-Atlantic communities in New Orleans, Havana, and Lagos created spaces for freedom through movement, exchange, and collaboration.

The influence and interchange among the multiplicity of peoples in the Atlantic world during the mid- to late-nineteenth century included Black, white, mulatto, native, and Asian communities whose members were working for freedom, but also laboring as servants, slaves, and free people of color in a variety of capacities. If racial paradigms based on stark notions of whiteness and blackness existed, these were being selectively used by either those in power or by those trying to organize against that power. In other words, whiteness and blackness here signified much more than racial categories; they represented ideologies that imagined the world outside of its lived context. That is, notions of racial purity were constantly challenged in terms of day-to-day living and the reality of an ethnically mixed folklife such as that found in the Atlantic world. The development of intercultural aesthetics that characterized the lived experience of creolized cultures is what seems to identify the Caribbean especially, and the circum-Atlantic in general.[18] We can look to language, art, music, local (market) economies, and religion as obvious examples of how lived culture in the Caribbean is unique because of its tendency toward unapologetic creolization.[19]

Many members of Afro-Cuban *cabildos* in Havana, and elsewhere on the island—especially in Oriente—felt that there was a need for separate Black political organizations during the early independence era in Cuba. The desire for visibility came from a feeling of engagement with the new civil society in a manner that highlighted a mutual fight against racism. This is not to say that all people of color involved in *cabildos* wanted to see Black organizations, or that they were a homogeneous group that understood blackness and African-ness in a single, unified way. The *cabildos*' own internal dynamics, as Childs has shown for earlier in the nineteenth century, indicated varying degrees of understanding African and Afro-Cuban identity in terms of membership, power within the associations, and the desire to work with other groups.[20] That is, *cabildo* members themselves already made up organizations of Blacks on the island that demonstrated a heterogeneity of ideas about how African-ness and blackness could and could not intersect in the creation of a social entity.[21] They navigated, for example, the role that ethnicity would play in accepting members, performing religious rites, and providing mutual economic aid. Though transnational notions of Black consciousness were indeed forming across the Atlantic in the late nineteenth and early twentieth centuries, these discourses were necessarily promblematized by groups within new nations, especially in the Spanish Caribbean, that were creating a space for their own civil discourse.[22] As with *cabildos* in Cuba and the Aguda in Lagos, the assertion to be recognized by the larger society forced members of these Afro-Atlantic communities to negotiate openly their ethnic, racial, cultural, and national identities. These groups necessarily came to this process from an Atlantic perspective in terms of explaining their origins, history of migration, and shared past.

The difficulty of mitigating cultural and racial identities in the context of Cuban civil society after independence was exemplified by the tensions that circulated around the idea of forming a Black political party. Many attempts were made to create a group that would speak to the racial problems present in Cuban society with varying results.[23] In 1908, the mobilization toward a Black party coalesced, and Evaristo Estenoz and others founded El Partido Independiente de Color in Oriente.[24] The party was closely linked to the fight for workers' rights, which also provided challenges in both rural and urban settings since the focus on race caused uneasiness because of the racially mixed nature in most workplaces.[25] Another challenge El Partido faced was criticism by important Afro-Cuban leaders and journalists, most notably Martin Morúa Delgado, Juan Gualberto Gómez, and Rafael Serra.[26] One dilemma facing people of color in the formation of a new Cuban nation was how to be included into civil society without creating political parties that focused solely on race. The heart of the problem here was that these parties could be used to exclude Blacks from public debate. In other words, some Afro-Cuban leaders saw talking about blackness as a way to remove themselves from the larger conversation over integration in Cuban society. It was not that they believed that Cuba was fully integrated; rather, they wanted to change the terms of the conversation because they understood how dangerous talking about racial solidarity could be for people of color in Cuba. Indeed, the brutal murder of members of El Partido Independiente de Color in 1912, as part of the so-called race wars, touched off a wave of rampant panic and fear on the part of whites. As with other cases of racial violence in the nineteenth century, Cuba's white rulers used the Haitian Revolution as a justification for repression of people of color in 1912.[27] These attacks on Afro-Cubans seemed to signal a reversion to colonial fears that manifested in narratives about maroonage, *palenquismo*, African conjure, and revolution that gripped the Atlantic world in previous centuries.[28]

These recurring instances of "white fear" force us to consider the ways people fought against slavery in their daily lives, employing a range of official and unofficial actions. What was the relationship between slaves and free people of color in urban settings like Havana? Cuban historians have noted that urban *cimarrones*, or runaway slaves, received aid from individuals, some belonging to *cabildos*, nestled in the *barrios negros*, or Black neighborhoods, of Havana.[29] Periodicals like *Diario de La Habana* ran advertisements by those asking for the return of runaway slaves that emphasized the punishment for those aiding runaways, because of the perceived connection between free people of color and slaves.[30] *Cimarrones* used a range of strategies to ensure that they could live free in places like Havana. They were often literate and felt a sense of entitlement to use the civic culture of colonial Cuba to ensure their freedom. Since many of these *cimarrones* were *criollo*, or Cuban-born, they had the ability to utilize the public culture of places like Havana to their advantage. For example, some urban slaves falsified documents like change of ownership or permission to rent out work, or simply passed themselves off as free or emancipated slaves in a manner that fooled authorities and helped them to continue to live as free people in an urban setting.[31] An example of how slaves were able to go to Havana and blend into the free Black population comes from *Diario de La Habana* of January 20, 1827, in which this advertisement was placed:

> Two months ago, a black African of the Mandigo Nation by the name of Cayetano came from Guanabacoa to earn his keep working as a tobacco roller, and he has not returned to his home: he is of a regular stature, thin and dark-skinned,

about 25 years old, he knows how to read and he seems like a *criollo*: a warning to those who harbor him in their homes for even one night: they will be held responsible for all accounts and consequences: at no. 65 Damas Street any information regarding his whereabouts would be appreciated.[32]

The advertisement indicates that Cayetano was able to read, write, and blend into the population of free *criollo* Afrocubanos living in Havana. It is interesting that this example of flight by a slave occurred within an urban context. The stereotypical trope of maroonage in the Caribbean included the flight of slaves from a plantation to a dense forested region. In this manner, the example above recontextualizes the range of slave resistance in Cuba by allowing us to imagine such acts taking place in a city like Havana. The advertisement situated one kind of public culture—that of the slave owners—which had to recognize Afro-Cubans as living in a context of being both slave and free. It alludes to the complicated and fluid arena of Havana's urban environment in terms of its Afro-Cuban population. The setting of urban Havana created a context in which the status of free and slave was not openly obvious in public culture. The claiming of a Cuban civil identity was an important tactic used by some Afrocubanos, whether slave or free, in circumventing and fighting the Spanish colonial slave system. However, whether they were in urban environments or in the country, and whether they were members of a *cabildo* or a *palenque*, Afrocubanos used communication and associations effectively to legally and physically combat slavery. Their effective methods of association were adopted in terms of the ways in which people imagined themselves to be Cubans in what would be postcolonial contexts later on.

Spanish colonial officials saw the effectiveness of these connections between free people of color and slaves, and reacted in ways that fostered the transatlantic migration of Afro-Cubans. In November 1843, Cuba was rocked by the upheaval known as La Escalera, which comprised a number of slave revolts.[33] There is much debate about whether or not there was a true conspiracy involving the British in fomenting the revolts.[34] Either way, the Spanish colonial response was brutal. Besides deporting more than four hundred free Afro-Cubans to Africa, the Spanish colonial government also sent hundreds of slaves and free people of color to prisons in Ceuta, in Spanish North Africa.[35] Indeed, by some accounts, the government executed a total of seventy-eight individuals—slaves, free people of color, and whites—in Mantanzas in 1844.[36] The reputation of the Spanish government in Cuba endured much negative international reaction during the "year of the lash," and abolitionists worldwide reported on the colony's activities.[37] It was in this context of terror that much of Cuba's Lagosian population decided to move back to Africa. The unpleasant official attitude toward Africans and Afro-Cubans, coupled with the British abolitionist desire to help those wanting to repatriate to Africa, certainly created a situation conducive to repatriation for those seeking it. It is significant to note that the Cuban Aguda moving to Lagos from 1844 on did so primarily by their own means and by working with British antislavery forces.[38] However, others were being simultaneously forced out of Cuba—whether African slave, free, or a *criollo* of color—because of the threat of slave revolts in the minds of many whites.

The colonists' recurring fear that Cuba would become another Haiti created a physical and social gap between white *criollos* and the Afro-Cuban population on the island that was pervasive well into the late nineteenth and early twentieth century. Louis Pérez Jr. argues that the paradigm equating both societies—the idea of "Cuba as Haiti"—was manipulated (especially by the United States) to reinforce racial separation on the island.[39] Yet, for Cuban independence and civil society to succeed, this gap had to be narrowed. Obviously, Spanish officials were interested in feeding the mutual fear between whites and people of color. The growing problem for the Spanish government, and for those who benefited from the colonial social system, was that the formation of a multiethnic and polyracial *criollo* culture on the island was becoming the fabric of everyday life for Cubans. A new kind of citizen, heterogeneous in ethnicity and race, was emerging. This new kind of *criollo* effectively negotiated the cosmopolitan reality of Cuba's colonial social world. The Spanish repeatedly sought to suppress associations that might encourage new and "uncontrollable" associations that would lead to unique Cuban identities. In other words, though the fear of slave revolts divided people in the realm of the social imagination, their shared folklife brought them together and created community. My argument here is that this sense of shared community created out of daily discourse replaced the tropes of fear with new significations that were amalgamated and unique. The growing practice of the religion of Santería in the late nineteenth century is a case in point here. These new cultural collaborations profanely touted miscegenation and mélange in terms that were revolutionary. In denying "pure" forms of culture, I am thinking especially of religion and music; Cuban *criollo* culture became a postcolonial condition in that it contained elements of both the colonizer and the colonized in its expression.[40]

What Is "Lo Criollo" in the Atlantic World?

The phenomenon of the "plantation complex" developed from its early Mediterranean roots to its American manifestations.[41] In the Portuguese and Spanish plantations, the net proportion of Africans to Europeans was fairly high. In Brazil and Cuba, large numbers of Africans brought their home languages, religions, and social organizations to these new contexts. Yet, Afro-Atlantic texts and cultures were present in both North and South

America, as well as the Caribbean, from colonial times well into the nineteenth century. Here, *texts* refer to a range of representations that include but are not exclusive to written works, performed customs, and items of material culture, such as religious objects.

Although different Afro-Atlantic experiences existed in Anglophone, Francophone, and Lusophone New World societies, similarities existed between the kinds of texts Africans were bringing to and creating within these contexts. For example, Gómez provides a reading of Islam from West Africa to the colonial and antebellum American South that included the continuous production of Muslim texts among slaves in the form of religious practices, writings, and the making of amulets and other products of material culture.[42] Another example of exchange among Islamic slaves and free people of color in the nineteenth century is the distribution of copies of the Koran in Rio de Janeiro.[43] In other words, Afro-Atlantic populations were creating a portable and "readable" culture in the form of religious texts. Though the above examples include Afro-Atlantic interactions involving Islam, the same kinds of readability and portability can be attributed to such forms of traditional religious culture as *orisha* worship or the belief in Zambi for slave communities creating new identities in the Atlantic world.[44] The social practices that reinvented these "African" cultural scripts in the Americas were the foundation for enacting creolized cultures in a manner that discerned new Afro-Atlantic societies. These scripts also informed literary production, public spheres, and civic discourse that articulated a postcolonial search for identity and nationhood.[45]

How do we interpret the ways in which people described these new societies in texts that emerged under the Spanish and Portuguese colonial plantation systems? The initial texts in these contexts were written by clerics, *conquistadores*, and other members of the ruling elite in these societies. Accounts of early Spanish America by Las Casas, Díaz del Castillo, and Cabeza de Vaca come to mind here as examples.[46] Angel Rama gives us considerations of the writing of encounter in *La ciudad letrada* (The Lettered City), in which he urges us to rethink the discourses Iberians carried with them in documenting their experiences in the Americas.[47] Here, imagined paradigms of "order" provided the impetus for "writing" new societies in the region. It was thought that these paradigms needed to be inscribed so that they would provide social trajectories for the new communities.

The very process of textualizing colonial discourses allowed for the construction of a transatlantic public sphere that encompassed African and European ideas about homelands, often using the image of the African and indigenous subject in order to demarcate these sites. Examples of a kind of "Cuban" colonial literature include travel accounts by Europeans, such as Alexander von Humboldt, who attempted to describe the places and peoples of the Atlantic world.[48] These types of writings mapped new places in the imagination of different publics. Instilling ideas of home and the exotic into the new spaces they inhabited, Europeans injected their own tropes about the formation of civic culture, and what constituted "viable" institutions, into American contexts.[49] These injections were initially infused with the contradictions and ambiguities that the encounter between diverse audiences, native and from outside, engendered for clerics and others writing to create an American public sphere.[50]

It had to be a transatlantic imaginary that helped to create the "American' public culture of the *ciudad letrada* in terms of providing portable tropes that referred to both colonial and creolizing discourses.[51] In this emerging public sphere, the negotiation of Latin American identities in relation to Spanish and Portuguese cultures was fraught with tension and an enforced hegemony. The transformation of colonial identities into American identities created societies that were made from European, African, Asian, and Native American miscegenation. Racial mixing was one site where the presentation of the "face" of national identity in Latin America was hotly contested.[52] For Cuba, before 1608, there was no real identification of a *vox populi* with a discrete Cuban sense of national identity.[53] However, there was a sense of localized identity that emerged in places like Havana in the process of fighting against the British, the French, and pirates from the mid-sixteenth century onward.[54] Yet, it was not until the end of the eighteenth century, when slavery became a debated issue on the island, that Cuban anti-Spanish sentiment became more vocal.[55]

Criollismo existed in different ways in Latin America, in which, as in Cuba, a conceptual shift occurred between associating the community or nation with *la ciudad letrada* of the colony and associating it with the land of their birth in the Americas. In this way the lettered city, with its institutions and civil societies mirroring that of the metropole, births itself into a revolutionary city, *la ciudad revolucionaria*, with an anticolonial sentiment that then gives birth to new nationalisms.[56] In this formation, how do we read texts that were being created for the purpose of decentering the projected *ciudad letrada*? In other words, how is the injection of creolized, "home-grown" cultural texts incorporated for use in *la ciudad revolucionaria*? Central to this process is the recognition that the civic ways and public cultures being produced by Native Americans and Africans in Latin America provided the stepping stones needed for the disassembly of the Spanish and Portuguese hegemonies that had been imposed on *criollo* public culture.

African and Afro-Atlantic writing about the experiences of slavery and diaspora, like that of Samuel Ajayi Crowther, give another perspective on the worlds alluded to in colonial accounts.[57] What we find is that African communities traversed and challenged the idea of unidirectional movement in the Afro-Atlantic diaspora.[58] As we have explored, Afrolatinos who hailed originally from Africa, but arrived in Cuba and Brazil in their youth as emancipated slaves, made their lives for over thirty years in most cases in these Latin lands. These individuals also moved back and forth between Brazil, Cuba, Sierra Leone, London, Ouidah, and Lagos during their lifetimes, challenging in the process notions of limited mobility.[59] This group of businesspeople, explorers, religious advocates, and others showed that a range of communities of African descent crossed boundaries and borders throughout the eighteenth and nineteenth centuries. Texts by Africans also include oral performances, music, dance, carnival, and other aesthetic productions communicated the discourses that were alive in colonial contexts but might not have made it into the colonial record per se. However, we can try to approach the texts we do have for groups like Afrolatinos in Cuba, looking toward an imaginative recovery of the complexity of these voices and the world they lived in.[60]

Emerging "Cuban" Perspectives

In the seventeenth century Sandoval wrote about slavery and Africans in Latin America, specifically Cartagena, Colombia, in a manner that fleshed out what later would be seen as a universalist idea of history that explained the enslavement of Africans through a "civilizing" discourse.[61] The works produced in this context mirrored Sandoval's studies in that they documented African culture brought to the Americas by reimagining slave life and African history and culture through this lens.[62] Accounts described the arrival of *bozales* of mainly central African origin during this era.

Early Portuguese and Dutch slaving in the sixteenth and seventeenth centuries created the backdrop for the negotiation of new African and Atlantic creole identities for people brought to and later born in the Americas.[63] It is important to note here that Brazil, Portugal's primary colony in the Americas, was producing the majority of sugarcane in the late seventeenth century and that the region contained many more plantations and Africans than did Cuba.[64] Thus, the arrival in Cuba of slaves from central Africa, and from Yorubaland in later centuries mirrored that of Brazil's layered amalgamation of African ethnicities through the colonial project of the plantation.

The Haitian Revolution created an opening for Cuba's growth in the global sugar market. Consequently, Africans began to be transported as slaves to Cuba for sugarcane production in larger and larger numbers in the late eighteenth and early nineteenth centuries.[65] The development of the Cuban railroad in the early nineteenth century created an infrastructure for transporting the increasing amounts of sugar and tropical products for export to European and North American markets.[66] The building of the railroads involved the use of salaried North American and Canary Island laborers, as well as slaves and *emancipados*.[67] In a specific case discussed in this volume, *emancipado* Lorenzo Clarke worked on the Havana–Güines Line, which proved to be an expensive and controversial rail to build.[68]

It is in this context of the growing importation of African people and cultures, albeit through slavery, that a literary context for what would become a Cuban nation and identity began. The start of Cuban writing about Cuba as a discrete national culture has been understood as including primarily the works of cultural analysts Caballero and Varela in the 1800s. Closely following Caballero and Varela is the work of de la Cruz.[69] These authors are hailed as the "first" Cuban writers, primarily because of their anti-Spanish, pro-*criollo* stances toward local cultural production. Father Caballero was a cleric whose antagonism toward the Spanish fueled much of the Cuban separatist movement that began in the early nineteenth century. Caballero wrote sympathetically about the plight of Africans forced into slavery, infusing the seeds of abolitionism into the public sphere. He wrote that slaves in Cuba in the nineteenth century were

> unos brazos que sostienen nuestros trenes, mueblan nuestras casas, cubren nuestras mesas, equipan nuestros roperos, mueven nuestros carruajes, y nos hacen gozar las placeres de la abundancia.
>
> [arms that support our trains, furnish our houses, cover our tables, fill our closets, drive our carriages, and help us enjoy the pleasures of abundance.][70]

Here Caballero uses the metaphor of *brazos* (literally, arms) to show that much of the wealth that citizens of the colony enjoyed was built on slave labor. His discourse is interesting because here he is simultaneously building a consensus about Cuban community and about Africans' roles in the yet to be formed nation. His textual strategy is also intriguing because he situated both white *criollos* and slaves in the same conceptual milieu. By doing this, he was also pushing the Spanish away from formation of a just Cuban society because of their roles as instigators and perpetuators of the unjust system of slavery.[71] Thus, Father Caballero is calling upon the "proto-Cubans" to rise above the morally bankrupt Spanish institution of slavery. This development foreshadows the call to arms for the emerging Cuban masses, as well as the sentiments expressed by Martí in the poem that begins this chapter.

Other strategies were also used by white *criollos* to build a heterogeneous textual Cuban community at the time. The textualization of a unique *criollista*, or local (that is, not Spanish), version of Cuban history was one way in which independent-minded writers built a sense of common identity. Both Felix Varela and Manuel de la Cruz were educators who wrote biographies of the great men of the island. They did this as their main method of building a Cuban national consciousness.[72]

Eighteenth- and nineteenth-century biographies like those in *Los Cromitos Cubanos* (The Cuban Archives) by de la Cruz were crucial in forming both anti-Spanish and antislavery sentiment on the island.[73] As Lugo-Ortiz aptly observes, the invention and textualization of a uniquely "Cuban" history helped place a textual, literary form on shared memory.[74] Manuel Sanguily, a contemporary of de la Cruz, wrote extensively in dialogue with de la Cruz about *Los Cromitos Cubanos* in Cuban newspapers of the day, creating an alternate, public, textual realm that reacted to Spanish publications of the day.[75] Sanguily's description, published after his death in 1893, of *Los Cromitos Cubanos* is interesting:

> En el libro de Sr. Cruz por lo visto, se plantea, y no se resuelve o prueba, una tesis radical y aventurada. Hay a su juicio, una tendencia antigua, tradicional que nos aleja de España, que nos desespañoliza. Es verdad. Lo malo es que hay efectivamente otras tendencias—antiguas, tradicionales también—que nos acercan a España, que nos españolizan.
>
> [In Mr. de la Cruz's book, a radical and adventurous thesis is planted, and it is neither resolved nor proven. There is, to his credit, an ancient and traditional tendency that moves us away from Spain, that makes us less Spanish. It is true. The problem is that there are effectively other tendencies—ancient, traditional as well—that move us closer to Spain, that make us more Spanish.][76]

Sanguily's comments are lucid. Here he observes that the act of textualizing the Cuban nation *through* the biography of great men behaves as a trope that both rejects and embraces the Spanish tradition. He pinpoints the fact that the very discourse of anticolonial nation building requires many of the strategies of nationalism that had been used by the former colony, and by the metropole. The shaping of a community of great men was the most obvious textual, rhetorical link to these European tropes of making history for Cuban writers. Sanguily also contributes to his own ambivalent discourse in the fact that he sees the tradition of moving away from the colony as ancient on some level as well. Here we can see that the Cuban textualization of community and nation was a self-reflexive endeavor that grew out of a multitude of discourses. A major way in which this debate moved from writing to revolutionary action was by incorporating Africans and Afro-Cubans into the texts, as well as into the community of lettered individuals, or *la comunidad letrada*, of the era. This also moved the contours of the discussion of local identity on the island away from talking about being more or less Spanish to talking about being Cuban.

Estudios Delmontianos, Negotiating Africans as Cubans

Writing about and by Africans in Cuba began in many ways with the patronage of white *criollo* Domingo del Monte. During the 1830s, del Monte hosted *tertulias*, or intellectual gatherings, on his estate.[77] His focus was to create an abolitionist movement in Cuba by writing and supporting writers with antislavery, proindependence sentiments. Del Monte was thought of as the "patron of African arts," since he supported not only white *criollo* abolitionists but mulatto and Black authors as well.[78] The Afrocubano poet Juan Francisco Manzano gained his freedom and fame through help from del Monte. One of Manzano's most noted works was *Zafira*, written in 1844, the same date of the "year of the lash." By supporting writers like Manzano, del Monte furthered his vision of the Cuban *pueblo*:

> Digo que es preciso los contrastes de los colores de nuestra población; los negros y los blancos trabajándose . . . de tal manera que en los blancos se vea a los negros y en los negros a los blancos.

> [I say that it is precisely the contrast of the colors of our population; the blacks and whites working . . . in such a manner that in whites we see blacks and in blacks we see whites.][79]

Del Monte here is calling for a creolization of sorts, a melding of cultures and peoples in order to construct a Cuban nationhood. He addresses the social reality of the difficulty of obtaining this vision. However, del Monte was aware that the reality of Cuban independence could not be conceptually or physically attained without the incorporation of the majority of the population on the island, Africans and Afrocubano *criollos* alike.

In the 1840s a large majority of the Afro-Cubans and people of color living in Havana were free laborers who contributed a great deal to the economy of the city. Added to this context was an influx of European immigrants from the Canary Islands and other regions of Spain. The clash of immigrant, African, and *criollo* cultures created a volatile and competitive atmosphere in the city. These hostilities ran through many different populations—between white *criollos* and Asian immigrants, for example, as well as between members of the elite *criollos* themselves, like del Monte.[80] Del Monte's vision illustrated one way in which proto-Cubans began to conceptually incorporate Africans as part of a *pueblo* or a local Latin American citizenry. Both the textualization of this dream and the lived reality of the mixed and complex social worlds created an atmosphere of a multifaceted movement that was tempered by discontent directed toward the Spanish.

The writers supported by del Monte included *criollo* authors like Anselmo Suárez y Romero, who wrote the influential novel *Francisco*, which was one of the most widely read abolitionist novels in circulation on the island in the 1800s.[81] Other novelists whose romantic visions of racial mixing in Cuba in the nineteenth century shaped the social imagination were Cirilo Villaverde, the author of *Cecilia Valdez*, written in 1834; revolutionary war veteran Martin Morúa Delgado, author of *Sofía*, published in 1891; and Gertrudis Gómez de Avellaneda, the author of *Sab*, published in 1841.[82] Works like *Francisco* and *Sofía* included as background material "ethnographic" descriptions of the "African" culture found in Cuba at the time.[83] Yet these *novelas* were mainly committed to romantically expressing the horrors of slave life.

Indeed, literary critic Doris Sommer believes that the "national intimacy" necessary for creating nineteenth-century Latin American nationalisms was expressed in the social imagination through novels like *Cecilia Valdez*, *Sofía*, and *Francisco*.[84] Further, novels in Latin America about love crossing the color and class lines, Sommer argues, moved the terms of civic engagement away from binaries inscribed by the colonial powers, and toward a sort of reconciliation through nationalism.[85] The "myth" of racial inclusion that stems from this branch of the literary and civic imagination is what Helg believes has held Black political parties back in terms of fighting the racism that was denied in postindependence discourses of the Cuban nation.[86] One can clearly see that abolitionist romances were texts written about Africans in Cuba for a white *criollo* audience. Thus, in a way, they contributed to certain abolitionist traditions by manipulating white *criollo* stereotypes and romantic images of Africans, rather than reevaluating or changing these stereotypes and images. However, these texts were certainly constructed in order to sway popular opinion on the island against slavery, albeit within a paternalistic framework. And, as Sommer argues, abolition was a condition and not a result of Cuban independence.[87]

The figure of the Afrocubano man of letters emerged in the person of Martín Morúa Delgado during this era. He was a highly educated former slave who attained a university education. Working in bakeries, as a *lector* in the tobacco factories, and as a newspaper editor, he managed to support his career as a writer.[88] He is a significant figure in Cuban history for a number of reasons. To many, he embodies the vision of the Afrocubano citizen described by del Monte. Morúa Delgado's writings were accessible to both Black and white *criollos* on the island because of his origins as a Cuban-born individual. He also adopted white *criollo* cultural tropes in his work. He tried to fit into the society of the rising Cuban elite by being both an intellectual renegade and a military general in the 1895 Cuban war of independence. Morúa Delgado contributed to and shaped some of the ways in which Afrocubanos were characterized as citizens in the emerging Cuban nation.

In 1872, Morúa Delgado moved to New York to work on planning the revolution with poet José Martí. Martí and Morúa Delgado launched, in 1880, from their position in exile, the revolutionary, anti-Spanish periodical

Revista Popular. Periodicals like *Revista Popular* provided an imagined textual space where Cuban exiles constructed a sense of *cubanidad*, or Cuban-ness, from afar. The members of this Cuban diaspora in the nineteenth century included a range of individuals of mixed cultural, ethnic, and racial ancestry who were working in a myriad of ways for Cuban independence. The *Revista Popular* was also a forum in which exiles especially in the North American diaspora hammered out strategies for implementing their future visions of Cuba. Morúa Delgado used these experiences in New York to paint a semiautobiographical picture of an exiled vanguard in his abolitionist novel *Sofía*.

As with del Monte's and Suárez y Romero's abolitionist works, *Sofía* made an important impression on white *criollos*, influencing their views on independence from colonial Spain and on abolitionism. In 1891, four years before the beginning of the second Cuban war of independence, *Sofía* was banned on the island.[89] The very act of reading *Sofía* was interpreted as rebellion against Spanish colonial power. The rising tension between local culture and colonial rule in the public sphere created this context in which acts of reading were seen as rebellious acts. In this manner, the turning of the lettered city (*ciudad letrada*) into the revolutionary city (*ciudad revolucionaria*) aided the development of a public culture that emphasized an anticolonial sentiment. The incorporation of individuals of African descent into the white elite Cuban vanguard who were leading the intellectual planning of the revolutionary campaigns became one major justification for seeing Cuba as a creolized nation. The construction of a new social reality needed to include Africans and Afrocubanos who were placed at various levels within the social hierarchy on the island, and also among their counterparts in the diaspora.

It is important to consider the options that Afrocubanos had in creating a space for themselves in the emerging Cuban civil society. One Afrocubano writer and political activist, Juan Gualberto Gómez, navigated the boundaries of what it meant to be a Black revolutionary in a white racist colonial society fighting for a new civic culture. His views revealed the challenge of building an independent Cuba as an integrated society. Gómez reacted strongly to the idea of a Cuba separated along racial lines, and he refused to support Black political parties in Cuba:

> No mi amigo, jamás, jamás, nos separemos de los blancos de Cuba. Aunque ellos no se han comportado con nosotros como hermanos, lo son en realidad, y ni ellos ni nosotros podemos deshacer lo que naturaleza ha formado. Nosotros ya no somos africanos. No nos separemos jamás.

> [No my friend, never, never shall we separate ourselves from whites in Cuba. Even though they have not behaved like our brothers, in reality they are just that, and neither they nor we can undo what nature has formed. We are no longer Africans. We will never ever be separated.][90]

128   *Creating Afrocubanos*

The statement "We are no longer Africans" is especially striking in its implication that both Afro-Cuban and white *criollos* should give up their ties to the past in order to forge a new Cuban nation.[91] According to Gómez, just as whites were asked to leave their Spanish identity behind in order to forge a new nation, Afrocubanos should also leave Africa in the "past." The problem with this notion was that neither group could readily abandon the complexity of the cultures that each brought to their new Cuban home. Rather, both the Spanish *criollo* and the Afro-Cuban *criollo* incorporated elements of their pasts into the cultures they were engaging on the ground in Cuban public culture to create a unique, new identity that contained elements of both. However, Gómez's sentiments reveal several aspects central to the 1890s Cuban independence movement, in that Martí and others were desperate to find discourses that would allow some kind of unity between white and Black *criollos*. As a member of the educated, wealthy Afro-Cuban "moderate" social elite, Gómez held views exemplifying a stance of negotiation. He and other Afrocubanos of his class declared their desire to unite with white *criollos* on the island as Cuban citizens in a new independent nation. The hope of those who espoused this perspective was to forge a new society that was based on shared values of patriotism that moved beyond race.

This view rested on a classic Latin American *criollista* stance in dealing with postcolonial identities in the region. The romantic myth of the postindependence Latin nations interpreted community formation and nation building as an organic, almost natural, mixture of disparate cultures in a "New World" social context.[92] The less idealistic result was often a postnational reality that saw stark racial and social stratification, which resembled that of the recent colonial past. In response to this emerging split, Gómez's goal was to forge, through his political writing, a remedy for what he saw as the "broken" *criollo* society of nineteenth-century Cuba.[93] He wanted to see true heterogeneity in Cuban society's racial structure that included Afrocubanos as full partners with white *criollos* in constructing the nation. Gómez felt this could only be achieved if Blacks were to set an example by leaving their racial and cultural identity, especially their ties to Africa, behind.

A Cuban Nation Emerges

> Aquí no hay blanquitos ni negritos, solo cubanos.
> There are no whites or blacks here, only Cubans.
> —General Antonio Maceo, in *El Cuba Libre*, May 2, 1870

The development of Cuban national consciousness in the nineteenth century encompassed a complex set of conceptual and social negotiations.

The groups involved in moving the conceptual locus away from a Spanish identity were heterogeneous and differed in their approaches and strategies. Generally, three distinct political positions have been recognized: *independista, autonomista,* and *reformista*.[94] Although all three approaches sought to change the island's relationship to Spain, the difference in the desired degree of the shift away from the colony was marked. The *independistas* by and large represented those who wanted to completely sever ties with Spain. The *autonomistas* were willing to accept a relationship with Spain like that of an annexed state, giving Spain the last word on Cuban international affairs. The last group, the *reformistas*, wanted to stay under the patronage of the Spanish crown, with some changes that would boost the rights of white *criollo* and Peninsular plantation owners. The strained negotiations between the three groups came to a halt in 1868 with the Grito de Yara, a plantation revolt that began the Cuban Ten Years' War.

The failure of the Ten Years' War was largely due to the lack of consensus among Cubans over how to proceed as a coherent nation of people. The three approaches outlined above helped to complicate the picture. The key element that forced the issue of independence from Spain was the development of a "national consciousness" that was moving toward Maceo's dream of integration. The *independistas* realized that there was no way to win a war against Spain without embracing the Afro-Cuban population on the island. This was true both in terms of building a spirit of nationalism, with the help of an Afrocubano vanguard including people like Gómez and Morúa Delgado, and in terms of finding the actual revolutionary soldiers needed to pose a real threat to the Spanish.

The great poet Martí was the key figure who textually and politically orchestrated this incorporation of culture and communities into Cuban memory. From his exile in New York, Martí wrote letters endorsing the Afrocubano general, Maceo. He conspired with prominent white and Black *criollos* on the island in a way that wove these influential characters into the *independista* camp. He focused on an emerging sense of patriotism and honor that created a Cuban sense of purpose and camaraderie.[95] The poem with which this chapter begins exemplifies some of the romantic tropes Martí used to urge white *criollos* in particular to embrace Africans as Cubans. This was important for the formation of a textualized Cuba, or the idea of a place and people called Cuba in the written record. In short, the national poet's writing fueled the necessary interest in incorporating African cultural production as part of a Cuban aesthetic language that set Cuba apart from Spain.

Other exiles were also writing and creating a public culture through periodicals that addressed independence, race, and Cuban national identity. Rodrigo Lazo, in *Writing Cuba: Filibustering and Cuban Exiles in the United States*, discusses this transnational Cuba that operated from exile in the

United States to help create a civil society on the island. Some of the main anti-Spanish discourses were aired in newspapers like *El Guao* and *La Verdad* edited by Pedro Santacilia in New York in 1853 and 1856, respectively.[96] Of particular note here is the periodical *El Mulato*, first published in 1854, which stressed the important connection of abolitionism to Cuban independence.[97] *El Mulato*, Lazo argues, served to place issues of race at the center of civic discourse about Cuba from a transnational perspective.[98] Thus, thinking and writing about Cuba and being Cuban was fostered within a context of diaspora, exile, and contention that was not just transnational, but transatlantic, in its essence. This is especially so because, to become a viable idea, the construction of the Cuban citizen had to somehow address the participation of Afro-Cubans.

This is the very context in which the Havana Lagosians lived and to which they contributed in terms of their understanding of community, diaspora, and transnational identity. Their lived experience as Cubans underscored the reality of Martí's expression of his dream of a Cuba where Africans also felt like Cubans. They also understood the importance of creating a civic culture from abroad to express that identification—much as the exilic periodicals *El Guao* and *El Mulato* did in various ways. The persistent identification with Cuba among the Aguda in Lagos shows that the creation of the idea of being Cuban was as diasporic as the creation of any other Atlantic identity. Yet, the Aguda's endeavors to reclaim their Cuban-ness and Brazilian-ness were couched in a larger "Yoruba" transnationalist fight against colonialism.[99]

What about the Aguda in Lagos and their Afrocubano family members in Cuba during this period of struggle for Cuban independence? As mentioned previously in their respective contexts, both groups considered themselves part of a transnational "Yoruba" community that included strong aspects of local affiliation to Cuba and Nigeria. From Sarracino's work and my own research, we know that members of the Campos family moved around freely between Cuba, London, and Lagos during the mid to late nineteenth century.[100] We also know that most Aguda families, from both Cuba and Brazil, spoke at least three languages, including English; were educated; and became financially prosperous.[101] The question of these Afrolatinos' role in the struggle for Cuban independence is an interesting one, and no definite answers can be ventured here. We can surmise, however, from looking at the contexts of the groups explored in this study, that some Lagosian Cubans certainly did identify with being Cuban and that this may have led to varying degrees of involvement in the independence struggle. Whether through physical combat, economic support, or the use of their Atlantic informational network, these communities most likely helped promote that struggle. And, it is just as probable that they associated their Afrolatino identity with a transatlantic stance against the colonial enterprise as a whole.

However, it can be said that the idea of Africans and Afrocubano *criollos* fighting in the Ten Years' War between 1868 and 1878, and in the Cuban war of independence that followed in 1895, is a strong nationalistic trope.[102] A character that epitomizes the Afrocubano veteran of these wars in the Cuban historical imagination was created by ethnologist Miguel Barnet. He wrote about this figure in the form of Estebán Montejo in *Biografía de un cimarrón* (*Biography of a Runaway Slave*).[103] It is interesting to note, as historian Michael Zeuske has discovered, that the accounts of Montejo in Barnet's biographical novel and the archive are conflicting at times.[104] Evidence of Montejo's life exists in the records, and these show that he was actually born after slavery was "officially" abolished in Cuba.[105] Barnet's use of the personage of Montejo is complicated, contradictory, and ironic in many ways. He uses the ethnologist's language of reflexivity coupled with a novelist's irreverent use of play in writing Montejo into being.[106]

I would argue that Barnet's understanding of the anthropological act of writing as the construction of character and culture is what compels him to say that he "created" Montejo—as many reflexive ethnologists see writing culture in this way.[107] More to the point here is Barnet's understanding that Montejo would represent an important figure of past Afro-Cuban resistance, a necessary character in the process of reclaiming Cuban identity from within the Black Atlantic transnational imaginary.[108] A similar discourse can be found in African postcolonial novels written in the same time period as *Biografía*, such as Chinua Achebe's *Things Fall Apart* and Ngugi wa Thiong'o's *The River Between*; these narratives reimagine past resistance to colonialism by employing the language of ethnographic description.[109]

Barnet's depiction of Montejo creates a typology for the life-cycle of an Afrocubano. Barnet uses the language of ethnography to re-create Montejo's life as a slave, as a *cimarrón* or maroon, and as a revolutionary in the Cuban wars of independence of the nineteenth century. This text symbolizes the process of becoming an Afrocubano in Cuba in a manner that displays an overtly optimistic path by comparison to the treatment in other works dealing with Black citizenship in Cuba in the nineteenth century.[110] However, the issue here is that Barnet is not writing about Black citizenship; rather, his re-creation of Montejo's life scripts the Cuban imaginary in the trajectory of *afro-crilloismo*. The text illustrates how popular Cuban discourse Africanizes *cubanidad* through a reinterpretation of history, especially through the incorporation of Afro-Cuban religious imagery.[111] This kind of characterization through descriptions of the Santería and Palo traditions is recognizable in cultural productions that attempt to make Afro-Cubans more "Cuban" and Cuba more "Afro-Cuban."[112] Barnet gives us an example when he depicts Montejo saying this about the Lucumí or Yoruba roles in forming the Cuban nation:

132 *Creating Afrocubanos*

> Los *lucumises* eran muy trabajadores. Hasta en la guerra hicieron un buen papel. En la guerra de Carlos Manuel.[113] Aun sin estar preparados para pelear se metían en las columnas y echaban candela. Luego, cuando esa guerra se acabó, volvieron a trabajar, a seguir esclavos. Por eso se desilusionaron con la otra guerra. Pero pelearon igual. Nunca yo vi un Lucumí echando para atrás. . . . Ahora, la mayoría de ellos [los africanos] echó cuerpo en la Independencia.

> [The Lucumí were very hardworking. Even in the war they played a great part. In the war of Carlos Manuel [the Ten Years' War]. Even though they were not prepared to fight they would enter into the rank and file and they fought with fervor. Later, when that war was over, they went back to work; they continued to be slaves. It was because of this that they became disillusioned with the other war. But they fought all the same. I have never seen a Lucumí fall behind. . . . Now, the majority of them [Africans in Cuba] gave their lives for independence.][114]

Barnet, through his characterization of Montejo, presents a set of views about the Lucumí, or ethnic Yoruba in Cuba. He situates tropes of hardworking, valiant Africans and Afrocubanos as collapsing into each other in this reconstructed memory. Barnet, through Montejo, names the specific ethnicity of different Africans in this recollection, which indicates an acknowledgment of the distinctiveness of African ethnic groups and their experiences in Cuba as part of the remembered discourse. In this context, Barnet/Montejo creates a view of the Yoruba-derived Lucumí in an especially valiant light—the crucial example of this is that they fought for Cuban independence even after being returned to slavery. The presentation of devotion to the cause of Cuban independence on the part of the Lucumí makes the case for imagining the Yoruba as proto-Afro-Cubans. The religion of Santería uses a similar method of *cubanizando,* or "Cubanizing" Yoruba mythology and folklore for a related purpose—that is, to legitimize the tradition on the island through the internalization of a postcolonial discourse.[115] These kinds of depictions show how the Lucumí are held as patriotic examples in retrospect: they are depicted as illustrating a high level of self-sacrifice and commitment to forming the Cuban nation. The Yoruba who returned to Lagos in this era had a dual frame of reference that helped to transform the societies they lived in, for both Cuba and Nigeria. The transformation of the concepts of African identity becomes extensive and can be structured across the Atlantic. The language of patriotism, here, takes on a range of meanings—depicting the same kinds of communities as Cuban and Yoruba simultaneously.[116]

Barnet's narrative, through Montejo's character, opens up avenues of inquiry about African cultures and experiences in the Americas. These reconstructed reflections play off and augment those available in the periodicals and other writings of Cuba's nineteenth-century *ciudad letrada.* Barnet's choice to use the voice of "lived experience" in re-creating Montejo's memory mirrors and plays with the use of the ethnographical present and fieldwork in a manner that highlights reflexive anthropology's concern over the writing of culture and use of informants.[117] Barnet creates a Montejo who contextualizes his memoir with ethnographical information about Africans and Afro-Cubans living in Cuba as slaves, *emancipados*, workers, and soldiers. The voice Barnet chooses for Montejo adds the element of personal affiliation with these communities to engage the reader with the narrative through a lived storyteller's bravado, by the use of Montejo's vernacular.[118] The author gives Montejo an ethnological memory and a historical imagination, using religion as a central model for speaking about African creolization in Cuba. As an example of this, he has Montejo speak about Congo religious rites he "witnessed" as a slave living in the barracks:

> Y el mayombe era un juego utilitario. Los santos tenían que estar presentes. Empezaban a tocar tambores y a cantar. Llevaban cosas para las ngangas.[119] Los negros pedían por su salud y la de sus hermanos y para conseguir la armonía entre ellos. Hacían *enkangues*, que eran trabajos con tierras del cementerio. Con esas tierras se hacían montoncitos en cuatro esquinas, para figurar los puntos del universo. . . . Cuando el amo castigaba a algún esclavo, los demás recogían un poquito de tierra y la metían en la cazuela. Con esa tierra resolvían lo que querían. Y el amo se enfermaba o pasaba algún daño en la familia. Porque mientras la tierra esa estaba dentro de la cazuela, el amo estaba apresado ahí y ni el diablo lo sacaba. Esa era la venganza del *congo* con el amo.
>
> [And *mayombe* was a utilitarian practice. The *santos* had to be present. They [the Congos] began to play drums and sing. They would take things to the *ngangas* [pot]. Blacks would ask for good health and that of their brothers and also for harmony between them. They would make *enkangues*, which were rituals performed with earth from the cemetery. With that earth one would make little mounds in the four corners, to represent the points of the universe. . . . When a master would punish a slave, the rest would collect a little bit of dirt and put it in the pot, With that dirt they would get what they wanted. And the master would get sick or there would be some tragedy in his family. Because while that dirt was inside the pot, the master was imprisoned there, and not even the devil could take him out. That was the vengeance of the Congo against the master.][120]

Barnet understands that for the Cuban popular imagination, the description of these cultural performances as used by slaves to build community echoes the kinds of syncretism we find in contemporary Afro-Cuban vernacular religion.[121] In the imagery that Barnet provides through Montejo's voice, slaves in the past combated wrongs done to the whole, multiethnic African community by performing folk religious rituals against the slave master. In this manner, Barnet/Montejo's imagined memory of the barracks situates Africans in Cuba within a zone of agency regarding belief that creates a metanarrative about the inevitability of conjuring and revolution as modes of social action in postcolonial Cuba. For contemporary Cubans, these kinds of "memories" create a continuum of acceptance of the efficacy of the power of conjuring that so permeates quotidian life on the island and in diasporic Cuban communities, like that of the Aguda in Lagos.[122]

The Cuban social imagination aside, or perhaps because of the possibility of manipulating its construction, Afrocubanos of a variety of ethnicities used these kinds of politico-religious strategies in ways that solidified and protected their communities on the island. For example, in the 1840s and 1850s, the Movimiento Catalino Fuentes advocated the use of *brujería,* or witchcraft, against whites for the purpose of destroying the plantation system on the island.[123] These kinds of performances of African-based magic in Cuba were flexible and adapted well to a multitude of situations. Many ethnic differences between Africans living in Cuba were negotiated for the common cause of fighting slavery and Spanish colonial rule.[124] A kind of syncretism between the ethnic Yoruba and Congo religions and Catholicism in Cuba became the basis for Cuban vernacular religion. Here, the practice of folk religion became an aesthetic template for social cohesion and nation building in a variety of contexts.[125] This religious negotiation between different Africans in Cuba mirrors that of the lived religious admixture found in Lagos, and became the organizing social principle of a civil religion with a proclivity toward tolerance. It would not be too far-fetched to say that the Havana Lagosians and the Aguda created crucial components of these Atlantic civil religions and thus contributed to the discourse of nationality in Cuba, Brazil, and Nigeria.[126]

Cuban Cultural Studies: Africans in Cuba, Cubans as Africans

The study of the African folklore, especially in African religious culture, found in societies of the Caribbean and Latin America has had a profound impact on the way these societies identify themselves in relation to the rest of the world. Conversely, Afrolatinos like the Aguda in Lagos and Benin also found that traditional African religious culture represented their identity both as African and as Caribbean people. As Gooding-King and Bamgboshe Martins expressed in interviews in Lagos, the Cuban and Brazilian reinterpretation of *orisha* worship created an expressive avenue for representing Aguda transatlantic cultural flows.[127] We find, then, that the study of religious culture in this context, and the resituating of identities through oral history, come together in locating culture through patterns of change, innovation, and movement.

In these ways, the study of local African and indigenous folklore has played a crucial role in providing points of reference of differentiation for creolized cultures. The study and description of African cultures, especially religious practices, in Cuba arose hand in hand with cultural production and the development of a national identity. The textualization of African cultures as Cuban was displayed in varied ways. From emic and etic contexts, "African" ways of living were incorporated into the public discourse and described in popular literature, periodicals, poetry, and travel journals from the eighteenth century onward.[128] These colonial texts became the sites where cultural contact and conflict was negotiated. For the early Cuban nation, what was perceived as African folklore, in writing and in the public performance of spectacle and popular religion, was institutionalized into the public discourse about identity.[129]

In 1627, Alonso de Sandoval published the seminal work *El mundo de la esclavitud negra* (The World of Black Slavery) about slavery in Cartagena.[130] Sandoval wrote at a time when Europeans, Africans, Asians, and Native Americans were situating themselves in the new Latin American colonial contexts.[131] Within the hegemonic structure of these colonial societies, people forged a shared, albeit stratified, quotidian existence and culture. As de la Fuente suggests for even as early as sixteenth-century Havana, negotiations between colonial elites on the island and the population of free Blacks, urban slaves, and the emerging mercantile class were not monolithic.[132] This early multiplicity in the understanding of identities and place and the intense negotiation for the construction of a new social order were characteristic of the Atlantic world, which had its origins in a range of African sensibilities that helped to create the creolized discourses that emerged from the various encounters.[133] Though colonial institutional frameworks may have attempted to divide and code clearly defined public spheres and notions of "place," the lived reality was one of cohabitation, intersection, and close proximity between people living in Havana.

To review what has been presented here, Cuban interest in writing about Africans and Afro-Cubans on the island expanded in the early nineteenth century with the *tertulias*, workshops of sorts, of del Monte.[134] Abolitionist writings, as well as writings by Afrocubanos of the time, flowered under the patronage of this powerful man of letters.[135] Suárez y Anselmo, Morúa Delgado, and Manzano were just a few of the *antiesclavista* authors that emerged from this period. After the Ten Years' War of 1868–1878, and the Cuban war of independence that followed in 1895, the incorporation of African identities as Cuban was a central strategy for building the imagined community of the Cuban nation. Martí, especially through his exilic writings, was instrumental in building the romantic link between nation, land, and community from his diasporic location in New York.[136] As Roger Abrahams has noted with regard to the construction of romantic nationalism, the Herderian connection between land and lore was the fertile soil in which folklore studies emerged.[137] Cuba, and especially Martí's concept of Cuba, was no exception to this imaginative and instrumental nationalistic practice. Martí, in poems like the one that opened this chapter, included Africans as Afrocubanos in his construction of what would become Cuban citizenship.

As discussed earlier, the construction of the trope of the Afrocubano, and especially the Yoruba as Afrocubano, takes on a life of its own at this point in the nineteenth century and later becomes an idiom by which Cubans express their national identity in diaspora.[138] Cuban authors, filmmakers, and artists quote and describe the practices of Yoruba-derived religions as a sort of shorthand for a kind of Cuban cultural identity that is both portable and perpetual. For example, novelists of contemporary Cuba and the Cuban diaspora like Zoé Valdés and Antonio José Ponte use an *orisha* aesthetic in their work when describing quotidian Cuban life, especially in Havana.[139] However, it is important to note that a range of African ethnic religious cultures exists in Cuba—and these cultures merge in practice and identify with Yoruba traditions to form a complicated web of ritual culture.[140]

This process of cultural recovery through remembering ritual comes full circle for the Cuban Aguda in contemporary Lagos. We see that Cuban and Brazilian identities are connected with both traditional Yoruba religion and Catholicism for this community. The legacy of the Aguda in Lagos is tied to their unique expression of Yoruba identity that incorporated the religious cultures of Latin America and the Caribbean in a manner that mirrors the Cuban use of Santería and Palo to signal identity, authenticity, and the portable nation. The discussion of the Campos and Bamgboshe Martins families' connection to traditional Yoruba religion and Catholicism in the previous chapter is a case in point. Their religious affiliations allowed them to signify their belonging to a range of communities that make up a larger Atlantic diaspora that claims Cuba, Brazil, and Nigeria as home. The use of the "Yoruba" incorporative model of community and family that comes exclusively from *orisha* worship allowed for this Atlantic diaspora to create new models of cultural admixture especially in Cuba. There is an interconnected flow between Aguda and Afrocubano use of religion as a viable conduit for recovering and expressing an Atlantic cultural memory.

Cuban Folkloristics in the Twentieth Century: Postindependence and Estudios Afrocubanos

The study of Cuban folklore, or Cuban folkloristics, from the early twentieth century onward is sensitive to diasporic creolization among Afro-Cuban, Spanish, Native American, and Asian *criollo* cultures on the island. As discussed above, the Afro-Cuban contributions to the formation of the Cuban nation clearly influenced the ways in which Cubans have imagined themselves as a distinct people.[141] In Fernando Ortiz's seminal essay "Los factores humano de la cubanidad" (The Human Factors of Cuban-ness), Cuba's first self-proclaimed folklorist outlined the *ajiaco*, a slow-cooking Cuban stew, as the founding metaphor for *cubanidad*, or Cuban-ness.[142] The melding of diverse European, Asian, Native American, and African cultures produced the sense of community expressed in Ortiz's notion of *cubanidad*. Unlike the American melting pot, the *ajiaco*'s ingredients, or distinct cultures, maintain their integrity, while still adding to the overall "flavor" of the mix. In other words, cultures are not destined to assimilate into one general way of being. Rather, different elements constantly mingle in the formation of a fluid national culture.

Through this trope of the *ajiaco*, Ortiz stressed his idea of transculturation over the concepts of acculturation and assimilation.[143] He differentiated transculturation from, especially, acculturation by emphasizing the former as a unique cultural intermixing that affected Cuban national culture across social strata. Unlike acculturation, transculturation was a process in which contact transformed social interactions into an amalgam of productions. Ortiz situated the formation of Cuban folklore and popular culture within this process. This contribution by Ortiz is significant in that it helps to explain why Afrocubano culture, especially the expression of folk religions like Santería, became a central metaphor for referencing *cubanidad* in general.

In 1917, Ortiz wrote *Hampa Afrocubana: Los Negros Brujos* (The Afro-Cuban Underworld: The Black Wizards). This was a criminological study of Afrocubanos living in Havana. Recently, scholars like Christine Ayorinde have taken Ortiz to task for his characterization of members of Afro-Cuban religious culture as pathological.[144] Ortiz, to his credit, however, changed his perspective drastically by the 1920s, moving from studies in pathological sociology to the study of folklore, and became the main advocate in his day for the study of Afro-Cuban culture. He established the pro-Afro-Cuban Sociedad de Estudios Afrocubanos and its journal in the early 1930s.[145] He was also the founder of the island's first La Sociedad del Folklore Cubano (Cuban Folklore Society), established in the 1920s. Perhaps it is the list of scholars and writers who built their work on Ortiz's extensive study of Afro-Cuban culture that is most impressive. Works that belong to this intellectual lineage include Lydia Cabrera's *Cuentos Negros de Cuba* (Black Stories from Cuba) and Romulo Lachateñere's *El Sistema Religioso de los Lucumí* (The Religious Systems of the Lucumí).[146] In terms of linguistic explorations of African dialects spoken in Cuba, Ortiz, Cabrera, Díaz Fabelo, and Olmstead provided some thorough inquiries that revealed the ritual use of the Lucumí dialect of the Yoruba language in the religion of Santería.[147]

Religious production was also the impetus for such novelists and poets as Alejo Carpentier, Guillermo Cabrera Infante, and Nicolás Guillén in their creation of works about Afro-Cuban culture in general. Others scholars in

Ortiz's lineage to emerge in the mid to late twentieth century include Isabel Castellanos, Natalia Bolívar, and Miguel Barnet. It is significant to mention these connections to Afro-Cuban culture here because of the self-reflexive nature of the Cuban public sphere, which relies heavily on both cultural performances and the texts produced about them. In the nineteenth century, people were reading and producing cultural performances about what being Cuban meant in relation to Afro-Cuban identity, and this process has continued in the twentieth and twenty-first centuries, magnified perhaps by the multifaceted nature of the worldwide Cuban diasporas. The construction of Afrocubano culture by the authors mentioned above has influenced and still influences Cuban identity on a number of levels, but especially as part of the *ciudad letrada* of Cuba as a nation. The process of creating the *ciudad letrada*, as well as the idea of Cuba, is largely an ongoing project of negotiation between those living the civic culture on the island and those reading and writing about that experience in diaspora.[148]

Since the Revolution of 1959, studies of Cuban culture have been divided in terms of sites of production. Cabrera, Castellanos, Cros Sandoval, and Benítez Rojo write about the island's culture from exile.[149] As could be expected, then, scholars negotiate Afro–Cuban–American diasporic culture and identity in their works.[150] In the literary realm, studies by Matibag and Hewitt discuss the central role that Yoruba and Congo religious metaphors play in forming Cuba's aesthetic language.[151] The contemporary writings of Ana Menendez, Cristina García, and Achy Obejas show how Cuban-American writers who came of age in the United States see their *cubanidad* as including the revolution. Of the three authors mentioned above, García and Obejas in particular situate their *cubanidad* by alluding to the African-ness of Cuban culture both on the island and in the United States diaspora.[152] In Cuba, we have writers like José Antonio Ponte writing about the *orisha* in the midst of a crumbling Havana.[153] Coco Fusco's transnational brand of Black cultural critique, which is informed by her Cuban identity, is illustrated by her performance pieces and analytical work, written in the United States.[154] Other authors and performers struggling with their Cuban identity from a position of exile include anthropologist Ruth Behar, playwright Eduardo Machado, author Zoé Valdés, literary critic Alan West-Durán, and performance artist Alina Troyano, a.k.a Carmelita Tropicana.[155] All these components make the construction of *cubanidad* from outside of the island, especially from the United States, a continuation of the conceptualization of "Cuba" that Martí began over a century ago.

We began with Martí's poem about the violence of slavery and the repercussions of such violence on the colonial states perpetuating the system. The making of societies in Latin America, the Caribbean, and the United States constituted a negotiation between this violence and the agency that Africans brought to the table. The study of African peoples in the Americas has been the foundation for the study of Black culture in the Atlantic world, but especially in Cuba. Africans played essential roles in creating Cuban national identities on conceptual and experiential levels. The creativity of Africans in the Americas also played a major part in advocating national consciousness in Africa, the creation of the Yoruba nation in the nineteenth century being a case in point.[156] The merging of new cultures from the eras of European expansion and the plantation economy in the Americas left behind a unique and conflicted legacy of creolization.

In this chapter, I have emphasized the creation of Cuban letters and consciousness in relation to vernacular practices, in order to illustrate that they are codependent. Writing, living, speaking one's language, creating an altar, narrating a memory—these activities were and are shared across an Afro-Cuban diaspora that spans all the shores of the Atlantic. In this book, the focus has been on how the construction of Afro-Cuban identity took place in both Cuba and Africa, and how the construction of Yoruba identity took place in both Cuba and Africa as well. Religion is a central component in any understanding of how people created these transnational communities across differences in language, society, and place. The *orisha* and the aesthetic universe people recognize from their worship are translatable and portable. In the construction of the idea of the Afrocubano in the nineteenth century, the religious culture of *orisha* worship became a movable force for organizing communities and creating new identities. By focusing on the range of ways in which, pervasively, Africans in Cuba helped to create public culture and identity, we see that the constant re-creation of "home," as an imagined space, a retrievable past, and a political mandate, is a collaborative venture between spheres of cultural production and lived communal experience, or folklife. Some of the texts were oral, performed, conjured, and written as well. They represent a range of cultural productions that signaled the construction of Cuban and Yoruba nationhood, which occurred in a scattered, and layered, postcolonial process.[157] By reconsidering especially the semiotics of Lucumí discourses, as potential languages and codes for resituating a Cuban identity, we discover that the utterances of Afrocubanos became the very seeds of the Cuban diasporic enterprise in the Atlantic world.

Conclusion

Flow, Community, and Diaspora

This volume has examined how the Yoruba in Cuba and the Cuban-Yoruba in Nigeria constructed communities across the Atlantic. This particular flow of people and culture was fueled by a social imagination that understood the other shores of the Atlantic as a sort of homeland. One homeland did not rule out the other, however. The Lagosians in nineteenth-century Cuba and the Aguda in nineteenth- and twentieth-century Lagos understood their identities as diasporic, as fluid, and as belonging to the processes of journey and relocation. The longing that made these communities articulate a sense of difference in their new environments was a way of understanding who they were in new contexts, of creating a sense of identity. Whether in Havana or Lagos, family history played a large role in how people came to understand why they moved from Nigeria, to Cuba, and back. In a sense, Cuba and Nigeria were situated as extensions of each other in terms of culture and belonging for the Lagosians in Havana and the Aguda of Lagos.

What occurred when these populations moved between Havana and Lagos, for example, was that the same families and communities coinhabited different borderlands and boundaries. They conceptually linked themselves with several different categories of people: Lagosian, Cuban, Lucumí, Yoruba, African. They made their connections to each other known primarily through the performance of folklore and other kinds of aesthetic production. An apt example of a cultural performance shared by Yoruba and Cubans is the calling or hailing of the ancestors, the *mojuba*, before any ceremony in Yoruba traditional religion and Cuban Santería.[1] Before any important religious or civic function can occur in these communities, one must first call upon the ancestors, and publicly note the genealogy of the community coming together. It is interesting that for Yoruba-Cubans and the Aguda, this kind of cultural performance created a spiritual link, ritually and in memory, between Cuba and Nigeria.

Some clarification with regard to the precarious and layered nature of naming different segments of Yoruba Afrolatino identity will help to provide another example. In the nineteenth century, the term "Lucumí" may have referred to Yoruba in Cuba, and the term "Aguda" may have referred to Yoruba-Cuban-Brazilians in Lagos.[2] The same individuals, or even portions of a community, could identify with these different ways of naming themselves at the same time. The process resembled the very common social practice of adding titles, *oye*, and special names, such as *oriki*, to oneself as one grows in honor and position in West African, especially Yoruba, society.[3] The ways in which diasporic populations like the Aguda and the Saro shifted their naming practices from English/Spanish/Portuguese to Yoruba reveals a movement toward identifying with a burgeoning neotraditionalism that began to express itself in Lagos toward the late nineteenth century.[4]

This kind of reexpression of Yoruba identity in Lagos had a great deal to do with the transnational movement that asserted a Yoruba nationhood in response both to colonialism in Africa and to a diasporic pan-African nationalism on the part of Lucumí Cubans and Nago Brazilians.[5] The accumulation of titles and names for these communities in flux included different categories of identity, as well as different kinds of experiences to be associated with. These associations were subject to change, often including layering, according to social contexts. The main factor influencing such choices, in Afrolatino-Yoruba contexts, at least, was the accumulation of social prestige. Thus, transnational terms of identification can refer loosely to a potential group of people who share a semiotic cluster of cultural symbols and practices in different lands. I say "potential" here because it was perhaps the assembling of different groups, actively choosing and making themselves—for example, Lucumí, Nago, or Aguda—through the social performance of naming, that "transnationalism" refers to here. In performances of the religious culture of the Yoruba diaspora, especially, fluid association in the use and utterance of names has been one of the main ways in which performers/members "do" community.[6]

Though separated by the Atlantic Ocean, Afrolatinos of Yoruba origin and Yoruba of Afrolatino origin merged, broke apart, and resided in spaces they made their own. This does not mean that such spaces went completely uncontested from within or outside the emergent diasporic communities. Rather, the terms of the negotiation of such spaces, as in a Yoruba marketplace, an *oja*, were reassembled to reflect an epistemology of pragmatic discourse.[7] This profoundly sound way of evaluating situations allowed Yoruba Afrolatino diasporas the flexibility to incorporate what was necessary for them to survive and thrive in new environments. And, of course, this also allowed for a keen selection of a useful traditionality that provided the basis for framing new interpretations of cultural identity.

This unique kind of cultural building based on Yoruba epistemologies occurs especially in traditional oral history, theater, and ritual performance.[8] This process is open ended, perpetual, and itself open to discursive critique.[9] For the Lucumí and Aguda, then, the nostalgic tropes of dispersal and relocation between Cuba and Africa provided the critical themes for their discursive performances. These performances occurred in a wide range of contexts, from the naming of children to the performance of Ifa divination, for example, which expressed the importance of folklore and folklife in providing opportunities for grassroots social agency, in both Cuba and Nigeria from the nineteenth century onward.[10]

This frame of referencing by the Lucumí and the Aguda in terms of Africa and Cuba challenges thinking about diasporas as being unidirectional. The ways in which these communities reinvented themselves in their new environments of Cuba and Africa was dialogic in character. That they shared a remembered trajectory connected them to each other, but also especially to the real and imagined movement between the different poles they called home. Routes here were multifaceted. Cities like Havana and Lagos represented new zones of congregation, where Yoruba-Cubans and Cuban-Yoruba populations used their skills as cultural innovators and resilient actors in social history. Theirs was a kind of diasporic practice, with portable diasporic sensibilities, that invented "home" in multiple kinds of constructions and deconstructions, in stages that negotiated, borrowed, and connected traditions with new social practices.

Creating Home in Diasporas

Diasporic communities invent narratives that signal home and reintroduce it into their lives.[11] Displacement and relocation create fodder for the reconstruction of memory. Dispersal also fuels the desire among diasporic communities like the Aguda to locate themselves not only within a particular set of narratives of the past but also within a particular set of places.[12] The creation of new customs in traditional ways helps to extend a community's sense of continuity.[13] Such marked customs exist in a continuum of performances across various subgroups that may claim access to a larger diasporic identity. For example, many perform Santería in Puerto Rico, Venezuela, Mexico City, New York, and so on, in a manner that suggests an association with a transnational "Latino" identity that is also Africanized.[14] Channeling into that religious identity is cross-cultural play at performing the Cuban, and the Yoruba. Both of these cultural locations hold certain kinds of mystic imaginaries for Latinos. This kind of performativity may become a hotbed of controversy for the negotiation of claims of legitimacy if we are dealing with layered religious identities that include a range of ethnicities.[15] In Santería in the United States, for example, many African Americans, other Latinos, and Puerto Ricans are important members of this religious culture.

Many cultural movements with political tendencies toward transnational Blackness in Africa and the African diaspora, were fostered by itinerant, exiled and repatriated groups or figures.[16] Sometimes itinerant communities on opposite shores of the Atlantic, like the Nago and Lucumí, and the Aguda, for example, made political connections across the Atlantic, forming transnational nationalisms. Two cases in point here are the role that the Aguda played in the formation of a pan-African notion of Yorubaland and the Lucumí contribution to the Cuban Revolutionary War of 1895.[17] Narratives of home, such as the ones we have explored in this volume, reinscribed space by concretizing images of home within a geographic place. These stories tie travel to past events, perpetually recasting the journey and resituating home on multiple fronts, creating a portable, reflexive history.[18] "Reflexive" here is to be understood in terms of home being seen as both a place left behind and a place where the community has just arrived, as in the case of the Aguda in Lagos and the way they saw Africa, Cuba, and Brazil.[19]

There are many kinds of home, and the idea and performance of being at home and going home acted as bordered frames of reference for diasporic populations like the Aguda. Going home and being at home were at times interchangeable, because they referred to each other in terms of how communities understood where and who they were. We can see how this process operated through Mrs. Ola Vincent's and Mrs. Gooding-King's narratives of their childhood, in which they remembered multiple homes and languages and a strong sense of nostalgia and pride issuing from Hilario Campos's *cubanidad*. They inherited a layered legacy in which their difference created their identity and sense of place in Lagos.

The multifaceted Yoruba-Aguda-Lucumí-Nago diaspora created beacons of home in collaboration with the transnational communities that this diaspora was simultaneously generating. The Aguda opened an array of channels that helped to circulate their unique identity as Africans and Afrolatinos.[20] Merging and emerging Afrocubano imaginaries (Lucumí, Congo, Abakua, and so forth) became the fabric of the diverse religious cultural universe of Cuban spirituality in the late nineteenth and early twentieth centuries.[21] These spheres were interlaced in one creolized context even as another context of admixture usually sat beneath its surface.[22] Though syncretism and creolization are different in many ways, the existence of both in African, especially Yoruba, contexts set the stage for a portable, cosmopolitan culture to be expressed in Cuba and Brazil, albeit also with African sensibilities.[23] Ortiz thought about this kind of admixture and its contours in Afrocubano culture. As discussed earlier, he used the idea of *kasha*, a religious performance where the words in Yoruba are interspersed with other African phrases, to show how Afrocubano syncretism and cultural admixture take their cues from a complex African context. He observed that the confusion about African ethnicity in Cuba

> can be explained by the syncretic formation of those [mixed] practices already in Africa. In the secret society of the abakuás or ñáñigos, diverse languages

are mixed and invented; [and] the rites of the Lucumís frequently introduce traditions and vocabulary from theararás, from the takús, from the iyesás, and from other neighboring towns [in Africa]. And, many Congo rites are *cruzados* [lit., crossed/mixed], that is how they are referred to, with others [other rites] from Africa.[24]

These observations about the *cruzado* or "crossed/mixed" nature of African customs in Afro-Cuban religious culture indicate that practitioners understood cultural admixture as a phenomenon that occurred in Africa as well, and that this cultural strategy was carried across the Atlantic to Cuba. The admixture that we see in the Caribbean was indeed unique in terms of the kinds of cultures created, but these grew out of other combinations that occurred in many different sociopolitical, cultural contexts, especially and primarily in Africa. Rather than assuming that any one kind of admixture signifies a defining moment of purity or pollution, Ortiz here understands the complex cultural negotiations that occurred between different African ethnic groups as a continuation of performative social mechanisms of inclusion.[25] In many ways, transnationalism, globalization, and hybridity are current methods of describing the kinds of culture building that were carried on for long periods, within the movement and resettlement of people across different kinds of borders.[26] More and more we see that explanations that emphasize a "modernist" framework over-determine industrialization as the primary factor influencing cultural processes in the Caribbean.[27] Indeed, technology does play a role, but it may be in communities using "postmodern" tools, like cyberspace, to refine, recycle, and define the contours of their identity, creativity, and culture.[28]

In the case of Cuba, as Ortiz suggests above, using African-based notions of culture building from influential religious practices makes sense in trying to achieve an understanding of the kinds of Afrolatino identities that were created on the island. The Afrocubano performance of a *cruzado* religious identity, for example, the cross-reference of Yoruba deities with Congo spirits, occurs in a realm that is dominated by what are thought of as "African" ways of hybridizing culture. These cultural marriages in religious semiotics and ritual performance became uniquely possible in the Caribbean as a whole, but were articulated especially well in Cuba. In these instances of religious admixture, the creation of innovative religious meaning becomes a challenge in interpretation and translation.[29] My approach has been to try to use folk etymology and cultural thinking as a source for working through these complex negotiations of cultural expression. Yet my idea is not to replace other terms for cultural admixture with terms like *cruzado*, or *asa*, but to open up the dialogue about what these kinds of words are meant to describe in their own social-cultural milieu. As noted above, new words are borrowed and melded to more adequately describe and perform the hybrid religious rites already being carried out in, for example, Santería, Palo, and Espiritismo. This understanding of religious admixing, from within different "African" religious spiritual spheres, was prominent not only in Cuba but in the larger Afro-Atlantic religious world as well.[30]

The actual words that are being created and performed in these Afro-Atlantic instances of admixture both describe and "do" the religious work discussed here. For example, the use of the Yoruba word *asé/aché*, "let it be," in Cuban instances, does the work of declaring into motion the desired results of a performed ritual. Folklorists and others interested in vernacular culture and linguistics often argue that the folk are aware of their own cultural creative work and well equipped to explain, define, and defend it.[31] One idea that comes to mind in this regard is the Yoruba idea of play, *sere*, as serious cultural work that is an important vernacular process based on a reflexivity of social performances.[32] We can argue that this process, among others, became an Atlantic process of culture building that informs the ways in which Afro-Cuban religious modes of *cruzando*, for example, have reiterated themselves in new contexts. Modes of combining and negotiating the performance of culture, like *sere* and *cruzando*, become part of the diasporic sensibilities of Afro-Cubans moving in the Atlantic world from the nineteenth century onward.

Thus, the people who were involved in creating the religious culture Ortiz was describing were mastering, playing at, and creating language and culture, consciously, for a myriad of purposes. Some may have been political, and some may have been personally political, but the nature of such performances certainly had real social consequences in terms of social power and prestige.[33] The folk, then, have understood the importance of the creative work they do, because this work affects their place in the world.

Marginality, Liminality, and Agency in Diasporic Settlement

Some researchers have suggested that the marginal status of diasporic communities in their new homes plays a significant role in the imagining of home for these groups.[34] Diasporas, especially in Afro-Atlantic contexts, use innovative approaches toward social organization because these allow them to navigate around and through their plight as slaves, exiles, and repatriates. Cohen noted that diasporas have "particularly adaptive forms of social organization."[35] Their flexible approaches to creating community are framed by the context of their distinction from "mainstream" culture, if not marginality.

The problem with this analysis of diasporas is that it cannot accurately account for the many levels of interaction between diasporic and "settled" populations. High levels of interaction between diasporic and "settled" communities, for example, were seen especially in the creation of public culture in the nineteenth century in both Havana, Cuba, and Lagos, Nigeria. As a case in point, I refer the reader to Ortiz's example, cited above, of ethnologists' confusion over Afro-Cuban ethnicity and the use of liturgical language. The vernacular language used in Palo rituals is a Bantu-Yoruba-Spanish-Arabic mixture, and it is a language that is creative, functional, and continuous.[36] The ritual language of Palo expresses a lasting engagement between different linguistic populations, "settled" and diasporic, and their perceived relationships to each other.[37] The utterances of a *muerto*, or ancestor, through a practitioner, reveal a historical relationship between the world of the living and the dead that is coded with the issues of slavery, race, and diaspora.[38] In order to understand the complex working of such combinations, one has to be involved in the emic cultural strategies at play in creating vernacular expressions in Palo's liturgical language.[39] Those engaged in Palo in Cuba, from some perspectives, may be seen to express "marginal" cultural practices emblematic of the diasporic creativity referred to above.

As I mentioned, I believe that this line of analysis for studying traditions like Palo vernaculars is problematic because it forces on a group a notion of displacement that seems artificial if one looks at quotidian practice in a performative context. The complex kinds of cultures being created are "central" to themselves in terms of being "locations" where meaning is made. It seems that the notion of an invisible cultural center blinds us to viewing the vibrant practices and histories, alive and interactive, like those of the Afro-Cuban tradition of Palo, that existed and exist between diasporas and "mainstream" cultures.[40] The marginality component of the analysis of diasporic populations relies on a falsely fixed paradigm of periphery and center. Such a separation does not fully describe the kinds of negotiation, conflict, and integration of the array of populations that live side by side—even if global centers are hegemonic by design.[41] The Cuban Aguda imagined themselves as Lagosians and Cubans in a manner that made each of these identities communicate with, rather than alienate, each other. The mediation by the Aguda of their own diasporic and settled identities allowed them to move through locked notions of periphery and center, and build a layered, transnational sense of community.

One particularly troubling assumption is that, in the periphery and center paradigm, communities and individuals are composed of discrete, centered entities. However, the ability of a single individual to claim multiple identities, such as Lucumí, Aguda, and Nago, reveals a high level of code switching and fluidity in national and cultural affiliation with Cuba, Brazil, and Nigeria, which plays a large role in creating the very contour of this diaspora.[42] Tropes of periphery and center, in short, have difficulty accounting for multiple and overlapping centers of cultural production.[43] What emerges in the study of the social contexts expressed in *lived* folk and vernacular cultures is a picture of diasporas as fluid highways creating further routes. This opening up of the ways of movement and creation challenges a central trope that we have discussed here: the very spaces of home and diaspora. The idea of the diaspora's journey helps provide, as do many paradigms, a range of description, or a model from which to speak through experience—but if used alone, it ignores the reality of the multiplicity of forms that defy or move beyond these two conceptual zones of home and diaspora, especially in the multifaceted context of the Atlantic world.[44]

Of course, there were cases in the past in which diasporic communities were marginalized, and there are cases of their maginalization now, especially in terms of economic disenfranchisement and international political visibility. Yet, even within these circumstances, there are ways to engage, interpret, and affect "mainstream" culture that are proactive for a "marginalized" community. The question to be asked is marginal to whom? In assuming only one frame of reference for an acceptable center, we ignore the reality of multiple centers for the creation of culture and meaning in complex and interconnected global and local societies. This is especially true in reconstructing the myriad of pasts found in the Atlantic world.[45] As we see especially with regard to Black Atlantic religions such as Candomblé and Santería, diasporic cultures from Africa used their capacity for "imagination as social practice" to challenge notions of their own marginality and deeply influence the nature of social and cultural identity in Brazil and Cuba.[46] Further examples of similar processes of the social imagination include Africans or Native Americans making representations of colonial figures, like explorers and missionaries, and recasting these into their own venues and contexts to create an alternative public sphere.[47] This space exists for an audience that can read coded, ironic, and satirical messages.[48] In a Cuban and Black Atlantic context, this play with the public sphere can surely be seen in the production of works like Coco Fusco's traveling "anthropological" exhibit.[49]

That some of these public spheres are hidden or exist under the radar of the "mainstream" does not mean that they do not exist. Nor does their exclusivity suggest that these vernacular publics are any less than central to the folk groups participating in their discourse and culture making—especially when the new counterperspectives are placed in publics that force all audiences to face the counter-performance and presentation of "marginality."[50] Appropriation, reversal, and reinterpretation in cultural production are among the diasporic and postcolonial sensibilities that create successful aesthetic strategies for "marginal" communities imagining and changing their host societies.[51] For example, the ongoing relationship between Santería and folk Catholicism in Cuba from the nineteenth century onward delineates and negotiates continuities and disruptions between formal and folk cultures, not unproblematically, of course.[52] One such line of continuity and disruption is found in the shared and layered iconography of the church and the *casa de santo*, with both Catholic objects and traditional

148 *Conclusion*

Yoruba objects being found in each other's public space. These conversing signs, as found on altars in both spaces, reveal a deep and complicated confluence of historical negotiations speaking to a social contract that privileges ritual practice and the efficacy of spiritual power.

Another example of the complexity of negotiating identity, power, and centrality in changing societies includes the changing ethnicity among Yoruba diasporas across the Atlantic and within Africa.[53] Especially in the nineteenth century, people from different ethnic Yoruba communities—from Oyo, for example—went through many different manifestations of Yoruba identity through their lifetimes. This was so especially in the context of the fall of Oyo and the subsequent civil wars.[54] An individual may conceivably have gone from being an *omo Oyo*, a citizen of Oyo, to a refugee or new citizen of Lagos, *omo Eko titun*.[55] Similarly, before arriving in or returning to the Bight of Benin, the Brazilian Yoruba, the Nago, embodied different kinds of transnational, Afrolatino citizenship before resettling in London, in Lagos, in Ouidah, or in Sierra Leone.[56] Thus, the assertion of the stability of a fixed, centralized, monolithic, Yoruba ethnic identity made little sense in lived practice.[57] Rather, the experiences of Nago, *omo Oyo*, *omo Eko*, and Lucumí Yoruba, for example, included a range of social and cultural performances and affiliations that were marked with a diasporic sensibility for change, for innovation, as well as key traditions that served as culture markers. And Yoruba traditional religion, in a semiotic and performed fashion, served as one powerful culture marker that helped the Yoruba, as well as diasporic Afrolatinos from the Caribbean, to reinvent themselves.[58]

As returnees who had lived in different places in Latin America and the Caribbean, the Aguda in Lagos embraced each other, merged with the local Yoruba, and championed their mixed version of Afrolatino culture, which included the Boa masquerade, also known as the "Carretas," and masking brought from Brazil.[59] The ways in which these people moved in and out of West Africa, Europe, the Caribbean, and the Americas highlight, over and over again, how the great work of creating home as a folk community was done in small ways. The Aguda, and diasporic groups like them, played and resituated social and cultural splits, established ethnic mergings, and displayed their ability to belong, not to a place, necessarily, but to themselves as a group, in small consistencies, or in the "simple forms" of folklore and performed culture.[60] The cultural signifiers used by the Nago Yoruba and the Aguda, for example, were portable and flexible. Customs like the Boa masquerade in Lagos, which has continued to this day with the display of the Carretas, illustrate the importance of creating performances that mark an environment with difference, and thereby claiming that space as their own.[61] Also, the public display of cultural objects as in murals and "tagging," represents a way for groups to mark and transform territory.[62] In this manner, the Aguda have been able to belong to multiple communities, places, and sites of cultural production.

This kind of creative construction of home for diasporic communities in the Atlantic world in the nineteenth century, especially in cosmopolitan centers like Havana and Lagos, also included a certain amount of contention over space with those already in place. That is, certain constituencies competing for power and prestige were already located in and associated with certain sites in urban Lagos and Havana. In Lagos, the most obvious site of traditional prestige would be the *oba*'s palace, the Iga Igandaran.[63] Prestige was also associated with the building of the Saro and Aguda neighborhoods in the city with their respective Victorian and Afrolatino cultural touches.[64]

In Havana, a range of African communities collaborated around ethnicity and other points of unification in creating community spaces that were identifiable in the public sphere. *Cabildos* are a case in point here in their geographic and social locations.[65] These fraternal organizations often were organized early on in a manner that reflected in-group aesthetics of prestige and power that were described as "African."[66] Thus, in Lagos and Havana, we see that the struggle over place and prestige was bound up in a combination of factors that communities brought to these sites. These factors included bringing aspects of culture, especially in the form of religious identity, attained from across the Atlantic, as markers of prestige for both the Aguda and Africans in Cuba. The new kinds of prestige generated by these incoming groups challenged the old order for space in interesting ways that also relied on the viability of the incorporative nature of the traditional religious and political system.[67]

When home becomes a new society, as was the case of the Aguda establishing the Popo Aguda in Lagos, communities use the aesthetic tools of difference to demarcate sites as their own.[68] In the process, the Aguda changed Lagos, as also the Lagosian *emancipados* changed Havana—in the realms of civic-religious folklore, popular culture, and vernacular economies.[69] The vernacular economies of the Aguda included both material and cultural productions, like the production of the batik and the *ese* produced at the Campos workshop, that created public cultures existing on various levels in Lagos and beyond. These local public cultures were engaged in larger transnational networks, especially in terms of identifying and imagining Cuba and Brazil as an extension of the kind of spheres that the Aguda could associate with and that could also be associated with them.[70]

The Ijebu Yoruba provide an example of a similar kind of creative economic control in the nineteenth century. Their exclusive access to, and internal management of, important trade routes between the Nigerian hinterland and Lagos brought the group into direct conflict with the British, as the Ijebu aligned themselves with the Portuguese and the Bini during a critical period of colonization.[71] The British eventually won this struggle, but the important points here are the competing and emerging notions of trade, involving, for example, the Yoruba ideas of *oja*, the market, and the Luso-European ideas of *mercado*, which became intermingled as a result of conflicts such as these.[72] Trade here signifies the social ritual of the exchange of material goods, and of narratives that perform communities to outsiders as well. Gifts associated with connecting certain histories together, like the Portuguese donation of the stucco tiles for the roof of the Lagosian royal palace (see chapter 2), provide a basis for understanding multiple identities that unfold histories and link them together, through different notions of trade.[73]

Trade in this Atlantic context does not mean the synthesizing of goods and cultural products solely for their market value. Though trade in palm oil and slavery did create the parameters of trade in the Bight of Benin during the eighteenth and nineteenth centuries, many other items of material culture were being exchanged and understood in new contexts as well.[74] Items of material culture, especially religious articles associated with *orisha* worship, were made and traded for multiple levels of reception and use in Nigeria, Cuba, and Brazil. Similarly, the performance of narratives and oral histories was exchanged in this Atlantic context, having multiple audiences with shifting frames of reference.[75] Exchange and consumption, on a vernacular level especially, were reimagined and implemented in contexts like *orisha* worship. These cultural performances extended and changed existing systems of ritualized social stratification based on ancient ideas of prestige, ritual obligation, and cultural ascendancy.[76] So the exchange of culture, in the form of recognizable material culture and traditions, became a conduit for reinvention, resistance, and retrieval for communities like the Havana Lagosians and the Aguda.[77] In the same way, diasporic cultures, like that of the Aguda in Lagos, continue to thrive and reinvent themselves in "late capitalism and (post)modernity," concepts that themselves reply on specific cultural and historical contexts.[78] These Atlantic communities were flexible in their approaches to society and culture, and the nature of their diasporic sensibilities reflected a tendency toward movement and transnational affiliation.[79]

The vernacular culture of diasporic communities like the Aguda and the Havana Lagosians was at least to an extent self-reliant and resilient.[80] Contrary to the view of many analysts, some diasporic communities in the Afro-Atlantic world of the past were able to display social agency in the face of colonialism, slavery, and other forms of institutional disenfranchisement.[81] Deconstruction of the narratives created to enforce European colonialism in the Caribbean and Africa reveals the tacit hegemonies that reinforce the dominance of certain spheres of cultural production. This placement of official colonial cultures as dominant over vernacular local cultures can be understood as the setting up of an imposed, fabricated cultural center.[82] Yet we also see that "marginal" communities like the Aguda in Lagos deeply influenced and transformed the fabric of the societies that they entered.

They, as diasporic newcomers, realigned the existing hierarchies of social relations that they encountered. This forces us to rethink the roles of local people in Africa and the Caribbean, and the connections they made to each other, in creating the routes of the Atlantic.[83]

Let us take, for example, the Lagosians who resided in Cuba in the shifting and uncertain social context of the nineteenth century: some lived in slavery, some were emancipated, most engaged in urban labor, and a few achieved repatriation back to Africa. Yet, after repatriation, some merged through marriage with Afro-Brazilians and with Saros (Sierra Leoneans), and became part of another complex set of enmeshed social communities. In this manner, both in Lagos and in Havana, multiplicities of "marginal" peoples created their whole image, their implied center of identity. In these social matrices, especially in the development of the notion of *cubanidad*, or Cuban-ness, the spaces for making social meaning and identity were in reality too abundant, too numerous, open, and influential to be silenced or collapsed into an invisible center.[84] Further, on the Lagosian side of this copenetration, evidence of the rich, complex fabric of Lagosian communities in the making, especially from the nineteenth century onward, has been clearly seen in detailed studies of linguistic and material cultural analysis of groups like the Aguda and the Saro, converging and realigning themselves in the region.[85] The phenomenon of moving in multiple centers of culture making left a marked social and architectural landscape in the entire region of the Bight of Benin, but especially in the intense points of merging for the Aguda diasporas: in Havana, Bahia, Queen's Terrace in Southampton, Lagos, and Ouidah.[86]

Diasporic communities like the Aguda and the Havana Lagosians used the processes of imagination and invention in order to place themselves in their new homes with a unique history about a home left behind. The present study of Havana Lagosians and Aguda Cubans has dealt with how the members of one *rama*, or branch, of this diasporic community conceptualized themselves and then tied these conceptualizations to geographic regions, cultural symbols, and areas of interest.[87] Narratives found in popular literature and myth played a large role in framing the aesthetics of the Afro-Cuban connections to "home" in Africa and eventually to Cuba as well.[88] The historical contexts of these Atlantic Afro-Cuban diasporas influenced the distinct linguistic textures of the narratives and religious practices carried back and forth through contact and resettlement.[89] Here, the multiplicity of languages, homelands, and ideas about origins, especially in a religious sense, in terms of Santería and Yoruba traditional religion, overlapped and diverged, but also agglomerated for the Aguda and the Havana Lagosians.[90]

The clues I use to explore the depths and contours of these Atlantic connections are provided by vernacular religious and social principles.[91] These principles serve as signposts that are often read by communities, like the

Aguda and the Havana Lagosians, as cultural metanarratives rooted in discourses that can transcend differences in languages and place. For example, the Yoruba creation myth that centers around the formation of the human body by the *orisha* Obatala is one of these narrative signposts, one that could be "read" simultaneously by the Aguda in Lagos, the Lucumí in Cuba, and the Nago of Brazil.[92]

The unifying factor here is knowledge of the religious cultures of *esin ibile*, Santería, and Candomblé, among the Aguda, the Lucumí, and the Nago, respectively. These narratives were particularly useful in forming the transnational connections that helped to loop together these three groups in their imagination of their primordial origins, their place in the world, and the ways in which they did and did not belong to each other. *Orisha* worship worldwide provides a template for the social imagination in offering fluid metanarratives that consist of portable codes.[93]

Diasporic communities like the Aguda and the Havana Lagosians force us to ask questions about nationality, identity, and the relationship between the global and the local. As these groups relocated, they brought their strategies of culture building and identity formation with them. The amalgamative task of constructing a narrative of a home culture and identity was central to the way Havana's Lagosians and the Aguda repositioned themselves in Cuba and Lagos.[94] These communities negotiated their outsider status with claims of belonging to the cultures and nationalities left behind, and also of belonging with each other. What was referred to as an "authentic" home culture in places like Bahia, Havana, and Lagos included earlier kinds of cultural admixture and diasporic experiences.[95] The language of home is imbued with an ironic sense of the unchangeable that can never fully be recaptured. I believe that the experiences of the Aguda teach us that this language of home served to motivate the construction of a new identity that could simultaneously embrace two nostalgic centers of cultural memory. We see that this process was deeply connected to the way the Yoruba affected the societies in Latin America and the Caribbean. As the Cuban Aguda were carrying their memories of home in Cuba back to Lagos, they thought about the ways in which they had changed and created their own worlds in both of these cultures. This became a template for the way they would use their imagination and sense of community when they returned to Lagos.

Anthropologist James Clifford believes that diasporic communities have cultures that travel. He emphasizes that culture is made in such cases very much like a textual product that is being mutually constructed between movement and culture.[96] If one considers the work that oral, discursive quotation does in the performance of Yoruba history (as in Prince Olusí's singing of the Ifa divination poem in chapter 3), then Clifford's assertion is an interesting starting point for further inquiry and discussion about the relationship of such narratives to the construction of culture.[97] Clifford looks at the way in which anthropologists have created texts as cultures, and cultures as texts. In African and Afro-Atlantic contexts, especially, anthropology and folklore have a complicated, sometimes colonizing, relationship to the cultures they have "textualized." Yet knowledge from both of these spheres of production has been recirculated into the very cultures explored.[98] And, the process of rearticulating these different modes of knowledge-production resembles that of the cultural bricolage or creolization. The use of Cabrera's ethnological work as a sort of ritual guide by North American Santeros is an example of this kind of transference of the knowledge collected from the folklorist or anthropologist back into the folk group.

Clifford Geertz, differently from Clifford, experiences a "there" where cultures are concerned.[99] Local knowledge, in a semiotic way, can be knowable for Geertz in emic and etic ways. One of the main issues in looking at the construction of culture, for anthropologists, then, is whether we need universals in order to communicate cross-culturally. Like the local and global paradigm so prevalent in discussions of diaspora, the particular and general paradigm also bifurcates the terms of engagement in the study of culture. For example, if we consider the Aguda, Lucumí, and Nago, as above, in terms of Yoruba religious metanarratives speaking through linguistic and cultural difference, the question concerning the terms of communication becomes more complicated. This kind of dilemma lies very close to the dilemma of the translatability of language and culture in diasporic contexts. The answer may lie in looking closely at how transnational communities like the Aguda, Nago, and Lucumí negotiated levels of meaning through the performance of discourses that were already layered with embedded meaning. These Yoruba metanarratives were not static or universal, but they could speak across cultural difference because they focused on the process of performing communication in a myriad of ways.

In the semiotics of cross-cultural *orisha* worship that we are considering here, the signification of symbols in ritual and narratives is polylingual in aspect through time, with layers of aesthetic translatability incorporated as different populations adopted these traditions in the Caribbean and Latin America.[100] This issue of translatability and language in the Cuban Aguda diaspora recalls the perpetual debate among anthropologists and linguists as to whether cultures can be understood outside of their conceptual and social contexts.[101] Yet, when we look at the way language and meaning work in the context we are considering here, that of an *orisha* semiotics, there is embedded in language a space for mis- or not-understood language. Some of the language and its intended meaning in sacred contexts is both secret, *awo*, and deep, *jinle*. This space for the unread is seen in Yoruba ritual, visual art, and music relating to traditional religion, but especially in the language of the *orisha*. What is deeply coded is often reserved for various levels of the priesthood and initiated participants.[102] Adherents to the religious traditions that were shared by the Aguda, the Lucumí, and the Nago successfully deciphered the meanings of "secret" religious significations for themselves, both synchronically and simultaneously.

However, reading religious signification—for example, in viewing Atlantic altars made for the ocean deities like Yemayá and Olokun—may result in similar understandings by different communities, but may also be dependent on different perspectives or starting points. For example, the altars found in Phyllis Galembo's *Divine Inspiration: From Benin to Bahia* may be read along nationalistic or sect-oriented lines, which may or may not be shared by Yemayá and Olokun priests, artists, and devotees in Nigeria, Cuba, Brazil, and Benin.[103] The reading of dense ritual practices and ornamentation relies largely on a composite set of tools that the viewer has on hand, or even tools that the viewer chooses to use at any given moment.[104] The readings are contextual in themselves in that they are always up for negotiation, incorporation, and discursive improvement.[105]

In Havana, Bahia, and Lagos in the nineteenth century, Santería, Candomblé, and *esin ibile* constructed unique but overlapping methods of cultural production.[106] The long and layered historical encounters between these three religious communities across the African diaspora strengthened cultural borrowings and sophisticated, "cosmopolitan" (re)associations.[107] Observations by Yoruba specialists like William Bascom, who in 1962 saw the need to rethink the paradigms of urbanity and sophistication in Africa, in his article "Some Aspects of Yoruba Urbanism," suggested that from early on, the "folk" were well ahead of the scholar or specialist in understanding, creating, and explaining the social fabric and context of their own lived culture and environment. What Bascom understood, by looking at the religious materials he was working with in terms of Ifa divination and *orisha* worship in Cuba, Nigeria, and the United States, was that new conceptual understandings of urbanism, and by implication cosmopolitanism, needed to be articulated with an eye toward folk and vernacular epistemologies. For Bascom, the issue focused on the diverse, open, and incorporative nature of Yoruba cultures in what were, because of population density and location, rural contexts. Bascom both called for a change in the criteria for social categorization based on cultural relativism and presented an objection to using a dyadic paradigm that limited the way we looked at the sophistication and scale of Yoruba cultural and religious practice in terms of its socio-cultural geographic context. Within past Yoruba and Afro-Cuban religious contexts, changes in the aesthetics, history, and social organization of *orisha* traditions occurred in the process of a lived society in Lagos and Havana. These religious changes, even within these very specific cultural contexts, developed a mode of readability and reinvention that was passed on in these locales.[108]

Diasporas like those of the Havana Lagosians and the Aguda operated in the social imagination as allegorical continua of home and return for each other.[109] These allegories of belonging worked as a dance, a fluid movement that occurs within discursive borders.[110] Religious performances found in Santería and in *esin ibile* express this movement, refer to origins, and look toward the formation of new communities. The imagining and performing of home in these allegorical ways was a means used by the Aguda—for example, in the yearly performance of the Boa masquerade from Bahia—to express an identity or experience of belonging and difference. However, performances like those of the Boa masquerade and of the Santería religious ceremonies that refer to home in either the African diaspora or Africa do not describe the distinctiveness of the Aguda in rigid ways. These performances display a freedom in their referential use of allegorical boundaries. The referencing of the Aguda and Havana's Lagosians to each other works like playing a tune in a particular key or writing in a particular language in their ability to play with the themes and symbols in Yoruba religious and nationalistic mythology. Also, many examples from the Aguda diaspora suggest that multiple poles of origin were understood as potential resources for this kind of play. This worked in terms of potential geographic connections and also in terms of religious and cultural alliances abroad, especially if we consider sites of departure and home like Bahia, London, and Ouidah.[111]

The cultural strategies of dispersed peoples like the Havana Lagosians and the Aguda in Africa focused on the reinvention of their communities, histories, and cultural legacies by using the notion of "home." As the Havana Lagosians and the Aguda relocated, they defined themselves in relation to the host societies in which they resided, designating difference as a means of creating identity. An inspiring irony was that they looked toward each other in ways that reasserted the similarities between the homes they left behind and the homes they would create. Central to weaving together Afro-Cuban-Yoruba and Yoruba-Cubans was the traditional belief in *orisha* worship and the nationalistic identity this religious culture engendered through its rituals and mythology. Indeed, it was because of the importance of *orisha* worship in Brazil, and among Brazilian Aguda, that the different prongs of this transnational community could come together.[112]

One also must recognize the deep significance of folk Catholicism as a viable source of spirituality and identity for the Aguda and Yoruba-Cubans.[113] Yoruba communities in Cuba and Cuban communities in Nigeria incorporated Catholic religious culture into their spiritual practices. Catholic culture included the veneration of local saints and virgins—like La Caridad del Cobre in both Lagos and Cuba—the Holy Trinity, going to Mass, assembling for festivals, and so on.[114] These rites were both public and private, at times syncretic and at other times seperated. A case in point from this study is the affiliation of Catholicism attributed to the Aguda in Lagos, and to the Campos family in particular, even by non-Catholic family members.[115] However, belief in either *orisha* traditions or in the ritual culture of Catholicism was not a mutually exclusive phenomenon. The spiritual worldviews and experiences of these communities displayed a complicated, open, and adeptly fluid frame of reference for working through religious discourses. These deep and personal approaches to cosmology are a mark of vernacular religion in general, which often focuses on ritual as a form of community formation.[116]

What continues to make the contemporary Aguda in Lagos, the Lucumí in Cuba, and the Nago in Brazil unique is their mutual sense of African and Latin American identities. Their ability to switch frames of reference and to fluidly reimagine their location in the trajectory of the Atlantic world they share make them a portable transnational community. They are Afrolatinos and Africans in all of the complicated senses of these shifting identities. And, as Afro-Atlantic communities with a sense of a shared past, they use narratives of difference and distinction as a means of organizing their social identities. At the heart of these diasporic cultural productions is an attempt to dialogue about the similarities and differences between their African and Latin American "home" societies. Their viability and strength resides in the ability to adopt flexible strategies of cultural negotiation.

These strategies are necessarily part of a transatlantic imagination that operates with a wide purview even within "localized" sites.[117] In the Afrolatino diasporas that spanned the shores of the Atlantic world in the nineteenth century, negotiations between distinct cultures took place in a way that emphasized a cosmopolitanism that, in some instances, may be characterized away from the West. In diasporic processes that challenge a "modernist" narrative, communities like the Aguda amalgamated disparate traditions in multiple ways. These communities from the diasporic past mimic but also go beyond the current context and understanding of the "postmodern."[118] The variety of strategies used by Afro-Cubans and by Afro-Brazilians in Africa, especially, existed in a continuum of cultural agency that began with their experiences of nationalizing African religious discourses in Cuba and Brazil.[119]

Afrolatinos in the Americas constructed themselves and home with the methodologies they brought with them from their African communities. And, in the continuum we have explored in this volume, Afro-Cuban methods of cultural and social amalgamation were brought back into Africa to be reinvented there as well. This resiliency in motion, this pliant cultural technique of traditional incorporation of the new, challenged the very contexts of servitude, exploitation, and racism that formed the social backdrop for Afro-Cuban diasporic communities in all of the Atlantic places they called home.

Appendix

Case Studies of Returnees to Lagos from Havana, Cuba

Sources

Macaulay, Zachary, ed. *The Anti-Slavery Reporter. Under the Sanction of the British and Foreign Anti-Slavery Society.* Vol 2, 3rd ser. London: Peter Jones Bolton, 1854, 234–39.

Pérez de la Riva, Juan. *Documentos para la historia de las gentes sin historia.* 1960. Reprint, Havana: Biblioteca Nacional de José Martí, 1969.

Joaquín Pérez

A native of Lagos, Joaquín Pérez was between fifty and sixty years old at the time of his journey back to the city of his birth. He had lived in Havana for about thirty years. Joaquín first arrived in Cuba with three hundred other enslaved Africans on a Spanish ship, on which there was an outbreak of smallpox. However, only four people were lost to the disease at sea. Upon reaching Cuba, Joaquín was taken to the Castillo Principe slave barracks, where he waited for three days before being sold to a businessman named Don Pérez. He worked as a dockworker with other slaves until he was sold to Joaquín Lupicio, under whom he worked for fifteen years before saving up enough money to buy his freedom for 550 pesos. His wife, Martina Seguí, and his eighteen-year-old son, Crescencio Seguí, accompanied him back to Africa. Joaquín paid a total of 300 pesos for their journey.

Martina Seguí

Martina Seguí was a child when she arrived in Havana, about thirty years before joining her husband, Joaquín Pérez, on their journey. She was between forty and forty-five years old when she made her declaration to ship officials upon boarding the repatriation vessel. Martina had been taken from Lagos to Havana with five hundred other captives. They were taken to a forested region on the Cuban coast. They were sold as slaves, and Martina went to work for Don José Morales, a landowner who put her to work selling his produce and goods on the streets of Havana. She stayed with Morales for a year and then was sold to a free person of Congo background named Seguí who had a good position working in the docks, where Martina's future husband also worked. Martina continued selling goods in Havana and saved up enough money to buy a different status from Seguí. She paid 200 pesos to move up to the status of *coartada,* or contract laborer, at which point she and Seguí agreed that she would pay him a sum of 3 pesos a week from her hawking until she had paid him the remaining 300 pesos she needed for her liberty. After twenty years of work under Seguí, she was sold to Joaquín Mandiola. Martina carried her paid balance over to Mandiola and finally paid him enough to buy her freedom three years after she had been sold to Mandiola. Her manumission was postponed because, before she had paid the entire amount to her new owner she used her savings to "buy" her son's freedom for 150 pesos. Her son worked as a tobacco roller in Havana before going with his mother and father back to their hometown of Lagos.

Augustín Acosta

Augustín Acosta was taken out of Lagos on a Spanish slave vessel. He was forty years old at the time of his repatriation to Africa. He lived in Havana for twenty-four years before deciding to return to Lagos. He arrived in Cuba, along with four hundred other Africans taken out of Lagos as slaves, and was sent to a slave barracks near Havana. Augustín and forty others were then sold to Tiburcio Yané, an individual who specialized in renting out his slaves' labor.

Augustín was repeatedly rented out to various sugar and coffee plantations in the island's interior. He worked in a rural sugar refinery, where he and other slaves spent long hours with little food and rest. Augustín was forced to work in these conditions for twelve months, after which he was sold to Lopez Diez, a wealthy landowner who used Augustín as a domestic servant. Lopez sold Augustín to another wealthy landowner, Manuel Acosta, who had both coffee and sugar plantations on the island.

After nine years, Augustín Acosta was able to buy his freedom for 50 pesos. He paid 100 pesos for his journey home to Lagos. Unfortunately, Augustín did not describe his life in Havana after working in the provinces on plantations, but we can infer that he was able to establish links with free people of color and slaves who also had ties to Lagos.

María Luisa Mazorra

María Luisa Mazorra and her husband, Gabriel Crusati, were Yoruba born in Lagos. María Luisa was forty years old when she and her husband returned to Africa, and she had lived in Cuba for seventeen years. She was brought to Cuba, along with 420 others, as a slave. The ship had problems due to conditions at sea. The ship was wrecked, and the survivors were brought to the slave barracks in Castillo Principe.

María Luisa was then bought by Don José Mazorra, a bookmaker who dealt in the lottery. She worked for Mazorra as a domestic servant for seven years. In her deposition, she complained of Don Mazorra's cruelty, and because of his abuse she demanded that he sell her. She got her wish, as Brigada Pina, a relative of hers, bought María and brought her to work in Brigada's store, where she sold sundries.

Here we see a case of an economically prosperous Havana Lagosian liberating a relative by buying her labor.[1] Most of the slaves who were bought by free relatives had to then "buy" their freedom by providing labor for the relatives. Obviously, these Havana Lagosian businesswomen retained some of the highly competitive Yoruba business behaviors commonly associated with the markets and trade of Lagos.

Pina died within a year, before María Luisa could pay off her entire debt. María Luisa was left as a *coartada*, or contract laborer. Her contract was valued at 300 pesos, and her family sold the contract to another relative named Mauricio Rodríguez. María Luisa contracted out her labor, lived on her own, but paid Rodríguez 9 pesos a month, as he "owned" the contract. She stayed under Rodríguez for three years, until she was "cut out" of the labor contract with Rodríguez for 100 hundred pesos, and was transferred to Don Alejandro Mínez. María Luisa was eventually able to buy her freedom after a year under Mínez, her monthly payments to Don Mínez being put toward her purchase of her freedom under the *coartada* system. At the time of her repatriation to Lagos, María Luisa had been free for over four years. She worked as a cook in Havana, and with her earnings she bought her passage back to Lagos for 100 pesos.

Ignacio Moni

Ignacio Moni was forty-one years old when he decided to return to Lagos, his native town. He was brought to Havana between 1834 and 1838, during Governor Tacón's era. Ignacio and 350 other slaves were taken to Castillo Principe, where most were moved to the barracks of an infamous slaver, Don Manuel Barriero. Ignacio was sold to Don Antonio Mayo, an architect, who later sold Ignacio to Don Pedro Moni. He worked under Don Moni for nine years.

During this time, Ignacio took a wife, another slave, and both worked toward their manumission by selling their labor to other patrons. Ignacio bought his wife first, then he bought his own freedom, in each case for 500 pesos. Ignacio had to appeal to *el síndico* in regard to buying his wife. The main problem was that her owner wanted 700 pesos, an illegal amount since there was a ceiling placed on the amount that an owner could ask for the emancipation of a slave. *El síndico*, through the international court system in place in Havana, had established 500 pesos as the maximum amount payable in *all* cases of manumission. After buying their freedom, Ignacio and his wife continued to work in Havana. Ignacio worked as a stevedore. From their labor, they earned enough money to pay for their passage back to Africa, which cost 200 pesos at the time.

Ignacio testified that he expected to find his mother and his sisters waiting for him in Lagos. He had kept in contact with them continuously for a period of eight to nine years, through word of mouth provided by slaves in Cuba and repatriates to Lagos who had lived in Havana. As early as 1835, people were utilizing this grassroots information network, which allowed slaves like Ignacio to keep in touch with the lives and people they had left behind in Africa. This helped make repatriation a reality for many Afrocubanos of Yoruba background.

María Rosalia García

María Rosalia García was thirty years old when she boarded the *Avon* in order to return to the city she considered home, Lagos. She was returning with her husband, Lorenzo Clarke, and her three Cuban-born children, José, Roue, and Isabel. Lorenzo and María Rosalia had arrived in Havana on the same slave ship, the *Negrito*, some twenty-odd years earlier.

María Rosalia was only eight years old when the *Negrito* was intercepted at sea. As with other people emancipated at sea by the British, María Rosalia was taken to the government barracks by the Spanish colonial government shortly after arriving in Havana. As discussed in chapter 1, mixed commission courts handled the people of undetermined status like Rosalia. She was sold to Dolores García, then taken away from Dolores García by the Spanish colonial government and sent to an orphanage; the reason for this was unclear from María Rosalia's testimony. She stayed in the orphanage for several days before being moved again.

María Rosalia was later sold to Francisco La Moneda, a shoemaker, who essentially rented out her labor in return for a percentage of her meager earnings. Her other main source of income while she was owned by La Moneda came from working as a laundress. After four years María Rosalia bought her freedom from La Moneda for 68 pesos. After this time, she lived as a free black person in urban Havana for about ten or eleven years before returning to Lagos with Lorenzo and their *criollo* children.

María Rosalia García's narrative reveals that the lives of *emancipados* from Lagos in Havana were often rough and changeable. Employment, personal status, and housing were constant concerns for urban slaves and free people of color during this era. That María García and Lorenzo Clarke found each other and started a family before going back to Africa is a testament to their spirit of survival, endurance, and renewal.

Catalina Bosc

Catalina Bosc was married to fellow passenger Ignacio Moni and accompanied him on the journey back to Lagos. She was forty years old at the time and had lived in Havana for twenty years. She was a native of Lagos who was taken to Havana as a slave along with six hundred other individuals by a Spanish slaver. In Havana, Catalina worked for Don Moni as a laundress and cook for four and a half years. She was then sold to an Afro-Cuban woman named Rosalia Aguirre. Aguirre was a worldly businesswoman, who owned her own restaurant and café at the time. Rosalia Aguirre was of Carabalí origin, an ethnic group from Camaroon and Southeastern Nigeria.

Catalina worked under Aguirre for five and a half years, until her husband, Moni, bought her freedom for 500 pesos. As was mentioned, Moni had to take Aguirre to *el síndico* because Aguirre refused to take the mandatory maximum of 500 pesos for Catalina's liberty. Catalina was clear in her testimony to ship officials about *el síndico*'s advocacy for slaves. *El síndico*, to the best of its ability, was enforcing legal codes set in place to protect the slaves and *emancipados* that made up a majority of Havana's urban labor force during the era.

Notes

Introduction

1. The notes in this volume refer to works cited in full detail in the bibliography. Sources not cited in the bibliography receive full citation treatment in the notes. Where two or more authors listed in the bibliography share the same surname, the full names of these authors are given in the notes, to aid the reader in locating the appropriate bibliography entry.
2. Otero, "Spirit Possession, Havana, and the Night," 45–74.
3. For previous studies of the importance of returnees to the region, see Law, "The Evolution of the Brazilian Community in Ouidah," 22–41; Smith, *The Lagos Consulate, 1851–1861*, 68–79; Yai, "The Identity, Contributions, and Ideology of the Aguda," 72–82; Sarracino, *Los Que Volvieron a Africa*, 47–63, 130–31; and Juan Pérez de la Riva, *Documentos para la historia de las gentes sin historia*. 42–44.
4. *Orisha* worship is the traditional Yoruba religion.
5. Glassie, "The Moral Lore of Folklore," 123–52; Abrahams, "Questions of Criolian Contagion," 73–87; Bauman and Briggs, "Poetics and Performances," 59–88; Ben-Amos, "Toward a Definition of Folklore in Context," 3–15; Magliocco, *Witching Culture*, 23–56; and Bendix, *In Search of Authenticity*.
6. See, for example, the following essays in *The Yoruba Artist: New Theoretical Perspectives on African Arts*, ed. Rowland Abiodun, Henry J. Drewal, and John Pemberton III: Abiodun, "An African (?) Art History," 37–47; Yai, "In Praise of Metonymy," 107–15; and Abimbola, "Lagbayi: The Itinerant Wood Carver of Ojowon," 137–42. See also Falola, *African Historiography*. And as examples of scholarship about Yoruba performance, see Karin Barber's works: *I Could Speak until Tomorrow* and *The Generation of Plays*.
7. Falola and Roberts, "Introduction," in *The Atlantic World, 1450–2000*, ix–xiv.
8. Abrahams, "Questions of Criolian Contagion," 73–87.
9. Mintz and Price, *An Anthropological Approach to the Afro-American Past*.
10. Apter, "Herskovits' Heritage," 235–60; and Apter, "Que Faire?" 87–105.
11. See David Hilary Brown, *Santería Enthroned*; and Christine Ayorinde, *Afro-Cuban Religiosity*.
12. See Yai, "The Identity, Contributions, and Ideology of the Aguda," 72–82.
13. See Law, "The Evolution of the Brazilian Community in Ouidah," 22–41, and Matory, "The English Professors of Brazil," 72–103.
14. See especially Matory, *Black Atlantic Religion*.
15. Luis, "Cultura Afrocubana en la revolución," 37–45; and Christine Ayorinde, *Afro-Cuban Religiosity*.

16. Ricoeur, *Memory, History, Forgetting*, 5–11; and Abiodun, "An African (?) Art History," 182–92.

17. See Yai, "The Identity, Contributions, and Ideology of the Aguda." See figures A, C, J, and K on author's website: http://www.lsu.edu/faculty/solimar.

18. Not all of the images/figures for this study could be published, due to loss of digital image quality through print publication. However, all of the figures are provided in clearly visible form on the author's website: http://www.lsu.edu/faculty/solimar/.

19. Laotan, "Brazilian Influence on Lagos," 156–65.

20. Otero, "*Iku* and Cuban Nationhood," 116–31; and Otero, "Rethinking the Diaspora," 54–56.

21. See Otero, "Spirit Possession, Havana, and the Night," 45–74; De la Campa, *Cuba on My Mind*; and Behar, "Going to Cuba," 136–60.

22. Ponte, "Las lágrimas en el congrí," 43–49; and Borchmeyer and Hentschler, *Havana*.

23. Murphy and Sanford, "Introduction," in *Osun across the Waters*, 1–9; Barnes, "Africa's Ogun Transformed," xiii–xxi; and Abimbola, "The Contribution of Diaspora Blacks," 79–89.

24. Alejandro de la Fuente, *Havana and the Atlantic in the Sixteenth Century*, 36–43.

25. See Law, "The Evolution of the Brazilian Community in Ouidah," 22–41.

26. Mann, "Shifting Paradigms in the Study of the African Diaspora," 3–21; Gilroy, *The Black Atlantic*; Foner, "What's New about Transnationalism?" 355–76; and Hannerz, "The World in Creolization," 546–59.

27. See Sheila S. Walker, "Introduction: Are You Hip to the Jive?" 1–44.

28. Bascom, "Oba's Ear," 1–16; and Dorson, "The African Connection," 260–65.

29. M. J. Herskovits, *The New World Negro*.

30. See Apter, "Herskovits' Heritage."

31. Gates, *The Signifying Monkey*; Abrahams and Bauman, "Sense and Nonsense in St. Vincent," 762–72; Brock and Bayne, "Not Just Black," 168–204; and Cros Sandoval, *Worldview, the Orichas, and Santería*, 323–42.

32. See Otero, "*Iku* and Cuban Nationhood," 116–31, Otero, "Rethinking the Diaspora," 54–56.

33. For more, consult Adorno's works: "Reconsidering Colonial Discourse for Sixteenth and Seventeenth-Century Spanish America," 134–45, and "The Discursive Encounter of Spain and America," 210–29.

34. Ortiz, "Brujos o Santos," 85–90; and Ortiz, "Los cabildos Afrocubanos," 54–63; Cabrera, *El Monte Igbo Finda Ewe Orisha*; and García Canclini, *Imaginarios Urbanos*.

35. Arrom, "Criollo: Definición y matices," 11–26.

36. Barnet, *Biografía de un cimarrón* (Biography of a Runaway Slave), 160–61. There has been some discussion of the issues of genre and historiographic detail in Barnet's "play" with writing the figure of Montejo into being. I am interested in what the figure of Montejo does for imagining Afro-Cuban resistance and citizenship in terms of a trope. For more on the discussion of genre play and the archives in Barnet's work, see Zeuske, "El Cimarrón y las Consecuencias de la Guerra del 95," 65–84.

37. Abrahams, "Questions of Criolian Contagion," 73–87.

38. Ferrer, *Insurgent Cuba*; Robin D. Moore, *Nationalizing Blackness*; and Christine Ayorinde, *Afro-Cuban Religiosity*.

39. See Otero, "Spirit Possession, Havana, and the Night," 45–74, and Otero, "*Iku* and Cuban Nationhood," 116–31.

40. Ortiz, "Los factores humano de la cubanidad," 1–20.

41. Lachateñere, "El sistema religioso de los Lucumí y otras influencias Africanes en Cuba I," 28–82; and Barnet, "Cuba: Tres disquisiciones etnológicas," 61–76.

42. Benítez Rojo, "La cultura criolla en Cuba," 69–76; and also Benítez Rojo, *La Isla Que Se Repite El Caribe*, 159–66.

43. Verger, "Nigeria, Brésil et Cuba," 125–36; Matory, "The English Professors of Brazil"; Matory, *Black Atlantic Religion*; and Law, "The Evolution of the Brazilian Community in Ouidah."

44. Benítez Rojo, *La Isla Que Se Repite El Caribe*, 1–29, 43–47.

45. See also the following for the density and heterogeneity of Yoruba cultures and languages found in Cuba: Bascom, "Yoruba Acculturation in Cuba," 163–67; Bascom, "The Yoruba in Cuba"; and Olmstead, "Comparative Notes on Yoruba and Lucumi," 157–64.

46. Ortiz, *La Africanía de la Música Folklórica de Cuba*, 86–135.

47. Ibid., 91–92 (my translation).

48. "Transculturation" is a term coined by Ortiz to refer to the transference of elements of any set of cultures into each other. Ortiz hoped to use the idea of "transculturation" to challenge the idea of the "acculturation" of any culture into another more dominant culture by stressing how any two cultures in contact with each other will be affected by that encounter. See Ortiz, *Contrapunteo Cubano del Tabaco y el Azúcar*, 97–103.

49. Barber, "Quotation and the Constitution of Yoruba Oral Texts," 1–17.

50. Flores-Peña and Evanchuck, *Santería Garments and Altars*; Thompson, "Divine Countenance," 1–17; and David Hilary Brown, *Santería Enthroned*.

51. Peel, "The Cultural Work of Yoruba Ethnogenesis," 65–75.

52. Law, *The Slave Coast of West Africa 1550–1750*; and Smith, *The Lagos Consulate, 1851–1861*. Also, prior to the late nineteenth century, "the Yoruba" referred only to the Yoruba-speaking peoples of Oyo; the term has been extended to include other ethnic groups speaking dialects of the same language. For more on this linguistic conglomeration of the Yoruba, see Law, *The Oyo Empire, c. 1600–c. 1836*.

53. See Alejandro de la Fuente, *Havana and the Atlantic in the Sixteenth Century*, 136–43; Michael A. Gomez, *Exchanging Our Country Marks*, 81; Da Costa e Silva, "Buying and Selling Korans in Nineteenth-Century Rio de Janeiro," 83–90; and Thornton and Heywood, *Central Africans, Atlantic Creoles, and the Foundation of the Americas, 1585–1660*.

54. Some examples of this process of African incorporation into nineteenth-century colonial society involve novels written by Afrocubanos. See, for example, Morúa Delgado's *Sofía*, written in 1891.

55. Abrahams, "Toward an Enactment-Centered Theory of Folklore and Folklife," 79–120.

56. Carlos Moore, Shawna Moore, and Tanya Sanders, "Introduction," in *Magical Interpretations, Material Realities*, 1–27; Bastian, "Vulture Men, Campus Cultists and Teenage Witches," 71–96.

57. Dayan, "Haiti, History, and the Gods," 66–97.

58. Comaroff and Comaroff, *Civil Society and the Political Imagination in Africa*, 1–44; and Apter, "IBB = 419," 267–309.

59. Matory, *Black Atlantic Religion*; Matory, "The English Professors of Brazil," 72–103; and Bay, "Protection, Political Exile, and the Atlantic Slave-Trade," 42–60.

60. Cabrera, *Yemayá y Ochún: Kariocha, Iyaloichas, y Olorichas*; Isabel Castellanos, "From Ulukumí to Lucumí," 39–50; and Cros Sandoval, "Afro-Cuban Religion in Perspective," 81–98.

61. Arrom, "Criollo: Definición y matices."

62. Barnet, "Cuba: Tres Disquisiciones Ethnológicas," 61–76; Cabrera, "Religious Syncretism in Cuba," 84–94; and Verger, "Nigeria, Brazil, and Cuba," 113–23.

63. Take, for example, the Catholic concept of transubstantiation, as well as the belief in miracles and spirit possession.

64. Michael A. Gomez, *Exchanging Our Country Marks*, 145–50; Thornton, *Africa and Africans in the Making of the Atlantic World*, 1400–1680.

65. For a good discussion of syncretism and religious admixture, see Shaw and Stewart, "Introduction: Problematizing Syncretism," 1–26. For religious syncretism and multifaith contexts in Africa, see Olabiyi Babalola Yai's "Religious Dialogue, Peace and the Responsibility of the Translator," 133–46. For a discussion of Yoruba attitudes toward Christianity, and toward Catholicism in particular, in Nigeria, see Kukah, "African Traditional Religion and Christianity."

66. For an interesting discussion of the complications between Black *criollo* and African members of *cabildos* in terms of authority and authenticity within the organizations, see Childs, "The Defects of Being a Black Creole," 209–25.

67. De la Fuente, *Havana and the Atlantic in the Sixteenth Century*, 179–81, 186–87, 220–21.

68. Ortiz, *Los cabildos y la fiesta del Día de los Reyes*; and Ortiz, "Los cabildos Afrocubanos," 54–63.

69. Howard, *Changing History*, 20–44.

70. Childs, "The Defects of Being a Black Creole," 209–25

71. Ortiz, *Los cabildos y la fiesta del Día de los Reyes*; and Ortiz, "Los cabildos Afrocubanos," 64–63

72. Verger, "Nigeria, Brazil, and Cuba," 113–23; Laotan, "Brazilian Influence on Lagos"; Matory, "The English Professors of Brazil"; Matory, *Black Atlantic Religion*, 38–72; and Bamgboshe Martins, "Legacy and Brazil," 15.

73. See chapter 3 in this volume for a discussion of Afrolatino religion in Lagos, Nigeria. Also see figures D and F, showing the "Brazilian" Egungun shrines in contemporary Lagos, on the author's website: http.www.lsu.edu.faculty/solimar/.

74. David Hilary Brown, "Toward an Ethnoaesthetics of Santeria Ritual Arts," 77–130.

75. Ortiz, *La Africanía de la Música Folklórica de Cuba*, 135–84.

76. A maternal deity associated with the sea and La Virgen de Regla in Cuba. See Cabrera, *Yemayá y Ochún: Kariocha, Iyaloichas, y Olorichas*.

77. Ortiz, in *La Africanía de la Música Folklórica de Cuba*, writes about this prayer: "The phrasing of [this] Afro-Cuban prayer is equal, then, to saying: 'It is here that I am saying to you, [as] your servile child. [It is]Your servile child, that is saying to you: I am reciting your sacred names [*kasha*]! Eternal and true mother! Give me health and food [and] joy," 142 n. 26, 180. The emphasis and the translation

from Lucumí to Spanish is Ortiz's, and the translation from Spanish to English is mine. I would translate the last Yoruba phrase, *gbe le yó*, as "bring joy with you," as I do not see the elision for *ounje* or food in the Lucumí phrase as given by Ortiz.

78. I use Lucumí to refer to both the Yoruba spoken in Cuba and the group of individuals who refer to themselves as such. For an example from popular music, see/listen to a rumba like "Rumba de los Rumberos," performed by Carlos Embale y los Roncos Chiquitos, on the compilation recording *La Rumba de Cuba*, Milan Records, New York, 1966, track 1. Also see Hagedorn, *Divine Utterances: The Performance of Afro-Cuban Santería*, for guides to the style and format of contemporary *oricha* music from Cuba, both in popular and in sacred contexts.

79. Ortiz, *La Africanía de la Música Folklórica de Cuba*, 142.

80. Barber, "Quotation and the Constitution of Yoruba Oral Texts," 1–17; Barber, "Polyvocality and Individual Talent," 151–160; Adedeji, "Oral Tradition and Contemporary Theater in Nigeria," 134–39, and Adedeji, "Folklore and Yoruba Drama," 321–39.

81. Akinaso, "Yoruba Traditional Names and the Transmission of Cultural Knowledge," 139–58; Babalola, *Awon Oriki Orile*; and Barber, *I Could Speak until Tomorrow*.

82. Babalola, *Ijala atenudenu*, and the Babalola, "Folk-tales from Yorubaland," 14–15.

83. Irele, "Dimensions of African Discourse," 67–81.

84. Peel, "The Cultural Work of Yoruba Ethnogenesis," 65–75.

85. Klor de Alva, "The Postcolonialization of the (Latin) American Experience," 241–73.

86. Rewt, "The African Diaspora and Its Origins," 3–15.

87. Adorno, "Reconsidering Colonial Discourse for Sixteenth and Seventeenth-century Spanish America," 134–45; Adorno, "The Discursive Encounter of Spain and America," 210–29.

88. Similarly, Sommer's work in *Foundational Fictions* adds to the discussion of the development of a civic culture through literature in Latin America, emphasizing that romance, intimacy, and racial mixing become merged with nationalist discourses that move themselves away from Spain and Portugal: see 114–37.

89. De la Fuente, *Havana and the Atlantic in the Sixteenth Century*, 36–43.

90. Thornton and Heywood, *Central Africans, Atlantic Creoles, and the Foundation of the Americas*, 1585–1660.

91. Folayan, "Yoruba Oral History: Some Problems and Suggestions," 95–114; Law, "Constructing 'a Real National History,'" 70–100; Johnson, *History of the Yorubas*; Falola, *Pioneer, Patriot, and Patriarch*; and Peel, "Making History," 111–32.

92. Schön and Crowther, *Journals of the Rev. James Frederick Schön and Mr. Samuel Crowther*; Johnson, *History of the Yorubas*; and Falola, *Pioneer, Patriot, and Patriarch*.

93. For a discussion of Cuban nostalgia from this perspective, see Behar, "Going to Cuba"; and Machado and Domitrovich, *Tastes like Cuba*, 62, 257.

94. Otero, "Dreaming the Barrio," 31–52; and Otero, "Spirit Possession, Havana, and the Night," 45–74.

95. Ricoeur, *Memory, History, Forgetting*. 96–132.

96. Saldívar, *The Borderlands of Culture*, 9–11, 390–94; and Giles, *Virtual Americas*, 1–21.

Chapter 1

1. These accounts were first reported in the abolitionist series edited by Zachary Macaulay, *Anti-Slavery Reporter: Under the Sanction of the British and Foreign Anti-Slavery Society*, vol. 2, 3rd ser., 234–39. They were later reprinted by Cuban historian Juan Pérez de la Riva in *Documentos para la historia de las gentes sin historia*, 27–51.
2. Christopher Leslie Brown, *Moral Capital*, 259–60.
3. Writings of this era included the following: John Wesley, *Thoughts on Slavery* (London: R. Hawes, 1774); Adam Smith, *Wealth of Nations* (London: W. Strahan; and T. Cadell, 1776); William Robertson, *History of America* (Dublin: Printed for Messrs. Whitestone, 1777); and Abbé Raynal, *A philosophical and political history of the British settlements and trade in North America* (Edinburgh: C. Denovan, 1779).
4. By "Atlantic world," I mean the emerging transnational cultural, social, and economic milieu that framed communities living in this era and region. Thus, I am using the term to describe a broad temporal, spatial, and qualitative entity.
5. Christopher Leslie Brown, *Moral Capital*, 327–30; and Coupland, *The British Anti-slavery Movement*, 66.
6. Christopher Leslie Brown, *Moral Capital*, 1–5, 29–30.
7. See Sarracino, *Los Que Volvieron a Africa*, 65–124, for a discussion of the diversity of motives in the British antislavery movements of the nineteenth century.
8. Christopher Leslie Brown, *Moral Capital*, 11.
9. Coupland, *The British Anti-slavery Movement*, 77.
10. For Nigerian examples, see Kukah, "African Traditional Religion and Christianity."
11. Coupland, *The British Anti-slavery Movement*, 81.
12. Ibid., 81–82.
13. Christopher Leslie Brown, *Moral Capital*, 314–16; and Adderley, *New Negroes from Africa*, 9, 51–52, 95–97, 102–3.
14. Alejandro de la Fuente argues that the correlation between the African and slavery was an Atlantic construction that was created in the late sixteenth and early seventeenth centuries for the purpose of fueling the economies of European empires. For more on this, see his *Havana and the Atlantic in the Sixteenth Century*, 145–85.
15. Manzano, "Carta de Juan Francisco Manzano a Domingo del Monte," 81.
16. Coupland, *The British Anti-slavery Movement*, 83.
17. Adderley, *New Negroes from Africa*, 9, 51–52, 95–97, 102–3.
18. Landers, "African Presence in Early Spanish Colonialization of the Caribbean and the Southeastern Borderlands," 315–27, and Landers, "*Cimarrón* and Citizen," 111–45.
19. Christopher Leslie Brown, *Moral Capital*, 260–61.
20. Ibid., 282–330.
21. Chambers, "The Black Atlantic: Theory, Method, and Practice," 151–73; Usman, "The Nineteenth-Century Black Atlantic," 114–34; and Adderley, *New Negroes from Africa*, 95–97, 102–3.
22. See Mann, "Shifting Paradigms in the Study of the African Diaspora," 3–21.
23. Adderley, *New Negroes from Africa*.

24. Coupland, *The British Anti-slavery Movement*, 54–55; and Christopher Leslie Brown, *Moral Capital*, 96–100.
25. Christopher Leslie Brown, *Moral Capital*, 290.
26. Ibid., 295.
27. Ibid., 287.
28. Ibid., 298; James C. Scott, *Domination and the Arts of Resistance*, 5–6, 37–42, 156–90, 198–201; and Fabian, *Moments of Freedom*, 41–69, 70–101.
29. Gilroy, *Against Race*, 178–206, 241–278; Otero, "Dreaming the Barrio," 31–52; and Kamari Maxine Clarke, "Yoruba Aesthetics and Trans-Atlantic Imaginaries," 290–315.
30. Childs, "The Defects of Being a Black Creole," 209–45.
31. Jean Herskovits, *A Preface to Modern Nigeria*; and Mann, *Slavery and the Birth of an African City*.
32. Martinez-Fernandez, *Fighting Slavery in the Caribbean*, 42; and Adderley, *New Negroes from Africa*. 9, 51–52, 95–97, 102–3.
33. Coupland, *The British Anti-slavery Movement*, 122.
34. Adderley, *New Negroes from Africa*, 46; and Otero, "A Tale of Two Cities," 79–124.
35. Adderley, *New Negroes from Africa*, 102–6.
36. Coupland, *The British Anti-slavery Movement*, 161; Adderley, *New Negroes from Africa*; and Christopher Leslie Brown, *Moral Capital*, 314–16.
37. Smith, *The Lagos Consulate, 1851–1861*, 68.
38. Juan Pérez de la Riva, *Documentos para la historia de las gentes sin historia*, 27–51; Coupland, *The British Anti-slavery Movement*, 163; and Adderley, *New Negroes from Africa*, 9, 51–52, 95–97, 102–3.
39. Adderley, *New Negroes from Africa*, 9, 51–52, 95–97, 102–3.
40. Coupland, *The British Anti-slavery Movement*, 164; Martinez-Fernandez, *Fighting Slavery in the Caribbean*, 53–8; and Adderley, *New Negroes from Africa*, 9, 51–52, 95–97, 102–3.
41. Martinez-Fernandez, *Fighting Slavery in the Caribbean*, 42 n. 5.
42. Alejandro de la Fuente, *Havana and the Atlantic in the Sixteenth Century*, 46; and Thornton and Heywood, *Central Africans, Atlantic Creoles, and the Foundation of the Americas, 1585–1660*, 5–48; 294–332.
43. Coupland, *The British Anti-slavery Movement*, 172.
44. Ibid., 179; and Adderley, *New Negroes from Africa*, 97–99, 128–29.
45. I use the term "Afrocubano" to refer to the sense of identity that emerges from within the community being discussed. I use "Afro-Cuban" to refer to a similar social and cultural grouping as seen from an observer's perspective. Both are used to indicate differences in registers that mirror the point of interconnection between micro- and macronarratives in history.
46. Martinez-Fernandez, *Fighting Slavery in the Caribbean*.
47. Ibid.; and Adderley, *New Negroes from Africa*, 44–47.
48. See Adderley, *New Negroes from Africa*, 51, 96.
49. For an alternative reading of slave revolts and the role of vanguards and intellectuals from abroad and within the region, with the Aponte conspiracy in mind, see Palmié, *Wizards and Scientists*, 79–158.

50. Martinez-Fernandez, *Fighting Slavery in the Caribbean*, 133; Paquette, *Sugar Is Made with Blood*, 131–82; and Adderley, *New Negroes from Africa*, 51.

51. Paquette, *Sugar Is Made with Blood*, 3–26.

52. Ibid., 261–66.

53. The "transnational imaginary" is a concept borrowed from cultural and film studies; it looks at transnational discourses that create direct and indirect links to shifting allegiances and identities in both contemporary and historical contexts. For examples of studies that use the notion of a transnational imaginary in Mexico, in Asia, and in popular culture, see Saldívar, *The Borderlands of Culture*; Wilson and Dissanayake, *Global/local*; and Giles, *Virtual Americas*.

54. Palmié, *Wizards and Scientists*, 79–158; and Paquette, *Sugar Is Made with Blood*, 123–26.

55. Childs, "The Defects of Being a Black Creole," 209–45.

56. Palmié, *Wizards and Scientists*, 79–158.

57. Adderley, *New Negroes from Africa*, 9, 51–52, 102–3.

58. Martinez-Fernandez, *Fighting Slavery in the Caribbean*.

59. Ibid., 19.

60. Howard, *Changing History*, 106–8.

61. Adderley, *New Negroes from Africa*, 4, 45; and Martinez-Fernandez, *Fighting Slavery in the Caribbean*, 40–58.

62. In *New Negroes from Africa*, Adderley asserts that the Mixed Commission Court in Havana played an especially central role in creating an avenue for the movement of liberated Africans through the Atlantic: into slave societies like Cuba, back and forth from Sierra Leone, and to Trinidad and the Bahamas; see esp. 45, 51, 95–97, 102–3.

63. Again, Alejandro de la Fuente, in *Havana and the Atlantic in the Sixteenth Century*, asserts that this process began as early as the sixteenth century.

64. See, for example, the following studies: Helg, *Our Rightful Share*; Robin D. Moore, *Nationalizing Blackness*; Ferrer, *Insurgent Cuba*; Matory, "The English Professors of Brazil," 72–103; Christine Ayorinde, *Afro-Cuban Religiosity, Revolution, and National Identity*; Rebecca J. Scott, *Degrees of Freedom*; and Adderley, *New Negroes from Africa*, 4.

65. Coupland, *The British Anti-slavery Movement*, 183.

66. Rebecca J. Scott, *Degrees of Freedom*, 5.

67. Ibid., 94–128.

68. Ibid., 129–53; Ayorinde, *Afro-Cuban Religiosity, Revolution, and National Identity*, 5, 10, 169–72, 184–202, 190–91; Ferrer, *Insurgent Cuba*, 112–40; and Louis Pérez, *On Becoming Cuban*, 104–25, 149–50.

69. Rebecca J. Scott, *Degrees of Freedom*, 269.

70. Matory, "The English Professors of Brazil," 77–103; Mann, "Shifting Paradigms in the Study of the African Diaspora," 3–21; and Adderley, *New Negroes from Africa*, 9, 52–55, 95–97.

71. Kipple, *Blacks in Colonial Cuba*, 1774–1899, 96.

72. Ibid., 95.

73. Deschamps Chapeaux, *El negro en la economía habanera del siglo XIX*; Howard, *Changing History*, 21–48; and Juan Pérez de la Riva, *Documentos para la historia de las gentes sin historia*, 27–51.

74. Alejandro de la Fuente, *Havana and the Atlantic in the Sixteenth Century*, 154–55.

75. See Adderley, *New Negroes from Africa*, 25.

76. Paquette, *Sugar Is Made with Blood*, 107; and Casanovas, *Bread or Bullets!* 35.

77. Juan Pérez de la Riva, *El Barracon y Otros Ensayos*.

78. Adderley, *New Negroes from Africa*, 9, 102–3.

79. An interest in investigating and imagining this Asian diaspora in Cuba has been developing among Cuban novelists. See, for example, Cristina García, *Monkey Hunting* (New York: Ballantine Books, 2004); and Zoé Valdés, *La Eternidad del Instante* (Mexico City: Plaza Janés/Mondadori, 2005).

80. This was also and especially the case for Brazilians who had bicoastal families in Lagos and Bahia. See Matory, "The English Professors of Brazil," 72–103. An interesting ethnographic description of the religious figure of Martiniano, who was deeply connected to the continent, can be found in Landes, *The City of Women*, 22–34. For a scathing critique of Landes's portrayal of men and women's roles in Candomblé, and her alleged (mis)use of Martiniano's voice, see Matory, *Black Atlantic Religion*, 190–224, esp. 193.

81. Smith, *The Lagos Consulate, 1851–1861*, 79; and Adderley, *New Negroes from Africa*, 95–97, 102–3.

82. For specific examples of Lagosians in Havana seeking council from *el síndico*, see Juan Pérez de la Riva, *Documentos para la historia de las gentes sin historia*, 27–51.

83. See ibid., 51 n. 8.

84. The nineteenth century in Yorubaland was a period of hotly contested civil war. It was not surprising that many of the recent arrivals in the Americas during this period were prisoners of war from the interior of Nigeria. For more on the highly religious nature of these conflicts, see Peel, *Religious Encounter and the Making of the Yoruba*. Also see Martinez-Fernandez, *Fighting Slavery in the Caribbean*, 56–8.

85. According to Dosalu, he was captured and sold by the "Dahominians" in 1855 after the invasion of Abeokuta. See Martinez-Fernandez, *Fighting Slavery in the Caribbean*, 57, 151. Also, for an account of Crowther's life, see J. F. A. Ajayi, "Samuel Ajayi Crowther of Oyo," 289–316.

86. Martinez-Fernandez, *Fighting Slavery in the Caribbean*, 56–60; and J. F. A. Ajayi, "Samuel Ajayi Crowther of Oyo," 289–316.

87. Lanier, *El directorio central de las sociedades negras de Cuba, 1886–1894*, 2.

88. As quoted in Juan Pérez de la Riva, *Documentos para la historia de las gentes sin historia*, 30.

89. The *real orden* documenting permission reads in translation: "I have notified Our Royal Highness of Communication from V. E. on the 21st of November, No. 85, in which he recognizes giving authorization for the bergantín *San Antonio* to ship to the coast of Africa seventy or eighty free Blacks who wish to return to their native land." RC, January 4, 1845, Archivo Nacional de Cuba, Reales Ordenes y Cédulas, leg. 139, no. 152.

90. Paquette, *Sugar Is Made with Blood*, Appendix II, Part B: General Regulations of the Slave Code of 1844, esp. regulations 1–5, 274.

91. See Sarracino, *Los Que Volvieron a Africa*, 65–124, for later dates.

92. Matory, "The English Professors of Brazil," 72–103; and Matory, *Black Atlantic Religion*.

93. Jean Herskovits, *A Preface to Modern Nigeria*.

94. One striking example of the importance of the symbolism of bringing Africa to the island in public spectacle is given by Cabrera in *Yemayá y Ochún*, 17–18.

95. This pattern was established as far back as the late sixteenth century, when emancipation for African-born slaves in Havana took relatively longer than for the *criollo* slaves. For more on the development of Havana's Black communities emerging from this particular pattern of manumission, see Alejandro de la Fuente, *Havana and the Atlantic in the Sixteenth Century*, 176–79.

96. This phrase is used in Cuban Santería to indicate the child of an *oricha*. For example, *omo* Chango is a child of Chango in the Cuban vernacular. For more on the use of Yoruba words in Cuban folk speech, see Cabrera, *Anagó*.

97. Otero, "Rethinking the Diaspora," 54–56.

98. Yai, "Les 'Aguda' (Afro-Brésiliens) du Golfe du Bénin," 275–284; Margaret Thompson Drewal, *Yoruba Ritual*; Abimbola, "Lagbayi," 137–142; Abiodun, "An African (?) Art History," 37–47; Matory, "The English Professors of Brazil," 72–103; Matory, *Black Atlantic Religion*; and Otero, "A Tale of Two Cities," 79–124.

99. See, for example, Barber and De Moraes Farias, *Self-Assertion and Brokerage*; and Falola, *Pioneer, Patriot, and Patriarch*.

100. Yai, "In Praise of Metonymy," 107–15.

101. Barber, "Quotation and the Constitution of Yoruba Oral Texts," 1–17; and Peel, "The Cultural Work of Yoruba Ethnogenesis," 65–75.

102. See, for example, the following: Verger, "Nigeria, Brazil, and Cuba," 113–23; Sarracino, *Los Que Volvieron a Africa*, 65–124; and Juan Pérez de la Riva, *Documentos para la historia de las gentes sin historia*, 27–51.

103. Adderley, *New Negroes from Africa*, 45, 94, 102–4.

104. Zachary Macaulay, *The Anti-Slavery Reporter*, vol. 2, 3rd ser., 234–9; and Juan Pérez de la Riva, *Documentos para la historia de las gentes sin historia*, 27–51.

105. Information on the company that operated these vessels is included because these were historically and economically significant in providing the political backdrop to the movement within the African diaspora. For more on their influence on the slave trade, repatriation, and the general tenor of the era, see Verger's *Bahia and the West African Slave Trade*.

106. Juan Pérez de la Riva, *Documentos para la historia de las gentes sin historia*, 36.

107. The passengers in many cases bear the surnames of their previous owners. According to Havana law around the early nineteenth century, owners were legally required to give slaves their surnames.

108. Apparently, some private organizations also obtained the services of *el síndico*.

109. This was a common practice among slave owners at the time; certain ethnic groups of Africans were selected for different kinds of tasks. This continued well into the late nineteenth century, even after the abolition of slavery. For more examples from a Cuban historical perspective, see Deschamps Chapeaux, *Los Cimarrones Urbanos*.

110. It is unclear in the record what type of "hard labor" Crusati engaged in. It is also unclear whether he worked exclusively in Havana during this period of his life. See Pérez de la Riva, *Documentos para la historia de las gentes sin historia*, 42–43.

111. Verger. *Bahia and the West-African Trade*, 1549–1851, and "Nigeria, Brazil, and Cuba," 113–23.

112. Law, "The Evolution of the Brazilian Community in Ouidah," 29–30, 38 n. 15; Smith, *The Lagos Consulate, 1851–1861*, 21, 30–31; and Yai, "The Identity, Contributions, and Ideology of the Aguda," 72–82.

113. Verger; Matory, "The English Professors of Brazil," 72–103; Matory, *Black Atlantic Religion*; and Prince T. Olusí, interview March 29, 2001, Isaleko, Lagos, Nigeria.

114. This freedom of movement was established early on in the colony's history, around the late 1500s. De la Fuente describes the development of this pattern for urban slaves in Havana in his *Havana and the Atlantic in the Sixteenth Century*, 151–61.

115. Juan Pérez de la Riva, *Documentos para la historia de las gentes sin historia*, 43; and Deschamps Chapeaux, *Los Cimarrones Urbanos*.

116. Zachary Macaulay, *The Anti-Slavery Reporter*, vol. 2, 3rd ser., as quoted in Juan Pérez de la Riva, *Documentos para la historia de las gentes sin historia*, 43 (my translation).

117. Juan Pérez de la Riva, *Documentos para la historia de las gentes sin historia*, 46.

Chapter 2

1. Abiodun, "Identity and the Artistic Process in Yoruba Aesthetic Concept of Iwa," 13–30; Bamgbose, "The Form of Yoruba Proverbs," 74–86; Barber, "Quotation and the Constitution of Yoruba Oral Texts," 1–17. Adeko, "Word's Horse, or the Proverb as a Paradigm of Literary Understanding"; Yai, "In Praise of Metonymy," 107–15; and Finnegan, *The Oral and Beyond*.

2. Doortmont, "The Invention of the Yorubas," 101–9; and Barber, "Quotation and the Constitution of Yoruba Oral Texts," 1–17.

3. See Smith, *Kingdoms of the Yoruba*, and Law, "The Evolution of the Brazilian Community in Ouidah," 29–37.

4. Smith, *The Lagos Consulate, 1851–1861*, 51.

5. "Yoruba" here refers to not one single ethnic group, but rather to the loose grouping of Yoruba-speaking peoples moving in and out of African and American diasporas. There is a large amount of variation within and between Yoruba groups.

6. Law, "The Evolution of the Brazilian Community in Ouidah," 21–41; and Smith, *The Lagos Consulate, 1851–1861*, 79–80, 97.

7. Mann, *Slavery and the Birth of an African City: Lagos, 1760–1900*, 23–27; Barnes and Agiri, "Lagos before 1603," 18–32; and Aderibigbe, "Early History of Lagos to about 1850," 1–26.

8. Patrick Dele Cole, *Modern and Traditional Elites in the Politics of Lagos*; Patrick Dele Cole, "Lagos Society in the Nineteenth-Century," 27–57; and Baker, *Urbanization and Political Change*.

9. The Yoruba and the Bini share a long history of cultural exchange. See Barnes and Agiri, "Lagos before 1603," 18.

10. Mann, *Slavery and the Birth of an African City*, 27–29, 120–21; and Smith, *The Lagos Consulate, 1851–1861*, 13.

11. Mann, *Slavery and the Birth of an African City*, 270; and Smith, *The Lagos Consulate, 1851–1861*, 16.

12. Smith, *The Lagos Consulate, 1851–1861*, 51.

13. Mann, *Slavery and the Birth of an African City*, 23–50.

14. Losi, *History of Lagos*, 3.

15. Verger, *Trade relations between the Bight of Benin and Bahia from the 17th to 19th Century*; and Saco, *Historia de la esclavitud de la raza africana en el nuevo mundo, y en especial en los paises Americo-hispanos*, vols. 1–4.

16. Bay, "Protection, Political Exile, and the Atlantic Slave-Trade," 42–60; Law, "The Evolution of the Brazilian Community in Ouidah," 22–24, 35–37; and Prince T. Olusí, interview, April 21, 2001, Isaleko, Lagos, Nigeria.

17. Barber, "Discursive Strategies in the Texts of Ifá and in the 'Holy Book of Odù,'" 196–240; and Barber, "Quotation and the Constitution of Yoruba Oral Texts," 1–17.

18. Apter, "The Historiography of Yoruba Myth and Ritual," 1–25.

19. Peel, "The Cultural Work of Yoruba Ethnogenesis," 65–75.

20. Doortmont, "The Invention of the Yorubas," 101–9

21. Otero, "Iku and Cuban Nationhood," 129–31.

22. Falola, *African Historiography*.

23. Aderibigbe, "Early History of Lagos to about 1850," 1–26; Law, "The Dynastic Chronology of Lagos," 46; and Doortmont, "The Roots of Yoruba Historiography," 52–63.

24. Barber, "Quotation and the Constitution of Yoruba Oral Texts," 1–17

25. Patrick Dele Cole, *Modern and Traditional Elites in the Politics of Lagos*, 19.

26. An *oba* was a Yoruba king. According to traditional belief, ideally an *oba* gained his legitimacy from Oduduwa, the first Yoruba king and creator of mankind who ruled in Ile Ife. For more on Yoruba folktales and myths, see Babalola, "Folk-tales from Yorubaland," 14–15; and Beier, *Yoruba Myths*.

27. Mann, *Slavery and the Birth of an African City*, 406 n. 36; Smith, *The Lagos Consulate, 1851–1861*, 16–17, 20; Law, "The Dynastic Chronology of Lagos," 49–51; and Law, "The Evolution of the Brazilian Community in Ouidah," 24–29.

28. Mann, *Slavery and the Birth of an African City*, 160–199; and Smith, *The Lagos Consulate, 1851–1861*, 13–15, 20.

29. Law, "Heritage of Oduduwa," 207–22; and Smith, *Kingdoms of the Yoruba*. In Yoruba mythology, Ile Ife is the primordial town from which all Yoruba and all humankind originate.

30. Blier, *African Vodun*, 3–20.

31. Losi, *History of Lagos*; Patrick Dele Cole, *Modern and Traditional Elites in the Politics of Lagos*; Patrick Dele Cole, "Lagos Society in the Nineteenth-Century," 27–57; Law, "Heritage of Oduduwa," 210–15; and Law, "The Dynastic Chronology of Lagos," 46–54.

32. Losi, *History of Lagos*, 1.

33. Ogunfunmire's reputation as a hunter also ties him to the god of iron, war, and hunting, Ogun. For more on the *orisha* Ogun and his symbolic properties, see Barnes, *Ogun: An Old God for a New Age*. See also Mann, *Slavery and the Birth of an African City*, 26; Aderibigbe, "Early History of Lagos to about 1850," 1–26; and Barnes and Agiri, "Lagos before 1603," 26–27.

34. Losi, *History of Lagos*, 2.

35. Folami, *A History of Lagos, Nigeria*, 7–8.

36. Ibid.; Patrick Dele Cole, *Modern and Traditional Elites in the Politics of Lagos*; and Patrick Dele Cole, "Lagos Society in the Nineteenth-Century," 27–57.

37. For more on the importance of formulaic structures in Yoruba oral tradition, see Abimbola, *Yoruba Oral Tradition*.

38. Literally meaning the "dancing body of people" in Standard Yoruba, this can be translated as "the body (community) that dances." Over time, as Olusí indicated, the expression was elided into one word. Decoding such Yoruba names is a matter of *ede jinle* or knowing the "deep language" that forms such words at various stages of merging. Olusí is privy to such "deep knowledge," or *imo jinle*, because of his leadership role in the community. For more on the idea of *jinle*, "deep" knowledge, and language in Yoruba philosophy and religion, see Hallen and Sodipo, *Knowledge, Belief, and Witchcraft*. Also of related interest is Apter, *Black Critics and Kings*.

39. Olusí, interview, April 21, 2001, Isaleko, Lagos, Nigeria.

40. Mann *Slavery and the Birth of an African City*; and Mann, "Shifting Paradigms in the Study of the African Diaspora," 9–13.

41. Mann, *Slavery and the Birth of an African City*, 23–27; and Law, "The Dynastic Chronology of Lagos," 51–52.

42. Smith, *The Lagos Consulate, 1851–1861*, 9, 13.

43. Ibid., 37.

44. Law, "The Dynastic Chronology of Lagos," 48–50; and Falola and Roberts, "Introduction," in *The Atlantic World, 1450–2000*, ix–xiv.

45. Austen, "'Africanist' Historiography and its Critics, " 203–17.

46. Ben-Amos, *Sweet Words*, 165–98.

47. Losi, *History of Lagos*, 7–8; Patrick Dele Cole, *Modern and Traditional Elites in the Politics of Lagos*; and Patrick Dele Cole, "Lagos Society in the Nineteenth-Century," 27–57

48. Patrick Dele Cole, *Modern and Traditional Elites in the Politics of Lagos*, 11.

49. Losi, *History of Lagos*, 11.

50. Patrick Dele Cole, *Modern and Traditional Elites in the Politics of Lagos*, 19.

51. For example, between about 1780 and 1805, during the reign of Oba Ologun Kutere, a second Ido war was diplomatically averted by creative trading with the Bini royal court. See Law, "The Dynastic Chronology of Lagos," 48; and Smith, *The Lagos Consulate, 1851–1861*, 14.

52. Mann, *Slavery and the Birth of an African City*, 238–240, 247; Aderibigbe, "Early History of Lagos to about 1850," 1–26; Patrick Dele Cole, *Modern and Traditional Elites in the Politics of Lagos*. 8–10; and Olusí, interview, May 5, 2001, Isaleko, Lagos, Nigeria.

53. Mann, *Slavery and the Birth of an African City*; and Mann, "Shifting Paradigms in the Study of the African Diaspora," 3–21.

54. Bay, "Protection, Political Exile, and the Atlantic Slave-Trade," 49–50.

55. Law, "The Evolution of the Brazilian Community in Ouidah," 23.

56. Mann, *Slavery and the Birth of an African City*, 92, 97, 125–26.

57. Law, "The Dynastic Chronology of Lagos," 46–47, 51; and Mann, *Slavery and the Birth of an African City*, 54–64; Smith, *The Lagos Consulate, 1851–1861*, 9.

58. Smith, Ibid.: Law, "The Evolution of the Brazilian Community in Ouidah," 23; and Olusí, interview, May 5, 2001, Isaleko, Lagos, Nigeria.

59. Smith, *The Lagos Consulate, 1851–1861*, 9–10.

60. Mann, *Slavery and the Birth of an African City*, 34, 36.

61. Smith, *The Lagos Consulate, 1851–1861*, 9–10.
62. The Bamgboshe Martins may be related to the Martinez family. I found instances during my fieldwork in Lagos in 1999 of families among the Aguda who had anglicized their names. See Law, "The Evolution of the Brazilian Community in Ouidah," 22–41; Law, "The Dynastic Chronology of Lagos," 46–54; and Laotan, A. B., *The Torch Bearers: The Old Brazilian Colony in Lagos*.
63. Smith, *The Lagos Consulate, 1851–1861*, 46.
64. Mann, *Slavery and the Birth of an African City*, 40, 74–76, 85–86, 134–36, 204–11, 238–44; and Law, "The Evolution of the Brazilian Community in Ouidah," 23–25.
65. Mann, *Slavery and the Birth of an African City*, 75–76, 215, 229.
66. Bamgboshe Martins, "Mabinouri Dawodu," 11–12.
67. Matory, *Black Atlantic Religion*, 38–72, 73–114, Matory, "The English Professors of Brazil," 72–103; Verger, "Nigeria, Brazil, and Cuba,"113–23; and Macaulay, *Justitia Fiat*.
68. Mann, "Shifting Paradigms in the Study of the African Diaspora," 11, 13–16.
69. Yai, "The Identity, Contributions, and Ideology of the Aguda," 78–81.
70. Bamgboshe Martins, interview, April 23, 2001, Popo Aguda, Lagos, Nigeria; and Olusí, interview, May 5, 2001, Lagos, Nigeria.
71. Verger, "Trance and Convention in Nago-Yoruba Spirit Mediumship," 50–66; Matory, *Black Atlantic Religion*, 73–114; Matory, "The English Professors of Brazil," 72–103; and Smith, *The Lagos Consulate, 1851–1861*, 13–15, 33.
72. Mann, *Slavery and the Birth of an African City*, 26, 30–31; Law, "The Dynastic Chronology of Lagos," 47–51; and Smith, *The Lagos Consulate, 1851–1861*, 13–15.
73. Mann, *Slavery and the Birth of an African City*, 45–47, 53, 60–62; and Smith, *The Lagos Consulate, 1851–1861*, 14.
74. Mann, *Slavery and the Birth of An African City*, 45–47, 53, 60–2; and Smith, *The Lagos Consulate, 1851–1861*, 16.
75. Mann, *Slavery and the Birth of an African City*, 45–7, 53, 60–2; and Bay, "Protection, Political Exile, and the Atlantic Slave-Trade," 42–60.
76. Law, "The Evolution of the Brazilian Community in Ouidah." 25–27; and Juan Pérez de la Riva, *Documentos para la historia de las gentes sin historia*, 43–46.
77. Mann, *Slavery and the Birth of an African City*, 94, 120, 247; and Smith, *The Lagos Consulate, 1851–1861*, 33.
78. Smith, *The Lagos Consulate, 1851–1861*, 33–5.
79. Yai, "The Identity, Contributions, and Ideology of the Aguda," 72–75.
80. J. F. A. Ajayi, "The Beginnings of Modern Lagos," 122–27.
81. Laotan, "Brazilian Influence on Lagos," 156–65.
82. Smith, *The Lagos Consulate, 1851–1861*, 39–40, 51; Mann, *Slavery and the Birth of an African City*, 125–26; and Mann, "Shifting Paradigms in the Study of the African Diaspora," 9, 14–16.
83. Yai, "The Identity, Contributions, and Ideology of the Aguda," 71–81; and Yai, "In Praise of Metonymy," 107–15.
84. Bauman and Briggs, "Poetics and Performances," 59–88.
85. Bay, "Protection, Political Exile, and the Atlantic Slave-Trade," 43, 49–58; Barber, "Polyvocality and Individual Talent," 151–60; Finnegan, *Oral Literature in Africa*; and Finnegan, *The Oral and Beyond*.

86. Bamgboshe Martins, "Mabinouri Dawodu," 11–12.
87. Juan Pérez de la Riva, *Documentos para la historia de las gentes sin historia*, 40–43; and Law, "The Evolution of the Brazilian Community in Ouidah," 22–24.
88. Included in this understanding of the Afro-Atlantic are ports in Europe, North Africa, and the Americas that were affected by the African diaspora, through trade and slavery.
89. Bamgboshe Martins, "Mabinouri Dawodu," 11–12.
90. Ibid.
91. Barber, "How Man Makes God in West Africa," 724–45.
92. Euba, "Dress and Status in Nineteenth-Century Lagos," 142–65.
93. Olupona, "Orisa Osun," 46–48.
94. Olusí, interview, June 3, 2001, Isaleko, Lagos, Nigeria.
95. Yai, "The Identity, Contributions, and Ideology of the Aguda," 78; Barber, *The Generation of Plays*, 22; and Mann, *Slavery and the Birth of an African City*, 229–30.
96. Mann, Ibid., and Smith, *The Lagos Consulate, 1851–1861*, 16.
97. Patrick Dele Cole, *Modern and Traditional Elites in the Politics of Lagos*, 19.
98. Mann, *Slavery and the Birth of an African City*, 45, 93–94, 231.
99. Ibid., 97–98; and Smith, *The Lagos Consulate, 1851–1861*, 55.
100. Mann, *Slavery and the Birth of an African City*, 95–98; and Smith, *The Lagos Consulate, 1851–1861*, 54.
101. Smith, *The Lagos Consulate, 1851–1861*, 16; and Mann, *Slavery and the Birth of an African City*, 84, 93.
102. Law, "The Evolution of the Brazilian Community in Ouidah," 25–27; and Mann, *Slavery and the Birth of an African City*, 66.
103. Smith, *The Lagos Consulate, 1851–1861*, 54; and Mann, *Slavery and the Birth of an African City*, 97–98.
104. Mann, *Slavery and the Birth of an African City*, 107–108; and Smith, *The Lagos Consulate, 1851–1861*, 3.
105. Olusí, interview, April 21, 2001, Isaleko, Lagos, Nigeria.
106. Losi, *History of Lagos*, 47. As stated earlier, according to Eko traditional law, the Idejo chiefs "own" the lands that make up Lagos. The *oba* has the right to rule, but he does not have the right to sell or buy the land. For more on the Idejo chiefs and the *oba* of Lagos, see Patrick Dele Cole, *Modern and Traditional Elites in the Politics of Lagos*, and Patrick Dele Cole, "Lagos Society in the Nineteenth-Century," 27–57.
107. Barnes, *Patrons and Power*, 19–23, 31–39, 97–125.
108. Ibid.; and Mann, *Slavery and the Birth of an African City*, 66, 109.
109. Patrick Dele Cole, *Modern and Traditional Elites in the Politics of Lagos*, 24, 32; Smith, *The Lagos Consulate, 1851–1861*, 51; and Mann, *Slavery and the Birth of an African City*, 66.
110. Losi, *History of Lagos*, 48–49; and Mann, *Slavery and the Birth of an African City*, 26, 49.
111. Olusí is an *omoba*, the son of a king, and a traditional ruler of the Isaleko neighborhood of Lagos.
112. Murphy and Sanford, "Introduction," in *Osun across the Waters*, 1–9.
113. Abimbola, *Ifa: An Exposition of Ifa Literary Corpus*; Bascom, *Ifa Divination*; and Barber, "Discursive Strategies in the Texts of Ifá and in the `Holy Book of Odù,'" 196–240.

114. For an explanation, see note 38, above.

115. These numbers are significant for the Yoruba, especially in terms of their relationship to history, mythology, and political power. See Bascom, *Sixteen Cowries*, for the way the numbers sixteen and thirty-two shape divination practices in Yorubaland, Cuba, and Brazil.

116. The Odun Ifa is an Ifa festival in Lagos.

117. Olusí, interview, April 21, 2001, Isaleko, Lagos, Nigeria.

118. Soyinka's memoir, *Ake: The Years of Childhood*, describes an interesting merging of gender, labor, and religion in the market women's rebellion against the traditional *oba*'s wishes: see 216–18. Soyinka's dramatic memory helps us to understand how alliances can be formed in spontaneous and powerful ways. For an analysis of this work in an Atlantic perspective, see Otero, "Getting There and Back," 274–92.

119. Hallen, *The Good, the Bad, and the Beautiful*, 11.

120. Yai, "The Identity, Contributions, and Ideology of the Aguda," 74–75.

121. Law, "The Evolution of the Brazilian Community in Ouidah," 30.

122. Hallen, *The Good, the Bad, and the Beautiful*; and Barber, "How Man Makes God in West Africa," 724–45.

123. Sheila S. Walker, "Introduction: Are You Hip to the Jive?" 1–44; and Howard, *Changing History*, 21–48.

124. Ortiz, "Los cabildos Afrocubanos," 54–63; and Howard, *Changing History*, 74.

125. Ramos, *The Negro in Brazil*.

126. Morton-Williams, "The Oyo Yoruba and the Atlantic Trade, 1670–1830," 25–45; Morton-Williams, "The Yoruba Ogboni Cult in Oyo," 362–74; Howard, *Changing History*; and Childs, "The Defects of Being a Black Creole," 209–45.

127. Alejandro De la Fuente, *Havana and the Atlantic in the Sixteenth Century*, 147–85.

128. See Childs, *The 1812 Aponte Rebellion in Cuba and the Struggle against Atlantic Slavery*.

129. Palmié, *Wizards and Scientists*, 135–42, 147.

130. An example here would be the nineteenth-century popularity of the deity Chango/Xango/Sòngó in Cuba, Brazil, and Trinidad. Sòngó is an *orisha* believed to be the *oba* of the great Oyo kingdom in the sixteenth century. See Peel, "The Cultural Work of Yoruba Ethnogenesis," 65–75; and Bascom, *Chango in the New World*. And, in a different ethnic vein, for examples of early exchanges between Europeans and central Africans in the 1500s, see Thornton and Heywood, *Central Africans, Atlantic Creoles, and the Foundation of the Americas, 1585–1660*, 5–48.

131. For a Haitian example of this Atlantic process, see Buck-Morss, *Hegel, Haiti, and Universal History*, 119–151. For a Cuban study considering Aponte and the religious culture of Havana in the nineteenth century, see Childs, *The 1812 Aponte Rebellion in Cuba and the Struggle against Atlantic Slavery*.

132. Childs, *The 1812 Aponte Rebellion in Cuba and the Struggle against Atlantic Slavery*, 22–24.

133. Ortiz, "Los cabildos Afrocubanos," 54–63; and Rebecca J. Scott, "Fault Lines, Color Lines, and Party Lines," 61–106.

134. See Ferrer, *Insurgent Cuba*; and Christine Ayorinde, *Afro-Cuban Religiosity, Revolution, and National Identity*. Also for a comparative discussion of a similar process of

selective remembering and an investigation of Afro-Atlantic political connections in the nineteenth century, see Scott, *Degrees of Freedom*.

135. Helg, *Our Rightful Share*; and Christine Ayorinde, *Afro-Cuban Religiosity*.

136. Matory, *Black Atlantic Religion*; and Matory, "The English Professors of Brazil," 72–103.

137. Verger, "Nigeria, Brésil et Cuba," 125–36; and Law, "The Evolution of the Brazilian Community in Ouidah," 22–41.

138. Martinez-Fernandez, *Fighting Slavery in the Caribbean*, 21.

139. See author's website, http://www.lsu.edu/faculty/solimar/, for Figure A—Community Center for the "Popo Aguda," the Afro-Cuban and Afro-Brazilian neighborhood in Lagos, 2001, photograph by author.

140. Patrick Dele Cole, *Modern and Traditional Elites in the Politics of Lagos*, 45.

141. Yai, "The Identity, Contributions, and Ideology of the Aguda," 79.

142. Patrick Dele Cole, *Modern and Traditional Elites in the Politics of Lagos*, 45–47; and Euba, "Dress and Status in Nineteenth-Century Lagos," 142–65.

143. *Popo* is a word that designates a neighborhood. Smith, *The Lagos Consulate, 1851–1861*, 97; Patrick Dele Cole, *Modern and Traditional Elites in the Politics of Lagos*, 45; Mann, *Slavery and the Birth of an African City*, 26, 250; and Otero, "Getting There and Back," 274–92

144. Laotan, "Brazilian Influence on Lagos," 156–65; Matory, *Black Atlantic Religion*, 39, 64–65; Matory, "The English Professors of Brazil," 72–103; Robin Cohen, "Diasporas, the Nation-State, and Globalization," 37; and Yai, "The Identity, Contributions, and Ideology of the Aguda," 76–80.

145. For Cuba, see Fernando Ortiz, "Los cabildos Afrocubanos,"54–63.

146. Ibid., 55.

147. The Saros are returnees to Lagos from Sierra Leone. They live in the Popo Maro area, where Olusí is the chief. For more on the Saros see Jean Herskovits, *A Preface to Modern Nigeria*; and Gibril Cole and Dixon-Fyle, *New Perspectives on Sierra Leone Krio*.

148. Prince T. Olusí interview, April 21, 2001, Isaluko, Lagos, Nigeria.

149. Yai, "The Identity, Contributions, and Ideology of the Aguda," 75–79.

150. Juan Pérez de la Riva, *Documentos para la historia de las gentes sin historia*, 27–51.

Chapter 3

1. Mann, "Shifting Paradigms in the Study of the African Diaspora," 3–21; and Falola and Roberts, "Introduction," in *The Atlantic World*, 1450–2000, ix–xiv.

2. Matory, "The English Professors of Brazil," 72–103.

3. Verger, *Bahia and The West African Slave Trade*, 1549–1851, 3, 5, 9, 30–33.

4. Bay, "Protection, Political Exile, and the Atlantic Slave-Trade," 57; and Law, "The Evolution of the Brazilian Community in Ouidah," 28–30.

5. Ibid.

6. Matory, "The English Professors of Brazil," 72–103; and Pérez de la Riva, *Documentos para la historia de gentes sin historia*, 30.

7. Smith, *The Lagos Consulate, 1851–1861*, 30–33.

8. In my interviews with Brazilian Aguda Lola Bamgboshe Martins, he referred to the Chachas as the Xa-Xas.
9. Law, "The Evolution of the Brazilian Community in Ouidah," 26.
10. Ibid.," 27.
11. Franco, *Los Palenques de los Negros Cimarrones*; Helg, *Our Rightful Share*, 45–47, 104–5; and Paquette, *Sugar Is Made with Blood*, 72–73, 104–5.
12. Pérez de la Riva, *Documentos para la historia de gentes sin historia*, 30–32.
13. Yai, "The Identity, Contributions, and Ideology of the Aguda," 75–77; and Mrs. Aderemi Gooding-King, interviews, August 7, 1999 and April 15, 2001, Cuban Lodge, Campos Square, Lagos, Nigeria.
14. See Margaret Thompson Drewal, *Yoruba Ritual*, 62–66; and Otero, "Getting There and Back," 274–92.
15. Yai, "The Identity, Contributions, and Ideology of the Aguda," 78; and Matory, "The English Professors of Brazil," 72–103.
16. Patrick Dele Cole, "Lagos Society in the Nineteenth-Century," 42; Echeruo, *Victorian Lagos*; Jean Herskovits Kayloff, *A Preface to Modern Nigeria*; and Gibril Cole and Dixon-Fyle, *New Perspectives on Sierra Leone Krio*.
17. Abner Cohen, *The Politics of Elite Culture*, 37.
18. Ibid., 165–67, 174–76, 208; and Gibril Cole and Dixon-Fyle, *New Perspectives on Sierra Leone Krio*.
19. Howard, *Changing History*, 73–99; Lanier, *El directorio central de las sociedades negras de Cuba*, 1886–1894; and Lanier, *Directorio central de las sociedades de color*, 1840–1878.
20. Christopher Leslie Brown, *Moral Capital*, 255, 297; Adderley, *New Negroes from Africa*, 3, 26; Jean Herskovits, *A Preface to Modern Nigeria*, 18–19; and see Crowther and Wright in Curtin, *Africa Remembered*, 289–333.
21. Johnson, *History of the Yorubas*; and Schön and Crowther, *Journals of the Rev. James Frederick Schön and Mr. Samuel Crowther*.
22. J. F. A. Ajayi, "The Beginnings of Modern Lagos," 122–27; and Jean Herskovits, *A Preface to Modern Nigeria*.
23. Peel, "The Pastor and the *Babalawo*," 338–369; and Matory, "The English Professors of Brazil," 77–103.
24. Herbert Macaulay, *Justitia Fiat*.
25. Olusanya, "Henry Carr and Herbert Macaulay," 281.
26. Ibid., 280–83.
27. Yai, "The Identity, Contributions, and Ideology of the Aguda," 81–82; Bamgboshe Martins, "Mabinouri Dawodu," 11–12; and Gooding-King, interviews, August 7, 1999 and April 15, 2001, Cuban Lodge, Lagos, Nigeria.
28. Law, "The Evolution of the Brazilian Community in Ouidah."
29. Yai, "The Identity, Contributions, and Ideology of the Aguda," 77, 79.
30. Law, "Constructing 'a Real National History'," 78–100; and Apter, "Herskovits' Heritage," 235–60.
31. Peel, "The Cultural Work of Yoruba Ethnogenesis," 65–75.
32. Peel, "The Pastor and the *Babalawo*," 338–69.
33. See Matory, "The English Professors of Brazil," 72–103; and Falola, *Pioneer, Patriot, and Patriarch*.

34. Apter, "The Historiography of Yoruba Myth and Ritual," 1–25; and Yai, "In Praise of Metonymy," 107–15.

35. Olupona, "Orisa Osun," 46–67.

36. For more on the origins of *orishas*, see, for example, Gleason's exploration of Oya as a "borrowed" deity, in *Oya: In Praise of an African Goddess*. For Cuban explorations of the Yoruba origins of *orishas*, see Bolívar and López Cepero, *Sincretismo Religioso?*.

37. Ortiz, "Los cabildos Afrocubanos," 54–63.

38. See, for example, Villumbrero in Cabrera, *Reglas de Congo*, 147. For a detailed discussion of the creation of Creole Atlantic identities from a central African perspective, see Thornton and Heywood, *Central Africans, Atlantic Creoles, and the Foundation of the Americas, 1585–1660*, 49–108.

39. Viarnés, "Cultural Memory in Afro-Cuban Possession," 127–60; and Cabrera, *El Monte Igbo Finda Ewe Orisha Vititi Nfinde*.

40. Francisco Pérez de la Riva, "*Cuban* Palenques," 49–59.

41. Bamgboshe Martins, interview, March 27, 2001, Victoria Island, Lagos, Nigeria.

42. Dimeji Ajikobi, personal communication, March 23, 2001, University of Lagos, Nigeria; and Dimeji Ajikobi, "African Folklore."

43. Gooding-King, interview, August 7, 1999, Cuban Lodge, Lagos, Nigeria.

44. Olusí performance, recorded on March 29, 2001, at the Iga Olusí in Isaleko, Lagos, Nigeria.

45. Ibid.

46. See Bay, "Protection, Political Exile, and the Atlantic Slave-Trade," 49–51.

47. Olusi's dates contradicted Law's date, which placed the narrative after 1760. See Law, "The Dynastic Chronology of Lagos," 49–50.

48. *Ebo* is the performance of sacrifice in traditional Yoruba religion.

49. For more on Olokun in Yorubaland, see Lawal, *The Gelede Spectacle*; and Henry John Drewal and Margaret Thompson Drewal, *Art and Female Power among the Yoruba*. For Cuban instances connected to other *orisha* and Olokun, see Cabrera, *Yemayá y Ochún*. David Hilary Brown's work on altars and Santería communities in the United States provides an excellent way of viewing the relationship between different *orisha*-related religions aesthetically, especially Brown's thorough Yale University doctoral dissertation, "The Garden in the Machine."

50. It is difficult to say when the first Portuguese explorations of Africa reached the western coast. Saco, in his *Historia de la esclavitud de la raza africana en el nuevo mundo*, places the first Portuguese sightings and settlement of Lagos at around 1443–44, with the voyages of Nuño Tistán establishing the links that would later make Lagos an international port of trade: see 36–37.

51. The Isaleko is the palace at Eko, on Lagos Island.

52. Olusí, Olusí performance, recorded on March 29, 2001, at the Iga Olusí in Lagos, Nigeria.

53. Finnegan, *Oral Literature in Africa*, 12–15, 105–7, 129–30, 491–92; and Barber, "Quotation and the Constitution of Yoruba Oral Texts," 1–17.

54. Bamgboshe Martins, "Mabinouri Dawodu," 11–12.

55. Otero, "*Iku* and Cuban Nationhood," 116–31; and Otero, "Rethinking the Diaspora," 54–56.

56. Howard, *Changing History*, 73–99; Ortiz, *Los cabildos y la fiesta del Día de los Reyes*; and Childs, "The Defects of Being a Black Creole," 209–45.

57. Laotan, "Brazilian Influence on Lagos," 156–65; Laotan, *The Torch Bearers*; and Matthew Kukah, interview, August 9, 1999, Cuban Lodge, Campos Square, Lagos, Nigeria.

58. This is a Brazilian masquerade of a bull, *boa*, figurine in an annual Lagosian carnival. The *carretas*, or masques, are brought out with the bull figurine and with Brazilian dance, song, and cuisine every year in Lagos. The activities are distinctly Bahian in origin, noting a cross-diasporic origin.

59. "Mother of the Orisha," a priestess of Yoruba traditional deities, or *orisha*. In this case, the *iyalosha* comes from the Brazilian Candomblé tradition, and her title would be *mae de Santo*. In Santería, the Cuban component of *orisha* worship in the diaspora, we could call a person of this rank an *iyalocha*. The parallels occur because the structure of *orisha* worship thrives in multiple contexts.

60. Gooding-King, interview, August 7, 1999, Cuban Lodge, Campos Square, Lagos, Nigeria.

61. Bamgboshe Martins, "Legacy and Brazil," 15; and interviews with Bamgboshe Martins, August 11, 1999 and April 23, 2001, Campos Square, Lagos, Nigeria.

62. Yai, "The Identity, Contributions, and Ideology of the Aguda," 82.

63. See author's website, http://www.lsu.edu/faculty/solimar/, for figure J—Grave of Cuban Aguda Mrs. Anastasia Gooding, Hilario Campos's daughter, Ikoyi Cemetery, Lagos; and figure K—Grave of Cuban Aguda brother and sister, Hilario Campos and Johana Cicelia Munis, Ikoyi Cemetery, Lagos, 2001, photographs by author.

64. See Landes, *The City of Women*, 42; Ramos, *O Folk-Lore Negro do Brasil*; and Matory, *Black Atlantic Religion*, 46–47.

65. Peel, "The Pastor and the *Babalawo*" 338–69; Matory, *Black Atlantic Religion*, 38–71; and Matory, "The English Professors of Brazil," 72–103.

66. Olusí's own pronunciation of *oosa*.

67. Olusí, interview, April 21, 2001, Isolako, Lagos, Nigeria; emphasis in original.

68. Olupona, "Orisa Osun," 46–67.

69. Ibid., 48–49.

70. See author's website, http://www.lsu.edu/faculty/solimar/, for the following: figure B—Omoba Prince T. Olusí and Solimar Otero, Ile Omoba Olusí, Lagos, 2001; figure C—Child devotee of Olokun preparing for the Eyo masquerade, Lagos, 2001; figure D—Chief Lola Bamgboshe Martins, *olowo* of the Songo Egungun and prominent member of the Bamgboshe family, Lagos, March 2001; figure E—the Bamgboshe Martins House, Lagos, 2001; figure F—Bamgboshe Egungun shrine, Lagos, 2001 (all photographs by author).

Chapter 4

1. Juan Pérez de la Riva, *Documentos para la historia de las gentes sin historia*, 30–31.
2. Sarracino, *Los Que Volvieron a Africa*, 47–64.
3. Sarracino, "Back to Africa," 67–76, esp. 71.

4. Juan Pérez de la Riva, *Documentos para la historia de las gentes sin historia*, 30–33, esp. 32.

5. Yai, "The Identity, Contributions, and Ideology of the Aguda," 73–76; Matory, *Black Atlantic Religion*, 38–72, 73–114; Matory, "The English Professors of Brazil," 72–103; Verger, "Nigeria, Brazil, and Cuba,"113–23; and Mann, *Slavery and the Birth of an African City*, 32, 92–97, 248–49, 360 n. 56.

6. *Lloyd's Register* (London: Lloyd's Register Group, 1843); *Southampton Street Directory* (Southampton: Southampton City Council, 1847–1857). Special Collections Library, Southampton City Council, Southampton, UK.

7. Mann, *Slavery and the Birth of an African City*, 92–97, 248–49; Law, "The Evolution of the Brazilian Community in Ouidah," 22–41; Bay, "Protection, Political Exile, and the Atlantic Slave-Trade," 42–60; and Yai, "The Identity, Contributions, and Ideology of the Aguda," 72–82.

8. Juan Pérez de la Riva, *Documentos para la historia de las gentes sin historia*, 34–35; Otero, "A Tale of Two Cities," 79–124; and Otero, "Dreaming the Barrio," 31–52.

9. Juan Pérez de la Riva, *Documentos para la historia de las gentes sin historia*, 34–38. See Alejandro De la Fuente, *Havana and the Atlantic in the Sixteenth Century*, 43–50, for an example of how slavery shaped the city of Havana in complicated ways as early as in the sixteenth century.

10. Ortiz, "Los cabildos Afrocubanos," 54–63; Cabrera, *El Monte Igbo Finda Ewe Orisha*; Cabrera, "Religious Syncretism in Cuba," 84–94; Jorge Castellanos and Isabella Castellanos, *Cultura Afrocubanoa*, vol. 1; Otero, "*Iku* and Cuban Nationhood," 116–31; Do Nascimiento, "The African Experience in Brazil," 97–118; Verger, "Nigeria, Brazil, and Cuba," 113–23; Landes, *The City of Women*; and Matory, *Black Atlantic Religion*, 73–114.

11. Otero, "Barrio, Bodega, and Botanica Aesthetics," 173–94. I am influenced by the ways in which the following use and critique the idea of the imaginary as an influential and portable social and civic process: Appadurai, *Modernity at Large*, 31–50, 52–61, 195; Appadurai "Grassroots Globalization and the Research Imagination," 1–20; Flores, *From Bomba to Hip Hop*, 191–203, 227–28; and Saldívar, *The Borderlands of Culture*, 12, 38–39, 59–62, 239, 436–37.

12. Hegel, *The Philosophy of History*, 1–110; Le Goff, *History and Memory*, 86, 120–21, 128–30, 116–98, 199–216.

13. Ricoeur, *Memory, History, Forgetting*, 5–55.

14. Ibid., 7.

15. Ibid.

16. Hallen, *The Good, the Bad, and the Beautiful*, 49, 65–67, 133–34; and Ortiz, *Contrapunteo Cubano del Tabaco y el Azúcar*, 3–102.

17. Ricoeur, *Memory, History, Forgetting*, 10–13.

18. Fabian, *Remembering the Present*, 253, 274–75, 311.

19. Ricoeur, *Memory, History, Forgetting*, 13.

20. Ibid., 22–23; 96–102.

21. Abiodun, "Riding the Horse of Praise," 182–92.

22. For a discursive model of a similar kind of Yoruba "literary" criticism in relation to oral literature, see Barber, "Quotation and the Constitution of Yoruba Oral Texts," 1–17.

23. Abiodun, "Riding the Horse of Praise," 183.

24. Nuttall, "Introduction: Rethinking Beauty," 6–29; Vogel, "Future Traditions," 94–113; and Blier, "Art Systems and Semiotics," 7–18.

25. Appadurai, "Introduction: Commodities and the Politics of Value," 3–63; and Burke, *Lifebuoy Men, Lux Women*, 166–216.

26. Barber, *The Generation of Plays*, 1–17, 306–47; and Ranger, "The Invention of Tradition in Colonial Africa," 211–62.

27. Abrahams, *Everyday Life*, 96–126, 127–48, 217–60; Bauman and Briggs, "Poetics and Performances," 59–88; and Glassie, *Passing the Time in Ballymenone*, 35–94, 602–8, 669–714.

28. Finnegan, *The Oral and Beyond*; Barber, "Quotation and the Constitution of Yoruba Oral Texts," 1–17; and Ngugi wa Thiong'o, *Moving the Centre*.

29. Yankah, *Speaking for the Chief*, 6–24, 107–26; and Barber, "Polyvocality and Individual Talent," 151–60.

30. Hymes, "Breakthrough into Performance," 79–141.

31. Sarracino also notes that Campos was a carpenter, and provides details of family connections in Mantanzas, Cuba. He also speaks of Munis's husband, Andrés Muniz, born in Cuba, who came to Lagos in the nineteenth century with Campos, returned to Matanzas in 1914, and died in Cuba 1944. See *Los Que Volvieron a Africa*, 52–55, 130–31.

32. Ibid., 47–50, 51–52, 54–62.

33. Ibid., 47–50; and Juan Pérez de la Riva, *Documentos para la historia de las gentes sin historia*, 27–33, esp. 30.

34. Sarracino, *Los Que Volvieron a Africa*, 47–48.

35. See author's website, http://www.lsu.edu/faculty/solimar/, for figure G—Hilario Campos, Afrocubano repatriate to Lagos. Campos, who was born in Cuba in 1878, became the founder of the Cuban Lodge and Campos Square in Lagos, Nigeria.

36. Briggs, "Metadiscursive Practices and Scholarly Authority in Folkloristics," 387–434.

37. Behar, "Going to Cuba," 136–60.

38. Otero, "Spirit Possession, Havana, and the Night," 45–74; and Ponte, "Las lágrimas en el congrí," 43–49.

39. Mrs. Ola Vincent, interview, April 25, 2001, Victoria Island, Lagos, Nigeria.

40. See Otero, "Iku and Cuban Nationhood," 116–31; Otero, "A Tale of Two Cities," 79–124; "Dreaming the Barrio," 31–52.

41. Sarracino, *Los Que Volvieron a Africa*, 47–64, 130–31; and Juan Pérez de la Riva, *Documentos para la historia de las gentes sin historia*, 27–35.

42. See Olusí's discussion of Lagosian *oba*-ship in chapter 2 and 3. Also see Olupona's use of the notion of "civil religion" in "Orisa Osun," 46–67.

43. Mr. Lola Bamgboshe Martins assisted me in this interview. As a prominent Aguda of Brazilian origin, he has been central in providing leadership for the repatriate community as a whole. The word choice, "hearing" Spanish, comes directly from the Yoruba concept of linguistic performance. A person *gbo*—hears—a language correctly rather than solely "speaking" it. This frame of reference is a significant one to keep in mind in terms of how performance and speech operate in Yoruba contexts. Mrs. Gooding-King interview, August 7, 1999, Cuban Lodge, Campos Square, Lagos, Nigeria. Mrs. Ola Vincent, interview, April 25, 2001, Victoria Island, Lagos, Nigeria.

44. Mrs. Ola Vincent, ibid. Emphasis added.

45. See Matory, "The Coast Revisited."

46. Mrs. Gooding-King does not mean, literally, her own "children" here. She is talking about the generations of relatives born after her father's arrival in Lagos in the late nineteenth century. Mrs. Gooding-King interview, August 15, 1999, Cuban Lodge, Campos Square, Lagos, Nigeria.

47. See also author's website, http://www.lsu.edu/faculty/solimar/, for figure H—The Cuban Lodge, Campos Square, Lagos, 1999; and figure I—Mrs. Catherine Aderemi Gooding-King and neighbors inside of the Cuban Lodge, Lagos, 1999 (photographs by author).

48. See also author's website, http://www.lsu.edu/faculty/solimar/, for figure J—Grave of Cuban Aguda Mrs. Anastasia Gooding, Hilario Campos's daughter, Ikoyi Cemetery, Lagos; figure K—Grave of Cuban Aguda brother and sister, Hilario Campos and Johana Cicelia Munis, Ikoyi Cemetery, Lagos; and figure L—Mrs. Ola Vincent, granddaughter of Hilario Campos, Ikoyi Cemetery, Lagos (all 2001, photographs by author).

49. Former Secretary General of the Catholic Bishops Secretariat, Matthew Hassan Kukah, personal communication, August 9, 1999, Campos Square, Lagos, Nigeria.

50. See Mann, *Slavery and the Birth of an African City*, 247, 360; Laotan, "Brazilian Influence on Lagos," 156–165; Laotan, *The Torch Bearers*; Matory, *Black Atlantic Religion*, 38–114; and Matory, "The Coast Revisited."

51. This location is nearby Isaleko, in close proximity to Prince Olusí's jurisdiction.

52. *Oyinbo* is a Yoruba slang term that refers to European/American foreigners. Mrs. Gooding-King, interview, April 15, 2001, Cuban Lodge, Lagos, Nigeria.

53. Laotan, *The Torch Bearers*, and Laotan, "Brazilian Influence on Lagos," 156–65.

54. Verger, "Nigeria, Brazil, and Cuba," 113–23; Juan Pérez de la Riva, *Documentos para la historia de las gentes sin historia*, 30–38; and Matory, *Black Atlantic Religion*, 115–48.

55. Gooding-King, interview, August 7, 1999, Cuban Lodge, Lagos, Nigeria.

56. During the interviews I conducted with Mr. Lola Bamgboshe Martins, August 11, 1999, Campos Square, Lagos, Nigeria, he indicated to me that his grandfather was the most important *babalawo*, or Ifa divination priest, in Saldaor (Bahia), Brazil, in the late nineteenth century. This information is corroborated by several sources, one inspired by Matory's own work with Lola Martins: see "The English Professors of Brazil," 72–103.

57. In both Cuba and Nigeria, one sign of a *babalawo* like other orisha priests, is the wearing of white garments. Complete attire in white may be reserved for special rituals, or may be worn every day by high-status individuals.

58. Yai, "The Identity, Contributions, and Ideology of the Aguda," 75–77; David Hilary Brown, *Santería Enthroned*, esp. 113–64; and Matory, *Black Atlantic Religion*, 73–115.

59. Bamgboshe Martins, personal communication, April 2001, Lagos, Nigeria.

60. Otero, "*Iku* and Cuban Nationhood," 116–31; and Yai, "Les 'Aguda' (Afró-Brésiliens) du Golfe du Bénin," 275–84.

61. Townsend, quoted in Smith, *The Lagos Consulate, 1851–1861*, 82.

62. Ibid.

63. Yai, "The Identity, Contributions, and Ideology of the Aguda," 72–82; and Yai, "Les 'Aguda' (Afro-Brésiliens) du Golfe du Bénin," 275–84.
64. Smith, *The Lagos Consulate, 1851–1861*, 38–41, 80–82.
65. Ogundipe, "A Brief History of the Archdiocese of Lagos and the Beginnings of the Catholic Church in Nigeria," 38.
66. Ibid.
67. Smith, *Kingdoms of the Yoruba*, 135; and Smith, *The Lagos Consulate, 1851–1861*, 39–40, 82.
68. Laotan, "Brazilian Influence on Lagos," 156–65; and Picton, "Keeping the Faith," 205.
69. For more on Islam in Lagos among the Brazilian Aguda, especially in regard to the city's architecture, see ibid.
70. Mrs. Ola Vincent, Interview, April 25, 2001, Victoria Island, Lagos, Nigeria; Mrs. Aderemi Gooding-King, interview, August 7, 1999, Cuban Lodge, Lagos, Nigeria; and Gooding-King, interview, Alril 15, 2001, Cuban Lodge, Lagos, Nigeria.
71. See, for example, the ways that Congo and Yoruba code switching occurs in Cuban Palo traditions as discussed by Cabrera in *Reglas de Congo*, 147.
72. See Olupona, "Orisa Osun," 46–67; and Olusí interview, April 21, 2001, Isaleku, Lagos, Nigeria. See also Olusí interview excerpts, chapter 3 of this volume.
73. Peel, "The Cultural Work of Yoruba Ethnogenesis," 65–75; and Yai, "In Praise of Metonymy," 107–15.
74. Robin Cohen and Vertovek, "Introduction: Conceiving Cosmopolitanism," 1–25.
75. Ortiz, *Los cabildos y la fiesta del Día de los Reyes*; Verger, "Trance and Convention in Nago-Yoruba Spirit Mediumship," 50–66; Laotan, "Brazilian Influence on Lagos," 156–65; and Laotan, *The Torch Bearers*.
76. Benítez Rojo, *La Isla Que Se Repite El Caribe*, 1–29, 43–47; Amselle, *Mestizo Logistics*, 117–64; Abiodun, "An African (?) Art History," 37–47; and Margaret Thompson Drewal, "Dancing for Ogun in Yorubaland and in Brazil," 199–234.
77. Smart, "The Importance of Diasporas," 288–97; and Otero, "Dreaming the Barrio," 31–52.

Chapter 5

1. In *José Martí: Major Poems*, 86–87. The translation provided here is Elinor Randall's authorized translation from the bilingual edition of the book.
2. On these two critical moments for the inscription of African identity, see these texts: Ada Ferrer, *Insurgent Cuba*; Aline Helg, *Our Rightful Share*; and Rebecca F. Scott, *Degrees of Freedom*.
3. Here I take Appadurai's notions of the "research imagination" and "public culture" to heart in reexamining the Cuban landscape in the development and reproduction of a national literature through public discourse. For more on public culture as understood in this manner, see Appadurai, "Grassroots Globalization and the Research Imagination," 1–20.

4. See Christine Ayorinde, *Afro-Cuban Religiosity, Revolution, and National Identity*, 7–24.

5. See Cabrera, *Yemayá y Ochún*, 17–18.

6. For Afro-Cubans, see Childs, "'The Defects of Being a Black Creole,'" 209–45; also, for creolization theory, see Abrahams, "Questions of Criolian Contagion," 73–87.

7. Childs, "The Defects of Being a Black Creole," 209–45.

8. Helg, *Our Rightful Share*, 2–21, 55–90; Ferrer, *Insurgent Cuba*, 15–42, 70–92, 112–40; Robin D. Moore, *Nationalizing Blackness*, 13–40, 114–65; and Christine Ayorinde, *Afro-Cuban Religiosity, Revolution, and National Identity*, 7–69.

9. Helg, *Our Rightful Share*, 147–50.

10. See Hellwig, "The African American Press and United States Involvement in Cuba, 1902–1912," 70–84; and Mirabal, "Telling Silences and Making Community," 49–69; both pieces are in *Between Race and Empire*, ed. Brock and Castañeda Fuertes. Also see Scott, *Degrees of Freedom*, 253–69.

11. See Moore, *Nationalizing Blackness*, 114–65; and Ayorinde, *Afro-Cuban Religiosity, Revolution, and National Identity*, 7–69.

12. For a classic discussion of this dilemma, see Sarduy and Stubbs, "Introduction: The Rite of Social Communion," in *Afrocuba*, 3–26. For a more personal reinvestigation of the topic, see Sarduy, "Writing from Babylon," in Behar and Suárez, *The Portable Island*, 153–60.

13. There has been a recent resurgence of discussions of the elusive nature of Cuba the place and Cuban-ness the identity. See the edited volume by Behar and Suárez, *The Portable Island*.

14. Rebecca J. Scott, *Degrees of Freedom*, 74–75, 94–128, 253–72.

15. Childs, "The Defects of Being a Black Creole," 209–45

16. Rebecca J. Scott, *Degrees of Freedom*, 88; and Helg, *Our Rightful Share*, 107.

17. Rebecca J. Scott, *Degrees of Freedom*, 2–5.

18. Abrahams, *Everyday Life*, 127–48; and Abrahams, "Questions of Criolian Contagion," 73–87.

19. For examples of women creating, writing, and explaining Caribbean culture, see Otero, "Region: The Caribbean," in *Encyclopedia of Women's Folklore and Folklife*, 528–31.

20. Childs, "The Defects of Being a Black Creole," 209–45.

21. Ibid.

22. Usman, "The Nineteenth-Century Black Atlantic," 114–34; and Childs, "The Defects of Being a Black Creole," 209–45.

23. Rebecca J. Scott, *Degrees of Freedom*, 229–45; and Helg, *Our Rightful Share*, 142–59.

24. Ibid.

25. Rebecca J. Scott, *Degrees of Freedom*, 227.

26. Ibid., 230; and Helg, *Our Rightful Share*, 132–35, 144–46.

27. Childs, "The Defects of Being a Black Creole," 209–45; and Helg, *Our Rightful Share*, 48–53, 176–77.

28. See Buck-Morss, *Hegel, History, and Universal History*, 119–51.

29. Deschamps Chapeaux, *Los Cimarrones Urbanos*, 15, 27–30; and Childs, "The Defects of Being a Black Creole," 209–45

30. Deschamps Chapeaux, *Los Cimarrones Urbanos*, 12; also see Franco, *Los Palenques de los Negros Cimarrones*.
31. Deschamps Chapeaux, *Los Cimarrones Urbanos*, 27.
32. As cited in ibid., 30 (my translation from Spanish).
33. Paquette, *Sugar Is Made with Blood*, 3–12.
34. Ibid., 3–26, 131–57.
35. In Juan Pérez de la Riva, *Documentos para la historia de las gentes sin historia*, 30; and Paquette, *Sugar Is Made with Blood*, 229.
36. Paquette, *Sugar Is Made with Blood*, 229.
37. Ibid.
38. Juan Pérez de la Riva, *Documentos para la historia de las gentes sin historia*, 30–33.
39. Louis Pérez, *Cuba in the American Imagination*, 40–43, 63, 100–1.
40. I am thinking especially of Memmi here in terms of breaking the dyadic cultural and psychological relationship of the colonizer and the colonized. See Memmi, *The Colonizer and the Colonized*, 119–54.
41. Curtin, *The Rise and Fall of the Plantation Complex*, 73–86, 103–8; and Curtin, *Why People Move*, 15–21.
42. Gómez, *Exchanging Our Country Marks*, 67, 249.
43. Da Costa e Silva, "Buying and Selling Korans in Nineteenth-Century Rio de Janeiro," 83–90.
44. See Cabrera, *Reglas de Congo*, 140–52, for cultural scripts about *congo* beliefs in Cuba concerning the high god Zambi.
45. See Glissant, "Towards a Theory of *Antiallanité*," 126–54.
46. See, for example, these early texts about Latin America: Díaz del Castillo, *The Conquest of New Spain*, trans. Cohen; Las Casas, *Brevísima relación de la destruicion de las Indias*; and Cabeza de Vaca, *The Narrative of Cabeza de Vaca*, trans. Adorno and Pautz, esp. 39–40, 48–53, 170, for references to Cuba.
47. Rama, *La Ciudad Letrada*, 16–29.
48. For travel accounts describing Cuba in the colonial era, see von Humboldt, *The Island of Cuba*, 104–7, 110–12, 211–15, 227–29.
49. Fernandez, *Persuasions and Performances*, 199–211.
50. Klor de Alva, "The Postcolonialization of the (Latin) American Experience," 241–73; and Adorno, "Reconsidering Colonial Discourse for Sixteenth and Seventeenth-Century Spanish America," 134–45. For primary texts see Las Casas, *Brevísima relación de la destruicion de las Indias*.
51. Giles, *Virtual Americas*, 1–21.
52. Lopez-Baralt, *Iconografia Politica del Nuevo Mundo*, 51–116.
53. Arrom, "Letras de Cuba antes de 1608," 67–85; and Arrom, "Criollo," 11–26.
54. Alejandro De la Fuente, *Havana and the Atlantic in the Sixteenth Century*, 1–10, 147–85; and Thornton and Heywood, *Central Africans, Atlantic Creoles, and the Foundation of the Americas*, 1585–1660, 169–235.
55. Aguirre, *Nacionalidad y Nación en el Siglo XIX Cubano*, 2–5.
56. Rama, *La Ciudad Letrada*, 137–76.
57. See J. F. A. Ajayi, "Samuel Ajayi Crowther of Oyo" and Crowther, in Curtin, *Africa Remembered*, 289–316; Morúa Delgado, *Sofía*, vii–x; Barnet, *Biografía de un cimarrón*, 159–200; and Zeuske, "El Cimarrón y las Consecuencias de la Guerra del 95," 65–84.

58. Matory, "The English Professors of Brazil," 72–103.
59. Law, "The Evolution of the Brazilian Community in Ouidah," 22–41; and Yai, "The Identity, Contributions, and Ideology of the Aguda," 72–82.
60. Falola and Roberts, "Introduction," *The Atlantic World*, 1450–2000, ix–xiv.
61. Sandoval, *Un tratado sobre la esclavitud*; and Buck-Morss, *Hegel, History, and Universal History*, 119–51.
62. Sandoval, *De Instauranda Aethiopum Salute*.
63. Thornton and Heywood, *Central Africans, Atlantic Creoles, and the Foundation of the Americas*, 1585–1660, 5–48, 236–93; and Adderley, *New Negroes from Africa*, 23–61, 234–40.
64. Verger, *Trade Relations between the Bight of Benin and Bahia from the 17th to 19th Century*.
65. See Moreno Fraginals, *El ingenio*; and Ortiz, *Contrapunteo Cubano del Tabaco y el Azúcar*.
66. Zanetti, *Sugar and Railroads*, 25–45.
67. Ibid., 29–32.
68. See chapter 1 of this volume; and ibid., 18–38.
69. Ballester, *Letras*, 230–38.
70. Caballero, quoted in ibid., 235.
71. Ballester, *Letras*, 236–38.
72. Ibid., 230–235.
73. Llorens, *Nacionalismo y Nacion*, 21–32; and Lugo-Ortiz, "Identidades Imaginarios," 64.
74. Lugo-Ortiz, "Identidades Imaginarios," 51.
75. Ballester, ed., *Letras*, 163.
76. Sanguily, quoted in ibid., 163.
77. Ballester, *Letras*, 493.
78. Ibid., 330–31; see also Manzano, "Carta de Juan Francisco Manzano a Domingo del Monte," 81.
79. Del Monte, quoted in Ballester, *Letras*, 493–94.
80. Ortiz, "Los factores humano de la cubanidad," 1–20.
81. An interesting Marxist rendition of the novel was presented in a 1974 film, *El Otro Francisco*, by Cuban director Sergio Giral. The film critiques both del Monte and Suárez y Romero for their bourgeois notions, especially in framing the novel as a romance. Giral uses a fascinating array of neosociological voiceovers and reenactments from the novel that contrasts with the nineteenth-century rendition of the novel.
82. See Aguirre, *Nacionalidad y Nación en el Siglo XIX Cubano*, 2–6; and Sommer, *Foundational Fictions*, 114–38.
83. For an interesting criticism of *Francisco* see Giral, *El Otro Francisco*.
84. Sommer, *Foundational Fictions*, 114–37.
85. Ibid., 121–24.
86. Helg, *Our Rightful Share*.
87. Sommer, *Foundational Fictions*, 125.
88. Morúa Delgado, *Sofía*, vii–x.
89. Ibid.
90. Gómez, *Preparando la Revolución*, 7–9.

91. Ironically, Gómez was accused by Spanish officials of trying to create an exclusively Black party that separated Afro-Cubans from others in Cuban society. See Helg, *Our Rightful Share*, 51.
92. Adorno, "Reconsidering Colonial Discourse for Sixteenth and Seventeenth-Century Spanish America," 134–45.
93. See Juan Gualberto Gómez, *Preparando la Revolución*, 7–9.
94. Aguirre, *Nacionalidad y Nación en el Siglo XIX Cubano*, 2.
95. Martí, *Obras Completas*, 8:43–44; and Martí, "Letter to General Máximo Gómez," 257–260.
96. Lazo, *Writing to Cuba*, 63–97.
97. Ibid., 142–67.
98. Ibid.
99. Matory, "The English Professors of Brazil," 72–103; Otero, "Dreaming the Barrio," 31–52; and Otero, "Rethinking the Diaspora," 54–56.
100. Ola Vincent, interview, 2001, Lagos, Nigeria. See also Sarracino, "Back to Africa," 67–70; and chapter 4 of this volume.
101. Sarracino, "Back to Africa," 67–70. See also Matory, "The English Professors of Brazil," 72–103.
102. See Ferrer, *Insurgent Cuba, 1868–1898*, 15–92.
103. Barnet, *Biografía de un cimarrón*, 17–60. See also Ferrer on Montejo in *Insurgent Cuba*, 96, 238.
104. Zeuske, "El Cimarrón y las Consecuencias de la Guerra del 95," 65–84.
105. Ibid.
106. Ibid.
107. Clifford, "Introduction: Partial Truths," in *Writing Culture*, 1–26; and Behar, "Going to Cuba," 136–160.
108. Giles, *Virtual Americas*, 18, 22–46, 107–8, 270–80.
109. Achebe, *Things Fall Apart*; and Ngugi wa Thiong'o, *The River Between*.
110. Ferrer, *Insurgent Cuba*, 112140, and Helg, *Our Rightful Share*, 51–60.
111. On history and race in the creation of Cuban nationality, see Ferrer, *Insurgent Cuba*, 1–14.
112. Otero, "Spirit Possession, Havana, and the Night," 45–74, and Otero, "*Iku* and Cuban Nationhood," 116–31.
113. This refers to the Ten Years' War. Carlos Manuel de Céspedes, who was among the revolutionaries that initiated the war in 1868, was declared the Padre de la Patria (Father of the Nation). See Ibarra, *Ideologia mambisa*; and Ibarra, *Nación y Cultura Nacional, 1868–1930*.
114. Barnet, *Biografía de un cimarrón*, 160–61.
115. Otero, "Spirit Possession, Havana, and the Night," 45–74, and Otero, "*Iku* and Cuban Nationhood," 116–131.
116. Ibid.
117. Behar, "Going to Cuba: Writing Ethnography of Diaspora, Return, and Despair," in *The Vulnerable Observer: Anthropology that Breaks Your Heart*, 136–60.
118. See Bauman and Briggs, "Poetics and Performances," 59–88.
119. *Nganga* is the name for the sacred pots used in Congo religion. *Nganga* are usually made of iron and contain various herbs, bones, and other materials. They

are usually associated with either a deity or a *muerto*, the spirit of a dead person. For more on *nganga*, see Cabrera, *Reglas de Congo*, 130–48.

120. Barnet, *Biografía de un cimarrón*, 35.
121. Viarnés, "Cultural Memory in Afro-Cuban Possession"," 127–60.
122. Otero, "Dreaming the Barrio," 31–52.
123. Howard, *Changing History*, 94.
124. Ortiz, *Los cabildos y la fiesta del Día de los Reyes*.
125. Cabrera, "Religious Syncretism in Cuba," 84–94.
126. See Matory, *Black Atlantic Religion*, 38–72; and Matory, "The English Professors of Brazil," 72–103.
127. Gooding-King, interview, April 15, 2001, Cuban Lodge, Lagos, Nigeria,; Bamgboshe Martins, interview, March 27, 2001, Campos Square, Lagos, Nigeria.
128. Villaverde, *Cecilia Valdes o la loma del angel*; Calcagno, *Poetas de color*; and Sainz, *La literatura cubana de 1700 a 1790*.
129. Suárez y Romero, *Francisco*.
130. Sandoval, *De instauranda aethiopum salute*.
131. Saco's work was done in the mid-nineteenth century; Ortiz compiled and wrote a prologue for Saco's *Historia de la esclavitud* in 1938.
132. Alejandro De la Fuente, *Havana and the Atlantic in the Sixteenth Century*, 11–50.
133. Thornton and Heywood, *Central Africans, Atlantic Creoles, and the Foundation of the Americas, 1585–1660*, 5–48.
134. Del Monte y Anselmo, "Moral religiosa," 82–86.
135. Calcagno, *Diccionario biografico cubano*.
136. Martí, *Inside the Monster*, 209–43, 325–28.
137. Abrahams, "Phantoms of Romantic Nationalism in Folkloristics," 3–37.
138. Otero, "Spirit Possession, Havana, and the Night," 45–74; and Otero, "*Iku* and Cuban Nationhood," 116–31.
139. Otero, "Spirit Possession, Havana, and the Night," 45–74, and Otero, "*Iku* and Cuban Nationhood," 116–31. See also Ponte, "A petición a Ochún," in *Un arte de hacer ruinas y otros cuentos*, 74–87.
140. See Viarnés, "Cultural Memory in Afro-Cuban Possession," 127–60.
141. Ortiz, "Los factores humano de la cubanidad," 1–20.
142. Ibid., 3–10.
143. Ibid., 3–8.
144. Christine Ayorinde, *Afro-Cuban Religiosity, Revolution, and National Identity*, 40–69.
145. See, for example, Ortiz, "Brujos o Santos," 85–90.
146. Cabrera, *Cuentos Negros de Cuba*; Lachateñere, "El sistema religioso de los Lucumí y otras influencias africanes en Cuba I, 28–82"; and Lachateñere, "El sistema religioso de los Lucumí y otras influencias Africanes en Cuba II," 8–32.
147. See these early studies of Afro-Cuban language: Ortiz, *Glosario de Afronegrismos*; Cabrera, *Anagó*; Díaz Fabelo, *Lengua de Santeros, Guiné Gongorí*; and Olmstead, "Comparative Notes on Yoruba and Lucumi," 157–64.
148. See Behar, "After the Bridges," 3–8, and Suárez, "Our Memories, Ourselves," 9–16, in Behar and Suárez, *The Portable Island*.

149. See, for example, Cabrera's *Yemayá y Ochun*, Castellanos's *Cultura Afrocubana* series, Cros Sandoval's *La Religión Afrocubana*, and Benítez Rojo's *La Isla Que Se Repite*, all of which concern the formation of Afrocubano culture written outside of Cuba. For more on the trope of exile in Cuban writing, see Behar, "After the Bridges," 3–8, in Behar and Suárez, *The Portable Island*.

150. Of note here are the following studies: Sarduy and Stubbs, *AfroCuba*; Benavides, *Enigmatic Powers*; Behar, *Bridges to Cuba*; David Hilary Brown, *Santería Enthroned*; and Cros Sandoval, *Worldview, the Orichas, and Santería*.

151. Matibag, *Afro-Cuban Religious Experience*, 1–85; and Hewitt, *Aché, presencia africana*, 16–25, 75–82. For a good discussion of central African relationships with Europeans in the sixteenth century that illuminates the creation of "Atlantic Creoles," see Thornton and Heywood, *Central Africans, Atlantic Creoles, and the Foundation of the Americas, 1585–1660*, 5–48, 109–68.

152. García, *Dreaming in Cuban*; and Obejas, "We Came All the Way from Cuba So You Could Dress Like This?" 113–31.

153. Ponte, "Las lágrimas en el congrí," 43–49; "Un arte de hacer ruinas," 56–72; "A petición a Ochún," 74–87; and "El frío del Malecón," 125–27, all in *Un arte de hacer ruinas y otros cuentos*.

154. See Fusco, *English Is Broken Here*, 37–64.

155. Behar, *An Island Called Home*, 1–35; Machado and Domitrovich, *Tastes like Cuba'*, esp. 61–75, and 298–344; Zoé Valdés, *Te di la vida entera*, 339–62; West-Durán, "Going Home via Africa and Cayo Hueso," 145–52; and Alina Troyano (a.k.a. Carmelita Tropicana), "Milk of Amnesia/Leche de Amnesia," in Alina Troyano, *I, Carmelita Tropicana*, 52–71.

156. Matory, *Black Atlantic Religion*, 73–114; and Matory, "The English Professors of Brazil," 72–103.

157. See Ñgugi wa Thiong'o, *Moving the Centre*, 5–11.

Conclusion

1. Babalola, *Awon Oriki Orile*; Bascom, "The Yoruba in Cuba," 14–24; and Cabrera, *El Monte Igbo Finda Ewe Orisha*, 5–25.

2. Verger, "Nigeria, Brésil, et Cuba," 125–36; Matory, "The English Professors of Brazil," 72–103; and Yai, "The Identity, Contributions, and Ideology of the Aguda," 72–82.

3. Barber, *I Could Speak until Tomorrow*, 25–34, 87–104, 249–60; and Akinaso, "Yoruba Traditional Names and the Transmission of Cultural Knowledge," 139–58.

4. Akere, "Linguistic Assimilation in Socio-Historical Dimensions," 164–91.

5. Matory, "The English Professors of Brazil," 72–103; Mann, *Slavery and the Birth of an African City*, 1–50; Akere, "Linguistic Assimilation in Socio-Historical Dimensions," 164–91; and Jean Herskovits, *A Preface to Modern Nigeria*, 5–26.

6. Margaret Thompson Drewal, "Dancing for Ogun in Yorubaland and in Brazil," 199–234; and Barber, "Polyvocality and Individual Talent," 151–60.

7. Hallen, *The Good, the Bad, and the Beautiful*, 133–34, 137.

8. Adedeji, "The Church and the Emergence of the Nigerian Theatre," 23–45; Barber, *The Generation of Plays*, 1–18, 348–98; Barber, "Quotation and the Constitution of Yoruba Oral Texts," 1–17; and Yai, "In Praise of Metonymy," 107–15.

9. Margaret Thompson Drewal, "Dancing for Ogun in Yorubaland and in Brazil," 199–234; Barber, *The Generation of Plays*, 348–98; and Barber, "Quotation and the Constitution of Yoruba Oral Texts," 1–17.

10. Akinaso, "Yoruba Traditional Names and the Transmission of Cultural Knowledge," 139–58; Bascom, *Sixteen Cowries*, 3–52; and Margaret Thompson Drewal, "Embodied Practice/Embodied History," 171–90.

11. Bay, "Protection, Political Exile, and the Atlantic Slave-Trade," 42–60; Gilroy, *Against Race*, 278–356; and Matory, "The English Professors of Brazil," 72–103

12. Abrahams, "Phantoms of Romantic Nationalism in Folkloristics," 3–37; and Featherstone, *Global Culture: An Introduction*," 1–14.

13. Yai, "The Identity, Contributions, and Ideology of the Aguda," 72–82; and Yai, "*In Praise of* Metonymy: The Concepts of 'Tradition' and 'Creativity' in the Transmission of Yoruba Artistry over Time and Space," 107–15, and Appadurai, *Modernity at Large*, 48–65.

14. Canizares, "Santería," 59–63; and Perez Mena, "Cuban Santeria, Haitian Vodun, Puerto Rican Spiritualism," 15–28; see also the anthology *Osun across the Waters*, edited by Murphy and Sanford.

15. Palmié, "Against Syncretism," 73–105.

16. Comaroff and Comaroff, "The Madman and the Migrant," 155–80; Edwards, *The Practice of Diaspora*, 16–68, 241–305; and Kelley, *Freedom Dreams*, 1–12, 157–98.

17. Matory, "The English Professors of Brazil," 72–103; Ferrer, *Insurgent Cuba*, 1–69, 170–94; and Barnet, *Biografía de un cimarrón*, 159–202.

18. Juan Pérez de la Riva, *Documentos para la historia de las gentes sin historia*, 27–51; and Otero, "Barrio, Bodega, and Botanica Aesthetics," 173–94.

19. Law, "The Evolution of the Brazilian Community in Ouidah," 22–41.

20. Da Costa E Silva, "Buying and Selling Korans in Nineteenth-Century Rio de Janeiro," 83–90; Abimbola, "Lagbayi: The Itinerant Wood Carver of Ojowon," 137–42; and Appadurai, *Modernity at Large*, 48-65.

21. Cabrera, "Religious Syncretism in Cuba," 84–94; Lachatenere, "El Sistema Religioso de los Lucumí y otras Influencias Africanes in Cuba I," 28–82; Lachateñere, "El Sistema Religioso de los Lucumí y otras Influencias Africanes in Cuba II," 8–32; Lachateñere, "El Sistema Religioso de los Lucumis y otras Influencias Africanas en Cuba III," 208. Abakua here refers to Afro-Cubans who associate with an all-male society known as the ñáñigos and are of Ékpè origin. For more on the Abakua see Ivor L. Miller's recent book, *Voice of the Leopard: African Secret Societies and Cuba*, esp. 89–101.

22. Foner, "What's New about Transnationalism?" 355–76.

23. See Bascom, *Chango in the New World*, 4–8; Bascom, "Folklore and the Africanist," 253–59; Baron and Cara, "Introduction: Creolization and Folklore," 4–8; Kapchan and Turner Strong, "Theorizing the Hybrid," 239–53; and Barber, "Popular Arts in Africa."

24. Ortiz, *La Africanía de la Música Folklórica de Cuba*, 143 (my translation into English). Ortiz mentions the *iyesás* (Ijesha) as an ethnicity "separate" from the Lucumí,

with both groups belonging to the Yoruba "kingdoms." For more on ethnic formation, history, and the reconstruction of the "kingdoms" of the Yoruba, see: Peel, "Making History," 111–32; and also the informative compilation *Pioneer, Patriot, and Patriarch,* edited by Toyin Falola.

25. Browning, *Infectious Rhythm,* 17–32.

26. Fusco, *English Is Broken Here,* 279–84; Baron and Cara, "Introduction: Creolization and Folklore," 4–8; Kapchan and Turner Strong, "Theorizing the Hybrid," 239–53; and Foner, "What's New about Transnationalism?"

27. Benítez Rojo, *La Isla Que Se Repite El Caribe,* 1–81.

28. Baron and Cara, "Introduction: Creolization and Folklore," 4–8; Goldman, "Virtual Islands," 375–400; Kapchan and Turner Strong, "Theorizing the Hybrid," 239–53.

29. Quine, *Word and Object,* 1–21, 226–32; Hallen and Sodipo, *Knowledge, Belief, and Witchcraft,* 40–85; and Oke, "Towards an African (Yoruba) Perspective on Empirical Knowledge," 205–17.

30. Ortiz, *La Africanía de la Música Folklórica de Cuba,* 143; and Romberg, "Today, Changó Is Changó," 75–106.

31. Abrahams and Bauman, "Sense and Nonsense in St. Vincent," 762–72; Benavides, "Syncretism and Legitimacy in Latin American Religion," 19–46; and Isabel Castellanos, "From Ulukumí to Lucumí," 39–50.

32. Henry John Drewal and Margaret Thompson Drewal, "Composing Time and Space in Yoruba Art," 225–50.

33. Carlos Moore, Shawna Moore, and Tanya Saunders, *African Presence in the Americas*; Barber, *The Generation of Plays,* 1–18, 348–98; Barber, "Quotation and the Constitution of Yoruba Oral Texts," 1–17; Bastian, "Vulture Men, Campus Cultists and Teenage Witches," 71–96; Howard, *Changing History,* 48–72; and Matibag, *Afro-Cuban Religious Experience,* 75–85.

34. Robin Cohen, "Diasporas, the Nation-State, and Globalization," 117–43; Azevedo, "Images of Africa and the Haitian Revolution in American and Brazilian Abolitionism," 167–77; and Anthias, "Evaluating 'Diaspora'" 557–81.

35. Robin Cohen, *Global Diaspora,* 176.

36. See the following works by Lydia Cabrera: *Reglas de Congo,* 21–23; *Anagó,* 7–9; *El Monte Igbo Finda Ewe Orisha,* 21–27, 246–66, 485–505; and "Religious Syncretism in Cuba," 84–94.

37. Romberg, "Today, Changó Is Changó," 75–106.

38. Otero, "Spirit Possession, Havana, and the Night," 45–74.

39. Abrahams, "The Complex Relations of Simple Forms," 193–214.

40. Some have argued that this liminality may even be the case with regard to Palo in relation to Yoruba Afro-Cuban religion in terms of the creation of a hegemony of Lucumí ritual practices in some ritual circles. See Viarnés, "Cultural Memory in Afro-Cuban Possession," 127160.

41. Appadurai, "Grassroots Globalization and the Research Imagination," 1–20.

42. Matory, "The English Professors of Brazil," 72–103; and Juan Pérez de la Riva, *Documentos para la historia de las gentes sin historia,* 7–14.

43. Rama, *La Ciudad Letrada,* 16–29; and Appadurai, *Modernity at Large,* 32.

44. Benítez Rojo, *La Isla Que Se Repite El Caribe,* 1–32; and Abrahams, "Questions of Criolian Contagion," 73–87.

45. Falola and Roberts, "Introduction," in *The Atlantic World,* 1450–2000, x.
46. Appadurai, *Modernity at Large,* 31; Matory, *Black Atlantic Religion,* 38–72, 73–114; and Otero, "Dreaming the Barrio," 31–52.
47. Vogel, "Future Traditions," 94–113.
48. Otero, "Barrio, Bodega, and Botanica Aesthetics," 173–94; and Gilbert, "Things Ugly," 340–371.
49. Fusco, *English Is Broken Here,* 37–65.
50. Ibid.
51. Mbembe, "Provisional Notes on the Postcolony," 3–37; Mbembe, "Belly Up," 46–145; Ibarra, *Ideologia mambisa,* 12–18; Ferrer, *Insurgent Cuba,* 195–202; and Otero, "Rethinking the Diaspora," 54–56.
52. Benítez Rojo, *La Isla Que Se Repite El Caribe,* 31–81; Benítez Rojo, "The Role of Music in the Emergence of Afro-Cuban Culture," 197–203; and Hewitt, *Aché, presencia africana,* 25–40, 57–60.
53. Ortiz, *Los cabildos y la fiesta del Día de los Reyes*; Bascom, "Yoruba Acculturation in Cuba," 163–67; Verger, "Yoruba Influences in Brazil," 3–11; Peel, "The Cultural Work of Yoruba Ethnogenesis," 65–75; Peel, "Making History," 111–32; Law, "Heritage of Oduduwa," 207–22; Falola, *Pioneer, Patriot, and Patriarch*; and Johnson, *History of the Yorubas*.
54. See Law, *The Oyo Empire c.1600–1836*; J. F. A. Ajayi and Smith, *Yoruba Warfare in the Nineteenth Century*; and Matory, *Sex and the Empire That Is No More,* 28–61.
55. Aderibigbe, "Early History of Lagos to about 1850," 1–26.
56. Law, "The Evolution of the Brazilian Community in Ouidah," 22–41; Juan Pérez de la Riva, *Documentos para la historia de las gentes sin historia,* 27–33; Verger, *Trade relations between the Bight of Benin and Bahia from the 17th to 19th Century,* 17; and Matory, "The English Professors of Brazil," 72–103.
57. Apter, "Que Faire?" 87–105.
58. Matory, "The English Professors of Brazil"; Benavides, "Syncretism and Legitimacy in Latin American Religion," 19–46; Perez Mena, "Cuban Santeria, Haitian Vodun, Puerto Rican Spiritualism," 15–28; David Hilary Brown, *Santería Enthroned,* 165–209; and Quiñonez, *Chango's Fire,* esp. 125–255.
59. Laotan, "Brazilian Influence on Lagos," 156–65.
60. Abrahams, "The Complex Relations of Simple Forms," 193–214; Amselle, *Mestizo Logistics,* 136–150; Margaret Thompson Drewal, "Dancing for Ogun in Yorubaland and in Brazil, 199–234"; and Otero, "Dreaming the Barrio," 31–52.
61. Otero; "Dreaming the Barrio," 31–52; Laotan, *The Torch Bearers*; and Lasebikan, "The Yoruba in Brazil," 843.
62. See Rama, *La Ciudad Letrada,* esp. his discussion, 52–53, of sixteenth-century graffiti in Mexico City, where indigenous groups protested Cortés's stay by writing obscenities on a public wall. This was first described by Bernal Díaz del Castillo in *Historia verdadera de la conquista de la Nueva España,* 430–31.
63. Folami, *A History of Lagos, Nigeria,* 7–8.
64. Echeruo, *Victorian Lagos,* 1–16; and Otero, "Dreaming the Barrio," 31–52.
65. Howard, *Changing History,* 21–48.
66. Childs, "The Defects of Being a Black Creole," 209–45.
67. Olupona, "Orisa Osun," 46–67.
68. Radano, "Denoting Difference," 506–44.

69. Appadurai, "Grassroots Globalization and the Research Imagination," 1–20; and Barber, "Popular Arts in Africa," 1–78, 113–32.

70. Verger, *Trade Relations between the Bight of Benin and Bahia from the 17th to 19th Century*; Appadurai and Breckenridge, "Why Public Culture?" 5–9; and Foner, "What's New about Transnationalism?" 355–76.

71. Mann, *Slavery and the Birth of an African City*, 25–26, 30–31, 54; Smith, *The Lagos Consulate*, 1851–1861; Aderibigbe, "Early History of Lagos to about 1850, 1–26; Patrick Dele Cole, "Lagos Society in the Nineteenth-Century," 27–57; and Peel, "Making History, 111–32"

72. Awolalu, "Aiyelala—a Guardian of Social Morality," 79–89; Barnes and Agiri, "Lagos before 1603," 18–32; and Bamgboshe Martins, "Mabinouri Dawodu," 11–12.

73. Fox, "Diasporicentrism and Black Aural Texts," 367–78.

74. Mann, *Slavery and the Birth of an African City*, 93–96; Law, *The Slave Coast of West Africa, 1550–1750*, 33–69, 116–224; and Smith, *The Lagos Consulate, 1851–1861*, 22–41.

75. Adorno, "Reconsidering Colonial Discourse for Sixteenth and Seventeenth-Century Spanish America," 134–145; Hymes, "Breakthrough into Performance," 79–141; Matibag, *Afro-Cuban Religious Experience*, 1–75; and Law, "The Evolution of the Brazilian Community in Ouidah."

76. Abiodun, "Identity and the Artistic Process in Yoruba Aesthetic Concept of Iwa," 13–30; Bascom, "The Sanctions of Ifa Divination," 43–54; Barber, "Discursive Strategies in the Texts of Ifá and in the `Holy Book of Odù,'" 196–240; and Olupona, "Orisa Osun," 46–67.

77. By retrieval, I mean the commodification of temporal and cultural nostalgia as described by authors like Appadurai in *Modernity at Large*, 7–8, 66–86, and also Stewart, *On Longing*, 3–36.

78. Appadurai, *Modernity at Large*. 27–47, 158–77; and García Canclini, *Imaginarios Urbanos*. 74–78.

79. Appadurai, "Grassroots Globalization and the Research Imagination"; Bendix, *In Search of Authenticity*, 27–44, 159–87; Apter, "Que Faire?"; Peel, "Making History"; and Bamgboshe Martins, "Mabinouri Dawodu."

80. Otero, "Barrio, Bodega, and Botanica Aesthetics."

81. David Scott, "This Event, This Memory." 261–83; Hall, "Negotiating Caribbean Identities," 3–15; and Gikandi, "Introduction: Africa, Diaspora, and the Discourse of Modernity," 1–6.

82. Ngugi wa Thiong'o, *Moving the Centre*, 2–11, 25–29.

83. Feierman, "Colonizers, Scholars, and the Creation of Invisible Histories," 182–215; Barber, "Discursive Strategies in the Texts of Ifá and in the `Holy Book of Odù,'" 196–240; Appadurai and Breckenridge, "Why Public Culture?" 5–9; Fusco, *English Is Broken Here*, 279–84 Dayan, "Haiti, History, and the Gods," 66–97; and Juan Pérez de la Riva, *Documentos para la historia de las gentes sin historia*, 32.

84. See esp. Sarduy and Stubbs, "The Rite of Social Communion," 3–26; and Ortiz, "Los factores humano de la cubanidad," 1–20.

85. Akere, "Linguistic Assimilation in Socio-Historical Dimensions," 164–91; and Euba, "Dress and Status in Nineteenth-Century Lagos," 142–65.

86. Juan Pérez de la Riva, *Documentos para la historia de las gentes sin historia*. 27–33; Matory, "The English Professors of Brazil," 72–103; Yai, "The Identity, Contributions,

and Ideology of the Aguda," 72–82; Law, "The Evolution of the Brazilian Community in Ouidah," 22–41; Otero, "Dreaming the Barrio," 51–52; and Mann, *Slavery and the Birth of an African City*, 200–36.

87. I use the term *rama*, which stems from Afrocubano folk religion, because it commonly describes the different "branches" stemming from a conglomerate of similar sets of markedly distinct religious practices. It is an especially apt term since it also relates to the religious epistemology of the "road," or *ona*, in Yoruba traditional religion and the idea of the *camino*, or road, in Santería and Palo. For more on religious terminology, ritual, and *orisha* metalanguage in diasporic perspective, see these comprehensive anthologies: Lindsay, *Santeria Aesthetics*; Abiodun, Drewal, and Pemberton, *The Yoruba Artist*; Barnes, *Africa's Ogun*; and Murphy and Sanford, *Osun across the Waters*.

88. Matibag, *Afro-Cuban Religious Experience*, 35–50; and Cabrera, *Cuentos Negros de Cuba*.

89. Mann, *Slavery and the Birth of an African City*, 51–83; Mann, "Shifting Paradigms in the Study of the African Diaspora and of Atlantic History and Culture," 3–21; Isabel Castellanos, "From Ulukumí to Lucumí," 39–50; Isabel Castellanos, *The Use of Language in Afro-Cuban Religion*, 10–22; Olmstead, "Comparative Notes on Yoruba and Lucumi," 157–64; and Cabrera, *Reglas de Congo*, 6–18.

90. Otero, "Rethinking the Diaspora," 54–56.

91. Abiodun, "Identity and the Artistic Process in Yoruba Aesthetic Concept of Iwa," 13–30; Hallen, *The Good, the Bad, and the Beautiful*, 139–48; Cabrera, *Koeko Iyawó*. 3–17; and Cabrera, *Yemayá y Ochún*, 7–21.

92. For an example of this narrative, see Pemberton, "The Dreadful God and the Divine King," 124–25.

93. Otero, "Barrio, Bodega, and Botanica Aesthetics," 173–94; and Otero, "Dreaming the Barrio,"31–52.

94. See Yai, "The Identity, Contributions, and Ideology of the Aguda," 72–82; Abimbola, "Lagbayi," 137–42; and Matory, "The English Professors of Brazil," 72–103.

95. Apter, "Herskovits' Heritage," 235–60; Peel, "The Pastor and the *Babalawo*," 338–69; and Matory, "The English Professors of Brazil," 72–103

96. Clifford, "Diasporas," 302–38.

97. Barber, *The Generation of Plays*, 1–18; and Barber, "Quotation and the Constitution of Yoruba Oral Texts," 1–17.

98. Fabian, *Moments of Freedom*, 41–69; Comaroff and Comaroff, "Introduction," in *Civil Society and the Political Imagination in Africa*, 1–43; Baron and Cara, "Introduction: Creolization and Folklore," 4–8; Kapchan and Turner Strong, "Theorizing the Hybrid," 239–53; and Feierman, "Colonizers, Scholars, and the Creation of Invisible Histories," 182–215.

99. Geertz, *Local Knowledge*, 36–54.

100. Sanford and Murphy, "Introduction," in *Osun across the Waters*, 1–9; Yai. "In Praise of Metonymy," 107–15; Blier, "Art Systems and Semiotics," 7–18; and Robert Farris Thompson, "The Three Warriors," 225–39.

101. Hallen and Sodipo, *Knowledge, Belief, and Witchcraft*, 34–39, 60–81; and Hountondji, *African Philosophy*, 47–70.

102. Isabel Castellanos, "The Use of Language in Afro-Cuban Religion," 28–42; Abiodun, "Ifa Art Objects," 421–69; and Awobuluyi, *Yoruba Metalanguage I*.

103. Galembo, *Divine Inspiration*, 121–30.

104. On fate and choice, see esp. Sodipo, "Notes on the Concept of Cause and Chance in Yoruba Traditional Thought," 12–20.

105. Barber, *The Generation of Plays*, 1–18; Barber, "Quotation and the Constitution of Yoruba Oral Texts," 1–17; Otero, "Barrio, Bodega, and Botanica Aesthetics," 173–94; and Otero, "Dreaming the Barrio," 31–52.

106. Verger, "Nigeria, Brésil, et Cuba," 125–36; and Adebanjo, *Iwe adura*.

107. Yai, "The Identity, Contributions, and Ideology of the Aguda," 72–82; and Otero, "Dreaming the Barrio," 31–52.

108. Peel, "Making History," 111–32; Law, "Traditional History," 25–41; and Law, "My Head Belongs to the King," 399–415.

109. Breckenridge et al., "Introduction: Cosmopolitanisms," in *Cosmopolitanism*, 1–14; and Sennett, "Cosmopolitanism and the Social Experience of Cities," 42–48.

110. Skinner, "The Dialectic between Diasporas and Homelands," 17–45.

111. Yai, "The Identity, Contributions, and Ideology of the Aguda," 72–82; Law, "The Evolution of the Brazilian Community in Ouidah," 27–41; Juan Pérez de la Riva, *Documentos para la historia de las gentes sin historia*, 27–33; Sarracino, *Los Que Volvieron a África*, 47–64; Verger, "Nigeria, Brazil, and Cuba," 113–43; and Matory, "The English Professors of Brazil," 72–103.

112. Matory, ibid; and Otero, "Barrio, Bodega, and Botanica Aesthetics," 173–94.

113. Otero, "Dreaming the Barrio," 31–52; and Isabel Castellanos, "From Ulukumí to Lucumí," 39–50.

114. For Ochún in Cuba see Castellanos, "A River of Many Turns," 34–45; and Murphy, "Yéyé Cachita," 87–101.

115. See chapter 4 of this volume.

116. For a thoughtful discussion of methods, terminology, and vernacular religion, see Primiano, "Vernacular Religion and the Search for Method in Religious Folklife," 37–56.

117. See Appadurai, *Modernity at Large*, 27–65; and Appadurai, "Grassroots Globalization and the Research Imagination," 1–20.

118. Gikandi, "Introduction: Africa, Diaspora, and the Discourse of Modernity," 1–6.

119. See, for example, Law, "The Evolution of the Brazilian Community in Ouidah," 22–41.

Appendix

1. On the establishment of ganadoras, African woman as prosperous merchants in Havana beginning in the late sixteenth century, see Alejandro De la Fuente, *Havana and the Atlantic in the Sixteenth Century*, 150–60, 177–81, 197–98, 213, 222.

Bibliography

Interviews

Ajikobi, Dimeji, interview, March 23, 2001, University of Lagos, Lagos, Nigeria.
Bamgbose-Martins, Lola, interview, August 11, 1999, Campos Sqaure, Lagos, Nigeria.
———, interview, March 27, 2001, Campos Square, Lagos, Nigeria.
———, interview, April 23, 2001, Campos Square, Lagos, Nigeria.
Gooding-King, Aderemi, interview, August 7, 1999, Cuban Lodge, Lagos, Nigeria.
———, interview, April 15, 2001.
Kukah, Matthew, interview, August 9, 1999, Campos Square, Lagos, Nigeria.
Olusí, T. Omoba, interview, March 29, 2001, Isaleko, Lagos, Nigeria.
———, interview, April 21, 2001, Isaleko, Lagos, Nigeria.
———, interview, May 5, 2001, Isaleko, Lagos, Nigeria.
———, interview, June 3, 2001, Isaleko, Lagos, Nigeria.
Vincent, Ola, interview, April 25, 2001, Victoria Island, Lagos, Nigeria.
———, interview, May 3, 2001, Ikoyi, Lagos, Nigeria.

Archival Sources

Cuba Archivo Nacional, Leg. 139/152. January 4, 1845. "Real Orden Al Sr. Capitán de la Isla de Cuba." *Autorizado la salida de negros para Africa* Primera secretaria del Despacho de Estado. Madrid, S.A.
Cuba Archivo Nacional. "La Real Cédula de 31 de Mayo de 1789, Capítulo XIII."
Cuba Archivo Nacional. "Reglamento de 14 de Noviembre de 1842, articulo 37."

Secondary Sources

Abdul, M. O. A. "Ifa Divination and Islam." *Orita* 4, no. 1 (1970): 17–26.
Abimbola, Wande. "The Contribution of Diaspora Blacks to the Development and Preservation of Traditional African Religion in the Americas." In *Cultures Africaines: Documents de la réunion d'experts sur "Les apports culturels des noirs de la Diaspora à l'Afrique,"* 79–89. Paris: UNESCO, 1983.
———. *Ifa: An Exposition of Ifa Literary Corpus*. Ibadan, Nigeria: Oxford University Press, 1997.
———. *Ifa Divination Poetry*. Lagos: NOK Publishers, 1977.
———. *Ijinle Ohun Enu Ifa*. Glasgow, UK: Collins, 1968.

———. "Lagbayi: The Itinerant Wood Carver of Ojowon." In *The Yoruba Artist: New Theoretical Perspectives on African Arts*, edited by Rowland Abiodun, Henry J. Drewal, and John Pemberton III, 137–42. Washington, DC: Smithsonian Institution Press, 1994.

———. "The Literature of the Ifa Cult." In *Sources of Yoruba History*, edited by Saburi O. Biobaku, 41–63. Oxford: Clarendon Press, 1973.

———. *Sixteen Great Poems of Ifa.* Zaria, Nigeria: UNESCO, 1975.

———. "Stylistic Repetition in Ifa Divination Poetry." *Lagos Notes and Records* 3, no. 1 (1971): 38–53.

———. *Yoruba Oral Tradition: Poetry in Music, Dance and Drama.* Ile-Ife, Nigeria: University of Ife, Department of African Languages and Literatures, 1975.

Abiodun, Rowland. "An African (?) Art History: Promising Theoretical Approaches in Yoruba Art Studies." In *The Yoruba Artist: New Theoretical Perspectives on African Arts*, edited by Rowland Abiodun, Henry J. Drewal, and John Pemberton III, 37–47. Washington, DC: Smithsonian Institution Press, 1994.

———. "Identity and the Artistic Process in Yoruba Aesthetic Concept of Iwa." *Journal of Cultures and Ideas* 1, no. 1 (1983): 13–30.

———. "Ifa Art Objects: An Interpretation Based on Oral Traditions." In *Yoruba Oral Tradition: Poetry in Music, Dance and Drama*, edited by Wande Abimbọla, 421–69. Ile-Ife, Nigeria: University of Ife, Department of African Languages and Literatures, 1975.

———. "Riding the Horse of Praise: The Mounted Figure Motif in Ifa Divination Sculpture." In *Insight and Artistry in African Divination*, edited by John Pemberton III, 182–92. Washington, DC: Smithsonian Institution Press, 2001.

Abiodun, Rowland, Henry J. Drewal, and John Pemberton III, eds. *The Yoruba Artist: New Theoretical Perspectives on African Arts.* Washington, DC: Smithsonian Institution Press, 1994.

Abraham, R. C. *Dictionary of Modern Yoruba.* London: University of London Press, 1958.

Abrahams, Roger D. "The Complex Relations of Simple Forms." In *Folklore Genres*, edited by Dan Ben-Amos, 193–214. 1969. Reprint, Austin: University of Texas Press, 1976.

———. "'The Dunghill of the Universe': Creolization in the Greater Caribbean." Unpublished manuscript provided by author, 2002.

———. *Everyday Life: A Poetics of Vernacular Practices.* Philadelphia: University of Pennsylvania Press, 2005.

———. *The Man-of-Words in the West Indies.* Baltimore: Johns Hopkins University Press, 1983.

———."Phantoms of Romantic Nationalism in Folkloristics." *Journal of American Folklore* 106, no. 419 (1993): 3–37.

———."Questions of Criolian Contagion." *Journal of American Folklore* 116, no. 459 (2003): 73–87.

———. "Toward an Enactment-centered Theory of Folklore and Folklife." In *Frontiers of Folklore*, edited by W. R. Bascom, 79–120. Washington, DC: American Association for the Advancement of Science (AAAS), 1977.

Abrahams, Roger D., and Richard Bauman. "Sense and Nonsense in St. Vincent: Speech Behavior and Decorum in a Caribbean Community." *American Anthropologist* 73, no. 3 (1971): 762–72.

Abrahams, Roger D., and John F. Szwed. *After Africa*. New Haven, CT: Yale University Press, 1983.
Achebe, Chinua. *Things Fall Apart*. New York: W. W. Norton & Co., 2008.
Acosta Saignes, Miguel. "Las Cofradías Coloniales y el Folklore." *Cultura Universitaria* 47 (1955): 79–99.
Adderley, Rosanne M. *New Negroes from Africa: Slave Trade Abolition and Free African Settlement in the Nineteenth-Century Caribbean*. Bloomington: Indiana University Press, 2007.
Adebanjo, Emanual. *Iwe adura: Kokoro ona Igbala ati Idajo pelu atunda aiye titan*. Lagos: Ano-Oluwa Press, 1934.
Adedeji, Joel. "The Church and the Emergence of the Nigerian Theatre, 1866–1914." *Journal of the Historical Society of Nigeria* 4, no. 1 (1971): 23–45.
———. "Folklore and Yoruba Drama: Obatalá as a Case Study." In *African Folklore*, edited by Richard Dorson, 321–39. Bloomington: Indiana University Press, 1972.
———. "Oral Tradition and Contemporary Theater in Nigeria." *Research in African Literature* 2, no. 2 (1971): 134–49.
Adediran, Biodun. "Research on Pre-colonial Western Yorubaland: A Note on Source Materials." *Anthropos* 80, nos. 4–6 (1985): 545–54.
Adeko, Adeleke. "Word's Horse, or the Proverb as a Paradigm of Literary Understanding." PhD diss., University of Florida, 1991.
Ademakinwa, J. A. *Ife, Cradle of the Yoruba: A Handbook on the History of the Origin of the Yorubas, Parts I, II, II*. Lagos: Pacific Printing Works, 1959.
Aderibigbe, A. B. "Early History of Lagos to about 1850." In *Lagos: The Development of an African City*, edited by A. B. Aderibigbe, 1–26. London: Longman, 1975.
———. "Expansion of the Lagos Protectorate, 1863–1900." PhD diss., University of London, 1959.
———. *Lagos: The Development of an African City*. London: Longman, 1975.
Adesanya, Adebayo. "Yoruba Metaphysical Thinking." *Odu* 5 (1958): 36–41.
Adorno, Rolena. "The Discursive Encounter of Spain and America: The Authority of Eyewitness Testimony in the Writing of History." *William and Mary Quarterly* 49, no. 2 (1992): 210–29.
———. "Reconsidering Colonial Discourse for Sixteenth and Seventeenth-Century Spanish America." *Latin American Research Review* 28, no. 3 (1993): 134–45.
Agiri, Babatunde. "Aspects of Socio-economic Changes among the Awori, Egba, and Ijebu-Remo Communities during the Nineteenth Century." *Journal of the Historical Society of Nigeria* 7, no. 3 (1974): 385–402.
———. "The Ogboni among the Oyo-Yoruba." *Lagos Notes and Records* 3, no. 2 (1972): 50–59.
———. "Yoruba Oral Tradition with Special Reference to the Early History of Oyo." In *Yoruba Oral Tradition: Poetry in Music, Dance and Drama*, edited by Wande Abimbọla, 157–97. Ile-Ife, Nigeria: University of Ife, Department of African Languages and Literatures, 1975.
Agiri, Babatunde, and A. B. Aderibigbe, eds. *The History of the Peoples of Lagos State*. Lagos: Lantern Books, 1987.
Aguilera Patton, Pedro P. *Religion y arte Yorubas*. Havana: Editorial de Ciencias Sociales, 1994.

Aguirre, Sergio. *Eco de caminos*. Havana: Editorial de Ciencias Sociales, 1974.

———. *Nacionalidad y Nación en el Siglo XIX Cubano* [Nationality and Nation in Nineteenth-Century Cuba]. Havana: Editorial de Ciencias Sociales, 1990.

Ajayi, Bade. *Ifa Divination: Its Practice among the Yoruba of Nigeria*. Ilorin, Nigeria: University of Ilorin, 1996.

Ajayi, J. F. A. "The Beginnings of Modern Lagos." *Nigeria Magazine* 69 (1961): 122–27.

———. "The British Occupation of Lagos, 1851–1861: A Critical Review." *Nigeria Magazine* 69 (1961): 96–105.

———. "Samuel Ajayi Crowther of Oyo." In *Africa Remembered: Narratives by West Africans from the Era of the Slave Trade*, edited by Philip Curtin, 289–316. Madison: University of Wisconsin Press, 1967.

Ajayi, J. F. A., and Robert Smith. *Yoruba Warfare in the Nineteenth Century*. Cambridge: Cambridge University Press, 1964.

Ajikobi, Dimeji. "African Folklore: Its Importance in Our Development." Unpublished manuscript provided by author, University of Lagos, Nigeria, 2001.

Akere, Fusco. "Linguistic Assimilation in Socio-historical Dimensions in Urban and Sub-urban Lagos." In *The History of the Peoples of Lagos State*, edited by Ade Adefuye, Babatunde Agiri, and Akinjide Osuntokun, 164–91. Lagos: Lantern Books, 1987.

Akinaso, Niyi. "Yoruba Traditional Names and the Transmission of Cultural Knowledge." *Names: Journal of the American Name Society* 31, no. 3 (1983): 139–58.

Akinjogbin, I. A. "Dahomey and the Yoruba in the Nineteenth Century." In *A Thousand Years of West African History*, edited by J. F. A. Ajayi and I. Espie, 314–31. Ibadan, Nigeria: Ibadan University Press, 1965.

———. "Western Nigeria, Its History, Its People, and Its Culture." In *An Introduction to Western Nigeria: Its People, Culture, and System of Government*, edited by I. A. Akinjogbin, 8–19. Ife-Ile, Nigeria: University of Ife Institute of Administration, 1966.

Akinsemoyin, K., and A. Vaughn Richards. *Building Lagos*. Lagos: F & A Services, 1976.

Allison, Philip A. "Travelling Commissioners of the Ekiti Country." *Nigerian Field* 17 (1952): 100–15.

Amselle, Jean-Loup. *Mestizo Logistics: Anthropology of Identity in Africa and Elsewhere*. Stanford, CA: Stanford University Press, 1998.

Anderson, Benedict. *Imagined Communities: Reflections on the Origins and Spread of Nationalism*. London: Verso, 1983.

Andrews, George Reid. "Black Political Protest in São Paulo, 1888–1988." *Journal of Latin American Studies* 24, no. 1 (1992): 147–71.

Anthias, Floya. *Ethnicity, Class, Gender and Migration: Greek Cypriots in Britain*. Aldershot, UK: Avebury, 1992.

———. "Evaluating 'Diaspora': Beyond Ethnicity?" *Sociology* 32, no. 3 (1998): 557–81.

Appadurai, Arjun. "Grassroots Globalization and the Research Imagination." *Public Culture* 12, no. 1 (2000): 1–20.

———. "Introduction: Commodities and the Politics of Value." In *The Social Life of Things: Commodities in Cultural Perspective*, edited by Arjun Appadurai, 3–63. Cambridge: Cambridge University Press, 1986.

———. *Modernity at Large: Cultural Dimensions of Globalization.* Minneapolis: University of Minnesota Press, 1996.
———. *The Social Life of Things: Commodities in Cultural Perspective.* Cambridge: Cambridge University Press, 1986.
Appadurai, Arjun, and C. Breckenridge. "Why Public Culture?" *Public Culture* 1, no. 1 (1988): 5–9.
Appiah, Anthony Kwame. *In My Father's House.* New York: Oxford University Press, 1992.
Apter, Andrew. *Black Critics and Kings: The Hermeneutics of Power in Yoruba Society.* Chicago: University of Chicago Press, 1992.
———. "Herskovits' Heritage: Rethinking Syncretism in the African Diaspora." *Diaspora* 1, no. 3 (1991): 235–60.
———. "The Historiography of Yoruba Myth and Ritual." *History in Africa* 14 (1987): 1–25.
———. "IBB = 419: Nigerian Democracy and the Politics of Illusion." In *Civil Society and the Political Imagination in Africa: Critical Perspectives,* edited by John and Jean Comoroff, 267–309. Chicago: University of Chicago Press, 1999.
———. "Que Faire? Reconsidering Inventions of Africa." *Critical Inquiry* 19, no. 1 (1992): 87–105.
Arrom, Juan José. *Certidumbre de America: Estudios de Letras, Folklore y Cultura.* Madrid: Editorial Gredos, 1971.
———. "Letras de Cuba antes de 1608." *Revista Cubana* 18 (1944): 67–85.
Asiegbu, Johnson U. J. *Slavery and the Politics of Liberation 1787–1861: A Study of African Emigration and British Anti-Slavery Policy.* New York: Africana Publishing Corporation, 1969.
Asad, Talal. *Genealogies of Religion: Discipline and Reasons of Power in Christianity and Islam.* Baltimore: Johns Hopkins University, 1993.
Austen, Ralph E. "'Africanist' Historiography and Its Critics: Can There be an Autonomous African History?" In *African Historiography: Essays in Honour of Jacob Ade Ajayi,* edited by Toyin Falola, 203–17. Harlow, UK: Longman, 1993.
Awe, Bolanle. "Praise Poems as Historical Data: The Example of the Yoruba Oriki." *Africa* 44 (1974): 331–49.
Awobuluyi, O., ed. *Yoruba Metalanguage I.* Ibadan, Nigeria: Ibadan University Press, 1990.
Awolalu, J. Omosade. "Aiyelala—A Guardian of Social Morality." *Orita* 2, no. 2 (1968): 79–89.
———. "Sacrifice in the Religion of the Yoruba." PhD diss., University of Ibadan, Nigeria, 1970.
———. *Yoruba Beliefs and Sacrificial Rites.* London: Longman, 1979.
Ayandele, Emmanuel A. "The Aladura Movement among the Yoruba." *The Nigerian Christian* 3, no. 7 (1969): 15–16; 3, no. 9 (1969): 14.
———. "The Nigerian Church and Reformed Ogboni Fraternity." *Nigerian Baptist,* June 1966, 19–23.
Ayorinde, Christine. *Afro-Cuban Religiosity, Revolution, and National Identity.* Gainesville: University Press of Florida, 2004.
Ayorinde, J. A., Chief. "*Oriki.*" In *Sources of Yoruba History,* 63–76. Oxford: Clarendon Press, 1973.

Azevedo, Celia. "Images of Africa and the Haitian Revolution in American and Brazilian Abolitionism." In *The African Diaspora: African Origins and New World Identities*, 167–77. Bloomington: Indiana University Press, 1999.
Babalola, Adeboye. *Awon Oriki Orile*. Glasgow, UK: Collins, 1967.
———. *The Content and Form of Yoruba Ijala*. Oxford: Oxford University Press, 1966.
———. "Folk-tales from Yorubaland." *West African Review* 23, no. 292 (1952): 14–15.
———. *Ijala atenudenu*. Ibadan, Nigeria: Ministry of Education, General Publications Section, 1956.
———. "The Portrait of Ogun as Reflected in Ijala Chants." In *Africa's Ogun*, edited by Sandra T. Barnes, 147–72. 2nd ed. Bloomington: Indiana University Press, 1996.
———. "'Rara' Chants in Yoruba Spoken Art." *African Literature Today* 6 (1973): 79–92.
———. "Yoruba Folk-tales." *West African Review* 33, no. 415 (1962): 48–49.
———. "Yoruba Poetry." *Présence Africaine* 19, no. 47 (1963): 184–90.
Back, L. *New Ethnicities and Urban Culture*. London: University College London Press, 1996.
Baker, Pauline H. *Urbanization and Political Change: The Politics of Lagos, 1917–1967*. Berkeley: University of California Press, 1974.
Baldwin, David E., and Charlene M. Baldwin. *The Yoruba of Southwestern Nigeria: An Indexed Bibliography*. Boston: G. K. Hall, 1976.
Ballester, Ana, ed. *Letras: Cultura en Cuba*. Havana: Editorial Pueblo y Educación, 1989.
Bamgbose, Ayo. "The Form of Yoruba Proverbs." *Odu* 4 (1968): 74–86.
———. "The Meaning of Olodumare: An Etymology of the Name of the Yoruba High God." *African Notes* 7, no. 1 (1971): 25–32.
———. "Yoruba Folk-tales." *Ibadan* 27 (1969): 6–12.
———. *Yoruba Metalanguage, II*. Lagos: Nigerian Educational Research Council, 1984.
Bamgboshe Martins, Lola. "Legacy and Brazil." *Legacy Magazine* 1, no. 1 (1997): 15.
———. "Mabinouri Dawodu: The Merchant of Ologbowo." *Legacy Newsletter* 2, no. 3 (2000): 11–12. Published in Lagos by LEGACY Historical and Environmental Interest Group of Nigeria.
Barber, Karin, ed. *Africa's Hidden Histories: Everyday Literacy and Making the Self*. Bloomington: Indiana University Press, 2006.
———. "Discursive Strategies in the Texts of Ifá and in the `Holy Book of Odù' of the African Church of Orunmila." In *Self-Assertion and Brokerage*, edited by Karin Barber and P. F. De Moraes Farias, 196–240. Birmingham University African Studies 2. Birmingham, UK: Centre of West African Studies, 1990.
———. *The Generation of Plays: Yoruba Popular Life in Theater*. Bloomington: Indiana University Press, 2000.
———. "How Man Makes God in West Africa: Yoruba Attitudes towards the *Orisa*." *Africa* 51, no. 3 (1981): 724–45.
———. *I Could Speak until Tomorrow: Oriki, Women, and the Past in a Yoruba Town*. Washington, DC: Smithsonian Institution Press, 1991.
———. "Polyvocality and Individual Talent: Three Women Oriki Singers in Okuku." In *The Yoruba Artist: New Theoretical Perspectives on African Arts*, edited by Rowland Abiodun, Henry J. Drewal, and John Pemberton III, 151–60. Washington, DC: Smithsonian Institution Press, 1994.

---. "Popular Arts in Africa." *African Studies Review* 30 (1988): 1–78.
---. "Quotation and the Constitution of Yoruba Oral Texts." *Research in African Literatures* 30, no. 2 (1999): 1–17.
Barber, Karin, and P. F. De Moraes Farias, eds. *Self-Assertion and Brokerage*. Birmingham University African Studies 2. Birmingham, UK: Centre of West African Studies, 1990.
Barnes, Sandra. "Africa's Ogun Transformed: An Introduction to the Second Edition." In *Africa's Ogun: Old World and New*, edited by Sandra Barnes, xiii–xxi. 2nd ed. Bloomington: Indiana University Press, 1997.
---. "Becoming Lagosian." PhD diss., University of Wisconsin, 1974.
---. "The Many Faces of Ogun." In *Africa's Ogun: Old World and New*, edited by Sandra Barnes, 1–28. 2nd ed. Bloomington: Indiana University Press, 1989.
---. *Ogun: An Old God for a New Age*. Philadelphia: Institute for the Study of Human Issues, 1980.
---. *Patrons and Power: Creating a Political Community in Metropolitan Lagos*. Bloomington: Indiana University Press, 1986.
Barnes, Sandra, and A. B. Agiri. "Lagos before 1603." In *The History of the Peoples of Lagos State*, edited by Ade Adefuye, Babatunde Agiri, and Akinjide Osuntokun, 18–32. Lagos: Lantern Books, 1987.
Barnes, Sandra, and Paula Girshick Ben-Amos. "Ogun the Empire Builder." In *Africa's Ogun: Old World and New*, edited by Sandra Barnes, 39–64. 2nd ed. Bloomington: Indiana University Press, 1989.
Barnet, Miguel. *Apuntes sobre el folklore cubano*. Havana: Editorial de Ciencias Sociales, 1966.
---. *Biografía de un cimarrón* [Biography of a Runaway Slave]. 1964. Reprint, Madrid: Ediciones Alfaguara, 1984.
---. "Cuba: Tres disquisiciones etnológicas." *Ibero Americana* 13, no. 2 (1984): 61–76.
Baron, Robert, and Ana C. Cara. "Introduction: Creolization and Folklore: Cultural Creativity in Process." *Journal of American Folklore* 116, no. 459 (2003): 4–8.
Barret, Leonard. "African Religion in the Americas: The Islands in Between." In *African Religions: A Symposium*, edited by N. Booth, 183–215. New York: NOK Publishers, 1977.
Barth, F. *Ethnic Groups and Boundaries*. London: Allen & Unwin, 1969.
Basch, L,, G. Schiller, and C. Szanton Blanc. *Nations Unbound: Transnational Projects, Postcolonial Predicaments, and Deterritorialized Nation-states*. Basel, Switzerland: Gordon & Breach, 1994.
Bascom, William Russell. *Chango in the New World*. Austin: University of Texas African and Afro-American Research Institute, 1972.
---. "The Focus of Cuban Santería." *Southwestern Journal of Anthropology* 6, no. 1 (1958): 64–68.
---. "Folklore and the Africanist." *Journal of American Folklore* 86, no. 341 (1973): 253–59.
---. "Folklore Research in Africa." *Journal of American Folklore* 77, no. 303 (1964): 12–31.
---. "The Forms of Folklore: Prose Narrative." *Journal of American Folklore* 78, no. 307 (1965): 3–20.
---. "Four Functions of Folklore." *Journal of American Folklore* 67, no. 266 (1954): 333–49.

———. *Frontiers of Folklore*. Washington, DC: American Association for the Advancement of Science, 1977.

———. *Ifa Divination: Communication between Gods and Men in West Africa*. Bloomington: Indiana University Press, 1969.

———. "Oba's Ear: A Yoruba Myth in Cuba and Brazil." In *African Folktales in the New World*, foreword by Alan Dundes, 1–16. Bloomington: Indiana University Press, 1992.

———. "Odu Ifa: The Names of the Signs." *Africa* 36, no. 4 (1966): 408–21.

———. "The Relationship of Yoruba Folklore to Divining." *Journal of American Folklore* 56, no. 220 (1943): 127–131.

———. "The Sanctions of Ifa Divination." *Journal of the Royal Anthropological Institute* 71, nos. 1–2 (1941): 43–54.

———. *Sixteen Cowries: Yoruba Divination from Africa to the New World*. Bloomington: Indiana University Press, 1980.

———. "Some Aspects of Yoruba Urbanism." *American Anthropologist* 64 (1962): 699–709.

———. "Urbanism as a Traditional African Pattern." *Sociological Review* 7, no. 1 (1959): 29–43.

———. "Yoruba Acculturation in Cuba." *Les Afro-Américains*, edited by Pierre Verger. Memoir 27. Dakar: IFAN, 1953: 163–67.

———. "The Yoruba in Cuba." *Nigeria Magazine* 37 (1951): 14–24.

———. *The Yoruba of Southwestern Nigeria*. New York: Holt, Rinehart and Winston, 1959.

Bastian, Misty L. "Vulture Men, Campus Cultists and Teenage Witches: Modern Magics in Nigerian Popular Media." In *Magical Interpretations, Material Realities*, edited by Henrietta Moore and Todd Sanders, 71–96. New York: Routledge, 2002.

Bastide, Roger. *African Civilizations in the New World*. Translated by Peter Green. London: C. Hurst and Company, 1971.

———. *Sociologia do folclore brasileiro*. São Paulo, Brazil: Universidade Anhembi Morumbi, 1959.

Bauman, R., and C. L. Briggs. "Poetics and Performances: Critical Perspectives on Language and Social Life." *Annual Review of Anthropology* 19 (1990): 59–88.

Baumann, M. "Conceptualising Diaspora: The Preservation of Religious Identity in Foreign Parts, Exemplified by Hindu Communities outside India." *Temenos* 31 (1995): 19–35.

Bausinger, Hermann. *Folk Culture in a World of Technology*. Bloomington: Indiana University Press, 1986.

Bay, Edna G. "Protection, Political Exile, and the Atlantic Slave-Trade: History and Collective Memory in Dahomey." In *Rethinking the African Diaspora: The Making of a Black Atlantic World in the Bight of Benin and Brazil*, edited by Kristin Mann and Edna G. Bay, 42–60. Portland, OR: Frank Cass, 2001.

Beckles, Hilary. "Caribbean Anti-Slavery: The Self-Liberation Ethos of Enslaved Blacks." *Journal of Caribbean History* 22, nos. 1–2 (1988): 1–19.

Behar, Ruth, "After the Bridges." In *The Portable Island: Cubans at Home in the World*, edited by Ruth Behar and Lucia M. Suárez, 3–8. New York: Palgrave Macmillan, 2008.

———. "Going to Cuba: Writing Ethnography of Diaspora, Return, and Despair." In *The Vulnerable Observer*, 136–160. Boston: Beacon Press, 1996.
———, ed. *An Island Called Home: Returning to Jewish Cuba*. London: Rutgers University Press, 2007.
Behar, Ruth, and Lucia M. Suárez, eds. *The Portable Island: Cubans at Home in the World*. New York: Palgrave MacMillan, 2008.
Beier, H. Ulli. "Before Oduduwa." *Odu* 3 (1956): 25–32.
———. "The Egungun Cult among the Yoruba." *Présence Africaine* 17–18 (1958): 33–36.
———. "The Historical and Psychological Significance of Yoruba Myths." *Odu* 1 (1955): 17–25.
———. "Obatala: Five Myths about the Yoruba Creator God." *Black Orpheus* 7 (1960): 34–35.
———. "Olokun Festival." *Nigeria Magazine* 49 (1956): 168–83.
———. "Oshun Festival." *Nigeria Magazine* 53 (1957): 170–87.
———. *The Return of the Gods: The Art of Susan Wenger*. Cambridge: Cambridge University Press, 1975.
———. "Spirit Children among the Yoruba." *African Affairs* 53, no. 213 (1954): 328–31.
———. *A Year of Sacred Festivals in One Yoruba Town*. Lagos: Nigerian Printing and Publishing, 1959.
———. *Yoruba Myths*. Cambridge: Cambridge University Press, 1980.
Ben-Amos, Dan. "'Context' in Context." *Western Folklore* 52 (1993): 209–26.
———. "Folklore in African Society." *Research in African Literatures* 6 (1971): 165–98.
———. "The Seven Strands of Tradition: Varieties in Its Meaning in American Folklore Studies." *Journal of Folklore Research* 21 (1984): 97–131.
———. *Sweet Words: Storytelling Events in Benin*. Philadelphia: Institute for the Study of Human Issues, 1975.
———. "Toward a Definition of Folklore in Context." *Journal of American Folklore* 84, no. 331 (1971): 3–15.
———. "Tradition and Identity: The Seven Strands of Tradition; Varieties in Its Meaning in America Folklore Studies." *Journal of Folklore Research* 21, no. 2/3 (1984): 97–131.
Benavides, Gustavo. "Syncretism and Legitimacy in Latin American Religion." In *Enigmatic Powers: African and Indigenous Peoples' Religions among Latinos*, edited by Gustavo Benavides, 19–46. New York: Bildner Center for Western Hemisphere Studies, 1995.
Bendix, Regina. *In Search of Authenticity: The Formation of Folklore Studies*. Madison: University of Wisconsin Press, 1997.
Beniste, José. *Orun Aiye: O encontro de dois mundos*. Rio de Janeiro, Brazil: Bertrand Brasil, 1997.
Benítez Rojo, Antonio. "La cultura criolla en Cuba." *Taller de Letras* 22 (1994): 69–76.
———. *La Isla Que Se Repite: El Caribe y La Perspectiva Posmoderna* [The Repeating Island: The Caribbean and the Postmodern Perspective]. 1989. Reprint, Hanover, NH: Ediciones del Norte, 1992.

———. "The Role of Music in the Emergence of Afro-Cuban Culture." In *The African Diaspora: African Origins and New World Identities*, edited by Isadore Okpewho, Carole Boyce Davies, and Ali A. Mazrui, 197–203. Bloomington: Indiana University Press, 1999.
Berlin, Ira, and Philip D. Morgan. "Introduction." In *The Slaves' Economy: Independent Production by Slaves in the Americas*, edited by Ira Berlin and Philip D. Morgan. London: Frank Cass, 1995.
Beyioku, Akin F. *Ifa: Basic Principles of Ifa Science*. Lagos: Tika-Tore Press, 1940.
———. *Ifa, Its Worship, and Prayers*. Lagos: Salako Press, 1971.
Bhabha, Homi. *The Location of Culture*. New York: Routledge, 1994.
———, ed. *Nation and Narration*. New York: Routledge, 1990.
Biobaku, S. O. *The Egba and Their Neighbors, 1842–1872*. Oxford: Oxford University Press, 1957.
———. "Myths and Oral History." *Odu* 1 (1955): 12–17.
———, ed. *Sources of Yoruba History*. Oxford: Clarendon Press, 1973.
Biobaku, S. O., and Ulli Beier. "The Use and Interpretation of Myths." *Odu* 1 (1955): 12–25.
Birman, Patricia. *O que e Umbanda*. São Paulo, Brazil: Editora Brasilense, 1983.
Blassingame, John. *The Slave Community and Plantation Life in the Antebellum South*. Rev. ed. New York: Oxford, 1979.
Blier, Suzanne Preston. "African Art at the Crossroads: An American Perspective." In *African Art Studies: The State of the Discipline*, 91–107. Washington, DC: National Museum of African Art, Smithsonian Institution, 1990.
———. *African Vodun: Art, Psychology, and Power*. Chicago: University of Chicago Press, 1995.
———. "Art Systems and Semiotics: The Question of Art, Craft, and Colonial Taxonomies in Africa." *American Journal of Semiotics* 6, no. 1 (1988): 7–18.
———. "Melville J. Herskovits and the Arts of Ancient Dahomey." *Res: Anthropology and Aesthetics* 16 (1988): 125–42.
———. "Shadow Plays: Reading between the Lines in Postmodernist Criticism." *African Arts* 25, no. 3 (1992): 26, 29–30.
Bolívar, Natalia. *Los Orishas en Cuba*. Havana: Ediciones Unión, 1990.
———. *Ifá: Su historia en Cuba*. Havana: Ediciones Unión, 1996.
Bolívar, Natalia, and Mario López Cepero. *Sincretismo Religioso? Santa Barbara Chango*. Havana: Pablo de la Toriente Editorial, 1995.
Borchmeyer, Florian, and Matthias Hentschler. *Havana: The New Art of Making Ruins*. Berlin: Raros Media, 2007; 85 min., Spanish, German, and English.
Bordinat, Philip, and Peter Thomas. *Revealer of Secrets*. African Reader's Library 24. Lagos: African Universities Press, 1973.
Borrego Pla, María del Carmen. *Palenques de negros en Cartagena de Indias a fines del siglo XVII*. Seville, Spain: Publicaciones de la Escuela de Estudios Hispano-Americano de Sevilla, 1973.
———. "Papers Bearing on the Negros of Cuba of the Seventeenth Century." *Journal of Negro History* 12 (1927): 55–95.
Botkin, B. A. *A Treasury of American Folklore*. 1944. Reprint, New York: Crown, 1966.
Bottomly, Gillian. "Culture, Ethnicity, and the Politics/Poetics of Representation." *Diaspora* 1 (1991): 303–20.

Bradbury, R. E. "The Kingdom of Benin." In *West African Kingdoms in the Nineteenth Century*, edited by Daryll Forde and Phyllis Mary Kaberry, 1–35. London: Oxford University Press, 1967.

Brah, Avatar. *Cartographies of Diaspora: Contesting Identities*. New York: Routledge, 1996.

Brandon, George. *Santería from Africa to the New World: The Dead Sell Memories*. Indianapolis: Indiana University Press, 1993.

Breckenridge, C., Homi K. Bhabha, Sheldon Pollock, and Dipesh Chakrabarty, eds. *Cosmopolitanism*. Durham, NC: Duke University Press, 2002.

Briggs, Charles. "Metadiscursive Practices and Scholarly Authority in Folkloristics." *Journal of American Folklore* 106, no. 422 (1993): 387–434.

Brock, Lisa, and Bijan Bayne. "Not Just Black: African-Americans, Cubans, and Baseball." In *Between Race and Empire: African-Americans and Cubans before the Cuban Revolution*, edited by Lisa Brock and Digna Castañeda Fuertes, 168–204. Philadelphia: Temple University Press, 1998.

Brock, Lisa, and Digna Castañeda Fuertes, eds. *Between Race and Empire: African-Americans and Cubans before the Cuban Revolution*. Philadelphia: Temple University Press, 1998.

Brown, Christopher Leslie. *Moral Capital: Foundations of British Abolitionism*. Chapel Hill: University of North Carolina Press, 2006.

Brown, David Hilary. "The Garden in the Machine: Afro-Cuban Sacred Art and Performance in Urban New Jersey and New York." PhD diss., Yale University. Ann Arbor, MI: University Microfilms, 1989.

———. *Santería Enthroned: Art Ritual and Innovation in an Afro-Cuban Religion*. Chicago: University of Chicago Press, 2003.

———. "Toward an Ethnoaesthetics of Santería Ritual Arts: The Practice of Altar Making and Gift Exchange." In *Santería Aesthetics*, edited by Arturo Lindsay, 77–130. Washington, DC: Smithsonian Institution Press, 1996.

Browning, Barbara. *Infectious Rhythm: Metaphors of Contagion and the Spread of African Culture*. New York: Routledge, 1998.

Buckley, Anthony D. *Yoruba Medicine*. Oxford: Clarendon Press, 1985.

Buck-Morss, Susan. *Hegel, Haiti, and Universal History*. Pittsburgh: University of Pittsburgh Press, 2009.

Bueno, Salvador. "La Primitiva Narrative Antiesclavista en Cuba (1835–1839)." In *Letras: Cultura en Cuba*, edited by Ana Cairo Ballesyer, 487–505. 1980. Reprint, Havana: Editorial Pueblo y Educación, 1989.

———. *Temas y Personajes de la Literatura Cubana*. Havana: Ediciones Sociales, 1964.

Burke, Timothy. *Lifebuoy Men, Lux Women: Commodification, Consumption, and Cleanliness in Modern Zimbabwe*. Durham, NC: Duke University Press, 1996.

Burnett, Paula. "'Where Else to Row but Backward?' Addressing Caribbean Futures through Re-visions of the Past." *Ariel* 30, no. 1 (1999): 11–38.

Cabeza de Vaca, Alvar Núñez. *The Narrative of Cabeza de Vaca*. Translated by Rolena Adorno and Patrick Charles Pautz. Lincoln: University of Nebraska Press, 2003.

Cabral, Amilcar. "The Weapon of Theory." In *Revolution in Guinea: An African People's Struggle*. New York: Monthly Review Press, 1969.

Cabrera, Lydia. *Anagó: Vocabulario Lucumí el Yoruba que se habla en Cuba*. Miami: Ediciónes Universal, 1986.

———. *Los Animales en el folklore y la magia de Cuba*. Miami: Colección de Chicherukú en el exilio, Ediciones Universal, 1988.
———. *Cuentos Negros de Cuba*. Preface by Fernando Ortiz. Miami: Colección del Chicherukú en el Exilio, Ediciones Universal, 1972.
———. *Koeko Iyawó: Pequeño Trato de Regla Lucumí*. Miami: Colección del Chicherukú en el Exilio, Ediciones Universal, 1980.
———. *La Medicina Popular de Cuba*. Miami: Colección de Chicherukú en el Exilio, Ediciones Universal, 1984.
———. *El Monte Igbo Finda Ewe Orisha: Vititi Nfinde*. Miami: Colección de Chicherukú en el Exilio, Ediciones Universal, 1968.
———. *Por Qué . . . Cuentos negros de Cuba*. Miami: Colección de Chicherukú en el Exilio, Ediciones Universal, 1972.
———. *Refranes de negros viejos*. Havana: Ediciones C. R., 1955.
———. *Reglas de Congo: Palo Monte, Mayombe*. Miami: Ediciones Universal, 1986.
———. "Religious Syncretism in Cuba." *Journal of Caribbean Studies* 10, nos. 1–2 (1995): 84–94.
———. *Yemayá y Ochún: Kariocha, Iyaloichas, y Olorichas*. Miami: Colección de Chicherukú en el Exilio, Ediciones Universal, 1980.
Cabrera Infante, Guillermo. *Ella cantaba boleros*. New York: Vintage Español, Random House, 1996.
———. *Tres Tristes Tigres*. 1967. Reprint, Barcelona: Biblioteca del Bolsillo, 1995.
Calcagno, Francisco. *Diccionario biografico cubano*. New York: Imprenta de N. Ponce de León, 1878.
———. *Poetas de color*. Havana: Imprenta Mercantil de los Herederos de SS Spencer, 1887.
Camnitzer, Luis. "The Eclecticism of Survival: Today's Cuban Art." In *The Nearest Edge of the World, Art, and Cuba Now*, edited by Rachel Weiss, 18–23. Brookline, MA: Polarities, 1990.
Campbell, Robert. "Arrival at Lagos." In *Always Elsewhere: Travels of the Black Atlantic*, edited by Alastair Pettinger, 205–8. 1860. Reprint, New York: Cassell, 1998.
———. *A Few Facts Relating to Lagos, Abeokuta, and Other Sections of Central Africa*. Philadelphia: King & Baird, 1860.
———. *A Pilgrimage to My Motherland: An Account of a Journey among the Egbas and Yorubas of Central Africa in 1859–60*. New York: Thomas Hamilton, 1861.
Canizares, Raul José. "Santería: From Afro-Cuban Cult to World Religion." *Caribbean Quarterly* 40, no. 1 (1994): 59–63.
Cantwell, Robert. *Ethnomimesis: Folklore and the Representation of Culture*. Chapel Hill: University of North Carolina, 1993.
Caponi, Gena Dagel, ed. *Signifyin(g), Sanctifyin' and Slam Dunking: A Reader in African American Expressive Culture*. Amherst: University of Massachusetts Press, 1999.
Carneiro, A. J. Souza. *Os mitos africanos no Brasil*. São Paulo, Brazil: Companhia Editora Nacional, 1937.
Carneiro, Edison. *Candombles da Bahia*. Bahia, Brazil: Publicações do Estado 8, 1948.
Carpentier, Alejo. *El reino de este mundo*. 1967. Reprint, Barcelona: Biblioteca de Bolsillo, 1996.
Carreta Masquerades of Lagos. Archives of the Department of African Languages and Literature. Lagos: University of Lagos, 1986.

Casanovas, Joān. *Bread or Bullets! Urban Labor and Spanish Colonialism in Cuba, 1850–1898*. Pittsburgh: University of Pittsburgh Press, 1998.
Casas, Padre Juan. *La Guerra Separatista de Cuba*. Madrid: Imp. San Francisco de Sales, 1896.
Cassanelli, Lee V. *The Shaping of Somali Society: Reconstructing the History of a Pastoral People, 1600–1900*. Philadelphia: University of Pennsylvania Press, 1982.
Castellanos, Isabel. "From Ulukumí to Lucumí: A Historical Overview of Religious Acculturation in Cuba." In *Santería Aesthetics in Contemporary Latin American Art*, 39–50. Washington, DC: Smithsonian Institution Press, 1996.
———. "A River of Many Turns: The Polysemy of Ochún in Afro-Cuban Tradition." In *Osun across the Waters*, edited by Mei Mei Sanford and Joséph Murphy, 34–45. Bloomington: Indiana University Press, 2001.
———. "The Use of Language in Afro-Cuban Religion." PhD diss., Georgetown University. Ann Arbor, MI: University Microfilms, 1978.
Castellanos, Jorge, and Isabel Castellanos. *Cultura Afrocubana: El Negro en Cuba 1492–1844*. Vol. 1. Miami: Ediciones Universal, 1988.
Cedrón, Jorge. "Que el pueblo se narre a si mismo." *Cine Cubano*, nos. 86–88 (ca. 1972): 62–68.
Cepeda, Rafael, ed. *La múltiple voz de Manuel Sanguily*. Havana: Palabra de Cuba, Editorial de Ciencias Sociales, 1988.
Chambers, Douglas B. "The Black Atlantic: Theory, Method, and Practice." In *The Atlantic World, 1450–2000*, edited by Toyin Falola and Kevin D. Roberts, 151–73. Bloomington: Indiana University Press, 2008.
Chanan, Michael. *The Cuban Image*. Bloomington: Indiana University Press, 1985.
Chatelan, Henry. *Folk Tales of Angola*. New York, 1894.
Childs, Matthew D. "'The Defects of Being a Black Creole': The Degrees of African Identity in the Cuban *Cabildos de Nación*, 1790–1820." In *Slaves, Subjects, and Subversives: Blacks in Colonial Latin America*, edited by Jane Landers and Barry Robinson, 209–45. Albuquerque: University of New Mexico Press, 2006.
———. *The 1812 Aponte Rebellion in Cuba and the Struggle against Atlantic Slavery*. Chapel Hill: University of North Carolina Press, 2006.
Clarke, Kamari Maxine. "Yoruba Aesthetics and Trans-Atlantic Imaginaries." In *Beautiful/Ugly: African and Diaspora Aesthetics*, edited by Sarah Nuttall, 290–315. Durham, NC: Duke University Press, 2006.
Clarke, Kenneth W. "A Motif Index of the Folklore of Culture Area V West Africa." PhD diss., Indiana University, 1958.
Clifford, James. "Introduction: Partial Truths." In *Writing Culture: The Poetics and Politics of Ethnography*, 1–26. Berkley: University of California Press, 1986.
———. "Diasporas." *Cultural Anthropology* 9 (1994): 302–38.
Clifford, James, and George Marcus, eds. *Writing Culture: The Poetics and Politics of Ethnography*. Berkeley: University of California Press, 1986.
Cohen, Abner. *The Politics of Elite Culture: Explorations in the Dramaturgy of Power in a Modern African Society*. Berkeley: University of California Press, 1981.
Cohen, Robin. "Diasporas, the Nation-State, and Globalization." In *Global History and Migration*, edited by Wang Gungwu, 117–43. Boulder, CO: Westview Press, 1997.
———. *Global Diaspora: An Introduction*. London: UCL Press, 1997.

Cohen, Robin, and Steven Vertovec. "Introduction: Conceiving Cosmopolitanism." In *Conceiving Cosmopolitanism: Theory, Context, and Practice*, edited by R. Cohen and S. Vertovec, 1–25. New York: Oxford University Press, 2002.

Cole, Gibril, and Maz Dixon-Fyle, eds. *New Perspectives on Sierra Leone Krio.* New York: Peter Lang, 2005.

Cole, Patrick Dele. "Lagos Society in the Nineteenth-Century." In *Lagos: The Development of An African City*, edited by A. B. Aderibigbe, foreword by J. F. Ade Ajayi, 27–57. London: Longman, 1975.

———. *Modern and Traditional Elites in the Politics of Lagos.* London: Cambridge University Press, 1975.

Comaroff, J., and J. L. Comaroff, eds. *Civil Society and the Political Imagination in Africa: Critical Perspectives.* Chicago: University of Chicago Press, 1999.

———. "The Madman and the Migrant." In *Ethnography and Historical Imagination*, edited by John and Jean Camaroff, 155–80. Boulder, CO: Westview Press, 1992.

Comhaire, Jean. "A Propos des Brésiliens de Lagos." *Grands Lacs* (March 1949): 41–43.

———. "La Vie Religieuse à Lagos." *Zaire*, March 1949, 549–56.

Consentino, Donald J. "Repossession: Ogun in Folklore and Literature." In *Africa's Ogun*, edited by Sandra Barnes. 2nd ed. Bloomington: Indiana University Press, 1997.

Coupland, Sir Reginald. *The British Anti-Slavery Movement.* 1933. Reprint, London: Frank Cass, 1964.

Courlander, Harold. *A Treasury of Afro-American Folklore.* New York: Crown, 1976.

Coven, David. "Narrative, Free Spaces, and Communities of Memory in the Brazilian Black Consciousness Movement." *Western Journal of Black Studies* 21, no. 4 (1997): 272–80.

Cros Sandoval, Mercedes. "Afro-Cuban Religion in Perspective." In *Enigmatic Powers: Syncretism with African and Indigenous Peoples' Religions among Latinos*, edited by Antonio M. Stevens Arroyo, Andreãs Isidoro Peãrez y Mena,81–98. New York: Bildner Center for Western Hemisphere Studies, 1995.

———. *La Religion Afrocubana.* Madrid: Player, 1975.

———. *Worldview, the Orichas, and Santería: Africa to Cuba and Beyond.* Gainesville: University Press of Florida, 2007.

Crowley, Daniel J. *African Folklore in the New World.* Austin: University of Texas Press, 1977.

———. "Negro Folklore: An Africanist's View." *Texas Quarterly* 5 (1962): 65–71.

Curtin, Philip. *Africa Remembered: Narratives by West Africans from the Era of the Slave Trade.* Madison: University of Wisconsin Press, 1967.

———. *Cross-Cultural Trade in World History.* Cambridge: Cambridge University Press, 1984.

———. *The Rise and Fall of the Plantation Complex: Essays in Atlantic History.* Cambridge: Cambridge University Press, 1990.

———. *Why People Move: Migration in African History.* The Sixteenth Charles Edmondson Historical Lectures. Waco, TX: Baylor University, 1995.

Da Costa E. Silva, Alberto. "Buying and Selling Korans in Nineteenth-Century Rio de Janeiro." In *Rethinking the African Diaspora*, edited by Kristin Mann and Edna Bay, 83–90. London: Frank Cass, 2001.

Dana, Richard Henry. *Two Years before the Mast: A Personal Narrative of Life at Sea.* London: Folio Society, 1986.
Davidson, A. M.. "The Origin and Early History of Lagos." *Nigerian Field* 19, no. 2 (1954): 52–69, 139–188.
Davis, Mike. *Magical Urbanism: Latinos Reinvent the U.S. Big City.* New York: Verso, 2000.
Dayan, Joan. "Haiti, History, and the Gods." In *After Colonialism*, edited by Gyan Prakash, 66–97. Princeton, NJ: Princeton University Press, 1995.
———. "Paul Gilroy's Slaves, Ships and Routes: The Middle Passage as Metaphor." *Research in African Literatures* 27, no. 4 (1996): 7–14.
De Bustamente Montoro, A. S. "La Polemica filosofica de 1838–1840 en Cuba." In *Letras: Cultura en Cuba*, ed. A. C. Ballester, 313–25. Havana: Editorial Pueblo y Educación, 1989.
De la Campa, Román. *Cuba on My Mind.* New York: Verso, 2000.
De la Cruz, Manuel. *Obras de Manuel de la Cruz.* Madrid: Editorial Saturnino Calleja, 1926.
De la Fuente, Alejandro. *Havana and the Atlantic in the Sixteenth Century.* Chapel Hill: University of North Carolina Press, 2008.
———. "Race, National Discourse and Politics in Cuba." *Latin American Perspectives* 25, no. 3 (1998): 43–60.
De la Fuente, Jorge. *Arte, Ideología, y Cultura.* Havana: Editorial Letras Cubanas, 1992.
Degler, Carl N. *Neither Black nor White: Slavery and Race Relations in Brazil and the United States.* Madison: University of Wisconsin Press, 1972.
Del Monte y Anselmo, Domingo. *Escritos de Domingo del Monte.* Edited by José Fernandez de Castro. Havana: Cultural, S. A., 1926.
———. "Moral religiosa." *El Plantel* 1, no. 3 (1838): 82–86.
Deniga, Adeoye. *The Nigerian Who's Who for 1920.* Lagos: Tika-Tore Press, 1919.
———. *Notes on Lagos Streets.* Lagos: Jehova-Shalom Printing Press, 1921.
Dennett, R. "How the Yoruba Count: And the Universal Order in Creation, etc." *Journal of the African Society* 16, no. 63 (1917): 242–50.
———. *Nigerian Studies, or the Religious and Political Systems of the Yoruba.* London: Macmillan Brothers, 1910.
———. "The Ogboni and Other Secret Societies in Nigeria." *Journal of the African Society* 16, no. 61 (1916): 16–29.
———. "West African Categories and the Yoruba Language." *Journal of the African Society* 14, no. 53 (1914): 75–80; 16, no. 63 (1917): 242–50; 17, no. 65 (1917): 60–71.
Deren, Maya. *Divine Horsemen: Voodoo Gods of Haiti.* New York: Dell, 1970.
Deschamps Chapeaux, Pedro. "Autenticidad de algunos negros y mulatos de Cecilia Valdes." *La Gaceta de Cuba* 81 (February–March 1970).
———. *Los Cimarrones Urbanos.* Havana: Editorial de Ciencias Sociales, 1983.
———. *El negro en la economia Habanera del siglo XIX.* Havana: Ediciones Union, 1971.
Díaz, María Elena. *The Virgin, the King, and the Royal Slaves of El Cobre: Negotiating Freedom in Colonial Cuba, 1670–1780.* Stanford, CA: Stanford University Press, 2002.
Díaz del Castillo, Bernal. *The Conquest of New Spain.* Translated by John M. Cohen. New York: Penguin Classics, 1963.

Díaz Fabelo, Teodoro. *Cincuenta y un Patakies Afroamericanos.* Caracas, Venezuela: Monte Avila Editores, 1983.

———. *Lengua de Santeros, Guiné Gongorí.* Havana: Las Ideas, 1956.

Do Nascimiento, Abdias. "The African Experience in Brazil." In *African Presence in the Americas,* 97–118. Trenton, NJ: Africa World Press, 1995.

Doortmont, Michel. "The Invention of the Yorubas: Regional and Pan-African Nationalism versus Ethnic Provincialism." In *Self-Assertion and Brokerage,* edited by P. F. de Moraes Farias and Karin Barber, 101–9. Birmingham, UK: University of Birmingham, Centre of West African Studies, 1990.

———. "The Roots of Yoruba Historiography: Classicism, Traditionalism, and Pragmatism." In *African Historiography: Essays in Honour of Jacob Ade Ajayi,* edited by Toyin Falola, 52–63. Harlow, UK: Longman, 1993.

Dornbach, María. *Orishas en Soperas: Los cultos de origen Yoruba en Cuba.* Hungria: Centro de Estudios Historical de America Latina, 1993.

Dorson, Richard. "African and Afro-American Folklore: A Reply to Bascom and Other Misguided Critics." *Journal of American Folklore* 88, no. 348 (1975): 151–64.

———. "The African Connection: Comments on 'African Folklore in the New World.'" *Research in African Literatures* 8 (1977): 260–65.

———. *American Negro Folktales.* Greenwich, CT: Fawcett, 1967.

———. "A Theory for American Folklore Reviewed." *Journal of American Folklore* 82, no. 325 (1969): 226–44.

Dosumu, Abiola Elegbede-Fernandez. *Lagos: A Legacy of Honor.* Ibadan, Nigeria: Spectrum Books, 1992.

Dosumu, Gbadebo Adeoye. *The Origin of Mankind: The Yorubas, Binis, Dahomians, etc.* Ibadan: Church of Africa, 1951.

Douglass, Frederick. *Narrative of the Life of Frederick Douglass, an American Slave.* Boston: Anti-Slavery Office, 1845.

Drake, St. Clair. "Diaspora Studies and Pan-Africanism." In *Global Dimensions of the African Diaspora,* edited by Jospeh E. Harris, 451–514. Washington, DC: Howard University Press, 1992.

Drewal, Henry John. "Art and Divination among the Yoruba: Design and Myth." *Africana Journal* 14, nos. 2–3 (1983): 136–56.

———. "Beauty and Being: Aesthetics and Ontology in Yoruba Body Art." In *Marks of Civilization: Artistic Transformations of the Human Body,* edited by Arnold Rubin, 83–96. Los Angeles: Museum of Cultural History, University of California, Los Angeles, 1988.

———. "Meaning in Osogbo Art among the Ijebu Yoruba." In *Man Does Not Go Naked: Textilien und Handwerk aus Afrikanischen und Anderen Landern,* edited by B. Engelbrecht and B. Gardi, 151–74. Basel, Switzerland: Basler Beitrage zur Ethnologie, 1989.

———. "Yoruba Body Artists and Their Deity Ogun." In *The Yoruba Artist: New Theoretical Perspectives on African Arts,* edited by Rowland Abiodun, Henry J. Drewal, and John Pemberton III, 237–57. Washington, DC: Smithsonian Institution Press, 1994.

Drewal, Henry John, and Margaret Thompson Drewal. "Composing Time and Space in Yoruba Art." *Word and Image* 3, no. 3 (1987): 225–50.

———. *Gelede: Art and Female Power among the Yoruba.* Bloomington: Indiana University Press, 1983.

———. "An Ifa Diviner's Shrine in Ijebuland." *African Arts* 16, no. 2 (1983): 60–67, 99–100.

Drewal, Margaret Thompson. "Dancing for Ogun in Yorubaland and in Brazil." In *Africa's Ogun,* edited by Sandra Barnes, 199–234. 2nd ed. Bloomington: Indiana University Press, 1996.

———. "Embodied Practice/Embodied History: Mastery of Metaphor in the Performances of Diviner Kolawole Ositola." In *The Yoruba Artist: New Theoretical Perspectives on African Arts,* edited by Rowland Abiodun, Henry J. Drewal, and John Pemberton III, 171–190. Washington, DC: Smithsonian Institution Press, 1994.

———. *Yoruba Ritual: Performers, Play, Agency.* Bloomington: Indiana University Press, 1992.

Droogers, Andre. *Black Reconstruction: An Essay toward a History of the Part Which Black People Played in America,* 1860–1880. New York: Russel and Russel, 1935.

Du Bois, W. E. B. *The Souls of Black Folk.* 1903. Reprint, Millwood, NJ: Kaus-Thompson, 1973.

Duncan, John. *Travels to Western Africa.* London: Richard Bentez, 1846.

Dundes, Alan. "African Tales among the North American Indians." *Southern Folklore Quarterly* 29 (1965): 207–19.

———. "Folk Ideas as Units of Worldview." *Journal of American Folklore* 84, no 331 (1971): 93–103.

Echeruo, Michael J. "An African Diaspora: The Ontological Project." In *The African Diaspora: African Origins and New World Identities,* edited by Isidore Okpewho, 3–18. Bloomington: Indiana University Press, 1999.

———. *Victorian Lagos: Aspects of Nineteenth Century Lagos Life.* London: MacMillan Education, 1977.

Edwards, Brent Hayes. *The Practice of Diaspora: Literature, Translation, and the Rise of Black Internationalism.* Cambridge: Harvard University Press, 2003.

Edwards, Gary, and John Mason. *Black Gods: Orisa Studies in the New World.* New York: Yoruba Theological Ministry, 1985.

Ellis, George R. "Black Gods and Kings: Yoruba Art at U.C.L.A." *African Arts* 4, no. 3 (1971): 16–21.

———. "West African Folk-lore." *Popular Science Monthly* 45 (1894): 771–83.

———. *The Yoruba-Speaking Peoples of the Slave Coast of West Africa.* London: Chapman and Hall, 1894.

Entralgo, Elias José. *La liberacion etnica Cubana.* Havana: Universidad de La Habana, 1953.

Epega, Afolabi A., and Philip John Neimark. *The Sacred Ifa Oracle.* San Francisco: Harper San Francisco, 1995.

Euba, Titi. "Dress and Status in Nineteenth-Century Lagos." In *The History of the Peoples of Lagos State,* edited by Ade Adefuye, Babatunde Agiri, and Akinjide Osuntokun, 142–65. Lagos: Lantern Books, 1987.

Ewart, J. H. "Lagos: Its Hinterland, Its Products, and Its People." *Journal of the Royal Society of Arts* 50 (1903): 650–59.

Fabian, Johannes. *Moments of Freedom: Anthropology and Popular Culture.* Charlottesville: University Press of Virginia, 1998.

———. *Remembering the Present: Painting and Popular History in Zaire.* Berkeley: University of California Press, 1996.

———. *Time and the Other: How Anthropology Makes Its Object.* New York: Columbia University Press, 1983.

Fabiyi, R. F., and H. Sawyer. "The Sense of 'Concreteness' in Yoruba Worship." *Sierra Leone Bulletin of Religion* 7, no. 1 (1965): 13–22.

Faduma, Orishatukeh. "Religious Beliefs of the Yoruba People in West Africa." In *Africa and the American Negro: Addresses and Proceedings of the Congress on Africa, held under the Auspices of the Stewart Missionary Foundation for Africa of Gamon Theological Seminary, in Connection with the Cotton States and International Exposition, December 13–15, 1895,* 31–36. Atlanta: Gammon Theological Seminary, 1895.

Falola, Toyin, ed. *African Historiography: Essays in Honour of Jacob Ade Ajayi,* edited by Toyin Falola. Harlow, UK: Longman, 1993.

———, ed. *Pioneer, Patriot, and Patriarch: Samuel Johnson and the Yoruba People.* Madison: University of Wisconsin, African Studies Program, 1993.

Falola, Toyin, and Kevin D. Roberts, eds. *The Atlantic World, 1450–2000.* Bloomington: Indiana University Press, 2008.

Fagan, Brian. "Brazil's Little Angola (Palmares, Settlements of Escaped Slaves)." *Archeology* 46, no. 4 (1993): 14–20.

Fagg, William Butler. "Ife and Benin: Two Pinnacles of African Art." *UNESCO Courier* 12, no. 10 (1959): 15–19.

Fatunmbi Awo F. *Ògún: Ifá and the Spirit of Iron.* Plainview, NY: Original Publications, 1992.

Featherstone, M., ed. *Global Culture: Nationalism, Globalization, and Identity.* London: Sage, 1990.

Featherstone, M., S. Lash, and R. Robertson, eds. *Global Modernities.* London: Sage, 1995.

Feierman, Steven. "Colonizers, Scholars, and the Creation of Invisible Histories." In *Beyond the Cultural Turn,* edited by Lynn Hunt and V. E. Bonnell, 182–215. Berkeley: University of California Press, 1999.

Feld, S. "Notes on World Beat." *Public Culture* 1, no. 1 (1988): 31–37.

Ferguson, John. *The Yoruba of Nigeria.* Bletchley, UK: Open University Press, 1970.

Fernandez, James. *Persuasions and Performances: The Play of Tropes in Culture.* Bloomington: Indiana University Press, 1986.

Fernandez de Castro, José Antonio. *Temas negros en las letras de Cuba.* Havana: Editorial Letras Cubanas, 1936.

Ferrer, Ada. *Insurgent Cuba: Race, Nation, and Revolution, 1868–1898.* Chapel Hill: University of North Carolina Press, 1999.

Finnegan, Ruth H. *The Oral and Beyond: Doing Things with Words in Africa.* Chicago: University of Chicago Press, 2007.

———. *Oral Literature in Africa.* 1970. Reprint, Nairobi, Kenya: Oxford University Press, 1976.

Flores, Juan. *From Bomba to Hip Hop: Puerto Rican Culture and Latino Identity.* New York: Columbia University Press, 2000.

Flores-Peña, Ysamur. "Osayin, the One Legged Man Worth Two." *ASHE Newsletter* 1, no. 2 (1996): 3–5.
Flores-Peña, Ysamur, and Roberta J. Evanchuck. *Santería Garments and Altars: Speaking without a Voice.* Jackson: University Press of Mississippi, 1994.
Folami, Takiu. *A History of Lagos, Nigeria: The Shaping of an African City.* Smithtown, NY: Exposition Press, 1982.
Folayan, Kola. "Yoruba Oral History: Some Problems and Suggestions." In *Yoruba Oral Tradition,* edited by Wande Abimbola, 91–114. Ife African Languages and Literatures 1. Ile-Ife, Nigeria: University of Ife, 1975.
Foner, Nancy. "West Indian Identity in the Diaspora: Comparative and Historical Perspectives." *Latin American Perspectives* 25, no. 3 (1998): 173–89.
———. "What's New about Transnationalism? New York Immigrants Today and at the Turn of the Century." *Diaspora* 6, no. 3 (1997): 355–76.
Fornet, Ambrosio. *Antologia del cuento Cubano contemporaneo.* Mexico City: Ediciones Era, 1967.
Fox, Robert Elliot. "Diasporicentrism and Black Aural Texts." In *The African Diaspora: African Origins and New World Identities,* edited by Isidore Okpewho, 367–78. Bloomington: Indiana University Press, 1999.
Franco, José L. *Folklore Criollo y Afrocubano.* Havana: Publicaciones de la Junta Nacional de Arqueologia y Etnologia, 1959.
———. *Los Palenques de los Negros Cimarrones.* Havana: Coleccion Historica, Comision de Activistas de Historia, PCC, 1973.
Frazier, E. Franklin. "The Negro Family in Bahia, Brazil." *American Sociological Review* 7, no. 4 (1942): 465–78.
Freyre, G., ed. *Novos Estudos Afri-Brasileiros.* Rio de Janeiro, Brazil: Civilizaçâo Brasileira, 1937.
Friedeman, Nina S., and Richard Cross. *Ma Ngombe: Guerreros y Ganaderos en el Palenque.* Bogota, Columbia: Carlos Valencia Editores, 1979.
Friol, Roberto. "La novela Cubana en el siglo XIX." In *Letras: Cultura en Cuba,* edited by A. C. Ballester, 463–86. Havana, Cuba: Editorial Pueblo y Educación, 1989.
Frobenius, Leo. *The Voice of Africa.* Vols. 1–2. Translated by R. Blind. London: Hutchinson, 1913.
Fusco, Coco. *English Is Broken Here: Notes on Cultural Fusion in the Americas.* New York: New Press, 1995.
Galembo, Phyllis. *Divine Inspiration: From Benin to Bahia.* Albuquerque: University of New Mexico Press, 1993.
García, Cristina. *Dreaming in Cuban.* New York: Albert Knopf, 1995.
García Canclini, Néstor. *Arte Popular y Sociedad en América Latina: Teorías Estéticas y Ensayos de Transformación.* Mexico City: Editorial Grijalbo, 1977.
———. *Hybrid Cultures: Strategies for Entering and Leaving Modernity.* Minneapolis: University of Minnesota Press, 1995.
———. *Imaginarios Urbanos.* Buenos Aires, Argentina: Editorial Universitaria de Buenos Aires, 1997.
———. "Que preferie, arte o artesanías?" *Areito* 9, no. 34 (1983): 26–29.
García Márquez, Gabriel. "El Drama de las Dos Cubas." *Areito* 9, no. 36 (1984): 64–66.

Gates, Jr., Henry Louis. *The Signifying Monkey: A Theory of African-American Literary Criticism*. New York: Oxford University Press, 1988.
Gbadamosi, Bakare. *Oriki*. Ibadan, Nigeria: Mbari Publications, 1961.
Geertz, Clifford. *Local Knowledge: Further Essays in Interpretive Anthropology*. New York: Basic Books, 1983.
Genovese, Eugene. *From Rebellion to Revolution: Afro-American Slave Revolts in the Making of the New World*. Baton Rouge: Louisiana State University Press, 1979.
———. *Roll Jordan Roll: The World the Slaves Made*. New York: Vintage Books, 1972.
Gikandi, Simon, ed. "Introduction: Africa, Diaspora, and the Discourse of Modernity." *Research in African Literatures* 27, no. 4 (1996): 1–6.
Gilbert, Michelle. "Things Ugly: Ghanaian Popular Painting." In *Beautiful/Ugly: African and Diaspora Aesthetics*, edited by Sarah Nuttall, 340–71. Durham, NC: Duke University Press, 2006.
Giles, Paul. *Virtual Americas: Transnational Fictions and the Transatlantic Imaginary*. Durham, NC: Duke University Press, 2002.
Gilroy, Paul. *Against Race: Imagining Political Culture beyond the Color Line*. Cambridge: Belknap Press, a division of Harvard University Press, 2000.
———. *The Black Atlantic: Modernity and Double Consciousness*. Cambridge: Harvard University Press, 1993.
———. "Roots and Routes: Black Identity as an Outernational Project. In *Racial and Ethnic Identity: Psychological Development and Creative Expression*, edited by Herbert Harris, Howard Blue, and Ezea Griffith, 15–30. New York: Routledge, 1995.
Glasser, Ruth. *My Music Is My Flag: Puerto Rican Musicians and Their New York Communities, 1917–1940*. Berkeley: University of California Press, 1997.
Glassie, Henry. "The Moral Lore of Folklore." *Folklore Forum* 16 (1983): 123–52.
———. *Passing the Time in Ballymenone: Culture and History of an Ulster Community*. Bloomington: Indiana University Press, 1995.
Glazier, Stephen D. "New World African Ritual: Genuine and Spurious." *Journal for the Scientific Study of Religion* 35, no. 4 (1996): 420–32.
Gleason, Judith. *Orisha: The Gods of Yorubaland*. New York: Atheneum, 1971.
———. *Oya: In Praise of an African Goddess*. New York: Harper Collins Press, 1992.
Glissant, Edouard. "Towards a Theory of *Antiallanité: La case du commandeur, Le discours antillais*." In *Edouard Glissant: Cambridge Studies in African and Caribbean Literature*, edited by J. Michael Dash, 126–54. Cambridge: Cambridge University Press, 1995.
Goldman, Dara E. "Virtual Islands: The Reterritorialization of Puerto Rican Spatiality in Cyberspace." *Hispanic Review* 72, no. 3 (2004): 375–400.
Gomez, Georgina Grande. "La casa de cultura Cubana: Instituto para la participacion masiva del pueblo." In *Cultura transnacional y culturas populares*, edited by Nestor García Canolini and Rafeal Roncagliolo, 335–67. Lima, Peru: Instituto Para América Latina, 1988.
Gomez, Juan Gualberto. *Preparando la Revolución*. c. 1890s. Reprint, Havana: Publicaçiõnes de la Secretaria de Educación, Direccion de Cultura, 1936.
Gomez, Michael A. *Exchanging Our Country Marks: The Transformation of African Identities in the Colonial and Antebellum South*. Chapel Hill: University of North Carolina Press, 1998.

Gomez, Nery Abreu. "Estudio de una casa templo de la cultura Yoruba: El Ile-Ocha 'Tula.'" *Islas* 71 (1982): 113–37.
Gómez de Avellaneda, Gertrudis. *Sab*. 1841. Reprint, Barcelona: Linkgua, 1997.
Gómez y Arias, Miguel Maríano, Alcalde. *La dominación inglesa en La Habana: Libro de cabildos 1762–1763, Edición Oficial*. Preface by Emilio Roig de Leuchsenring, Comisionado Intermunicipal de La Habana. Havana: Imprenta Molina y CIA, 1929.
Gonzalez del Valle, José Z. *La vida literaria en Cuba*. Havana: Cuadernos de Cultura, 1938.
González-Wippler, Migene. "Santería: Its Dynamics and Multiple Roots." In *Enigmatic Powers: African and Indigenous Peoples' Religions among Latinos*, 99–111. New York: Bildner Center for Western Hemisphere Studies, 1995.
Gordon, Edmund T., and Mark Anderson. "The African Diaspora: Toward an Ethnography of Diasporic Identification." *Journal of American Folklore* 112, no. 445 (1999): 282–96.
Granda, German, ed. *Español de América, el Español de Africa y hablas Criollas Hispánicas: Cambios, contactos, y contextos*. Madrid: Editorial Gredos, 1994.
Greenberg, Joséph H. *Studies in African Linguistic Classification*. New Haven, CT: Compass Publishing Company, 1955.
Griaule, Marcel. *Conversations with Ogotemmêli*. London: Oxford University Press, 1965.
Habermas, Jürgen. *The Structural Transformation of the Public Sphere*. Cambridge: MIT Press, 1989.
Hagedorn, Katherine J. *Divine Utterances: The Performance of Afro-Cuban Santería*. Washington, DC: Smithsonian Institution Press, 2001.
Hall, Stuart. "Cultural Identity and Diaspora." In *Identity: Community, Culture, Difference*, edited by J. Rutherford. London: Lawrence and Wishart, 1990.
———. "Negotiating Caribbean Identities." *New Left Review* 209 (1995): 3–15.
Hallen, Barry. *The Good, the Bad, and the Beautiful: Discourse about Values in Yoruba Culture*. Bloomington: Indiana University Press, 2001.
Hallen, Barry, and O. Sodipo. *Knowledge, Belief, and Witchcraft: Analytic Experiments in African Philosophy*. Stanford, CA: Stanford University Press, 1997.
Hand, Wayland, ed. *The Frank C. Brown Collection of North Carolina Folklore, Superstitions from North Carolina*. Durham, NC: Duke University Press, 1952.
Hannerz, Ulf. "Notes on Global Ecumene." *Public Culture* 1, no. 2 (1989): 66–75.
———. "The World in Creolization." *Africa* 57, no. 4 (1987): 546–59.
Harris, Joséph. *Global Dimensions of the African Diaspora*. Washington, DC: Howard University Press, 1993.
Hegel, Georg Wilhelm Friedrich. *The Philosophy of History*. 1820. Reprint, Buffalo, NY: Prometheus Books, 1991.
Helg, Aline. *Our Rightful Share: The Afro-Cuban Struggle for Equality, 1886–1912*. Chapel Hill: University of North Carolina Press, 1995.
Hellwig, David J. "The African American Press and United States Involvement in Cuba, 1902–1912." In *Between Race and Empire: African-Americans and Cubans before the Cuban Revolution*, edited by Lisa Brock and Digna Castañeda Fuertes, 70–84. Philadelphia: Temple University Press, 1998.

Helmrich, S. "Kinship, Nation and Paul Gilroy's Concept of Diaspora." *Diaspora* 2 (1992): 2.
Heredia, José María. *Poesias, discursos, y cartas de José María Heredia.* 1836. Reprint, Havana: Cultural, 1939.
Herskovits, Jean. *A Preface to Modern Nigeria: The "Sierra Leonians" in Yoruba, 1830–1890.* Madison: University of Wisconsin Press, 1965.
———. "Liberated Africans and the History of Lagos Colony to 1886." PhD diss., Oxford University, 1960–61.
Herskovits, M. J. *Dahomey: An Ancient West African Kingdom.* 2 vols. New York: J. J. Augustin, 1938.
———. *The Myth of the Negro Past.* 1941. Reprint, Boston: Beacon Press, 1958.
———. *The New World Negro.* Bloomington: Indiana University Press, 1966.
Herskovits, M. J., and W. R. Bascom. *Continuity and Change in African Cultures.* Chicago: University of Chicago Press, 1971.
Herskovits, M. J., and Frances Herskovits. *Dahomean Narrative: A Cross-Cultural Comparison.* Evanston, IL: Northwestern University Press, 1958.
Hewitt, Julia Cuervo. *Aché, presencia africana: Tradiciones Yoruba-Lucumí en la narrativa Cubana.* New York: Peter Lang, 1988.
Hobsbawm, Eric, and Terence Ranger, eds. *The Invention of Tradition.* Cambridge: Cambridge University Press, 1983.
Holt, Thomas. "The Essence of the Contract: The Articulation of Race, Gender, and Political Economy in British Emancipation Policy, 1838–1866." In *Beyond Slavery: Explorations of Race, Labor, and Citizenship in Postemancipation Societies,* edited by Fredrick Cooper, Rebecca Scott, and Thomas Holt, 33–60. Chapel Hill: University of North Carolina Press, 2000.
Houk, James. "Afro-Trinidadian Identity and the Africanization of the *Orisha* Religion." In *Trinidad Ethnicity,* edited by Kevin A. Yelvington, 161–79. London: Macmillan, 1993.
———. *Spirits, Blood, and Drums.* Philadelphia: Temple University Press, 1995.
Hountondji, Paulin J. *African Philosophy: Myth and Reality.* Bloomington: Indiana University Press, 1996.
Howard, Philip A. *Changing History: Afro-Cuban Cabildos and Societies of Color in the Nineteenth Century.* Baton Rouge: Louisiana State University Press, 1998.
Hufford, David J. "Traditions of Disbelief." *New York Folklore Quarterly* 8, nos. 3–4 (1982): 47–55.
Hulme, Peter. *Colonial Encounters: Europe and the Native Caribbean, 1492–1797.* New York: Routledge, 1992.
Hulme, Peter, Francis Barker, and Margaret Iversen. *Cannibalism and the Colonial World.* Cambridge: Cambridge University Press, 1998.
———. *Uses of History: Marxism, Postmodernism, and the Renaissance.* Manchester, UK: Manchester University Press, 1991.
Hurston, Zora Neale. *Mules and Men.* New York: Harper and Row, 1990.
Huyssen, Andreas. *Present Pasts: Urban Palimpsests and the Politics of Memory.* Stanford, CA: Stanford University Press, 2003.
Hymes, Dell. "Breakthrough into Performance." In *"In Vain I Tried to Tell You": Essays in Native American Poetics,* edited by Dell Hymes, 79–141. Philadelphia: University of Pennsylvania Press, 1981.

Ibarra, Jorge. *Ideologia mambisa.* Havana: Instituto Cubano del Libro, 1972.
———. *Nación y Cultura Nacional:* 1868–1930. Havana: Editorial Letras Cubanas, 1981.
Idowu, Bolaji. *Olodumare: God in Yoruba Belief.* London: Longmans, 1962.
———. "Religion, Magic, and Medicine." *Orita* 1 (1967): 62–77.
———. "The Study of Religion with a Special Reference to African Traditional Religion." *Orita* 1 (1967): 3–12.
———. "Traditional Religion and Christianity." In *The City of Ibadan,* edited by P. C. Lloyd, A. L. Mabogunje, and B. Awe, 235–48. London: Cambridge University Press, 1967.
Irele, F. Abiola. "Dimensions of African Discourse." In *The African Imagination: Literature in Africa and the Black Diaspora,* edited by Abiola Irele. Oxford: Oxford University Press, 2001.
Jackson, Michael. *Paths toward a Clearing.* Bloomington: Indiana University Press, 1989.
Jackson, Michael, and Ivan Karp. "Introduction." In *Personhood and Agency: The Experience of Self and Other in African Cultures,* edited by Michael Jackson and Ivan Karp, 15–30. Uppsala, Sweden: Acta Universitatis Upsalensis, 1990.
James, Joel. *Sobre dioses y muertos.* Santiago de Cuba: Caserón, 1989.
Jameson, Robert Francis. "Letters from Havana, during the Year 1820." In S*laves, Sugar, and Colonial Society: Travel Accounts of Cuba,* 1801–1899, edited by Louis A. Pérez, Jr., 225–227. Wilmington: Scholarly Resources, Inc., 1992.
Jegede, Dele. "Popular Culture in Urban Africa." In *Africa,* edited by P. Martin and P. O'Meara, 273–294. 3rd ed. Bloomington: Indiana University Press, 1995.
Jiménez, Rafael Duharte. "Dos viejos temores de nuestro pasado colonial," In *Seis ensayos de interpretación histórica,* edited by Duharte Rafael Jiménez, 83–100. Santiago de Cuba: Editorial Oriente, 1983.
Johnson, Samuel. *History of the Yorubas, from Earliest Times to the Beginning of the British Protectorate.* Edited by O. Johnson. London: George Routledge & Sons, 1921.
Jorge, Angela. "Cuban Santería: A New World African Religion." In *African Creative Expressions of the Divine,* edited by K. Davis, 105–120. Washington, DC: Howard University School of Divinity, 1991.
Kapchan, Deborah A., and Pauline Turner Strong. "Theorizing the Hybrid." *Journal of American Folklore* 112, no. 445 (1999): 239–53.
Karp, Ivan. "Power and Capacity in Rituals of Possession." In *The Creativity of Power: Cosmology and Action in African Societies,* edited by W. Arens and Ivan Karp, 91–112. Washington, DC: Smithsonian Institution Press, 1989.
Kelley, Robin D. G. *Freedom Dreams: The Black Radical Imagination.* Boston: Beacon Press, 2003.
———. *Yo' Mama's Disfunktional! Fighting the Culture Wars in Urban America.* Boston: Beacon Press, 1998.
Khane, A. "Religions et traditions d'Afrique Noire: Au Pays des Orishas et des Voudons." *Africa en Marche* 10–11 (1958): 4–5.
Kidder, Rev. D. P., and Rev. J. C. Fletcher. *Brazil and the Brazilians, Portrayed in Historical and Descriptive Sketches.* Philadelphia: Childs & Peterson, 1857.
Kilson, Martin L. "The Rise of Nationalist Organizations and Parties in British West Africa." In *Africa from the Point of View of American Negro Scholars,* edited by John A. Davis, 35–70. Paris: Présence Africaine, 1958.

Kingsley, Mary. *West African Studies*. London: MacMillan, 1899.
Kipple, Kenneth F. *Blacks in Colonial Cuba, 1774–1899*. Gainesville: University of Florida Press, 1976.
Klor de Alva, Jorge. "The Postcolonialization of the (Latin) American Experience: A Reconsideration of 'Colonialism,' 'Postcolonialism,' and 'Mestizaje.'" In *After Colonialism: Imperial Histories and Post-colonial Displacements*, edited by Gyan Prakesh, 241–73. Princeton, NJ: Princeton University Press, 1996.
Kubayanda, Joséphat Bekunuru. "Minority Discourse and the African Collective: Some Examples from Latin American and Caribbean Literature." *Cultural Critique* 6 (1987): 113–30.
Kukah, Matthew. "African Traditional Religion and Christianity: Dialogue or Confrontation?" Master's thesis, University of Bradford, UK, 1980.
Kutzinski, Vera M. *Sugar's Secrets: Race and the Erotics of Cuban Nationalism*. Charlottesville: University of Virginia Press, 1993.
Lachateñere, Romulo. *El sistema religioso de los Afrocubanos*. Havana: Editorial de Ciencias Sociales, 1992.
———. "El sistema religioso de los Lucumí y otras influencias Africanas en Cuba I." *Estudios Afrocubanos* 3, no. 4 (1939): 28–82.
———. "El sistema religioso de los Lucumí y otras influencias Africanas en Cuba II." *Estudios Afrocubanos* 4, no. 2 (1940): 8–32.
———. "El sistema religioso de los Lucumí y otras influencias Africanas en Cuba III." *Estudios Afrocubanos* 5 (1945–46): 208.
Ladipo, Duro. *Oba ko so*. Ibadan, Nigeria: University of Ibadan, Institute of African Studies, 1968.
Laitin, David D. *Hegemony and Culture: Politics and Religious Change among the Yoruba*. Chicago: University of Chicago Press, 1986.
Landers, Jane. "African Presence in Early Spanish Colonialization of the Caribbean and the Southeastern Borderlands." In *Columbian Consequences*, edited by David Hurst Thomas, 315–327. Vol. 2. Washington, DC: Smithsonian Institution Press, 1990.
———. "*Cimarrón* and Citizen: African Ethnicity, Corporate Identity, and the Evolution of Free Black Towns in the Spanish Circum-Caribbean." In *Slaves, Subjects, and Subversives: Blacks in Colonial Latin America*, edited by Jane Landers and Barry Robinson, 111–45. Albuquerque: University of New Mexico Press, 2006.
Landes, Ruth. *The City of Women*. 1947. Reprint, Albuquerque: University of New Mexico Press, 1992.
Lanier, Oilda Havier, ed. *Directorio central de las sociedades de color, 1840–1878*. Havana: Editorial de Ciencias Sociales, 1996.
———. *El directorio central de las sociedades negras de Cuba, 1886–1894*. Havana: Editorial de Ciencias Sociales, 1996.
Laotan, A. B. "Brazilian Influence on Lagos." *Nigeria Magazine* 69 (1961): 156–65.
———. *The Torch Bearers: The Old Brazilian Colony in Lagos*. Lagos: Ife-Olu Printing Works, 1943.
Las Casas, Bartolomé de. *Brevísima relación de la destrucción de las Indias*. Madrid: Catedra, 2006.
Lasebikan, Ebenezer Latunde. "The Yoruba in Brazil." *West Africa*, no. 2357 (1962): 843.

Lavie, Smadar, and Red Swedenberg. *Displacement, Diaspora, and Geographies of Identity.* Durham, NC: Duke University Press, 1996.
Law, Robin. "Constructing 'A Real National History': A Comparison of Edward Blyden and Samuel Johnson." In *Self-Assertion and Brokerage*, edited by P. F. de Moraes Farias and Karin Barber, 78–100. Birmingham, UK: University of Birmingham, Centre of West African Studies, 1990.
———. "The Dynastic Chronology of Lagos." *Lagos Notes and Records* 2, no. 2 (1968): 46–54.
———. "The Evolution of the Brazilian Community in Ouidah." In *Rethinking the African Diaspora: The Making of a Black Atlantic World in the Bight of Benin and Brazil*, edited by Kristin Mann and Edna Bay, 22–41. Portland, OR: Frank Cass, 2001.
———. "Heritage of Oduduwa: Traditional History and Political Propaganda among the Yoruba." *Journal of African History* 14, no. 2 (1973): 207–22.
———. "My Head Belongs to the King: On the Political and Ritual Significance of Decapitation in Pre-colonial Dahomey." *Journal of African History* 30 (1990): 399–415.
———. *The Oyo Empire, c. 1600–c. 1836: A West African Imperialism in the Era of the Atlantic Slave Trade.* Oxford: Clarendon Press, 1977.
———. *The Slave Coast of West Africa 1550–1750: The Impact of the Atlantic Slave Trade on African Society.* Oxford: Clarendon Press, 1991.
———. "Traditional History." In *Sources of Yoruba History*, 25–41. Oxford: Clarendon Press, 1973.
Lawal, Babatunde. "From Africa to the Americas: Art in Yoruba Religion." In *Santería Aesthetics*, edited by Arturo Lindsay, 3–37. Washington, DC: Smithsonian Institution Press, 1996.
———. *The Gelede Spectacle: Art, Gender, and Social Harmony in an African Culture.* Seattle: University of Washington Press, 1996.
———. "The Living Dead: Art and Immortality among the Yoruba of Nigeria." *Africa* 47, no. 1 (1977): 50–61.
———. "Some Aspects of Yoruba Aesthetics." *British Journal of Aesthetics* 14, no. 3 (1974): 239–49.
Lazo, Rodrigo. *Writing to Cuba: Filibustering and Cuban Exiles in the United States.* Chapel Hill: University of North Carolina Press, 2005.
Leante, Cesar. *Los guerrilleros negros.* Madrid: Siglo Veinteuno Editores, 1979.
Le Goff, Jacques. *History and Memory.* New York: Columbia University Press, 1996.
Lehman, Sophia. "In Search of Mother Tongue: Locating Home in Diaspora." *MELUS* 23, no. 4 (1998): 101–21.
Lemelle, S., and Kelly R., eds. *Imagining Home: Class, Culture, and Nation in the African Diaspora.* London: Verso, 1994.
Le Riverend, Julio. "Conciencia de la contradiccion: El padre Caballero y esclavitud." In *Letras: Cultura en Cuba*, edited by A. C. Ballester, 233–39. 1976. Reprint, Havana: Editorial Pueblo y Educación, 1989.
Levine, L. W. *Black Culture and Black Consciousness: Afro-American Folk Thought from Slavery to Freedom.* Oxford: Oxford University Press, 1977.
Levine, Robert M. *Tropical Diasporas: The Jewish Experience in Cuba.* Miami: University of Florida Press, 1993.

Ligiero, Zeca. "Candomble is Religion-Life-Art." In *Divine Inspiration*, edited by Phyllis Galembo, 97–120. Albuquerque: University of New Mexico Press, 1983.
Lindfors, Bernth, ed. *Forms of Folklore in Africa*. Austin: University of Texas Press, 1977.
Lindsay, Arturo. "Orishas: Living Gods in Contemporary Latin Art." In *Santería Aesthetics*, 201–23. Washington, DC: Smithsonian Institution Press, 1996.
Little, K. L. "The Significance of West African Creole for Africanist and Afro-American Studies." *African Affairs* 59 (1950): 197.
Llorens, Irma. *Nacionalismo y Nacion*. Lleida, Spain: Universidad de Lleida, 1998.
Lloyd, P. C. "Installing the Awujale (of Ijebu-Ode)." *Ibadan* 12 (1961): 7–10.
———. "Sacred Kingship and Government among the Yoruba." *Africa* 3, no. 3 (1960): 221–37.
———. "The Traditional Political System of the Yoruba." *Southwestern Journal of Anthropology* 10, no. 4 (1954): 366–84.
———. "The Yoruba of Nigeria." In *Peoples of Africa*, 547–82. New York: Holt, 1965.
Long, Carolyn Morrow. *Spiritual Merchants: Religion, Magic, and Commerce*. Knoxville: University of Tennessee Press, 2001.
López, Ana. "Greater Cuba." In *The Ethnic Eye: Latino Media Arts*, edited by Chon A. Noriega and Ana M. López, 38–58. Minneapolis: University of Minnesota Press, 1996.
Lopez-Baralt, Mercedes. *Iconografia Politica del Nuevo Mundo*. Rio Piedras, Puerto Rico: University of Puerto Rico, 1990.
Lorenzo, Raúl. *Sentido nacionalista del pensamiento de Saco*. Havana: Editorial Trópico, 1942.
Losi, John. *History of Lagos*. 1914. Reprint, Lagos: African Education Press, 1967.
Lucas, J. Olumide. "The Cult of the 'Adamu Orisha.'" *Nigerian Field* 11 (1943): 184–96.
———. *Oduduwa*. Lagos: Twentieth Century Press, 1949.
———. *Religion of the Yorubas*. Lagos: CMS Bookshop, 1948.
Lugo-Ortiz, Agnes. "Identidades Imaginarios: Biografia y Nacionalidad en Cuba, 1860–1898." PhD diss., Princeton University, 1990.
Luis, William. "Cultura Afrocubana en la revolución: Entrevista a Elio Ruiz." *Afro-Hispanic Review* 13, no. 1 (1994): 37–45.
———. "La novela antiesclavista: Texto, contexto, y esclavitud." In *Esclavitud y narrativa en el siglo XIX cubano: Enfoques reientes*, edited by Salvador Arias, 43–57. Havana: Editorial Academica, 1995.
Luz y Caballero, José de la. *Impugnacion a Cousin*. 1840. Reprint, Havana: Editorial de la Universidad de La Habana, 1948.
Macaulay, Herbert. *Justitia Fiat: The Moral Obligation of the British Government to the House of King Docemo of Lagos: An Open Letter*. Lagos, Nigeria, 1921.
Macaulay, Zachary, ed. *The Anti-Slavery Reporter: Under the Sanction of the British and Foreign Anti-Slavery Society*. Vol. 2, 3rd ser. London: Peter Jones Bolton, 1854.
Machado, Eduardo, and Michael Domitrovich. *Tastes like Cuba: An Exile's Hunger for Home*. New York: Gotham Books, 2007.
Magliocco, Sabina. *Witching Culture: Folklore and Neo-paganism in America*. Philadelphia: University of Pennsylvania Press, 2004.

Mann, Kristin. "Shifting Paradigms in the Study of the African Diaspora and of Atlantic History and Culture." In *Rethinking the African Diaspora: The Making of a Black Atlantic World in the Bight of Benin and Brazil*, edited by Kristin Mann and Edna Bay, 3–21. Portland, OR: Frank Cass, 2001.
———. *Slavery and the Birth of an African City: Lagos, 1760–1900*. Bloomington: Indiana University Press, 2007.
Manzano, J. Francisco. "Carta de Juan Francisco Manzano a Domingo del Monte." In *Autobiografia, cartas, y versos, 1791–1854*, edited by Fransisco Mazano, 81. Havana: Cuadernos de Historia Habanera, 1937.
———. *Poems by a slave in the Island of Cuba, recently liberated. Translated from the Spanish by R. R. Maddler, M.D., with the early life of the Negro poet written by himself, to which are prefixed two pieces descriptive of Cuban slavery and the slave traffic*. London: Thomas Ward, 1840.
———. *Poesia de Juan Francisco Manzano*. Havana: Biblioteca Nacional de "José Marti," Departemento de Colección Cubana, Colección de manuscritos, Box 1. 1831.
Marruz, Fina García. "De estudios delmontinos." In *Letras: Cultura en Cuba*, edited by A. C. Ballester, 327–64. 1969. Reprint, Havana: Editorial Pueblo y Educación, 1989.
Martí, José. *En los Estados Unidos*. Madrid: El Libro de Bolsillo, 1968.
———. *Inside the Monster: Writings on the United States and American Imperialism*. Edited by Philip S. Foner. Translated by Elinor Randall. New York: Monthly Review Press, 1975.
———. *José Martí: Major Poems*, e   dited by Philip S. Foner. Teaneck, NJ: Holmes and Meier Publishers, 1982.
———. "Letter to General Máximo Gómez." In *José Martí: Selected Writings*, translated by Esther Allen, 257–260. New York: Penguin Classics, 2002.
———. *Obras Completas*. Havana Cuba: Editorial Obras Completas National de Cuba, 1963.
Martinez Echazabal, Lourdes. "The Politics of Afro-Cuban Religion in Contemporary Cuban Cinema." *Afro-Hispanic Review* 13, no. 1 (1994): 16–22.
Martinez-Fernandez, Luis. *Fighting Slavery in the Caribbean: The Life and Times of a British Family in Nineteenth-Century Havana*. Armonk, NY: M. E. Sharpe, 1998.
Mason, John. *Orin Orisa*. New York: Yoruba Theological Archministry, 1992.
———. "Yoruba-American Art." In *The Yoruba Artist: New Theoretical Perspectives on African Arts*, edited by Rowland Abiodun, Henry J. Drewal, and John Pemberton III, 240–250. Washington, DC: Smithsonian Institution Press, 1994.
Mason, Michael Atwood. "'I Bow My Head to the Ground': The Creation of Bodily Experience in a Cuban American Santería Initiation." *Journal of American Folklore* 107, no. 423 (1994): 23–39.
Matibag, Eugenio. *Afro-Cuban Religious Experience: Cultural Reflections in Narrative*. Gainesville: University of Florida Press, 1996.
Matory, James L. *Black Atlantic Religion: Tradition, Transnationalism, and Matriarchy in Afro-Brazilian Candomble*. Princeton, NJ: Princeton University Press, 2005.
———. "The Coast Revisited: The Lagosian Bourgeoisie and the Making of the Yoruba-Atlantic Complex, 1840–1950." Unpublished paper provided by author, 1995.
———. "The English Professors of Brazil: On the Diasporic Roots of the Yoruba Nation." *Comparative Studies in Society and History* 41 (1999): 72–103.

———. "Government by Seduction: History and the Tropes of 'Mounting' in Oyo-Yoruba Religion." In *Modernity and its Malcontents*, edited by Jean and John Camaroff, 58–88. Chicago: University of Chicago Press, 1993.

———. "Rival Empires: Islam and the Religions of Spirit-Possession among the Oyo-Yoruba." *American Ethnologist* 21, no. 3 (1994): 495–515.

———. *Sex and the Empire That Is No More: Gender and the Politics of Metaphor in Oyo Yoruba Religion*. Minneapolis: University of Minnesota Press, 1994.

Mbembe, Achille. "Belly Up: More on the Postcolony." *Public Culture* 5, no. 1 (1992): 46–145.

———. "Provisional Notes on the Postcolony." *Africa* 62, no. 1 (1992): 3–37.

Mbiti, John S. *Introduction to African Religion*. Oxford: Heinemann Educational Books, 1975.

McClelland, E. *The Cult of Ifa among the Yoruba: Folk Practice and the Art*. London: Ethnographica, 1982.

———. "The Significance of Number in the Odu of Ifa." *Africa* 36, no. 4 (1996): 421–31.

McKenzie, P. R. "Dreams and Visions from 19th Century Yoruba Religion." In *Dreaming Religion and Society in Africa*, 126–135. New York: E. J. Brill, 1992.

———. *Hail Orisha! A Phenomenology of West African Religion in the Mid-nineteenth Century*. Leiden, Netherlands: Brill, 1997.

McLeod, Marc C. "Undesirable Aliens: Race, Ethnicity, and Nationalism in the Comparison of Haitian and British West Indian Immigrant Workers in Cuba, 1912–1939." *Journal of Social History* 31, no. 3 (1998): 599–624.

Melgar, Ricardo. "Los *Orishas* y la Ciudad de la Habana en Tiempos de Crisis." *Cuadernos Americanos* 5 (1994): 165–84.

Memmi, Albert. *The Colonizer and the Colonized*. Boston: Beacon Press, 1991 [1957].

Metraux, Alfred. *Voodoo in Haiti*. 2nd ed. New York: Schocken Books, 1972.

Milburn, S. "Magic and Charms of the Ijebu Province, Southern Nigeria." *Man* 32 (1932): 158–60.

———. "A Yoruba Household Altar." *Nigerian Field* 7, no. 1 (1952): 43–44.

Miller, Ivor L. *Voice of the Leopard: African Secret Societies and Cuba*. Jackson: University Press of Mississippi, 2009.

Miller, N. S. "The Beginnings of Modern Lagos." *Nigeria Magazine* 69 (1961): 107–12.

Mintz, Sidney W., and Richard Price. *An Anthropological Approach to the Afro-American Past: A Caribbean Perspective*. Philadelphia: Institute for the Study of Human Issues, 1976.

Mirabal, Nancy Raquel. "Telling Silences and Making Community: Afro-Cubans and African Americans in Ybor City and Tampa, 1899–1915." In *Between Race and Empire: African-Americans and Cubans before the Cuban Revolution*, edited by Lisa Brock and Digna Castañeda Fuertes, 49–69. Philadelphia: Temple University Press, 1998.

Mitchell, Robert Cameron. "Religious Change and Modernization: The Aladura Churches among the Yoruba in Southwestern Nigeria." PhD diss., Northwestern University, 1970.

———. "Religious Protest and Social Change: The Origins of the Aladura Movement in Western Nigeria." In *Protest and Power in Black Africa*, edited by Robert I. Rotberg, 458–95. New York: Oxford University Press, 1970.

Moloney, Alfred C. "Cotton Interests, Foreign and Native, in Yoruba, and Generally in West Africa." *Journal of Manchester Geographical Society* 5 (1889): 265–76.
Moore, Carlos, Shawna Moore, and Tanya Saunders, eds. *African Presence in the Americas.* Trenton, NJ: Africa World Press, 1995.
Moore, Carlos and Todd Sanders. "Introduction." In *Magical Interpretations, Material Realities*, edited by Henrietta Moore, and Todd Sanders, 1–27. New York: Routledge, 2002.
Moore, Robin D. *Nationalizing Blackness: Afrocubanismo and Artistic Revolution in Havana, 1920–1940.* Pittsburgh: University of Pittsburgh Press, 1997.
Morejón, Nancy. *Fundación de la imagen.* Havana: Editorial Letras Cubanas, 1988.
Moreno Fraginals, Manuel. *The Sugarmill: The Socioeconomic Complex of Sugar in Cuba, 1760–1860.* Translated from Spanish by Cedric Belfrage. New York: Monthly Review Press, 1976.
Morton-Williams, Peter. "The Oyo Yoruba and the Atlantic Trade, 1670–1830." *Journal of the Historical Society of Nigeria* 3, no. 1 (1964): 25–45.
———. "The Yoruba Ogboni Cult in Oyo." *Africa* 30 (1960): 362–374.
Morúa Delgado, Martin. *Sofia.* 1891. Reprint, Havana: Instituto Cubano del Libro, 1972.
Mosquera, Gerardo. "'Eleggua' at the (Post?)Modern Crossroads: The Presence of Africa in the Visual Art of Cuba." In *Santería Aesthetics*, edited by Arturo Lindsay, 225–58. Washington, DC: Smithsonian Institution Press, 1996.
Moys, Elizabeth Mary. *Union Catalogue of Bibliographies in Lagos Libraries.* Lagos: Standing Joint Committee on Library Cooperation in Lagos, 1965.
Mudimbe, V. Y. *The Idea of Africa.* Bloomington: Indiana University Press, 1994.
———. *The Invention of Africa.* Bloomington: Indiana University Press, 1988.
Muheenudeen Society, Lagos. *The Faurabay Mosque.* Lagos: Tika-Tore Press, 1949.
Mullen, E. J. *Afro-Cuban Literature: Critical Junctures.* Westport, CN: Greenwood Press, 1998.
Murphy, Joséph. "Ritual Systems in Cuban Santería." PhD diss., Temple University, 1980.
———. "Yéyé Cachita: Ochún in a Cuban Mirror." In *Osun across the Waters: A Yoruba Goddess in Africa and the Americas*, edited by Joséph M. Murphy and Mei-Mei Sanford, 87–101. Bloomington: Indiana University Press, 2001.
Murphy, Joséph M., and Mei-Mei Sanford, eds. *Osun across the Waters: A Yoruba Goddess in Africa and the Americas.* Bloomington: Indiana University Press, 2001.
Murray, Jack. "Old Lagos." *Nigeria Magazine* 38 (1952): 122–30.
Nandy, A. "Dialogue and Diaspora." *Third Text* 11 (1990): 99–108.
National Library of Nigeria. *Lagos Past and Present: An Historical Bibliography.* National Library Occasional Publications 1. Lagos, 1968.
Nevadomsky, Joséph. "Religious Symbolism in the Benin Kingdom." In *Divine Inspiration*, edited by Phyllis Galembo, 17–32. Albuquerque: University of New Mexico Press, 1989.
Newell, William Wells. "On the Field and Work of a Journal of American Folklore." *Journal of American Folklore* 1, no. 1 (1888): 3–7.
Ngugi wa Thiong'o. *Moving the Centre: The Struggle for Cultural Freedoms.* Portsmouth, NH: Heinemann, 1993.
———. *The River Between.* Portsmouth, NH: Heinemann, 1990.

Niven, C. R. *A Short History of Nigeria.* London: Longmans, 1957.
Nuttall, Sarah, ed., "Introduction: Rethinking Beauty." In *Beautiful /Ugly: African and Diaspora Aesthetics,* edited by Sarah Nuttall, 6–29. Durham, NC: Duke University Press, 2006.
Obayemi, Ade. "The Yoruba and Edo-Speaking Peoples and Their Neighbours before 1600." *History of West Africa,* edited by J. F. A. Ajayi and Michael Crowder, 196–263. 2nd ed. London: Longman, 1976.
Obejas, Achy. *We Came All the Way from Cuba So You Could Dress like This?* San Francisco: Cleis Press, 1994.
Oduyoye, Modupe. *The Vocabulary of Yoruba Religious Discourse.* Ibadan, Nigeria: Daystar Press, 1971.
Ogmefu, M. I. *Yoruba Legends.* London: Sheldon Press, 1929.
Ogunba, O. "The Agemo Cult in Ijebuland." *Nigeria Magazine* 86 (1965): 176–86.
Ogundipe, F. B. A. "A Brief History of the Archdiocese of Lagos and the Beginning of the Catholic Church in Nigeria." *Lagos Courier,* [sponsored by] St. Ferdinand's Catholic Church (1998): 38.
Ogunkoya, Olatunji. "Yoruba Ancient Religion and Mythology." *Africana* 1, no. 3 (1949): 14–15.
Ogunlusi, Jola. "Igunnuko Festival: Lagos, Abeokuta, Badagry, Offa, etc." *African Arts* 4, no. 4 (1971): 60–61.
Oinas, Felix, ed. *Folklore, Nationalism, and Politics.* Columbus, OH: Slavica, 1978.
Ojo, G. J. A. *Yoruba Culture: A Geographical Analysis.* London: University of London Press, 1966.
———. *Yoruba Palaces.* London: University of London Press, 1966.
Oke, Moses. "Towards an African (Yoruba) Perspective on Empirical Knowledge: A Critique of Hallen and Sodipo." *International Philosophical Quarterly* 35, no. 2 (1995): 205–17.
Okpewho, Isadore. *Myth in Africa.* Cambridge: Cambridge University Press, 1983.
———, ed. *The Oral Performance in Africa.* Ibadan, Nigeria: Spectrum Books Limited, 1990.
Okpewho, Isidore, C. B. Davies, and A. Mazrui, eds. *The African Diaspora: African Origins and New World Identities.* Bloomington: Indiana University Press, 1999.
Oladapo, I. O. "Eko Bridge." *Nigeria Magazine,* July 1969, 421–31.
Olaleye, A. M. "A Philosophy of the Yoruba Religion." Master's thesis, Howard University, 1956.
Olinto, Antonio. *Brasileiros na África.* 2nd ed. São Paulo, Brazil: G. R. Dorea, 1980.
Olmstead, David. "Comparative Notes on Yoruba and Lucumi." *Language* 29, no. 2 (1953): 157–64.
Olupona, Jacob K. "Orisa Osun." In *Osun across the Waters: A Yoruba Goddess in Africa and the Americas,* edited by Joséph M. Murphy and Mei-Mei Sanford, 46–67. Bloomington: Indiana University Press, 2001.
Olusanya, G. O. "Henry Carr and Herbert Macaulay: A Study in the Conflict of Principles and Personalities." In *The History of the Peoples of Lagos State,* edited by Ade Adefuye, B. Agiri, and A Osuntokun, 279–89. Lagos: Lantern Books, 1987.
Omoregie, S. *Binis Own Lagos.* Benin City, Nigeria: 1954.
Ortiz, Fernando. *La Africanía de la música folklórica de Cuba.* Havana: Letras Cubanas, 1993. Originally published in *Revista Bimestre Cubana,* 1947–49.

———. *Los bailes y el teatro de los negros en el folklore de Cuba*. Havana: Ediciones Cardenas, 1951.

———. "Brujos o Santos." *Estudios Afrocubanos* 3, no. 4 (1939): 85–90.

———. "Los cabildos Afrocubanos." In *Etnia y Sociedad*, edited by Isaac Barreal, 54–63. 1921. Havana: Editorial de Ciencias Sociales, 1993.

———. *Los cabildos y la fiesta del Día de los Reyes*. 1921. Reprint, Havana: Editorial de Ciencias Sociales, 1992.

———. *Contrapunteo Cubano del Tabaco y el Azúcar*. 1940. Reprint, with introduction by Bronislaw Malinowski; Havana: Editorial de Ciencias Sociales, 1983.

———. "Los factores humano de la cubanidad." In *Etnia y Sociedad*, edited by Isaac Barreal, 1–20. Havana: Editorial de Ciencias Sociales, 1993.

———. *Glosario de Afronegrismos*. Havana: Imprenta El Siglo XX, 1924.

———. *Hampa Afrocubana: Los Negros Brujos*. Madrid: Editorial America, 1917.

———. *Historia de una pelea Cubana contra los demonios*. 1959. Reprint, Madrid: Ediciones ERRE, 1973.

———. "La Música Religiosa de los Yoruba (entre los Negros Cubanos)." *Estudios Afrocubanos* 5, no. 1 (1940): 190–99.

———. "La Religión en la Poesía Mulata." *Estudios Afrocubanos* 1, no. 1 (1937): 15–62.

Ositola, Kolawole. "On Ritual Performance: A Practitioner's Point of View." *The Drama Review: A Journal of Performance Studies* 32, no. 2 (1988): 31–41.

Osuntokun, Jide. "Introduction of Christianity and Islam in Lagos State." In *The History of the Peoples of Lagos State*, 128–41. Lagos: Lantern Books, 1987.

Otero, Solimar. "Barrio, Bodega, and Botanica Aesthetics: The Layered Traditions of the Latino Imaginary." *Atlantic Studies* 4, no. 2 (2007): 173–94.

———. "Dreaming the Barrio: *Afrolatinos* and the Shaping of Public Space in Africa." *Phoebe: Gender and Cultural Critiques* 18, no. 2 (2006): 31–52.

———. "Getting There and Back: The Road, the Journey and Home in Nuyorican Diaspora Literature." In *Writing Of(f) the Hyphen: Critical Perspectives on the Literature of the Puerto Rican Diaspora*, edited by José L. Torres-Padilla and Carmen H. Rivera, 274–292. Seattle: University of Washington Press, 2008.

———. "*Iku* and Cuban Nationhood: The Use of Yoruba Mythology in the Film 'Guantanamera.'" *Africa Today* 46, no. 2 (1999): 116–31.

———. "Rethinking the Diaspora: African, Brazilian, and Cuban Communities in Africa and the Americas." *The Black Scholar* 30, nos. 3–4 (2000): 54–56.

———. "El sistema de la salud y el bienestar en la religión de la santería cubana." *Revista de Investigaciones Folclóricas* 21 (2006): 144–58.

———. "Spirit Possession, Havana, and the Night: Listening and Ritual in Cuban Fiction." *Western Folklore* 66, nos. 1–2 (2007): 45–74.

———. "'A Tale of Two Cities': 'Ethnic' Yoruba in 19th Century Havana." *Wadabagei: A Journal of the Caribbean and Its Diaspora* 2 (2003): 79–124.

Owomoyela, Oyekan. "From Folklore to Literature: The Route from Roots in the African World." In *The African Diaspora: African Origins and New World Identities*, edited by I. Okpewho, A. A. Mazrui, and C. B. Davies, 275–89. Bloomington: Indiana University Press, 2001.

Oyelaran, Olasope. "Was Yoruba a Creole?" *Journal of the Linguistic Association of Nigeria* 1 (1982): 89–99.

Palmié, Stephan. "Against Syncretism: 'Africanizing' and 'Cubanizing' Discourses in American Orisa Worship." In *Counterworks: Managing the Diversity of Knowledge*, edited by Richard Fardon, 73–105. New York: Routledge, 1995.

———. *Wizards and Scientists: Explorations in Afro-Cuban Modernity and Tradition*. Durham, NC: Duke University Press, 2002.

Paquette, Robert L. *Sugar Is Made with Blood: The Conspiracy of La Escalera and the Conflict between Empires over Slavery in Cuba*. Middletown, CT: Wesleyan University Press, 1988.

Parkinson, John. "Yoruba Folklore." *Journal of African Society* 8, no. 30 (1909): 165–86.

Parratt, John K. "Religious Change in Yoruba Society—a Test Case." *Journal of Religion in Africa* 2, no. 2 (1969): 113–28.

Parratt, John. K., and A. R. I. Doi. "Some Further Aspects of Yoruba Syncretism." *Practical Anthropology* 16, no. 6 (1969): 252–56.

———. "Syncretism in Yorubaland: A Religious or Sociological Phenomenon?" *Practical Anthropology* 16, no. 3 (1969): 109–113.

Parrinder, Geoffrey. *West African Religion: Illustrated from the Beliefs and Practices of the Yoruba, Ewe, Akan, and Kindred Peoples*. London: Epworth Press, 1949.

Paul, Jutta. "La santería como resultado del proceso de transculturación en Cuba." *Biblioteca Nacional de José Martí* 23, no. 3 (1981): 123–36.

Peek, Philip M. *African Divination Systems: Ways of Knowing*. Indianapolis: Indiana University Press, 1991.

Peel, J. D. Y. "The Cultural Work of Yoruba Ethnogenesis." In *Pioneer, Patriot, and Patriarch: Samuel Johnson and the Yoruba People*, edited by Toyin Falola, 65–75. Madison: University of Wisconsin, African Studies Program, 1993.

———. "Making History: The Past in the Ijesha Present." *Man* 19, no. 1 (1984): 111–32.

———. "The Pastor and the *Babalawo*: The Interactions of Religions in Nineteenth-Century Yorubaland." *Africa* 60, no. 3 (1990): 338–69.

———. *Religious Encounter and the Making of the Yoruba*. Bloomington: Indiana University Press, 2001.

———. "Syncretism and Religious Change." *Comparative Studies in Society and History* 10, no. 2 (1968): 121–41.

Pelton, Robert. *The Trickster in West Africa: A Study of Mythic Irony and Sacred Delight*. Berkeley: University of California Press, 1980.

Pemberton, John, III. "The Dreadful God and the Divine King." In *Africa's Ogun*, edited by Sandra T. Barnes, 105–46. 2nd ed. Bloomington: Indiana University Press, 1997.

Pérez, Louis A., Jr. *Cuba in the American Imagination: Metaphor and the Imperial Ethos*. Chapel Hill: University of North Carolina Press, 2008.

———. *On Becoming Cuban: Identity, Nationality and Culture*. Chapel Hill: University of North Carolina Press, 2007.

———, ed. *Slaves, Sugar, and Colonial Society: Travel Accounts of Cuba, 1801–1899*. Wilmington: Scholarly Resources, Inc., 1992.

Pérez, Nancy. *El Cabildo Carabalí Isuama*. Santiago de Cuba: Editorial Oriente, 1982.

Pérez de la Riva, Francisco. *El Conde de Pozos Dulces: Un Revolucionario Sin Fuso*. Havana: Sociedad Economicas de Amigos del Paiz, 1950.

———. "Cuban *Palenques*." In *Maroon Societies: Rebel Slave Communities in the Americas*, edited by Richard Price, 49–59. 3rd ed. Baltimore: Johns Hopkins University Press, 1996.
Pérez de la Riva, Juan. *El Barracon y Otros Ensayos*. Havana: Editorial de Ciencias Sociales, 1975.
———. *Cuadro sinoptico de la esclavitud en Cuba y de la cultura Occidental*. Suplemento de la Revista Actas de Folklore. Havana: Seccion de Publicaciones del TNC, 1961.
———. *Documentos para la historia de las gentes sin historia*. 1960. Reprint, Havana: Biblioteca Nacional de José Martí, 1969.
Perez Mena, Andres I. "Cuban Santería, Haitian Vodun, Puerto Rican Spiritualism: A Multiculturalist Inquiry into Syncretism." *Journal for the Scientific Study of Religion* 37, no. 1 (1998): 15–28.
Pettinger, Alasdair, ed. *Always Elsewhere: Travels of the Black Atlantic*. London: Cassell, 1998.
Picton, John. "Keeping the Faith." In *Islamic Art in the 19th Century: Tradition, Innovation, and Eclecticism*, edited by Doris Behrens-Abouseif and Stephen Vernoit, 191–229. Leiden and Boston: Brill Academic Publishers, 2005.
Ponte, Antonio José. "Las lágrimas en el congrí," "Un arte de hacer ruinas," "A petición a Ochún," and "El frío del Malecón," In *Un arte de hacer ruinas y otros cuentos*, 43–49, 56–72, 74–87, 125–27. Mexico City: Aula Atlántica, Fondo de Cultura Económica, 2005.
Porter, James A. "The Trans-cultural Affinities of African Art." In *Africa from the Point of View of American Negro Scholars*, 119–30. Paris: Présence Africaine, 1958.
Prakash, Gyan, ed. *After Colonialism: Imperial Histories and Postcolonial Displacements*. Princeton, NJ: Princeton University Press, 1995.
Price, Richard. *Maroon Societies: Rebel Slave Communities in the Americas*. New York: Anchor, 1973.
Price, Sally, and Richard Price. *Maroon Arts: Cultural Vitality in the African Diaspora*. Boston: Beacon Press, 1999.
Primiano, Leonard Norman. "Vernacular Religion and the Search for Method in Religious Folklife." *Western Folklore* 54, no 1 (1995): 37–56.
Quine, W. V. *Word and Object*. Cambridge: MIT Press, 1960.
Quiñonez, Ernesto. *Chango's Fire*. New York: Rayo Imprint of Harper Collins Publishers, 2004.
Quirós, Oscar E. "Values and Aesthetics in Cuban Arts and Cinema." In *Artistic Representations of Latin American Diversity: Sources and Collections*, 151–71. Albuquerque: SALALM Secretariat, University of New Mexico, 1989.
Raboteau, Albert J. "African Religions in America: Theoretical Perspectives." In *Global Dimensions of the African Diaspora*, edited by Jospeh E. Harris, 65–82. Washington, DC: Howard University Press, 1993.
Radano, Ronald M. "Denoting Difference: The Writing of the Slave Spirituals." *Critical Inquiry* 22 (1966): 506–544.
Rahier, Jean. "Blackness as a Process of Creolization: The Afro-Esmeraldian *Decimas* (Ecuador)." In *The African Diaspora: African Origins and New World Identities*, edited by Isadore Okpewho, Carole Boyce Davies, Ali A. Mazrui, 290–314. Bloomington: Indiana University Press, 1999.

Rama, Angel. *La Ciudad Letrada.* Hanover, NH: Ediciones del Norte, 1984.
Ramos, Arthur. *The Negro in Brazil.* Translated from Portuguese by Richard Pattee. Washington, DC: Associated Publishers, 1939.
———. *O Folk-Lore Negro do Brasil: Demopsychologia e Psychanalyse.* Rio de Janeiro, Brazil: Civilização Brasileira, 1935.
Ranger, Terence. *Dance and Society in Eastern Africa, 1890–1970: The Beni Ngoma.* Berkeley: University of California Press, 1975.
———. "The Invention of Tradition in Colonial Africa." In *The Invention of Tradition,* edited by Eric Hobsbawm and Terence Ranger, 211–62. Cambridge: Cambridge University Press, 1983.
Rewt, Polly T. "The African Diaspora and Its Origins." *Research in African Literatures* (Winter 1998): 3–15.
Ribeiro, João. *O Elemento Negro: Historia, Folklore, Linguistica.* Rio de Janeiro, Brazil: Record, 1939.
Ribeiro, Rene. *Cultos Afrobrasileiros do Recife: Un Estudo Adjustamento Social.* Recife, Brazil: Boletim do Instituto Joaquim Nabuco, 1952.
———. "Significado socio-cultural das ceremonias de Ibeji." *Revista de Antropologia* 5, no. 2 (1957): 129–44.
Ricoeur, Paul. *Memory, History, Forgetting.* Translated by Kathleen Blamey and David Pellauer. Chicago: University of Chicago Press, 2006.
Riesch, Flavio. "Political and Cultural Cross-Dressing: Negotiating a Second-Generation Cuban-American Identity." In *Bridges to Cuba/Puentes a Cuba,* edited by Ruth Behar, 57–71. Ann Arbor: University of Michigan Press, 1996.
Rivas, Mercedes. "El texto como discurso en el relato antiesclavista cubano." In *Esclavitud y narrativa en el siglo XIX cubano: Enfoques reientes,* edited by Salvador Arias, 1–42. Havana: Editorial Academica, 1995.
Roach, Joséph. *Cities of the Dead: Circum-Atlantic Performance.* New York: Columbia University Press, 1996.
Roberts, John Smith. *The Impact of Latin American Music.* Tivoli, NY: Original Music, 1985.
Roberts, John W. *From Trickster to Badman: The Black Folk Hero in Slavery and Freedom.* Philadelphia: University of Pennsylvania Press, 1990.
Robertson, R. *Globalisation.* London: Sage, 1992.
———. "Globalisation: Time-Space and Homogeneity-Heterogeneity." In *Global Modernities,* edited by Mike Featherstone, Scott Lash, and Roland Robertson, London: Sage, 1995.
Rodrigues, Raymundo Nina. *O animismo fetichista dos negros bahianos.* Preface by Arthur Ramos. Rio de Janeiro, Brazil: Civilização Brasileira, 1935.
Rodríguez, Enrique Sosa. *Negreros catalanes y gaditanos en la trata Cubana, 1827–1833.* Colección la Fuente Viva. Havana: Fundación Fernando Ortiz, 1998.
Romberg, Raquel. "'Today, Changó is Changó': How Africanness Becomes a Ritual Commodity in Puerto Rico." *Western Folklore* 66, nos. 1–2 (2007): 75–106.
———. *Witchcraft and Welfare: Spiritual Capital and the Business of Magic in Modern Puerto Rico.* Austin: University of Texas Press, 2003.
Rosaldo, R. *Culture and Truth: The Remaking of Social Analysis.* Boston: Beacon Press, 1989.
Roth, H. Ling. *Great Benin: Its Customs, Art, and Horrors.* London: Routledge and Kegan Paul, 1968.

Saco, José Antonio. *Coleccion de papeles cientificos, historicos, politicos, y de otros ramos sobre la isla de Cuba*. Havana: Editorial Nacional de Cuba, 1962.

———, ed. *Historia de la esclavitud de la raza Africana en el nuevo mundo, y en especial en los paises Americo-hispanos*. Prologue and compiled by Fernando Ortiz. 4 vols. Havana: Coleccíon de Libros Cubanos, vol. 37, 1938.

Safran, W. "Diasporas in Modern Societies: Myths of Homeland and Return." *Diaspora* 1 (1991): 83–99.

Sainz, Enrique. *La literatura cubana de 1700 a 1790*. Havana: Editorial Letras Cubanas, 1983.

Saldívar, Ramón. *The Borderlands of Culture: Américo Paredes and the Transnational Imaginary*. Durham, NC: Duke University Press, 2006.

Sandoval, Alonso de, S. J. *De instauranda aethiopum salute: El mundo de la esclavitud negra en America*. (1627). Reprint, Bogota, Colombia: Empresa Nacional de Publicaciones, 1956.

———. *Un tratado sobre la esclavitud*. Tranlated, edited and with an introduction by Enriqueta Vila Vilar. Madrid: Alianza Editorial, 1987.

Sangode, H. L., and Iyalosa Ayobunmi Sosi. *The Cult of Sango*. Brooklyn, NY: Athelia Henrietta Press, 1996.

Sanguily, Manuel. "Cromitos Cubanos." In *Letras: Cultura en Cuba*, edited by A. C. Ballestoer, 149–64. 1893. Reprint, Havana: Editorial Pueblo y Educación, 1989.

Sansone, Livio. "The New Blacks from Bahia: Local and Global in Afro-Bahia." *Identities* 3 (1997): 457–94.

Santa Cruz y Mallen, Francisco Javier de. *Historia de familias cubanas*. Havana: Editorial Hercules, 1940.

Sapir, Edward. "Culture, Genuine, and Spurious." In *The Selected Writings of Edward Sapir*, edited by David G. Mandelbaum, 308–31. 1924. Reprint, Berkeley: University of California Press, 1951.

Sarduy, Pedro Pérez. "Writing from Babylon." In *The Portable Island: Cubans at Home in the World*, edited by Ruth Behar and Lucía M. Suárez, 153–160. New York: Palgrave Macmillan, 2008.

Sarduy, Pedro Pérez, and Jean Stubbs. "The Rite of Social Communion." In *AfroCuba: An Anthology of Cuban Writing on Race, Politics, and Culture*, edited by Pérez Sarduy and J. Stubbs, 3–26. New York: Ocean Press, 1993.

Sarracino, Rodolfo. "Back to Africa." In *AfroCuba: An Anthology of Cuban Writing on Race, Politics, and Culture*, 67–76. New York: Ocean Press, 1993.

———. *Los que volvieron a Africa*. Havana: Editorial de Ciencias Sociales, 1988.

Scher, Philip. "Unveiling the Orisha." In *Africa's Ogun*, edited by Sandra Barnes, 315–31. 2nd ed. Bloomington: Indiana University Press, 1996.

Scheub, Harold. *African Oral Narratives, Proverbs, Riddles, Poetry, and Song*. Boston: G. K. Hall, 1977.

Schön, James Frederick, and Samuel Crowther. *Journals of the Rev. James Frederick Schön and Mr. Samuel Crowther, who, with the Sanction of Her Majesty's Government, accompanied the Expedition up the River Niger in 1841, on behalf of the Church Missionary Society*. London: Hatchard and Son, 1842.

Schwab, William B. "The Growth and Conflicts of Religion in a Modern Yoruba Community." *Zaire* 6, no. 8 (1952): 829–35.

Schwartz, Ronald. *Latin American Films, 1932–1994: A Critical Filmography.* London: McFarland, 1997.
Scott, David. "This Event, This Memory: Notes on the Anthropology of African Diasporas in the New World." *Diaspora* 1 (1991): 261–83.
Scott, James C. *Domination and the Arts of Resistance: Hidden Transcripts.* New Haven, CT: Yale University Press, 1990.
Scott, Rebecca J. *Degrees of Freedom: Louisiana and Cuba after Slavery.* Cambridge, MA: Belknap Press, 2005.
———. "Fault Lines, Color Lines, and Party Lines: Race, Labor, and Collective Action in Louisiana and Cuba, 1862–1912." *Beyond Slavery: Explorations of Race, Labor, and Citizenship in Postemancipation Societies,* edited by Frederick Cooper, Thomas C. Holt, and Rebecca J. Scott, 61–106. Chapel Hill: University of North Carolina Press, 2000.
Segal, R. *The Black Diaspora.* London: Faber and Faber, 1995.
Sennett, Richard. "Cosmopolitanism and the Social Experience of Cities." In *Conceiving Cosmopolitanism: Theory, Context, and Practice,* edited by Steven Vertorec and Robin Cohen, 42–48. New York: Oxford University Press, 2002.
Serviat, Pedro. *El problema negro en Cuba y su solución definitiva.* Havana: Editora Política, 1986.
Sewell, William H. "The Concept(s) of Culture." In *Beyond the Cultural Turn,* edited by Lynn Hunt and V. E. Bonnell, 35–61. Berkeley: University of California Press, 1999.
Shaw, Rosalind. "Cannibal Transformations: Colonialism and Commodification in the Sierra Leone Hinterland." In *Magical Interpretations, Material Realities,* edited by Henrietta L. Moore and Todd Sanders, 50–70. New York: Routledge, 2002.
Shaw, Rosalind, and M. C. Jedrej. *Dreaming Religion and Society in Africa,* 1–20. New York: E. J. Brill, 1992.
Shaw, Rosalind, and Charles Stewart, eds. "Introduction: Problematizing Syncretism." In *Syncretism/Anti-syncretism: The Politics of Religious Synthesis,* 1–26. New York: Routledge, 1994.
Simpson, George E. "Religious Changes in Southwestern Nigeria." *Anthropological Quarterly* 43, no. 2 (1970): 79–92.
———. "Selected Yoruba Rituals: 1964." *Nigerian Journal of Economic and Social Studies* 7, no. 3 (1965): 311–24.
———. "The Shango Cult in Nigeria and Trinidad." *American Anthropologist* 64, no. 6 (1962): 1204–19.
———. *The Shango Cult in Trinidad.* Rio Piedras, Puerto Rico: Institute of Caribbean Studies, 1965.
———. "The Vodun Cult in Haiti." *African Notes* 3, no. 2 (1965): 11–21.
Skinner, Elliot P. "The Dialectic between Diasporas and Homelands." In *Global Dimensions of the African Diaspora,* edited by J. Harris, 17–45. Washington, DC: Howard University Press, 1982.
———. "The Restoration of African Identity for a New Millennium." In *The African Diaspora: African Origins and New World Identities,* edited by I. Okpewho, C. Boyce Davies, A. A. Mazrui, 28–48. Bloomington: Indiana University Press, 1999.

Smart, N. "The Importance of Diasporas." In *Gilgul: Essays on Transformation, Revolution and Permanence in the History of Religions*, edited by S. Shaked, D. Shulman, and G. A. G. Stoumsa, 288–97. Leiden, Netherlands: E. J. Brill, 1987.

Smith, Robert S. *Kingdoms of the Yoruba*. 3rd ed. Madison: University of Wisconsin Press, 1988.

———. *The Lagos Consulate, 1851–1861*. London: Macmillan; and Lagos: University of Lagos Press, 1978.

Smythe, Hugh H. "The African Elite in Nigeria." In *Africa from the Point of View of American Negro Scholars*, 71–82. Paris: Présence Africaine, 1958.

Sodipo, J. O. "Notes on the Concept of Cause and Chance in Yoruba Traditional Thought." *Second Order* 2, no. 2 (1973): 12–20.

Soledad, R. de la, and M. J. Sanjuan. *Ibó: Yorubas en Tierras Cubanas*. Miami: Ediciónes Universal, 1988.

Sommer, Doris. *Foundational Fictions: The National Romances of Latin America*. Berkeley: University of California Press, 1991.

Sonuga, Gbenga. *Lagos State: Life and Culture*. Vol. 1. Ikeja, Lagos: Ministry of Information and Culture, Government of Lagos State of Nigeria, 1987.

Soyinka, Wole. *Aké: The Years of Childhood*. New York: Vintage, 1989.

Spivak, Gayatri C. "Can the Subaltern Speak? Speculations on Widow-Sacrifice." *Wedge* 7–8 (1985): 120–30.

Stephens, John, ed. *African Attitudes towards Health and Healing*. Ibadan, Nigeria: 1964.

Stern, Peter A. "Art and State in Postrevolutionary Mexico and Cuba." In *Artistic Representations of Latin American Diversity: Sources and Collections*, 17–32. Albuquerque: SALALM Secretariat, University of New Mexico, 1989.

Stern, Stephen, and J. A. Cicala, eds. *Creative Ethnicity*. Logan: Utah State University Press, 1991.

Stewart, Susan. *On Longing: Narratives of the Miniature, the Gigantic, the Souvenir, the Collection*. Baltimore: John Hopkins University Press, 1984.

Stone, R. H. *Yoruba Lore and the Universe*. Ibadan, Nigeria: Institute of Education University of Ibadan, 1965.

Suárez, Lucia M. "Our Memories, Ourselves." In *The Portable Island: Cubans at Home in the World*, edited by Ruth Behar, Lucia M. Suárez, 9–16. New York: Palgreve Macmillan, 2008.

Suárez y Romero, Anselmo. *Francisco: Novela Cubana*. New York: Imprenta y Libreria de N. Ponce de León, 1880.

———. "José de la Luz y Caballero." In *Letras: Cultura en Cuba*, 281–84. 1865. Reprint, Havana: Editorial Pueblo y Educación, 1989.

Sydow, Carl Wilhelm von. *Selected Papers on Folklore*. Copenhagen: Rosenkilde and Bagger, 1948.

Tannenbaum, Frank. *Slave and Citizen*. 1946. Reprint, Boston: Beacon Press, 1992.

Thomas, David H. *Columbian Consequences*. Washington, DC: Smithsonian Institution Press, 1990.

Thompson, Robert Farris. *Black Gods and Kings: Yoruba Art at UCLA*. Bloomington: Indiana University Press, 1971. Reprint, 1976.

———. "Divine Countenance: Art and Altars of the Black Atlantic World." In *Divine Inspiration: From Benin to Bahia*, edited by Phyllis Galembo, 1–17. Albuquerque: University of New Mexico Press, 1989.

———. *Flash of the Spirit: African and Afro-American Art and Philosophy*. New York: Vintage, 1984.

———. "The Three Warriors: Atlantic Altars of Esu, Ogun, and Osoosi." In *The Yoruba Artist: New Theoretical Perspectives on African Arts*, edited by Rowland Abiodun, Henry J. Drewal, and John Pemberton III, 225–39. Washington, DC: Smithsonian Institution Press, 1994.

Thompson, Vincent B. *The Making of the African Diaspora in the Americas, 1441–1900*. New York: Longman, 1987.

Thornton, John K. *Africa and the Africans in the Making of the Atlantic World, 1400–1680*. New York: Cambridge University Press, 1992.

Thornton, John K., and Linda M. Heywood. *Central Africans, Atlantic Creoles, and the Foundation of the Americas, 1585–1660*. Cambridge: Cambridge University Press, 2007.

Troyano, Alina. *I, Carmelita Tropicana: Performing between Cultures*. Boston: Beacon Press, 2000.

Turner, Harold Walter. "African Religious Movements." *Comparative Studies in Society and History* 8, no. 3 (1966): 281–94.

———. "Pagan Features in West African Independent Churches." *Practical Anthropology* 12, no. 4 (1965): 145–51.

Turner, Jerry M. "Les Brésiliens: The Impact of Former Brazilian Slaves upon Dahomey." PhD diss., Boston University. Ann Arbor, MI: University Microfilms, 1975.

Turner, Lorenzo. "African Survivals in the New World with Special Emphasis on the Arts." In *Africa from the Point of View of American Negro Scholars*, 101–16. Paris: Présence Africaine, 1958.

———. "Some Contacts of Brazilian Ex-Slaves with Nigeria, West Africa." *Journal of Negro History* 27 (1942).

Usman, Aribidesi A. "The Nineteenth-Century Black Atlantic." In *The Atlantic World, 1450–2000*, edited by Toyin Falola and Kevin D. Roberts, 114–34. Bloomington: Indiana University Press, 2008.

Valdés, Nelson P. "Cuban Political Culture: Between Betrayal and Death." In *Cuba in Transition*, edited by Sandor Halebsky and John M. Kirk, 207–29. San Francisco: Westview Press, 1992.

Valdés, Zoé. *Te di la vida entera: Una vida truncada por un beso*. 1996. Reprint, Barcelona: Editorial Planeta, 1998.

Van de Veer, Peter. "Syncretism, Multiculturalism and the Discourse of Tolerance." In *Syncretism/Anti-syncretism: The Politics of Religious Synthesis*, edited by Charles Stewart and Rosalind Shaw, 196–211. New York: Routledge, 1994.

Van Gennep, A. *The Rites of Passage*. 1908. Reprint, London: Kegan Paul, 1965.

Varela y Morales, Felix. *El Habanero: Papel politico, cientifico y literario, Vol. 9 (1824–28)*. Seria Biblioteca de Autores Cubanos 4. Havana: Editorial Nacional, La Universidad de la Habana, 1945.

Varona, José Enrique. "La arte de la vida." In *Letras: Cultura en Cuba*, edited by A. C. Ballester, 25–26. Havana: Editorial Pueblo y Educación, 1989.

———. "La importancia social del arte." In *Letras: Cultura en Cuba*, edited by A. C. Ballester, 5–14. Havana: Editorial Pueblo y Educación, 1989.
Verger, Pierre Fatumbi. *Bahia and the West African Trade, 1549–1851*. Ibadan, Nigeria: Ibadan University Press, 1964.
———. *Dieux d'Afrique*. Paris: Paul Hartman, 1954.
———. *Ewe: The Use of Plants in Yoruba Society*. São Paulo, Brazil: Odebrecht, 1995.
———. "Influence du Brésil au Golfe du Benin." *Les Afro-Américains*. Memoir 27. Dakar: IFAN, 1953.
———. "Nigeria, Brazil, and Cuba." *Nigeria, 1960: A Special Independence Issue of Nigeria Magazine*, 113–123. Lagos: Federal Ministry of Information, 1960.
———. "Nigeria, Brésil et Cuba." *Le Nigeria: Edition Spéciale du Nigeria Magazine Independent*, March 1962, 125–36.
———. *Notes sur le culte des Orisa et Vodu a Bahia . . . au Brésil et a l'Ancienne Côte des Esclaves en Afrique*. Memoir 51. Dakar: IFAN, 1957.
———. "Oral Tradition in the Cult of the Orishas and Its Connection with the History of the Yoruba." *Journal of the Historical Society of Nigeria* 1, no. 1 (1956): 61–64.
———. *Trade Relations between the Bight of Benin and Bahia from the 17th to 19th Century*. Translated by Evelyn Crawford. Ibadan, Nigeria: Ibadan University Press, 1976.
———. "Trance and Convention in Nago-Yoruba Spirit Mediumship." In *Spirit Mediumship and Society in Africa*, edited by John Beattie, 50–66. London: Routledge and Kegan Paul, 1969.
———. "The Yoruba High God: A Review of the Sources." *Odu* 2 (1966): 19–40.
———. "Yoruba Influences in Brazil." *Odu* 1 (1955): 3–11.
Viarnés, Carrie. "Cultural Memory in Afro-Cuban Possession: Problematizing Spiritual Categories, Resurfacing 'Other' Histories." *Western Folklore* 66, nos. 1–2 (Winter 2006–Spring 2007): 127–60.
Villaverde, Cirilo. *Cecilia Valdes*. 1830. Reprint, Lima: Primer Festival del Libro Cubano, 1959.
———. *Cecilia valdes o la loma del angel: Novela de costumbres cubanas*. Havana: Talleres Tipograficos de la Academia America Arias, 1830.
Voeks, Peter M. *The Sacred Leaves of Candomblé*. Bloomington: Indiana University Press, 1997.
———. *Slave and Soldier: The Military Impact of Blacks in the Colonial Americas*. New York: Garland, 1993.
Vogel, Susan. "Future Traditions." In *Africa Explores: 20th Century African Art*, edited by Susan M. Vogel, 94–113. New York: Center for African Art, 1991.
Von Humboldt, Alexander. *The Island of Cuba*. Translated by J. S. Thrasher. New York: Derby and Jackson, 1801, 1856.
Wade, Peter. *Race and Ethnicity in Latin America*. London: Pluto Press, 1997.
Wafer, J., and Hedimo Rodrigues Santana. "Africa in Brazil: Cultural Politics and the Candomblé Religion." *Folklore Forum* 23 (1990): 1–2, 98–114.
Wagner, Roy. *The Invention of Culture*. Chicago: University of Chicago Press, 1981.
Walker, Barbara K., and W. Walker. *Nigerian Folk Tales*. New Brunswick, NJ: Rutgers University Press, 1961.

Walker, Sheila S. "Introduction: Are You Hip to the Jive? (Re)Writing/Righting the Pan-African Discourse." In *African Roots/American Cultures: Africa in the Creation of the Americas*, edited by Sheila S. Walker, 1–44. Lanham, MD: Rowman & Littlefield, 2001.

Walvin, James. *Questioning Slavery*. New York: Routledge, 1996.

Warner-Lewis, Maureen. "Cultural Reconfigurations in the African Caribbean." In *The African Diaspora: African Origins and New World Identities*, edited by Isidore Okpewho, Carole Boyce Davies, and Ali A. Mazrui, 19–27. Bloomington: Indiana Unversity Press, 1999.

———. *Trinidad Yoruba: From Mother Tongue to Memory*. Tuscaloosa: University of Alabama Press, 1996.

———. *Yoruba Songs in Trinidad*. London: Karnak House, 1995.

Waterman, Christopher. *Jùjú: A Social History and Ethnography of an African Popular Music*. Chicago: University of Chicago Press, 1990.

Welch, David Baillie. "Aspects of Vocal Performance in Sango Praise-Poetry and Song." PhD diss., Northwestern University, 1972.

Welch, Kimberly. "Our Hunger Is Our Song: The Politics of Race in Cuba, 1900–1920." In *The African Diaspora: African Origins and New World Identities*, edited by Isidore Okpewho, Carole Boyce Davies, and Ali A. Mazrui, 178–96. Bloomington: Indiana University Press, 1999.

Werner, Alice. "African Folklore." *Contemporary Review* 70 (1896): 377–90.

———. "Language and Folklore in West Africa." *Journal of the African Society* 6 (1906–1907): 65–83.

West, Dennis. "Slavery and Cinema in Cuba: The Case of Gutiérrez Alea's The Last Supper." *Western Journal of Black Studies* 3, no. 2 (1979): 128–33.

Westcott, Joan A. "The Sculpture and Myths of Eshu Elegba, the Yoruba Trickster: Definition and Interpretation in Yoruba Iconography." *Africa* 32, no. 4 (1962): 336–54.

West-Dúran, Alan. "Going Home via Africa and Cayo Hueso." In *The Portable Island: Cubans at Home in the World*, edited by Ruth Behar and Lucía M. Suárez, 145–52. New York: Palgrave Macmillan, 2008.

Whorf, Benjamin. *Language, Thought, and Reality*. New York: MIT Press, 1956.

Willett, Frank. *Ife in the History of West African Sculpture*. London: Thames and Hudson, 1967.

———. "A Missing Millennium? From Nok to Ife and Beyond." In *Arte in Africa*, edited by Ezio Bassani, 87–100. Modena, Italy: Edizioni Panini, 1986.

———. "New Light on the Ife-Benin Relationship." *African Forum* 3, no. 4 (1970): 28–34.

Wilson, Rob, and Wimal Dissanayake, eds. *Global/local: Cultural Production and the Transnational Imaginary*. Durham, NC: Duke University Press, 1996.

Witte, Hans. "Fishes of the Earth: Mudfish Symbolism in Yoruba Iconography." *Visible Religion: Annual for Religious Iconography* 1 (1982): 154–74.

———. *Ifa and Esu: Iconography of Order and Disorder*. Soest, Netherlands: Kunsthandel Luttik, 1984.

———. "Images of a Yoruba Water-Spirit." In *Effigies Dei: Essays on the History of Religions*, edited by D. van der Plas. Leiden, Netherlands: Brill, 1987.

———. "La quête du sens dans le symbolisme Yoruba: Le cas d'Erinle." *International Review for the History of Religions* 38, no. 1 (1991): 59–79.

Wood, J. B. *Awon akiyesi nipa itan ilu Eko*. Lagos: Church Missionary Society Bookshop, 1934.

———. *Historical Notices of Lagos, West Africa and on the Inhabitants of Lagos*. 1878. Reprint, Lagos: Church Missionary Society Bookshop, 1933.

Wright, Irene, ed. "Dispatches of Spanish Officials Bearing on the Free Negro Settlement of Gracia Real de Santa Teresa de Mose, Florida." *Journal of Negro History* 9 (1924): 144–96.

Wyndham, John. *Myths of Ife*. London: Erksine Macdonald, 1921.

———. "Yoruba Folklore: The Creation." *Man* 19 (1919): 107–8.

Yai, Olabiyi Babalola. "Les 'Aguda' (Afró-Brésiliens) du Golfe du Bénin." *Lusotopie* (1997): 275–84.

———. "From Vodun to Mawu: Monotheism and History in the Fon Cultural Area." In *L'Invention religieuse: histoire et religion en Afrique noir*, edited by Jean-Pierre Chretien, 241–65. Colloque du Centre de Recherches Africaines, Universite de Paris III, 1992.

———. "The Identity, Contributions, and Ideology of the Aguda (Afro-Brazilians) of the Gulf of Benin: A Reinterpretation." In *Rethinking the African Diaspora: The Making of a Black Atlantic World in the Bight of Benin and Brazil*, edited by Kristin Mann and Edna G. Bay, 72–82. Portland, OR: Frank Cass, 2001.

———. "'The Path Is Open': The Legacy of Melville and Frances Herskovits in African Oral Narrative Analysis." *Research in African Literatures* 30, no. 2 (1999): 1–16.

———. "In Praise of Metonymy: The Concepts of 'Tradition' and 'Creativity' in the Transmission of Yoruba Artistry over Time and Space." In *The Yoruba Artist: New Theoretical Perspectives of African Art*, edited by Rowland Abiodun, Henry J. Drewal, and John Pemberton III, 107–15. Washington, DC: Smithsonian Institution Press, 1994.

———. "Religious Dialogue, Peace and the Responsibility of the Translator: Some West African Examples." *Religion and Peace in Multi-Faith Nigeria*, edited by J. Olupona, 133–46. Ile-Ife, Nigeria: Obafemi Awolowo University, 1992.

Yankah, Kwesi. *Speaking for the Chief: Okyeame and the Politics of Akan Royal Oratory*. Bloomington: Indiana University Press, 1995.

Zanetti Lecuona, Oscar. *Sugar and Railroads: A Cuban History, 1837–1959*. Translated from Spanish by Franklin W. Knight and Mary Todd. Chapel Hill: University of North Carolina Press, 1998.

Zeuske, Michael. "'El Cimarrón y las Consecuencias de la Guerra del 95.' Un Repaso de la Biografía de Esteban Montejo." *Revista de Indias* 43, no. 212 (1998): 65–84.

Index

Note: Page numbers in *italics* indicate figures.

abakuás, 143–44, 193n21
Aberdeen, Lord, 33
Abiodun, Rowland, 93
Abrahams, Roger, 3, 11, 135–36
acculturation, 25, 50, 89; transculturation versus, 137, 165n48. *See also* creolization
Achebe, Chinua, 131
Acosta, Augustín, 158
Acosta, Manuel, 158
Adderley, Rosanne, 29, 170n62
Adele, Oba, 60
Adorno, Rolena, 10, 20
agbo, 55
Aguda, 2, 10–11, 88–110, 141–43; case studies of, 40–50, 157–61; cultural markers of, 99–103; Ikoyi Cemetery and, *96–98,* 103–4; Lagos neighborhood of, 71, 149; legacy of, 5, 54; religious practices of, 18–20, 106–10, 155–56; Saros and, 72, 104–6
Aguiar, Pancho, 43
Aguiar, Scipiano, 44
Aguirre, Rosalia, 161
Ajikobi, Dimeji, 79
Akinsemoyin, Oba, 58–59, 81, 82
Akitoye, 64
Akitoyi, Serafina, 95, 100
amalgamation: cultural, 12–13, 102, 119, 137, 152, 156; ethnic, 78, 86, 122, 173n5. *See also* creolization
Anti-Slavery Reporter (periodical), 28, 40, 72, 168n1
Anti-Slavery Squadron, 23, 29–30, 35, 77
Aponte, José Antonio, 32
Aponte rebellion, 31–32, 70, 169n49, 178n131

Appadurai, Arjun, 186n3, 196n77
Apter, Andrew, 3
ararás, 144
Aristotle, 92
asa, 18, 144
Aseru (warlord), 57
Asian immigrants, 14, 20; Chinese slaves in Cuba and, 35; Cuban novels on, 171n79; as indentured workers, 42
Asipa (chief), 57
atenedenu, 19
autonomistas, 129
awo, 16
Awori people, 51–53
Aye, Manuel, 48
Ayorinde, Christine, 70, 137

baba isale relationships, 65
babalawo. See Ifa priests
Backhouse, George C., 32, 36
Backhouse, Grace Catherine, 32
Bahamas, 27, 29
Bahia, Brazil, 151; Aguda and, 58, 59, 78, 88, 89; Candomblé and, 107; Lagos and, 85, 88; Mixed Commission Courts in, 33; Nago Yoruba of, 71; Ouidah and, 58–59, 74–75, 78, 88, 155; slave revolt in, 75
Banks, Joseph "Flycatcher," 26
Barber, Karin, 39, 69
Barnes, Sandra. *See baba isale* relationships
Barnet, Miguel, 11, 131–34, 138
Barriero, Manuel, 159
Bascom, William, 9, 154
batik cloth, 104–5, 149
Bauman, Richard, 2

Behar, Ruth, 5, 138
Ben-Amos, Dan, 2
Bendix, Regina, 2
Benezet, Anthony, 24
Benin Kingdom, 52, 56–57
Benítez Rojo, Antonio, 12, 138
Bini people, 51–53; Ijebu Yoruba and, 149; *oba*-ship and, 55
Boa masquerades, 79, 84–85, 88, 148, 155, 182n58. *See also* carnival
Bolívar, Natalia, 138
Borges da Silva, Lazaro, 107
Borghero, Francisco, 107
Bosc, Catalina, 161
bozales, 16, 35, 49, 122. *See also* slavery
Brazil. *See* Bahia
Briggs, Charles, 2
Brown, Christopher Leslie, 24, 26
Brown, David Hilary, 181n49

Caballero, Father, 123
Cabeza de Vaca, Alvar Núñez, 120
cabildos, 16–17, 28, 149; coalition building by, 69; heterogeneity of, 116; Lucumí identity in, 71, 77; runaway slaves and, 118; Síndico Protector de Esclavos and, 35; slave conspiracies and, 32. See also *sociedades de color*
Cabrera Infante, Guillermo, 137
Cabrera, Lydia, 137, 138, 153
Cabrera, Margarita, 43, 44
Camaroon, Carabali from, 44, 161
Campos family, 94–99, 104; Martins family and, 106, 136; religion of, 155–56. *See also* Cuban Lodge
Campos, Hilario, 14, 21–22, 50; family of, 6–7; father of, 95; granddaughters of, 61, 94–99; grave of, 95, *97, 98,* 103; religious practices of, 106, 110
Canary Islands, 122–23, 125
Candomblé, 17, 79, 147; creolization of, 76, 90, 107, 152; *iyalosha* in, 182n59; in Lagos, 85; Martiniano in, 171n80; masquerade in, 85. *See also* Palo Mayombe
Carabali people, 44, 161
La Caridad del Cobre, 15–16, 155

carnival, 38, 105; masquerades and, 79, 84–85, 88, 148, 155
Carpentier, Alejo, 137
Carrera, Pedro, 47
Carretas. *See* Boa masquerades
casa de santo, 147
Casanovas, Joān, 35
Castellanos, Isabel, 138
Catholicism, 7; Africanized forms of, 76, 107; *cabildos* and, 28, 84; folk, 15–18, 75–76, 113, 134, 147–48; Holy Cross Cathedral and, 71, 84, 104, 107; marriage in, 40; *orisha* worship and, 70, 84, 95, 107–10, 136, 155–56; saints of, 16–18, 84, 108–9, 113, 155; transubstantiation in, 166n63. *See also* Christianity
Chachas, 75
Chango, 178n130
Childs, Matt D., 70, 116
Christianity, 16, 25, 28, 62–63; diasporic, 62–63, 76–79, 84–86, 109. *See also* Catholicism
Church Missionary Society (CMS), 24, 36, 56; Egba Yoruba and, 60; founding of, 25; *orisha* worship and, 107; Saros and, 77, 78. *See also* missionaries
cimarrones, 11, 117–18, 131. *See also* slavery
Ciudad Letrada (Rama), 20, 120–21, 127, 132, 138
Clark, Joseph, 40
Clarke, Lorenzo, 41–43, 49, 123, 160, 161
Clarkson, Thomas, 24
Clifford, James, 152–53
CMS. *See* Church Missionary Society
coalition building, 68–70
coartadas, 47, 158, 159
Cohen, Abner, 76, 145
Cole, Patrick Dele, 54
"community-ship," 87
Congo, 13, 16, 44; religious beliefs from, 78–79, 133–34, 138, 143–44, 188n44, 190n119; Santería and, 90
Coupland, Reginald, 25
creoles, 70, 121; "Atlantic," 192n161; *reformistas,* 129; religious practices of,

16; runaway slaves and, 117–18; of Sierra Leone, 27, 76–77; stereotypes of, 126
creolization, 8, 119–22; Abrahams on, 3, 11; amalgamation and, 86, 89, 173n5; of Candomblé, 76, 90, 107, 152; *cruzado* identity and, 144–45; del Monte on, 125; folkloristics and, 136–39; postcolonial, 119; of Santería, 90
Cros Sandoval, Mercedes, 122, 138
Crowther, Samuel Ajayi, 21, 36, 63, 77, 121
Crusati, Gabriel, 44–45, 159
cruzado identity, 144–45. *See also* creolization
Cuba: *emancipados* of, 28–29; folkloristics of, 136–39; Haiti and, 119; migrants to U.S. from, 22; nationalist movement in, 128–36; 1959 Revolution of, 138; Spanish-American War and, 143; Ten Years' War of, 70, 112, 114, 129, 132, 135; U.S. campaign for annexation of, 32–33; virgin patron of, 15–16, 155; war of independence of, 112, 126–27, 131, 135
Cuban Lodge (Lagos), 66, 88; cultural mixing at, 104–6; founder of, 6–7; masquerades at, 85; photographs of, *91*, 185n47

dance, 17, 88, 105–6, 122, 155, 175n38
Da Silva, Lazaro Borges, 107
Da Silva family, 40; in Southampton, 45, 89, 99, 151
Da Souza family, 59, 75, 78
Dawodu, Fagbemi, 61–63
Dawodu, Mabinouri, 61–63, 83–84
de la Cruz, Manuel, 123–24
de la Fuente, Alejandro, 20, 135
del Monte, Domingo, 26, 31, 125–28, 135, 189n81
Deschamps Chapeaux, Pedro, 172n109
diasporic communities, 7, 101–2; approaches to, 9; Christianity in, 62–63, 76–79, 84–86, 109; creating home in, 142–45; marginality and, 145–56
diasporic sensibilities, 39–40, 48, 78, 145; creative elements in, 3–4, 60–61, 90, 101, 142; religious practices and, 6, 11, 62, 85–86, 99, 109, 147–48; Scott on, 115; social networks and, 56, 63, 68, 73, 76
Díaz del Castillo, Bernal, 120
Diaz Fabelo, Teodoro, 137
divination. *See* Ifa divination
Dorson, Richard, 9
Dosalu, John Baptiste, 36–37, 171n85
Dosumu, 64
Droseo, Luis, 44
Dundes, Alan, 2

ebo. *See* sacrifice
Egba Yoruba, 51, 53; British missionaries and, 60; religious practices of, 110
Egungun masquerade, 79, 85, 182n70
Egungun shrine, 182n70
Eko. *See* Lagos
emancipados, 123, 149; bribery of, 46; government terms for, 42
Embale, Carlos, 167n78
Equiano, Olaudah, 27
Escalera slave uprisings, 31, 32, 94, 118–19
Escovedo, Antonio, 42
ese, 104–5
esin ibile, 17, 152, 155
Espiritismo, 145
Estenoz, Evaristo, 116
Evangelical Movement, 24
Eyo masquerade, 182n70

Fabian, Johannes, 92
Ferrer, Ada, 70, 186n2
Fothergill, John, 24
Fusco, Coco, 138, 147

Gabarao, Oba, 58
Galembo, Phyllis, 154
ganadoras, 34
Garcia, Cristina, 138
Garcia, Dolores, 160
Garcia, Maria Rosalia, 42–43, 160–61
Geertz, Clifford, 153
Giral, Sergio, 189n81

Glassie, Henry, 2
globalization, 6, 8, 20–22, 144
Gómez, Juan Gualberto, 117, 127–29
Gomez, Michael A., 120
Gómez de Avellaneda, Gertrudis, 126
Gooding, Anastasia, 95; grave of, 96, 103–4, 185n48
Gooding-King, Aderemi, 6–7, 72–73, 76, 94–95; on Boa masquerades, 84; childhood of, 104–5, 143; on intermarriage, 79; on Lola Martins, 106; mother of, 95; on religious identity, 108–9; on returning to Cuba, 102–3; on speaking Spanish, 100
Guillén, Nicolás, 137

Haiti, 178n131; Cuba and, 119; Revolution of, 117, 122
Hallen, Barry, 69
Helg, Aline, 114, 126, 186n2
herbalists, 77
Herder, Johann Gottfried von, 135
Heywood, Linda M., 20–21
historiography, 21; Barnet and, 164n36; Ricoeur on, 92
Holy Cross Cathedral (Lagos), 71, 84, 104, 107
Humboldt, Alexander von, 120

idejo, 55–56, 58, 66–67, 177n106
Ido Island, 52
Ido wars, 175n51
Ifa divination, 54, 62; numbers in, 178n115; sacred rattle in, 93; song of, 80–84, 152
Ifa priests, 62–63, 68; alliances among, 77; clothing of, 185n57; worship of, 106–10
Iga Igandanran, 55, 60, 149
Ijebu Yoruba, 51–53, 60, 65, 149–50; religious practices of, 110
Ijesha, 68, 193n24
Ikoyi Cemetery, 95, *96–98*, 103–4
indentured workers, 34–35; Chinese, 42. *See also* slavery
independistas, 129
initiation rites, 17

intermarriage, 44, 66, 88, 104, 151; Gooding-King on, 79
iranjo, 76
iroke, 93
Islam. *See* Muslims
itan, 18, 53
iyaloja, 52, 68
iyalosha, 182n59
iyesás, 144, 193n24

jinle, 80, 153, 175n38
Johnson, Samuel (missionary), 21, 77
Judaism, 16

kasha, 18–20, 143
Klor de Alva, Jorge, 20
"Korin Itan ni Ebo Olokun," 80–84
Kosoko, 64

Lachatañere, Romulo, 11, 137
Lagos: Aguda in, 71, 88–110, 149; Brazilians in, 85, 88; founder of, 55–57, 174n33; Holy Cross Cathedral in, 71, 84, 104, 107; royal palace in, 55, 60, 149; Saros in, 71, 104–6, 179n47
La Moneda, Francisco, 160–61
Las Casas, Bartolomé de, 120
Law, Robin, 59
Lawson, Gerald, 87
Lazo, Rodrigo, 129–30
Lucumí, 140–44, 148; Barnet on, 131–32; definition of, 167n78; religious practices of, 18–20, 110; social organizations of, 71
Lupicio, Joaquín, 44–45, 157

Macaulay, Herbert, 62, 77
Macaulay, Zachary, 25, 28, 157, 168n2
Maceo, Antonio, 114–15, 128, 129
Machado, Eduardo, 138
Magliocco, Sabina, 2
Mandiola, Joaquín, 158
Mann, Kristin, 59
Manzano, Juan Francisco, 125, 135
Marino, Lucas, 45–46, 62
Marino, Manuel, 45
Marino, Martin, 4

Marino, Miguel, 43
maroon communities, 11, 117–18, 131
marriage. *See* intermarriage
Martí, José, 111–12, 123, 126–29, 135–36, 138
Martinez, Domingo, 60
Martinez family, 59, 176n62
Martinez-Fernandez, Luis, 30, 32
Martiniano, 171n80
Martins, Lola Bamgboshe, 61, 79, 83–84, 89, 100; on Candomblé, 107; grandfather of, 185n56; photographs of, 182n70; roles of, 106, 184n43
Martins, Ojo, 60
Martins family, 59, 85; Campos family and, 106, 136; Martinez family and, 176n62
masquerades: Boa, 79, 84–85, 88, 148, 155, 182n58; carnival and, 38, 105; Eyo, 182n70
Matory, J. Lorand, ix
Mayo, Antonio, 159
mayombe. *See* Palo Mayombe
Mazorra, Maria Luisa, 45, 159
memory, 142, 152; ethnographic, 6–7; folklore and, 53, 57, 102, 140; imagination and, 5, 22, 90–95, 110, 112; literary forms of, 112, 124, 129, 132–36, 139
Menendez, Ana, 138
mestizaje. *See* creolization
Minez, Alejandro, 159
missionaries, 26, 28, 56, 147. *See also* Church Missionary Society
Mixed Commission Courts, 28–34, 170n62; Síndico Protector de Esclavos and, 35–36
Moni, Ignacio, 159–61
Moni, Pedro, 159, 161
Monroe Doctrine, 33
Morales, José, 158
Morúa Delgado, Martin, 114, 117, 126–27, 129, 135
Movimiento Catalino Fuentes, 131–34
El Mulato (periodical), 130
Munis, Johanna Cicelia, 95, 100; grave of, *97, 98,* 103
Muniz, Andrés, 184n31

Muños, Manuela, 44
Muslims, 16, 61, 62; *orisha* worship and, 86, 107; of Rio de Janeiro, 120

Nago people, 71, 141, 143, 148, 152
ñáñigos, 143–44, 193n21
nationalism: Cuban, 128–36; folkloristics of, 137–39; transnational, 143
El Negrito (ship), 41
nganga, 133, 190n119
Ngugi wa Thiong'o, 131
Nigeria. *See* Lagos
Nobre, Francisco, 107
numerology, 178n115

*oba*s: history of, 54–55, 174n26; land ownership and, 177n106; palace of, 55, 60, 149; royal sagas of, 64
Obatala, 152
Obejas, Achy, 138
Ochún, 15–16
odu, 18
Oduduwa, 39, 54–56, 174n26
ofo, 19
Ogunfunmire, 55–57, 174n33
Ogunmade (chief), 62, 63
oja (marketplace), 1, 51, 61, 150
Oliviera, Joao de, 59
Olmstead, David, 137
olofin, 55–56
Ologun Kutere, 175n51
Olokun, 80–84, 154, 181n49, 182n70
Olupona, Jacob, 86
Olusí, T. (prince), 7, 56, 61; on Aguda versus Saros, 72; on Aguda work ethic, 105; on coalition building, 68–69; on community reintegration, 79–80; divination poem performed by, 80–84, 152; on *idejo* chiefs, 66–67; on *jinle,* 175n38; on *orisha* worship, 85–86; on Oshogbo cult, 68; photograph of, 182n70
Oluwole, 64
omoba, 80
omo eko, 39, 148
Ondo people, 53
onisegun, 77

Orgun Ajakaiye, 13
oriki, 19
orisha, 76, 107–10, 136, 139; Catholic saints and, 15–16, 84, 108, 113, 155; creation myth and, 152; cross-cultural, 153–54; multiple names of, 18–19; origins of, 181n36; Yemaya as, 18–19, 113, 154
orisha worship, 67, 76–79, 85–86, 120; Catholicism and, 70, 84, 95, 107–10, 136, 155–56
Ortiz, Fernando, 12, 136–38, 145; on *kasha*, 18–19, 143, 166n77; on syncretism, 18–19, 143–44
Oshinlokun, Oba, 60
Oshogbo cult, 68
Osinlokun, 64
Ouidah, 52, 122, 148, 151; Brazilians in, 58–59, 74–75, 78, 88, 155
Oya, 181
oyinbo, 105, 185n52
Oyo kingdom, 78, 148

palenques, 11, 118. *See also* maroon communities
palm oil trade, 59, 64, 150
Palo Mayombe, 11, 78–79, 136; Barnet on, 131, 133; code switching in, 146, 186n71. *See also* Santería
Paquette, Robert L., 31, 35
Partido Independiente de Color, 116–17
pataki, 18
Peel, J. D. Y., 20
Pérez, Joaquín, 157
Pérez, Louis A., Jr., 119
Pérez de la Riva, Juan, 72, 157; on Aguda, 88, 89; Sarracino and, 94, 99
Philippines, Chinese slave trade and, 35
Picard, Jose Maria, 47
Picard, Maria Luisa, 47–48
Pina, Brigada, 159
pipe, 19
plantation culture, 119–20, 122, 133–34
Plato, 92–93
Ponte, Antonio José, 136
Popo Aguda, 71, 107, 149, 179n139
Popo Maro, 71, 179n147

Postlethwayt, Malachy, 26
proverbs, Yoruba, 51, 112
el pueblo, 11, 125
Puerto Ricans, 142

Quakers, 24
quilombos, 11. *See also* maroon communities

Rama, Angel, 20, 120–21, 127, 132, 138
Ramsay, James, 24
Raynal, Abbé, 168n3
Real, Carmen, 23
Real, Dolores, 23, 41
reformistas, 129
Revista Popular, 127
Ricoeur, Paul, 92–93
Robertson, William, 168n3
Rodriguez, Mauricio, 159

Saavedra, Telesforo, 46, 49
sacrifice, 80–84, 181n48
saints, 15–16, 84, 108, 113, 155. *See also* Catholicism
samba, 105. *See also* dance
San Antonio (ship), 37–38, 75, 171n89
Sandoval, Alonso de, 135
Sanguily, Manuel, 124
Santacilia, Pedro, 130
Santería, 6, 11, 17, 79, 147; Afrolatino influences on, 142; Barnet on, 131, 132; Cabrera on, 153; creolization of, 90; as identity marker, 136, 137; *kasha in*, 19; *orisha* traditions in, 76; post-colonialism and, 119; Yoruba traditions and, 151–52, 155. *See also* Candomblé; Palo Mayombe
Saros, 14, 38, 54, 60, 151; Aguda and, 72, 104–6; creolization of, 27, 76–77; Lagos neighborhood of, 71, 179n147; Olusí on, 72; religious affiliations of, 77, 104. *See also* Sierra Leone
Sarracino, Rodolfo, 88, 94, 99, 130, 184n31
Scott, Rebecca, 34, 115, 186n2
secret societies, 143–44. *See also cabildos*
Seguí, Crescencio, 157
Seguí, Martina, 157–58

Senhor do Bonfin cult, 88
Serra, Rafael, 117
Shango, 79
Sharp, Granville, 24, 26
Sierra Leone, 14, 25; founding of, 26; Mix Commission Courts in, 30. *See also* Saros
Sierra Leone Company, 28
Síndico Protector de Esclavos, 35–36, 160, 161
slave revolts, 75. *See also* Aponte rebellion
slavery: *bozales* and, 15, 35, 49, 122; Caballero on, 123; *emancipados* and, 42, 46, 123, 149; escapees from, 11, 117–18, 131; ex-slaves as traffickers in, 75; indentured workers and, 34–35, 42; Martí on, 111–12; Yoruban civil wars and, 13
Slave Trade Act (1807), 29, 33
Smith, Adam, 168n3
Sociedad de Estudios Afrocubanos, 137
Sociedad del Folklore Cubano, 137
sociedades de color, 37, 71, 114. See also *cabildos*
Sociétés des Missions Africaines (SMA), 107
Somerset, James, 27
Sommer, Doris, 126, 167n88
Sòngó, 178n130
Songo Egungun, 79, 85, 182n70
Southampton, 1, 40, 105; Da Silva house in, 45, 89, 99, 151
Soyinka, Wole, 178n118
spirit possession, 166n63
Stewart, Charles, 27
Suárez y Romero, Anselmo, 125–26, 135, 189n81
syncretism, 3, 11, 109, 133–34, 155, 166n65; Ortiz on, 18–19, 143–44
Syndicate for the Protection of Slaves. *See* Síndico Protector de Esclavos

takús, 144

Ten Years' War (Cuba), 70, 112, 114, 129, 132, 135
Thornton, John K., 20–21, 25
Tinubu, Madam, 52
Townsend, Henry, 107
transculturation: acculturation versus, 137, 165n48; in music, 12
"transnational imaginary," 170n53
Trinidad, 27, 29
Troyano, Alina, 138
Turnbull, David, 31

Umbanda, 79

Valdes, Pedro Maximo, 47
Valdés, Zoé, 136, 138
Varela, Felix, 123–24
Verger, Pierre Fatumbi, 172n105
Vidau, Manuel, 46–48
Villaverde, Cirilo, 126
Vincent, Ola, 6–7, 72–73, 89, 94–102; childhood of, 104–6, 143; on Lagosian identity in Cuba, 101–2; mother of, 95; photograph of, *98,* 104; on religious identity, 108–9
Virgen de la Guadalupe, 16
Virgen de Regla, 113, 166n76
Vodoun, 79

Wesley, John, 168n3
West-Durán, Alan, 138
Wilberforce, William, 25
witchcraft, 134, 137
work ethic, 105, 132

Xango, 178n130
Xa-Xas, 75

Yané, Tiburcio, 158
Yemaya, 18–19, 113, 154

Zambi, 120, 188n44
Zeuske, Michael, 131

Rochester Studies in African History and the Diaspora

Toyin Falola, Senior Editor
The Frances Higginbotham Nalle Centennial Professor in History
University of Texas at Austin

(ISSN: 1092–5228)

Power Relations in Nigeria: Ilorin Slaves and their Successors
Ann O'Hear

Dilemmas of Democracy in Nigeria
Edited by Paul Beckett and Crawford Young

Science and Power in Colonial Mauritius
William Kelleher Storey

Namibia's Post-Apartheid Regional Institutions: The Founding Year
Joshua B. Forrest

A Saro Community in the Niger Delta, 1912–1984: The Potts-Johnsons of Port Harcourt and Their Heirs
Mac Dixon-Fyle

Contested Power in Angola, 1840s to the Present
Linda Heywood

Nigerian Chiefs: Traditional Power in Modern Politics, 1890s–1990s
Olufẹmi Vaughan

West Indians in West Africa, 1808–1880: The African Diaspora in Reverse
Nemata Blyden

The United States and Decolonization in West Africa, 1950–1960
Ebere Nwaubani

Health, State, and Society in Kenya
George Oduor Ndege

Black Business and Economic Power
Edited by Alusine Jalloh and Toyin Falola

Voices of the Poor in Africa
Elizabeth Isichei

Colonial Rule and Crisis in Equatorial Africa: Southern Gabon ca. 1850–1940
Christopher J. Gray

The Politics of Frenchness in Colonial Algeria, 1930–1954
Jonathan K. Gosnell

Sources and Methods in African History: Spoken, Written, Unearthed
Edited by Toyin Falola and Christian Jennings

Sudan's Blood Memory: The Legacy of War, Ethnicity, and Slavery in Early South Sudan
Stephanie Beswick

Writing Ghana, Imagining Africa: Nation and African Modernity
Kwaku Larbi Korang

Labour, Land and Capital in Ghana: From Slavery to Free Labour in Asante, 1807–1956
Gareth Austin

Not So Plain as Black and White: Afro-German Culture and History, 1890–2000
Edited by Patricia Mazón and Reinhild Steingröver

Writing African History
Edited by John Edward Philips

African Urban Spaces in Historical Perspective
Edited by Steven J. Salm and Toyin Falola

Yorùbá Identity and Power Politics
Edited by Toyin Falola and Ann Genova

Constructions of Belonging: Igbo Communities and the Nigerian State in the Twentieth Century
Axel Harneit-Sievers

Sufi City: Urban Design and Archetypes in Touba
Eric Ross

A Political History of The Gambia, 1816–1994
Arnold Hughes and David Perfect

The Abolition of the Slave Trade in Southeastern Nigeria, 1885–1950
A. E. Afigbo

HIV/AIDS, Illness, and African Well-Being
Edited by Toyin Falola and Matthew M. Heaton

Ira Aldridge: The African Roscius
Edited by Bernth Lindfors

Natural Resources and Conflict in Africa: The Tragedy of Endowment
Abiodun Alao

Crafting Identity in Zimbabwe and Mozambique
Elizabeth MacGonagle

Locality, Mobility, and "Nation": Periurban Colonialism in Togo's Eweland, 1900–1960
Benjamin N. Lawrance

Sufism and Jihad in Modern Senegal: The Murid Order
John Glover

Indirect Rule in South Africa: Tradition, Modernity, and the Costuming of Political Power
J. C. Myers

The Urban Roots of Democracy and Political Violence in Zimbabwe: Harare and Highfield, 1940–1964
Timothy Scarnecchia

Radicalism and Cultural Dislocation in Ethiopia, 1960–1974
Messay Kebede

The United States and West Africa: Interactions and Relations
Edited by Alusine Jalloh and Toyin Falola

Ben Enwonwu:
The Making of an African Modernist
Sylvester Okwunodu Ogbechie

Representing Bushmen:
South Africa and the Origin of
Language
Shane Moran

Afro-Brazilians: Cultural Production
in a Racial Democracy
Niyi Afolabi

Movements, Borders, and Identities
in Africa
Edited by Toyin Falola and
Aribidesi Usman

Africans and the Politics of
Popular Culture
Edited by Toyin Falola and
Augustine Agwuele

Political Culture and Nationalism in
Malawi: Building Kwacha
Joey Power

Women's Authority and Society in
Early East-Central Africa
Christine Saidi

Afro-Cuban Diasporas in the
Atlantic World
Solimar Otero